"Its great to see that (... ... voices, not normally heard, are ... ... ng social history."

CHIP HAMER, AU... ... 00-2015

"What a fantastic book this is — both a much needed history of a class claimed regularly not to exist, and a compendious, endlessly quotable book of facts, anecdotes and tales of the 'working class bohemia' that existed, and crucially still exists, and changes and grows and thrives, in the lands south of Watford, east of Staines, north of the Thames and west of the Lea."

OWEN HATHERLEY, CULTURE EDITOR, *TRIBUNE* AND AUTHOR OF *RED METROPOLIS: SOCIALISM AND THE GOVERNMENT OF LONDON*

"This is Dickens for a postwar North London. Not the mawkishness of *Old Curiosity Shop* but the mature journalism, in which he confronted the seeming ineffability of the metropolis to reveal the vital energy of its working population, and the callous brutalities to which it was routinely exposed. And, like Dickens, John Medhurst has walked the streets of his manor and listened to its residents. The result is an intimate letter to the North London working class, written out of a tough love, completely shorn of sentimentality. It is a kaleidoscopic anthropology of a culture striking in its diversity and dissonance, manifest in part by its darker inner workings. This is an important book. I know of no other quite like it. I wish I had written it."

JOHN MARRIOTT, VISITING FELLOW AT KELLOGG COLLEGE, OXFORD AND AUTHOR OF *BEYOND THE TOWER: A HISTORY OF EAST LONDON*

I COULD BE SO GOOD FOR YOU

I COULD BE SO GOOD FOR YOU

A PORTRAIT OF THE NORTH LONDON WORKING CLASS

JOHN MEDHURST

Published by Repeater Books

An imprint of Watkins Media Ltd

Unit 11 Shepperton House

89-93 Shepperton Road

London

N1 3DF

United Kingdom

www.repeaterbooks.com

A Repeater Books paperback original 2023

1

Distributed in the United States by Random House, Inc., New York.

ISBN: 9781914420344

Ebook ISBN: 9781914420351

Printed and bound in the United Kingdom by TJ Books Limited

MIX
Paper from
responsible sources
FSC® C013056

To my dad, 1938-2021

I had been born into a world that had learned to value important things. The Tories didn't dare mess with that infrastructure. An air of equality and tranquillity filled my world. Class would still be with us for another generation but it was disappearing and the evidence was everywhere... As a result of our first great socialist government we had become the freest people in the world, if not the richest. Sometimes you had to make a choice between a nice meal or a trip to a West End cinema. The wealth was spread, the country became stronger and, bit by bit, better off. For a while I saw working class London grow happier, better educated and more optimistic. Before they took it all away again.

Michael Moorcock, *The Whispering Swarm*, 2015

If you want to I'll change the situation
Right people, right time, just the wrong location.
I've got a good idea,
Just you keep me near,
I'll be so good for you.
I could be so good for you,
Love you like you want me to,
There ain't nothing I can't go through,
I'll be so good for you.

Minder, 1979-95

CONTENTS

Maybe It's Because
I'm a North Londoner

This book is an attempt to capture the life experience of North London's working class from the early 1950s through to the end of Ken Livingstone's second term as London Mayor in 2008, and to examine how it has been represented within our culture. It is inevitably partial and incomplete. Different biographies and personal stories could have been cited, other choices made about which cultural products to consider and a variety of approaches taken with the book's material. The final product is highly subjective although not, I hope, untrue or misleading.

There is a point to the period chosen. It runs from the beginning of an "affluent" post-war society through to the 2008 economic crash and other significant changes occurring in London around that time. It also, in my opinion, contains a particular period in the life of North London's working class qualitatively different from what came before the 1950s and to what by 2008 was fully emerging. The period is not absolutely demarcated, there are continuities on either end, but it provides a suitable framework for the book and its theme.

Why *North* London? Firstly, because I come from it and know it best. Secondly, because unlike East, South and West, there is an absurd yet widespread assumption that North London *has no working class*. The presence of working class communities in the heart of central London, especially, goes against the grain of common perception, sometimes even the perception of working class Londoners themselves. Ayesha Lorde Dunn, one of Stormzy's inner team, grew up on a council estate just off

Russell Square. When she told this to Stormzy, who hails from deepest South London, he was incredulous:

Whenever he introduces me to anyone, he's always like, "She's from central London! Did you know there were houses there?"[1]

For the purposes of this book I define its subject as that part of London's working class that live and work, or have lived and worked, within a large semi-circle of territory with the River Thames as its undulating base, the approximate border of which flows north-west-south from Shoreditch through Tottenham, Golders Green, Willesden and Hammersmith, i.e., the entire London Boroughs of Islington, Camden, Kensington & Chelsea, Hammersmith & Fulham, and the City of Westminster; most of Hackney and Haringey; enclaves of the City and a few western slivers of Tower Hamlets; and those parts of Enfield, Ealing, Barnet and Brent that closely attach to this inner core. I have used the obvious physical barriers — the River Thames, Hackney and Walthamstow marshes, the Tottenham reservoirs — as rough borders here, although no such obvious cut-off point exists in West London, and leads to a blurring of boundaries that I acknowledge.

This definition could be challenged on several fronts. Most obviously, the Thames is not a horizontal line, meaning that some parts of "South London" have a more northern latitude than some parts of "North London". Some areas south of the river, such as Borough, Vauxhall and Battersea, have by proximity and better transport links always had a North London air about them, and with the regeneration of the South Bank and Thames Footpath do so even more today. Many South Londoners, like other working class Londoners in Walthamstow or Finchley or Ealing, work and socialise within what I define as North London and are shaped by that experience as much as by where they live. Much of Hackney lies further east than Bethnal Green, yet Hackney lacks that close connection to Docklands that characterised the classic "East End" and is significantly further north.

These are fluid realities, made even more so by an ever-shifting workforce of new migrants in various stages of legality, working in a perpetual black economy of cleaning agencies, taxi firms and cash-in-hand builders and decorators. For most of these workers there is no differentiation between North and South London. A permanent home *anywhere* in London, but especially within the general area I have sketched out, is nearly impossible.

For all these reasons my fixing of the geographical boundaries of "North London" is a moveable feast, particularly in West London, historically more connected to the centre than the south and east (as a glance at the tube map demonstrates, although the London Overground is beginning to alter this dynamic). Nevertheless, and with all these caveats, I would argue that my definition does constitute an identifiable North London with a working class whose social and cultural history can be framed and examined. Beyond these porous borders sit Outer London, East London and South London, all of which have different stories to tell.

Defining place is simple compared to the problem of defining class. Marx's definition of the working class, i.e., the Proletariat, as those who do not own the Means of Production and are therefore compelled to sell their labour power in order to survive, is simplistic and unsatisfactory. Clearly, if taken literally, it would include most of the middle class as well, as Marx himself acknowledged in the unfinished Volume III of *Capital*. Considering England at the time, he concluded, "Middle and intermediate strata even here obliterate lines of demarcation everywhere".[2] In the twentieth century, under the great social democratic welfare states, these lines of demarcation continued to erode, although the neoliberal backlash that started in the 1980s attempted to stop and reverse this process, and in some countries, notably the US and the UK, it succeeded.

The socialist historian E.P. Thompson upended Marxist categorisation entirely when he proposed that "Classes do not exist as separate entities", instead suggesting that class is a relationship, a process, a mutual interaction in specific social circumstances.

In that sense, he believed, "Class eventuates as men and women live their productive relations, and as they handle these experiences in cultural ways".[3] This approach was expanded and deepened by the French sociologist Pierre Bourdieu and his development of a "cultural class analysis", in which a person is not defined solely by economic status but by an entire range of other indicators that he labelled social capital, cultural capital, financial capital and symbolic capital, which together provided a person with "pre-emptive rights over the future". These rights accrued naturally to the broad middle class while their absence defined the broad working class. Bourdieu grounded his analysis in what he called a "theory of practice", i.e., solid empirical research based on personal experience. This book, inasmuch as it has a theoretical underpinning, attempts to follow in that tradition.

So what *is* class in an "advanced" capitalist society like the UK, the cradle of the Industrial Revolution and the seedbed of Marx's work? In 2013, the BBC's Great British Class Survey, the largest and most rigorous investigation of class ever conducted in Britain, found seven different class formations:

1) a very wealthy elite of about 6% of the population, mostly inheriting their wealth, and the products of the country's top-rank public schools and universities
2) an affluent "established middle class" of senior professionals and managers within the legal, educational, medical, cultural and public policy professions, who make up 25% of the population
3) an intermediate middle class of technical experts within these professions, about 6% of the population, with high economic capital but low social and cultural capital
4) a layer of "new affluent workers" such as electricians, plumbers and other self-employed, as well as train drivers and other mid-level public sector workers with strong trade union protection, about 15% of British society
5) a mostly aging "traditional" working class, about 14% of the population, such as delivery, cleaning and care

workers with low social and cultural capital but some economic assets such as home ownership;

6) a group of emergent service workers such as bar staff, cooks, health trainers, customer service workers and musicians, about 19% of the total population, who have low economic capital but occasionally compensate with cultural capital which can be exploited for future gain;

7) a new, "precariat" working class with no savings or job security, who mostly rent and who have little to no capital of any kind, and who make up about 15% of modern Britain.

These categories are imposed on the data and should be treated accordingly. I find the survey results useful as a breakdown of the contemporary British working class, particularly its finding that in total it constitutes nearly 65% of the population, but feel it severely overestimates the proportion of the affluent middle class at the expense of its less well-off component. But one definitive finding, across all categories, was that most people do not consider themselves to have a particular class identity at all, and even if they do, they are wary of being defined in this way by others. Further, this was merely the confirmation of a trend that was evident from similar surveys since the 1960s. The survey found that in modern Britain more than two thirds of people resist class identification, and that

> Most people are now ambivalent and hesitant about which class they belong to, and when quizzed about it often prefer to reflect on the way that they straddle different classes.[4]

The political consequences of this fragmented view of class, of the loss of a cohesive working class with a clear sense of identity and interest, have been playing out since at least the 1980s. With the passage of time, it is getting clearer that "class consciousness" in the traditionally accepted sense, i.e., an innate collective politics intrinsic to working class communities and workplaces and expressed in mass-based trade unions and social democratic political parties, arose from the heavily concentrated industrial capitalism of the 1880s-1950s, and despite an upsurge of industrial militancy in the 1970s based on older industries now extinct, has been waning since then. It was, in any case, a far more complex phenomenon than commonly assumed, a reality explored by labour historians such as Thompson, Eric Hobsbawm and Raphael Samuel, and outstanding books on British working class culture like Jonathan Rose's *The Intellectual Life of the British Working Class* (2002), Michael Collins's *The Likes of Us* (2004) and Selina Todd's *The People: The Rise and Fall of the Working Class* (2014).

Working class women, especially, often had a different perspective on society than their fathers, brothers, husbands and sons. They worked less outside the home, and when they did their jobs were frequently part-time or subject to interruption due to domestic and child-caring responsibilities. Their identities therefore revolved less around the workplace and more around the family. Their role as primary carers, whether voluntary or involuntary, meant they engaged with different parts of the state than did working class men, such as hospitals, welfare services and schools. They often formed sisterhoods with subcultures and intimacies of their own, to parallel those formed by their men in the pub, the club, the trade union, the football team or the sound system.

Like working class women, working class men were a very mixed bag. In the period considered in this book most British working class men, especially in London, did not work in a factory. Not all were trade unionists and even fewer were socialists. While most voted Labour they seldom did so because of a consciously held ideology. Not all felt attachment to their local football team or their hometown. Not all were "good" husbands and fathers or demonstrated parental responsibility (one of the un-looked-for themes of this book, unpleasant but undeniable, is the large number who actively shunned it). Not all were heterosexual, or not exclusively. Some never married at all and lived primarily for themselves. Not all abided by the law.

Class is closely attached to occupation and income, to the extent that those on low incomes with no extra capital are almost all "working class". But it is not *solely* a result of them. Nor is it fixed and unalterable. There is and always has been fluctuation, e.g. social mobility. People can move up and down the class scale during their lives, fuelling the widespread uncertainty about class identity that all surveys discover. My own personal criteria for determining class has more to do with social and family background and the extent to which these factors continue through life as underlying values and attitudes. Even if economic, social and occupational barriers are surmounted, subtle and not-so-subtle cultural barriers will remain. A working class perspective and value system *can* be retained throughout higher education and a professional career but it will continually encounter social filters designed to diminish and ultimately erase it. Whether these filters succeed depend on a number of factors such as a person's job, social circle and political activity.

Class is also closely linked to ethnicity, at least in countries with deep colonial histories that still define and shape their cultures (the most obvious being the US and the UK, one as a result of domestic slavery and its legacy, the other as a result of a global empire and its legacy). It is not an absolute condition that if one is BAME one must therefore be working class. Clearly the UK has a BAME middle class. But it is undeniable that during the period considered here BAME Londoners were *far* more likely to be working class than were white Londoners. They were the most economically disadvantaged, they lived in the worst housing and they were subject to repressive and racist policing. London's large BAME population alone ensures it has a large working class.

In 1981, two years after the election of Margaret Thatcher and as the Right to Buy council tenancies was being introduced, 35% of London's population lived in social housing of one kind or another while 17% rented on the open market. By 2008 the percentage of people living in social housing had fallen to 24%, a still significant proportion, with 28% renting on the open market. While these figures conceal great variety in social and economic circumstances, they point to a large proportion of "working class" Londoners, if by working class we mean those with little spare capital to draw upon beyond the salary they receive for selling their labour power and which they rely on to survive.[5]

That working class has always been hard to classify. One reason for this is that London, like other major world cities like New York but unlike others such as Berlin, never went through an Industrial Revolution in the classic sense. Gareth Stedman Jones' *Outcast London* (1971) tells us that, excluding the building trade, most of London's working class in 1861 were employed in five industries — clothing, printing, wood and furniture, engineering and metalwork, and the skilled manufacture of items such as watches, precious metals, luxury goods and scientific instruments. This micro-economy was epitomised by Leather Lane, which in the 1860s contained a variety of specialist manufacturers such as organ grinders, glass blowers, picture frame-makers, mosaic makers and Italian plaster statuette makers.[6]

By the 1880s most of London's engineering was repair work, not manufacture from scratch. There were exceptions, though. From the 1880s to 1914 North London was the centre of the world's piano manufacturing industry, a tradition which persisted for some time after the First World War despite the increasing availability of recorded music. In 1919 the Imperial Piano and Organ Company relocated from Mare Street in Hackney to Perren Street, Kentish Town, and stayed there for several decades. In Stedman Jones' view, the predominance of this kind of skilled, small-scale production and the relative absence of large factories meant "the social character of London's industrial population was highly individual".[7] Certainly, this was the defining characteristic of my own family in the nineteenth and twentieth centuries (for a brief summary see the endnotes). It flourished in the crevices of London life, in self-employment, in delivery and transport, and in its entertainment, leisure and service industries, whose behaviour and ethos it often reflected.

The pattern continued in the post-war years. With the partial exception of the concentration of manufacturing at Park Royal and Tottenham Hale, North London's working class, unlike East London's centered on the docks and later on Ford

Dagenham and Beckton Gas Works, was seldom a product of big industry. Living and working in and around London's major cultural institutions, entertainment centres and grand public spaces, North London's working class had a radically different life experience than other working class people who lived and worked in one densely concentrated community and one dominant industry. Working in less regularised and predictable fashion, living in and amongst the urban middle class, aware of different lifestyles and opportunities, they *had* to adapt to survive. They also wanted to. If only by virtue of proximity, aspiration, imitation and lucky happenstance, they possessed or acquired more innate cultural capital than others not so fortunately situated.

This created a definite attitude that some find arrogant and self-involved. Like most other working classes in other cities and regions of the United Kingdom, North London's have a devotion to their home manor, so much so that they are notorious for a casual indifference to vast swathes of London east of the City and south of the river. But their sense of locality and community was not of the kind eulogised by the Raymond Williams school of class analysis, developed in the 1950s and based on a mostly non-urban culture that flourished in places like South Wales before the Second World War (whose modern, sentimentalised version is repeated by the likes of Jon Cruddas and Paul Embery, oblivious of any London working class west of the Lea). In contrast to older working class traditions examined by Williams and Richard Hoggart, North London's working class, in all its iterations over the past seventy years, has not celebrated or fetishised a class identity that was, in any event, heavily associated with white ethnicity. It had other things to do.

One of the foundations of North London working class life in the second half of the twentieth century was a network of council estates and council-owned properties that, despite some drear examples that failed catastrophically, provided council tenants with relatively decent homes in the heart of the city. To focus *only* on failed Brutalist experiments like the Heygate estate (Elephant and Castle), the Aylesbury estate

(Walworth) or the first Stonebridge estate (Harlesden) produces a skewed history. London, especially the area I define as North London, contains a multitude of very different council estates and many high-quality social housing schemes, including the magnificently restored Peabody estates. These are not ghettoes or "sink estates". Some never were, and those that declined badly have seen real efforts to improve and regenerate them. But those efforts require the support of a national housing policy that prioritises the building of new social housing, allied to an economic infrastructure that provides good-quality apprenticeships and full-time job opportunities for non-graduates. There is only so much municipal socialism can do.

"Gentrification", the other major threat to working class London, is presented in most left-wing commentary as an unadulterated evil, often by the same people who exemplify it. The reality is more complex. The first ten years of an area's gentrification is often a positive process, reclaiming urban dead space and giving it new life. But it invariably brings major problems in its wake, in particular the economic exclusion of working class Londoners through outrageously boosted property prices. At its worst it results in a Tory Borough like Kensington & Chelsea ghettoising a multi-ethnic working class into unsafe tower blocks, ignored and neglected as long as they do not disturb the view. It also brings an influx of middle class homeowners, renters, small businesses, shops and other outlets labelled "hipster" or "bohemian", although most middle class people are neither. Areas like Notting Hill, Camden and Islington have experienced this since the 1970s. Hackney went the same way in the 1990s and Shoreditch in the 2000s. It has led to the close proximity and parallel lives of working class and middle class, sometimes literally in the same street and the same block of flats.

Not *all* of this relationship is mutual antipathy. Working class Londoners, rightly, resent being priced out of their communities and public spaces by thoughtless gentrification. But not all working class people, especially in cities like London, want time to stand still. They are just as interested in new experiences and new opportunities as the middle class with whom they live in close proximity. They sample and sometimes even appreciate what "bohemians" and "hipsters" bring to their community, whether it be drinks at a new bar, visiting a trendy hairdresser or exploring an indie bookshop.

This is what an urban bohemia is, or should be. Not a bastion of middle class privilege but a fusion of the detritus of an older working class culture — its canals, warehouses, cafes, markets, garrets — with new immigrants and déclassé middle class elements seeking the freedom from bourgeois conventions offered by such environments. Past iterations were found on New York's Lower East Side; parts of 1920s Chicago like Bughouse Square and the Dil Pickle, a chaotic nightspot set up by the Industrial Workers of the World (IWW) where hobos, anarchists, jazz musicians and writers congregated; Berlin's Kreuezberg and Neukölln districts; and Paris's Montmartre when it was a working class area drawing middle class dissenters to it like moths to the flame. Soho was like this from the 1940s through to the 1980s. Camden Town had its time too. Today's equivalent is found in rough embryo in Harlesden and Tottenham and hitherto deeply unfashionable parts of South London. That kind of vibrant urban culture, of spaces where working class and middle class can meet as equals, is indisputably being pushed out of central London but not as far as commonly supposed. Even now London's working class, diminished as it may be, can still be found at the heart of the capital, living, working, surviving.

The underlying story of London's working class over the past seventy years is that whilst it has retained elements of its pre-existing identity, language and values it has also *transformed* into a new working class for a new century. It was always doing so. London's position in the eighteenth and nineteenth centuries as the largest and most important city in the world, the centre of the British Empire and of international capitalism, as well as a magnet for refugees seeking asylum, inevitably attracted workers of all nationalities and types.

Long before the arrival of the *Windrush*, London's working class was unusually heterodox and multicultural. Its nearest equivalents in the UK, Liverpool and Bristol, were also especially open to international trade and migration and also developed an ethnically diverse working class. As in London, this was not a peaceful process (in 1919 Liverpool's black population, already numbering around 5,000, became the target of white racist mobs). To this day there are deep social and cultural similarities between the working classes of Liverpool and Bristol and that of the capital, as there are with other British cities such as Manchester, Birmingham, Newcastle, Cardiff and Glasgow. If Britain has a "Red Wall", a reliable heartland for progressive politics and a broader anti-Tory coalition, that is where it is.

The most recent incomers to London in the last thirty years — Kurdish, Ghanaian, Somali, Polish, Bulgarian, Albanian — have followed in the wake of earlier waves of immigration of Huguenots, East European Jews, Irish, West Indian, Chinese, Greek and Turkish Cypriot, Indians, Pakistanis, Nigerians and Ugandans, all of whom settled, found work, raised families and became Londoners. It is a culture that traditionalists find baffling and even frightening (see Nigel Farage's frankly admitted relief as his stopping train out of London got south of Lewisham and he could hear "proper" English being spoken in the carriage). Attempting to explain his music to a live audience, where it came from and what it meant, Grime artist Skepta gave up the effort and told them simply, "It's a London thing".

At the time of writing there are no general histories of the London working class. What exists is either specialised, such as Stedman Jones' work or William Fishman's studies of East End Jewish radicalism; studies of aspects of London's culture such as black music that examine the social and economic conditions that produced it; local histories that contain interesting vignettes of working class life; or accounts that greatly simplify that life by concentrating only on political activity, such as John Rees' and Lindsay German's *A People's History of London* (2012). Of the broad histories of the capital, the best are Peter Ackroyd's *London: The Biography* (2001) and Jerry White's trilogy on the city in the eighteenth, nineteenth and twentieth centuries, but for the purposes of this book the most useful works have been personal memoirs, autobiographies and collected oral histories.

In bringing these together I am trying to identify a London working class experience and, in as much as possible, a specifically *North London* working class experience. I do this because, unlike, for example, East London — which already has excellent academic histories such as John Marriott's *Beyond the Tower: A History of East London* (2012), a surfeit of personal memoirs and an entire long-running TV soap opera devoted to establishing its place in our culture —it is a neglected and undervalued subject. Yet the story of the North London working class since the Second World War is a rich and fascinating one, alive with diversity and character and incident. It is a story that dispels lazy thinking and patronising stereotypes, not only about London but about how working class people are supposed to think and behave.

One final but important qualification. Writers who focus on London, especially if they make fine distinctions about which part of the city they are concerned with, will inevitably be labelled "London-centric". While this book is exactly that, I hope its focus does not disrespect or diminish other important areas of the English working class experience in the last seventy years, nor the rich history of the Welsh and Scottish working classes, intimately entangled as it is with nationalist resistance to the English state. These all have their own particular stories, idioms and histories, which I am not qualified to tell.

The working class considered here has a different story, at least from the beginning of the post-war welfare state. The conditions that gave rise to it are faltering now and have been since the 1980s, most particularly the large-scale, secure social housing embedded throughout central and North London in which it arose and thrived. But if there is one common experience in these years it is how the North London working class looked outward and grabbed what the city had to offer. In my view they personified the greatest working class virtue of all. They didn't let the bastards grind them down.

THE 1950s

"I love this place. It's just like home. Filthy and full of strangers."

Ronnie Scott

In 1950 twelve-year-old Edward "Ted" Medhurst, his older brother Ronnie and their mum Edith were still living in the "shared accommodation" to which they had been sent in 1945, a dilapidated four-storey house in Sidmouth Street, St Pancras, North London. Ted's first home, the ground floor of a small terraced house in Wakefield Street off Brunswick Square, was destroyed in January 1945 by a V2 rocket. Ted, six years old at the time, had been running out of Argyle Street Primary School opposite St Pancras station when the rocket landed. The shockwave blew him off his feet.

During the 1930s Ted's father was a timber merchant's lorry driver and general wide-boy working in central London, usually well suited and booted, while his mother worked as a warehouse cleaner and in the kitchen of the Princess Louise pub on High Holborn. During his deliveries Ted's dad would sometimes stop off at the Princess Louise to pick up newly cooked roast potatoes from Edith. At the end of the decade, after a short period living in the basement of a house on Balfe Street off the south end of Caledonian Road, they moved to Wakefield Street. In 1940 Ted's dad was drafted into the army, leaving his mum to look after him and his brother. In 1944, when the V2 bombing of London intensified, Ted was evacuated to Blackburn but after a few months his mum brought him back to London.

The V2s devastated large parts of the capital. During air raids Ted and his family took shelter in the crypt of Holy Cross Church in Cromer Street. When the bombers came, the anti-aircraft battery set up in Regent Square fired into the night sky but it was powerless against the V2s, which sometimes arrived with no warning in the middle of the day. After their house was destroyed the remains of the family were put up in a Displaced Persons Centre in Tavistock Square. At the end of the war they were relocated to Sidmouth Street. Ted's dad never came back to Edith, instead returning to his wife and three children in Hoxton whom he had temporarily abandoned in the 1930s. Ted never saw him again.

Ted, his mother and brother had some rooms to themselves, but only in a communal house where the common parts — the hall, kitchen, living room — were shared by other families made homeless by the bombing. Ted's room was at the rear of the house overlooking a derelict backyard. In a high wind the cheap lino covering the bare floor would lift and ripple from the draughts through the gaps in the floorboards. The single bed had sheets and blankets but in the cold winter months Ted's bed cover was a large British Army overcoat.

Ted spent his childhood much like any other working class kid in St Pancras in the late 1940s. Other than the annual hop-picking expedition to Paddock Wood in Kent, reached by train from London Bridge, he rarely ventured far from King's Cross. The highlight of his week was a trip to the King's Cross Cinema on Pentonville Road for the Saturday Morning Pictures. On Fridays he and his mum took a bus up to the Angel where after shopping in Chapel Street Market, they would have lunch in Manze's Pie and Mash Shop. In 1950 he, his mum and brother were rehoused by St Pancras Borough Council in a three-bedroom flat in a house on Bernard St between Russell Square and Brunswick Square. Things were finally looking up.[1]

Seventy years later Wakefield Street still wore the scars of the V2. In the 1950s, after the bomb site was cleared, a grey, pebble dashed four-storey council block with a small forecourt was constructed in its place. The block of flats backed on to Regent Square, two other sides of which have more modern and attractive 1960s council flats. Only the south side retained its original Georgian housing, a testament to the damage the area took during the war. In my childhood this was where most of my extended family lived. Edith's mother Phoebe, who helped raise Ted, was born in Holborn in 1883 and died there in 1974, hardly stepping foot outside London her entire life except for the annual trip to Paddock Wood, and even that, until the 1930s, was reached by the whole family walking all the way to Kent. They were the Bloomsbury working class, as much a part of central London as their wealthy bourgeois neighbours.

The social housing in which that class lived and still lives is peppered throughout Bloomsbury — the Tybalds Estate on Dombey Street off Great Ormond Street, completed in 1949 with two fourteen-storey tower blocks added in 1958; Culver and Brampton House, two social housing blocks on Red Lion Square built in the 1950s, and Beckley, built in the 1960s on Eagle Street just south of the square; the Devonshire Court buildings behind Unite's HQ on High Holborn; Winston House, the six-storey block on Endsleigh Street; the giant Peabody buildings of the Herbrand Estate off Woburn Place; the large Cromer Street Estate between Gray's Inn Road and Judd Street; and the modernistic Brunswick Estate on Brunswick Square. A recent history of the Bloomsbury area found that even in the twenty-first century it was "a hybrid neighbourhood with an economically diverse population" containing one of the densest levels of unprivatised social housing in central London. Despite many changes Bloomsbury in 2017 was characterised by

unpredictable and sometimes incongruous relationships... formed out of the collisions and collusions that result from such local demographic heterogeneity.[2]

The Second World War tore London's local demographics apart. During the first Blitz of 1940-41 the Luftwaffe's main targets in London were the East End, the core of London's industry and the docks, and central London and the City, the hub of its governing, financial and transport infrastructure. Toward the end of the war, in 1944 and 1945, V1 and V2 rockets brought renewed devastation. Working class Londoners, many of them residents of large estates and tenements packed tightly together, had less protection from the bombing than did middle class Londoners, with no large gardens in which to bury Anderson shelters and less resources to call upon if displaced.

Holborn and St Pancras, a major Luftwaffe target because of its mainline railway stations, was badly damaged, leaving a hollowed-out cityscape in which children played unsupervised for many years. During the war Holborn's population fell to about 18,700, only rising back to 25,000 by 1951, partly as a result of St Pancras Borough Council using its powers of requisition to take over abandoned properties and use them to house those still living in temporary accommodation. Even with that emergency measure, the housing problem in the borough remained acute. In 1947 3,500 families in Holborn had no bathroom, 2,000 had no separate toilet and 1,700 no water supply, a situation not improved until well into the 1950s.[3]

The common mythology of the Second World War, of how bombing laid waste to the East End and changed it forever, applied equally to central London. From the middle of the nineteenth century central London, outside of the West End and select areas of aristocratic housing such as Knightsbridge and Belgravia, had been transformed into a semi-industrial zone of warehouses, railway yards and small workshops, enhanced by London's major fruit and vegetable, meat and fish markets at Covent Garden, Smithfields and Billingsgate. With no mass transport and no money to afford it anyway, the capital's working class needed to live close to where they worked. Hence the appearance of large working class communities in Westminster, Islington, St Pancras, Holborn and Clerkenwell.

The bombing hit these communities hard. In total, it destroyed or severely damaged 3.5 million London homes, including 130,000 houses. By the end of the war 1.5 million Londoners were living in Displaced Persons Shelters, single rooms in temporary shared accommodation or with relatives. London housing had to be rebuilt or built anew. In March 1945 a government white paper estimated that the capital needed 750,000 new homes plus a further 500,000 to replace existing slums which were unfit for human habitation. This necessitated a vast new programme of council housing by local boroughs and the London County Council (LCC).

From its creation in 1889 the LCC was responsible for slum clearance and the creation of what today is called the capital's "social housing". Its pioneer estates — Arnold Circus in Shoreditch, Millbank in Pimlico directly behind the Tate Gallery, and the Bourne Estate in Clerkenwell — were remarkable examples of social housing, blocks of apartments in grandiose Edwardian style, superbly decorated in red and gold brick. They exist today, greatly enhanced by landscaping and regeneration. Despite inroads of private ownership most of them continue to provide affordable housing in central London for working class Londoners.

By the end of the 1930s the LCC had constructed 190 inner-London estates, including the huge White City Estate near Shepherd's Bush, which alone contained 2,300 flats, the beautiful Old Oak Estate in East Acton, and the Art Deco Ossulston Estate in Somers Town, and was responsible for maintaining them.[4] During the 1950s the LCC and local borough councils went into overdrive in the construction of new estates, including the Woodberry Down Estate at Manor House overlooking the New River reservoirs, and the Regent's Park Estate between Hampstead Road and Albany Street. These estates, and others like them, are what John Boughton has called

> the mark of an upwardly mobile working class and the visible manifestation of a state which took seriously its duty to house its people decently.[5]

In the immediate post-war years, following bomb damage to some of the Nash terraces surrounding Regent's Park, the Crown Commissioners planned to level the terraces and replace them with a ring of luxury flats. St Pancras Council, then under Labour control, had other ideas. In 1946 the Vice-Chair of the St Pancras Borough Labour Party, Eric Cook, wrote:

> The people of St Marylebone and St Pancras and their borough councils must persuade the Crown Commissioners...that something better can be done with this site. What an inspiration

it would be for the hundreds of thousands who come to Regent's Park every year... if they saw, instead of a restricted number of luxury flats for the very wealthy, right around the "outer circle" of the Park a magnificent sweep of modern flats where people like themselves, service couples and families, had their homes overlooking one of the loveliest of London's parks.

The vision of a council estate on the fringes of Regent's Park was never implemented. The Nash terraces remained and residents of the Regent's Park Estate did not have a view of the park. However, the estate —sixty-nine acres bought from the Crown Commissioners — was built across the road from the terraces, on the other side of Albany Street. The only through route from Albany Street to the park, Chester Gate, was a public right of way, so residents of the estate could reach the park in a few minutes. In the 1960s and 1970s my family lived on the estate, on the eighth floor of "Rydal Water" on Robert Street, five minutes' walk from Camden Town and fifteen minutes' walk from the West End. It seemed entirely natural to us that to see a film we went to Leicester Square and the weekly food shop was done in Marks & Spencer on Oxford Street.

The LCC's efforts were matched by new, architecturally innovative housing projects such as the Spa Green Estate near the Angel, the Holford Square Estate off Pentonville Road, and the Golden Lane Estate north of what is today the Barbican Centre. Golden Lane was built by the socialist-led Borough of Finsbury to cater for the needs of working class residents displaced by the bombing of the City. Influenced by Le Corbusier's work in Scandinavia, Golden Lane was unusual for the time in that most of the flats were designed for single people and couples rather than families with children, with studios and one-bedroomed flats making up the majority of its 554 units. Most of the Golden Lane Estate is now Grade II listed, a beacon of colourful, self-confident social housing providing high quality homes for approximately 1,500 people in the midst of gentrified Clerkenwell. Sadly, because of the effects of the Right to Buy scheme introduced by the first Thatcher government, about half of its flats have been sold on long leases and now command prices reflective of inner London's property market. The other half are still council flats for rent.

The Spa Green Estate was designed by the Constructivist architect Berthold Lubetkin, who in the 1930s designed London Zoo's iconic Penguin Pool and the modernist Finsbury Health Centre, which opened in 1938 and provided free healthcare in the borough ten years before the advent of the NHS. Spa Green was opened in 1949 by Herbert Morrison, leader of the London Labour Party and Deputy Prime Minister. It provided 126 flats in three attractive blocks no larger than eight storeys high, with lifts, balconies, central heating, plenty of natural light and a communal roof terrace directly opposite Sadler's Wells on Roseberry Avenue. Lubetkin practiced a more decorative and patterned style than the Brutalist aesthetic that drove later council housing, one that wasn't afraid to use splashes of colour, one reason his creations have been both durable and popular. Spa Green also asked more from tenants, stipulating that stairs and landing be swept every day and that music not be played between 10pm and 8am, a contract between responsible adults designed to ensure a civilised environment, and which did.

The Holford Square Estate on Holford Street at the King's Cross end of Pentonville Road, which opened in 1954, was designed and constructed by the same people on the same principles. The scheme arose from the almost complete destruction in the war of Holford Square, where Lenin had lived in 1902-4 while in exile. Because of this association, the estate's showpiece, Bevin Court, was originally to be called Lenin Court, but by the time it was completed political fashions had shifted and it was instead named after Ernest Bevin, a name far more in keeping with the character of British working class politics. As innovative as Spa Green, Bevin Court is a striking Y-shaped building with an elegant central staircase now regarded as a modernist masterpiece, the entire building sited so that no part of it faces north on to Pentonville Road. Its entrance hall contains a mural by the artist Peter Yates on the history of Finsbury. In their design, placement and social philosophy Bevin Court and Spa Green were symbols of a new world being born, a world that British Tories worked very hard over several decades to eradicate.

They have not quite succeeded. The massive thirty-acre Churchill Gardens Estate in Pimlico, run by Westminster City Council, still provides 1,600 homes in thirty-two blocks of flats for five thousand mostly working class people in central London. Constructed in phases between 1946 and 1962 as part of the LCC's aborted "Abercrombie Plan" for the capital's post-war housing, Churchill Gardens is distinctive for its variations of height and length, with tall slab-like blocks of between nine and eleven storeys surrounded by horizontal blocks of seven storeys, the whole interspersed by maisonettes and terraces. Its first four blocks, ready by 1950, won the Festival of Britain Architectural Award. The *Municipal Dreams* website found that

> *What is striking to any visitor to the Estate is — despite its size — its intimacy and humanity... And it seems clear that the Estate has worked — it has prospered as a decent place to live even as many other, superficially more grandiose post-war housing schemes have failed.*

Like Golden Lane, about half the flats have now been purchased under Right to Buy and some have subsequently been bought by middle class professionals, but it remains a predominantly working class community with a healthy social diversity.

There also existed in London, throughout and in the heart of the city, another network of up to eight thousand dwellings for working class families, although in the immediate post-war years its quality was variable and sometimes shockingly poor. The Peabody Estates arose from an endowment left by the American philanthropist George Peabody in 1862, turned into the Peabody Trust by an Act of Parliament that committed the Trust to work within London for the relief of poverty by constructing "model dwellings" for the poor. To get one of the homes a resident had to be a Londoner "by birth or residence".

By 1950 a large number of the Peabody Estates were in run-down condition, but they were still a step up from the private slum housing in which large numbers of London's working class lived. Alan Johnson, born in 1950, lived in a Rowe Housing Trust flat in Southam Street, W10, in North Kensington (or Kensal Town, as it was known at the time), a street whose houses had been condemned as uninhabitable in the 1930s and had deteriorated further since then. He recalled his nan's flat in Peabody Buildings, Delgano Gardens, as the "height of luxury". In comparison to his own two-room hovel, which had no electricity and no indoor toilet, his nan's had both, and "something called a living room".[6]

Today the Peabody Estate's 29,000 London homes are hardly recognisable from that time. In comparison to much of the social housing offered since the 1950s the estates are quiet, pleasant oases of attractive Victorian mansion blocks, many restored to their pristine state, built out of beautiful honey-coloured brick around lovingly maintained courtyards and playgrounds. Found throughout London — but also in great quantities in parts of central London otherwise far beyond the means of working class Londoners, such as Westminster, Drury Lane, Victoria and Farringdon — the Peabody buildings exemplify what progressive-minded housing associations can achieve for working class Londoners if allowed to do so.

But in 1950 it was not only those in Kensal Town who lived in Victorian conditions. Joyce O'Connell was born in 1940 in St Pancras. Her father Tom O'Connell, who had changed his name from Tom Connor, had arrived in London in the 1920s, an IRA hardman on the losing side of the Irish Civil War. In the 1930s he "married" Kathleen Delany, a young Irish woman from Waterford who was working as a cleaner and maid for an Irish London GP. In 1949 Joyce and her family (mother, two sisters and two brothers) moved from slum housing in Goldington Crescent, Somers Town, to slum housing in a terraced house at 5 Burton Street, which backed on to Tavistock Square.

The Burton Street flat had an outdoor toilet and no electricity (it did not get connected until 1961). Lit by candles, there was no heating except the fire in the living room. There were two bedrooms, one for the three girls and the other for mum and the boys. When they needed a bath they went to the Mary Ward youth club off Russell Square. The girls' bedroom looked on to the back of the British Medical Association's (BMA) large HQ on Tavistock Square, where in the 1950s Kathleen worked as a cleaner. On some evenings, gazing out from their cold bedroom window on to the BMA's well lit, opulent ballroom, Joyce and her sisters Kate and Anne watched doctors and their glamorously dressed wives dance the night away.

Joyce went to school at the St Aloysius Catholic Primary School in Somers Town and, later, the St Vincent De Paul Catholic School in Victoria. There she was taught by nuns who she remembered as bitter sadists who punished her relentlessly because, unlike her younger brothers and sisters, her birth certificate read "Father Unknown". Her ostensible father Tom O'Connell was also married (and married first) to another woman named Fifi who worked in Heals furniture store on Tottenham Court Road. Until the mid-1950s he was mostly away, living with Fifi in Brecknock Road, Kentish Town. Moving between cold house and cold school, Joyce became a teenager in the 1950s, gradually discovering a kind of freedom in the youth clubs of St Pancras where she learnt to dance and read music.

The centre of working class shopping in the St Pancras and Somers Town area was Chapel Street Market at the south end of Upper Street. By the early 1950s the market had hardly changed since the 1920s (in 1955 it still hosted a corn-cutter, operating on people's feet resting on upturned orange boxes). In 1951 Bert Lloyd, a London folk singer who joined the Communist Party in the 1930s and became a semi-professional chronicler of working class music and wrote for *Picture Post* in the 1940s, wrote about Chapel Street in a feature for *Illustrated* magazine called "Face of the Angel":

> *The eel man chinks a spoon against a basin. And, above all the human noises, from the record stalls rises the steel-stringed blatter of "Shotgun Boogie". The traders are having a thin time of it, with only fruit and vegetables selling well and other traders closing down.* [7]

Lloyd reported that the street violence and protection rackets of previous years were a thing of the past, but in this he was optimistic. Future years would see a formidable new criminal gang, the Adams, exert influence over Chapel Street before branching into more ambitious and lucrative crime.

In the 1950s the slums of Goldington Crescent were taken over by St Pancras Borough Council, which, aside from a few that later became extremely valuable, knocked most of them down to make way for the Goldington Street Estate. The estate consisted of the Goldington buildings and the Chenies, two monumental blocks of flats redeemed by flashes of Art Deco styling, sitting opposite St Pancras Old Church, one of the oldest churches in London, dating back to the thirteenth century and constructed partly out of abandoned Roman tiles and bricks (the name of the church and the borough derived from Pancratius, a third-century Christian martyr). In stark contrast to the rest of Somers Town, the Goldington Street blocks are dark, imposing hulks sitting on top of a few shops and offices, one of which is the constituency office of Holborn & St Pancras's Labour MP, Sir Keir Starmer.

In the nineteenth century Somers Town was a warren of slum streets whose life revolved around the Brill, a large, teeming general market for butchers' meat and provisions on its south-east corner where now sits the British Library. In the twentieth century it became a citadel of working class social housing with several large council estates, including the faded but still-impressive Ossulton Estate. In the early 1950s Somers Town was an overwhelmingly white working class area, but it was not divorced from other influences. From 1941 to 1957 the Trinidad-born Pan-Africanist socialist George Padmore lived with his partner, the white working class writer and activist Dorothy Pizer, in a small flat in Cranleigh House, a block of old "industrial dwellings" on Cranleigh Street. It was often visited by Afro-Caribbean opposition politicians such as Kwame Nkrumah, Jomo Kenyatta and Eric Williams, and functioned as a social and information hub for many anti-colonial movements. Just around the corner on Goldington Street, the left-wing Unity Theatre, an offshoot of the Workers' Theatre Movement, had since 1937 been promoting working class theatre and other agit-prop artistic projects, including hosting Paul Robeson in

1938 and over one hundred performances of the left-wing review *What's Left?* in 1948.

The Goldington Street Estate and the featureless blocks of Wakefield Street demonstrated that St Pancras, despite Camden Council's subsequent record, was just as capable of producing dispiriting council estates as any other borough. In the 1950s Camden itself was still semi-industrial, a hold-over from its role as the pioneer of railway expansion in London in the 1840s, when the London & Birmingham Railway (L&BR) drove a huge trench from Primrose Hill to Euston to carry its line deeper into the city. It was a mammoth project, necessitating a vast thirty-acre goods yard known as the Camden Goods Station to accommodate all its infrastructure, machinery, tools and waste products. The Goods Station, and the nearby railway sidings where queues of engines pumped smoke and soot into the air, remained the beating heart of transport and industry in Camden for the next century.

By the 1950s North London's once-thriving piano industry, in decline since the 1920s, was almost extinct. There were a few hold-outs scattered around Camden Town amongst a diverse range of small and medium-sized firms like motor body builders, glass and timber merchants, paint-makers, cardboard box-makers and a number of smaller engineering firms. The W. & A. Gilbey site, which took over the Camden Goods Station in the late nineteenth century, dominated the local economy. Gilbey, the largest drinks firm in the world, came to Camden in 1869. Its massive site encompassed a distillery, an ice wharf, coal yards, horse stables and numerous warehouses for blending, bottling and packing alcohol, the whole complex providing North London's working class with employment for nearly one hundred years until it finally closed down in 1963.

A large number of local working class people, mostly women, also held positions at the Arcadia Works factory of the Carreras Cigarette Company on Mornington Crescent, popularly known as the Black Cat Factory after the two ten-feet high bronze cast cats sitting outside its striking Art Deco building. At its height the Black Cat Factory employed over three thousand workers and provided four canteens, an on-site doctor and dentist, free legal advice, numerous social clubs and a convalescent home in Brighton. The factory closed in 1961 and relocated to Basildon. The building is now converted offices but the Black Cats remain, forever guarding the entrance to Camden Town.

Christine Kerr was born in 1947 and lived in two rooms on the top floor of 28 Greenland Road, adjacent to Camden Town tube station, with her dad, a greengrocer's barrow boy, and her mum, who worked in one of the few remaining piano factories, Herrburger Brooks at 31 Lyme Street, the world's oldest manufacturer of piano keyboards (and which remained so until it finally closed in 1998). In the 1950s Christine went with her dad to Covent Garden Market early every morning to stock up on fruit and veg for his stall. Of her upbringing she recalled:

> There was a tin bath in the basement which we brought up to the third floor for a bath, and my mum would boil water for it. The "kitchen" was a cooker on the landing and a cabinet for the food. Water was down one flight of stairs, from a corner sink. We never had water in the kitchen until I was five and they put in a big old butler's sink. My mum used to give me a bath in it. Anyway, we kept all our food in the kitchen cabinet since it was mostly in tins, we didn't have a fridge, and one day a tin of Spam or corned beef disappeared. My mum was going to do it for our tea and it wasn't there. So after that she planted food to see if it would disappear and everything went. We had locks put on the rooms then. The thief was a neighbour downstairs. She was a big drinker with a tiny husband she used to beat up.[8]

Victor Heath was a bit older, born in 1932 at the Mornington Crescent end of Arlington Road, one of eight children. The area took heavy damage in the war due to its proximity to the three big mainline stations of North London. Vic's older brother Jim, a young fireman, was killed in 1942 during a bombing raid. After the war Vic finished his education at Medburn Street School in Somers Town, which Ted also attended after it was renamed the Sir William Collins Secondary School for Boys. Leaving school at fourteen, Vic started work with FG Minter, a local construction firm, before moving in 1949 to work as a van delivery boy for Idris, a soft-drinks company. Naturally bright, he started to read the *Daily Worker* and went to meetings of the Young Communist League (YCL), although he did not join it. In 1950 he started as a labourer with a building firm renovating a large building on the Strand, where he joined the Transport and General Workers Union (TGWU). After a year he was elected shop steward.

In the 1950s Vic moved on to work for Costain and met Vera, the young woman who would become his wife. Short of money, one of their favourite outings was a walk over Primrose Hill to enjoy the view over London. Vic also introduced Vera to opera, a passion of his not always appreciated by his family. In the late 1950s the family home on Arlington Road was subject to a Compulsory Purchase Order from the council, who rehoused Vic, Vera and their young son in a flat in Kentish Town. In 1959 Vic went to work for St Pancras Borough Council, building flats on the Regent's Park Estate.[9]

Large parts of Hackney such as Stoke Newington, Stamford Hill and Green Lanes lay in a liminal zone between North and East London, uniquely suited to fractious politics. In March 1949 about 200 British fascists tried to intimidate the Orthodox Jewish area of Stamford Hill by marching straight through it from Dalston to Tottenham, but a large number of anti-fascists led by the 43 Group, a collection of Jewish ex-servicemen who fought frequent battles in Ridley Road Market with the remains of Mosley's Blackshirts, opposed them. Amongst the 43 Group's members was teenager Vidal Sassoon, a Jewish working class boy from Shepherd's Bush whose family arrived in London from Ukraine in the 1880s. Despite a ring of five hundred police protecting the marchers, hand-to-hand fighting broke out and the fascists had to retreat. In 1950 the 43 Group dissolved itself as it felt the immediate threat from domestic fascism had receded.

Jacky Hyams was born in 1944 in Hackney and grew up in a flat in a three-storey block just off Shacklewell Lane, in the midst of an area that in the 1950s was still a "shattered, wrecked wasteland" slowly recovering from the war.[10] The flat was heated by small coal fires. Although it had a bathroom it lacked hot running water, which was provided by boiling water on the gas stove. Jacky's father was a bookie working with his own father — known as the Old Man, a well-known figure in the East End and City gambling world, sufficiently respected to be left alone by the Krays — in a "commission agent" shop in Houndsditch near Liverpool Street station. Their customers were mainly City gents and traders. As a result, the local police turned a blind eye to the cash being exchanged in nearby pubs and street corners.

Jacky's dad was perfectly placed to benefit from the economic opportunities that were opening up in the 1950s to street-smart working class men. Jacky recalled that his daily routine, Monday to Saturday, remained unaltered throughout the 1950s and 1960s:

> *Each morning, my dad, smartly suited and booted, would take the number 649 bus down Kinglsand Road to Liverpool Street and make his way to the Lane and the "commission agent" office, to take bets from the more affluent punters who had a phone, could ring through their bets...all totally legit. Early evening — and at lunchtime — once the pubs were open, he'd stroll round the corner to Houndsditch and park himself at the corner of the George & Dragon, drinking, wisecracking, swapping stories or taking illegal bets from punters; his usual gang of cronies, small-time crooks, market stallholders and cops around him, ordering big rounds of drinks for all and generally having a whale of a time.[11]*

In the early 1950s the City itself was a land out of time, still battered from the war, still small and intimate, still organically linked to the Pool of London and the docks. The Port of London was severely damaged by the Blitz but although much of central London's industry around Shoreditch and Finsbury had been bombed out the Port still survived. From the 1950s until the mid-1960s it experienced an Indian summer, with shipping in those years reaching record levels before an abrupt and irreversible decline brought about by the arrival of containerisation and roll-on, roll-off ferries.

In 1953, at age fourteen, Michael Moorcock landed his first job as a messenger boy in the City. Of that time, he recalled:

> I could take a bus or a train down to the docks and then walk for miles looking for the appropriate ship or customs office: grey cranes, redbrick warehouses, endless rust-grimed ships. I never had any idea of where docklands ended. Apart from the great shipping lines, banks and insurance companies, the City was still an area of small businesses. There were scrap-yards, independent stationers, booksellers, printers, chophouses, eel and pie shops, tea shops.[12]

Moorcock moved on from the City for a while but by 1956, still only seventeen, he was back working in Holborn where by dint of precocious talent and chutzpah he became the editor of the popular juvenile magazine *Tarzan's Adventures*, the beginning of an astonishing career at the intersection of literary fiction and pulp SF.

Despite her dad's enjoyable masculine world on the fringes of the old City, Jacky's home life was not particularly comfortable. Surrounded by derelict ruins, the block they lived in was not well maintained and was dominated by the problems of "the Chute", an old rubbish chute which struggled to take the block's rubbish. There were small wall-mounted metal openings to the Chute on every other floor, but with the chute door and funnel too narrow for the amount of rubbish it took it was frequently blocked or over-spilling. In summer this meant the stairwells smelled awful and buzzed with flies.[13]

But for all its stark poverty, Hackney was not the "East End". It was much easier to transit to North London from Hackney than it was from Bow or Poplar, not just because of proximity but through use of the North London Line, an overground rail link that ran from Stratford through Hackney, Islington and Camden and on to Willesden Junction. Although the line was run-down, between 1952 and 1957 three of its stations — Willesden Junction, West Hampstead and Gospel Oak — received new platforms, staff offices and waiting rooms. Hackney's Jewish population, especially, felt the difference and put it to use. Throughout the twentieth century it progressively migrated north from Spitalfields and Shoreditch (the northern parts of which are in Hackney's southern spur) up Stoke Newington High Street to Stamford Hill and South Tottenham before transitioning west to Golders Green.

The young Steven Berkoff, born just before the war in Stepney, moved with his family to the Woodberry Down Estate in Manor House, but with his father still working as a tailor in Whitechapel he remained anchored to the East End. A quick journey on the 633 bus from Manor House took him to his father's shop. The flats of the Woodberry Down Estate had bathrooms and electricity, and were a step up from the poverty Berkoff had been born into. Although he attended Hackney Downs Boys School, Steven spent his teenage years moving between Manor House and Whitechapel. He spent free time and weekends at the small "beach" near Tower Bridge, in and out of Petticoat Lane Market, at the Stamford Hill Boys' Club or hanging about the Stamford Hill intersection, chatting up girls at the E&A Milk Bar on one side or with his mates in the Regent's Cinema on the other:

> This area became my university for the next half a dozen years and spawned many of the thoughts and ideas that were to become useful to me later on. I spent many evenings drifting around Stamford Hill and I might even go back to the East End to visit my old youth club.[14]

Even more so than Hackney, Paddington and North Kensington in the 1950s were notorious for the appalling conditions in which working class families lived. This was not a result of the poor quality of LCC housing estates, for aside from the enormous White City Estate they did not have many, but arose from the many private rented houses and flats that filled up the great urban sprawl between the Grand Union Canal in the north and Notting Hill Gate in the south. The local cinema, the Electric on Portobello Road, was known as "the Bughole". It was regularly sprayed with disinfectant by an attendant, sometimes during the film.

What at the time was known as "Notting Dale" was to all intents and purposes a vast slum, but one dense with extended white working class families who lived literally in and out of each other's homes and streets. Not many had bathrooms, the bath being (at best) a tin bath hung up over the sink and filled up once a week with hot water, with the family taking turns. Frank Hale's multi-occupancy house in Westbourne Park Road was owned by the London Co-Op:

> My aunt and uncle and brothers, Jim and Peter, lived in the two rooms on the top floor. They had a gas cooker in my uncle's bedroom. On the next floor down was my grandad and his daughter. There was a gas cooker in his room, and below on the ground floor there were two rooms portioned off with a toilet on the landing"[15]

Alan Johnson vividly recalled the winter in his small flat:

> Warmth was limited to a radius of about three feet around the coal fire and the vicinity of the stove. The bedrooms were iceboxes and we dreaded the moment when we had to get dressed or undressed...We had no carpet, save for a tatty scrap that served as a mat in front of the coal fire. Everywhere else the floor was covered with "lino", cold and cracked, cheap and nasty. Getting up to pee in a bucket in the middle of a frosty night was no fun, but it was infinitely preferable to having to go out to the back yard to use the toilet.[16]

Summer was at least warmer, but presented other problems:

> We were so used to swarms of flies we didn't register them. Like the trains clanking past at all hours on the line in and out of Paddington, we'd only have noticed them if they disappeared.[17]

The poverty imposed a particular lifestyle. Gwen Nelson, who lived in Golborne Road and whose father ran a local greengrocer's shop, recalled:

Few people owned cars in North Kensington. The few vehicles we did see were the totters' ponies and carts, the milkcart, men cycling to work, or delivery vans. Twice a week there was excitement in the form of a King's Troop clattering along Golborne Road on its way to Wormwood Scrubs...Following in their wake were locals with buckets and shovels to scoop up the horses' droppings because it was good manure.[18]

And yet, despite these enclaves of grim Edwardian poverty, in the 1950s an entirely new, post-war London working class was emerging. Even before *Blackboard Jungle* (1955) arrived and changed everything, adolescent Londoners were pushing against the pre-war conventions of their parents and creating a night-time economy of clubs and bars, particularly in central and North London. Sid Manning, who as a young lad worked in a shoe factory in Askew Road near Shepherd's Bush, used to meet his girlfriend and future wife Ann, a junior secretary in the West End, to go to the local clubs:

We used to head up to the Hammersmith Palais every Friday to listen to Joe Loss and Ken Macintosh... Unfortunately because of the new maple floor in the Palais the girls in stilettos weren't allowed on it as it would mark the floor, so we used to jive around the carpet edges...The music for me was redhot. They were more innocent times but we knew how to enjoy ourselves beyond a shadow of a doubt.

The impact of *Blackboard Jungle* and Bill Haley's "Rock Around the Clock" on British youth culture was revolutionary. It changed the traditional dance hall into something geared towards teenagers and their energy (even into their sixties my mum and dad, teenagers in the 1950s, would get up and do a remarkably fast jive should "Rock Around the Clock" come on). There were many dance halls catering for London's teenagers but the most popular were the Hammersmith Palais, the Lyceum off the Strand and, largest of them all, the Tottenham Royal on Tottenham High Road. In the early 1950s the Royal was home to big Dance Bands such as Joe Loss and Victor Sylvester, but from 1954 it was the place to go for more raucous rock n' roll. Teddy Boys flocked there and made it notorious.

Sid recalled that until he moved out of the family home he was constantly told off by his dad for playing the Dansette record player too loud. But times were changing rapidly, with the extra disposable cash earned by teenagers like Sid channelled into better clothing and sharper fashion:

> I used to get my clothes from John Silver on the Uxbridge Road. He had a massive sign on the front of his shop "Get the million dollar look from John Silver for a fiver"... Me and my mates looked smart when we went out, all in nice Italian suits.[19]

The basis for a new consumerism was already there. Rationing of clothes, made redundant by the widespread availability of forged clothing coupons on the black market, had ended in 1949. In 1954 rationing ceased entirely, although for many Londoners the black market had supplied food and other items "off the ration" right through the 1940s and early 1950s. London's street markets, especially Petticoat Lane, were a nexus for goods like cigarettes, cigars, nylons, cosmetics, alcohol and varieties of tinned food difficult to get elsewhere. The post-war black market was an integral part of London life and laid the groundwork for a vibrant cash-in-hand economy that permeated and sustained working class London for decades to come.

In the inter-war period large parts of London's economy underwent a belated industrialisation. Jolted into the modern world by the First World War and the need for accelerated war production, London became a national centre for the manufacture of cars and electrical goods. Park Royal industrial estate, previously a wasteland west of Willesden Junction, grew from eighteen factories in 1918 to 250 by 1939. In the 1920s London made a fitful attempt to give its new industries an improved transport infrastructure with the construction of the Great West Road and Western Avenue, the latter best known for the Art Deco-style Hoover Building which doubled as a corporate HQ and a modern construction plant employing 1,600 people. The Great West Road ran from Hounslow to Brentford and was littered with new factories and corporate offices for American firms like Gillette and Firestone Tyres as well as Smith's Crisps, Macleans Toothpaste and Curry's, which together employed over 11,000 people by the late 1930s.

Despite Park Royal's success, the working class of central and North London still worked mainly in retail, transport, construction and building maintenance, in printing and its allied trades, and in the servicing of the capital's large leisure and entertainment sector. Parts of central London such as Holborn, Finsbury and Clerkenwell contained a number of smaller factories and workshops, especially in the jewellery and furniture business. Before the war areas like Paddington and Marylebone contained an eclectic collection of micro-industries such as gunsmiths, feather bedders and assorted art supplies, small workhouses found in railway sidings and backstreet mews conveniently close to the West End's big stores.

Most of London's new industry was found outside what the 1951 Census called the "Central Area", an area of approximately ten square miles stretching from Kensington in the west to Aldgate in the east, and from the northern rail terminals of King's Cross and Euston to Elephant and Castle in the south. This area contained most of the city's academic, legal and government institutions, its print media and its entertainment and shopping centres, but conspicuously *not* the great docks, gasworks, ports and sewage outfalls that lay east of Tower Bridge on either side of the Thames. The Clean Air Acts of the 1950s, prompted by the Great Fog of December 1952 which killed over 4,000 people in London in four days, led to an exodus of metal casting and similar small industry from central London, pushing what remained out to the industrial estates of Edmonton and Park Royal.

By the 1950s Park Royal — conveniently situated between Western Avenue, the North Circular and the Grand Union Canal — had the biggest concentration of manufacturing industry in London and one of the largest in the country. Companies located in the area such as Heinz, Nestle, Hoover,

McVittee's, Lyons, Optrex, EMI, Gillette, Kodak and Guinness employed up to 45,000 people. The employees of Lucas Aerospace, Rolls Royce and GKN, which built the Routemaster buses introduced into the capital in 1956, were skilled engineers, but the majority of the other firms' workforces were either unskilled or semi-skilled, with many jobs filled by a largely migrant and female workforce. Acton was famous for its over fifty laundries, a significant employer of working class women from Kensal Town, Harlesden and Willesden.

Many factories in Cricklewood employed the newly arrived immigrant Irish, especially women. Mary Walker, a young Irish woman who upon arrival in London in 1959 worked for a French hairdressing salon in Hampstead and then for a Greek hairdresser in Cricklewood, recalled:

There were lots of factories around Cricklewood in those days. There was a big Smyth's that made clocks and speedometers, stuff like that. Another factory manufactured washing machines, Rose Razor, and then there was Frigidaire...It felt like the whole of London came out of Smith's on a Friday afternoon. You couldn't walk along the footpaths at quarter past four, when the factories finished.[20]

The large exhibition centres at White City, Earl's Court and Olympia in Kensington also employed hundreds of sub-contracted fitters, joiners and electricians. Most of these were protected by closed shop agreements and an active trade union presence. In 1953 two hundred electricians at Olympia and Earl's Court took part in national strike action by the Electrical Trade Union (ETU) over pay, resulting in the cancellation of that year's Cruft's Dog Show.

Whether it was in manufacturing, construction, public transport or the recently created National Health Service (NHS), there was work to be done and not enough labour to do it. This inevitably meant a large influx of immigrant workers to fill the gap, a process London had gone through several times before. Even in 1950 one in twenty Londoners were foreign-born, a historically high figure. Most of these came from other

European countries such as France, Italy, Greece, Spain and Germany. About four to five thousand were of West Indian or Indian/Pakistani origin. By 2011 white people, i.e. British, Irish and others, were still a majority (59%) of London's population, but they were heavily concentrated in Outer London boroughs such as Barnet, Enfield, Havering, Bexley, Bromley, Sutton, Kingston-upon-Thames and Richmond-upon-Thames. By contrast, Black and Asian Londoners, nearly 38% of the city's population, were concentrated in the six boroughs that form the core of North London; a block of similarly contiguous South London boroughs (Wandsworth, Lambeth, Southwark and Lewisham); plus other boroughs such as Tower Hamlets, Newham, Brent and Hounslow.[21] The cultural effect of this coalescence, over seventy years, has been profound.

The beginning of this process is usually cited as the arrival of the HMT *Empire Windrush* at Tilbury on 21st June 1948, bringing 693 West Indian men seeking work in England. But the *Windrush*, although historically important, did not open floodgates of immigration. By 1951 there had been only six similar voyages bringing a total of 1,800 Caribbean migrants. The numbers of West Indian migrants increased to 2,000 a year in 1952 and 1953 but only in 1954 did numbers jump to 10,000 and in 1955 to 27,000. Putting that in perspective, throughout the decade about 40,000 Irish immigrants arrived in the UK *every year*. There were lesser though still significant numbers of Greek Cypriot, Maltese and Italian immigrants.

London was hardly new to immigrant populations making certain areas of the city their own, from the French Huguenots in the seventeenth century to later influxes of Eastern European Jews and Chinese in the latter half of the nineteenth century. In the 1920s a significant number of Russian exiles, working class socialists fleeing the persecution of the new Bolshevik state, settled in an area on the border of Tottenham and Edmonton off Pretoria Road that became known as Little Russia, where many families kept horses, chickens and ducks in their backyards. The area survived that way until the 1970s, an urban ghetto so rough that the police would not venture there except in packs.

But it was the arrival of large numbers of Caribbean black immigrants that had the biggest impact on the social life of London, especially that of its working class. Half of the migrants from the West Indies who arrived in the UK between 1948 and 1962 settled in London, and of these more than 60% were from Jamaica. The new West Indian immigrants did not gravitate to comfortable middle class areas. Of necessity they went where rent and living was cheapest. Even there they were the victims of slum landlords, high rents and overcrowding, conditions for which they were then blamed. By 1953 there were four main West Indian communities in London, in Stepney, Brixton, Camden Town and Notting Dale. By the end of the decade these had reformed around the two much larger nexuses of Brixton in the south and Notting Hill/Bayswater in the north.

Outside of these "havens" the welcome from London landlords was as cold as the weather — "No Blacks, No Irish, No Dogs". Charlie Phillips' experience was not untypical. His parents journeyed to England in the early 1950s and in 1956, aged eleven, he travelled from Jamaica to join them. When he arrived his mother and father were still living in a single room in Paddington. After two nights they managed to get a double room at 15 Bassett Road in Kensal Town, a front room partitioned with a curtain. There was a communal kitchen on the landing and they shared a bathroom with sixteen other tenants. For Charlie the culture shock was intense:

> Coming out of your house straight onto the street. We never had that in the West Indies. It got warm four days after we arrived. In the Caribbean, automatically you'd take your shoes off and play. I got told off. "You're in England now. Put your shoes on."[22]

Later the family moved to a bigger basement flat but they still had to share a communal kitchen. The big turning point of his life occurred when an American GI, one of many who came to Notting Hill to party when stationed in London, pawned a Kodak camera to his father, who gave it to Charlie. Charlie taught himself how to use it, taking photographs and developing them in his bedroom. In the 1960s, after a spell in the Merchant

Navy, he walked around Notting Hill recording daily life for his friends and neighbours, in the process becoming a freelance photographer whose striking and atmospheric photos, like "Man in a Zoot Suit" and "The Piss House Pub", were picked up by *Harper's Bazaar* and *Life*.

The dislocating experiences of these new arrivals have been caught in several works, the first and best of which is Samuel Selvon's *The Lonely Londoners* (1956). Selvon, born in Trinidad, worked as a reporter for the *Trinidad Guardian* before coming to London in 1950 and working in a variety of unskilled jobs in order to survive. In his spare time he wrote *The Lonely Londoners*, the first literary examination, using West Indian creole and street slang for its narrative voice as well as the characters' dialect, of the experience of working class black Londoners, their daily lives and struggles and how they adapted to the challenges of white British society.

The Lonely Londoners does not tell a tale of triumph against the odds. On the contrary, its protagonist Moses has worn himself out on the cliff face of London's indifference and racism. Although he tries to prepare newer and more naïve arrivals for the rigours of London life, his own dreams of success get no nearer:

> *Daniel was telling him how over in France all kinds of fellas writing books what turning out to be best-sellers. Taxi-driver, porter, road-sweeper — it didn't matter. One day you sweating in the factory and the next day all the newspapers have your name and photo, saying how you are a new literary giant. He watch the tugboat on the Thames, wondering if he could ever write a book like that, what everybody would buy.*[23]

Selvon himself received no such acclaim, at least not in his lifetime, although *The Lonely Londoners* is now an acknowledged classic of both the post-war Caribbean immigrant experience and of the "London Novel". It laid the groundwork for later black British authors such as Zadie Smith and Andrea Levy, whose *Small Island* (2004), a similar work on a similar theme, finally received the plaudits and recognition denied Selvon.

Contrary to legend, most immigrants to London in the 1950s did not arrive in response to specific recruiting campaigns for the NHS or London Transport, although considerable numbers of Afro-Caribbean and Irish immigrants did end up working for one or the other (the men for LT, the women as nurses in the NHS). They weren't always welcome. In 1950, a number of white workers at King's Cross Goods Depot complained to the National Union of Railwaymen (NUR) that black men were being recruited above the basic entry grade which meant in some instances they had seniority or authority over white men. In response, the NUR's Assistant General Secretary Jim Campbell went personally to King's Cross and addressed a meeting of workers from six London depots, convincing them to support the union's opposition to the colour bar.

Integration took longer on the buses. In 1956, the same year it launched the iconic Routemaster bus, London Transport ran a recruitment campaign in Barbados for conductors and station masters but initially only hired 150 people. Despite this slow start, by 1961 LT was employing over 2,000 Barbadian immigrants and in the 1960s it sought to recruit directly from Trinidad and Jamaica.[24] The Post Office also became a major employer of West Indian and Irish workers. Because Afro-Caribbean and Irish workers had a common background and faced the same challenges — from predominantly rural societies, at the mercy of systems they did not understand, discriminated against by landlords and others — they often formed bonds of friendship and solidarity, especially within the big state employers.

From its inception in 1948 the NHS was in urgent need of more staff, particularly nurses, porters and cleaners. In the early 1950s it ran a high-profile recruitment campaign in Dublin which led to a large number of young Irish women working in NHS hospitals as newly recruited nurses, especially in London. Initially they met anti-Irish prejudice about their cleanliness and general ability but this rapidly dissolved as it became clear that they were, in the main, exceptionally efficient at the work.

The majority of Irish immigrants to London settled in Kilburn and Cricklewood with significant numbers in Camden Town and Kentish Town and, in South London, around Elephant and Castle. While the women found employment in the NHS or as domestic cleaners, the men worked mainly in construction. Early every morning the "Navvies" would congregate at the big pick-up points outside Camden Town tube station, the Crown pub on Cricklewood Broadway, the middle of Hammersmith Broadway and the Elephant and Castle roundabout, hoping for work with one of the big building firms that mainly employed Irish workers — John Laing, McAlpine, Balfour Beatty, Wimpey, Lowery, Murphy and Taylor Woodrow.

Many Irish labourers had little idea how English welfare and employment law operated and were easy meat for exploitative employers. Showing a fine sense for weakness, the construction firms often used Irish foremen, "gangers", to do the cheating. It was the gangers who decided on a whim who they wanted at the pick-up points in the early morning. They did well out of the system:

> On a Saturday night, a ganger would come into the Half Moon pub on Holloway Road and ask did you want a shift in the morning. If you did, you had to guarantee him a drink the next night. The shift might last from about seven o'clock to half past twelve, for about five pounds a shift. No documentation — just a bundle of fivers in the pub, and pay the men out. Afterwards, when you were driven back to London in the wagons, the foreman came in with you and had possibly ten shillings off each man, and he drank all day free, and if you didn't go along with it then there were no more Sunday shifts.[25]

It was a hard life made bearable by hard drinking, a life best caught by Dónall Mac Amhlaigh's powerful autobiography *An Irish Navvy: The Diary of an Exile* (1964) and by the Dubliner's immortal folk song "MacAlpine's Fusiliers", a slice of working class oral history patched together in ad hoc fashion by different labourers on different sites before being knocked into shape by Dominic Behan:

> Come all you pincher laddies
> And you long-distance men

Don't ever work for McAlpine
For Wimpey, or John Laing.
You'll stand behind a mixer
And your skin is turned to tan
And they'll say, Good on you, Paddy
With your boat-fare in your hand.

And not just the work, but the life in between:

The craic was good in Cricklewood
And they wouldn't leave the Crown
With glasses flying and Biddy's crying
'Cause Paddy was going to town.
Oh mother dear, I'm over here
And I'm never coming back
What keeps me here is the rake o' beer
The women and the craic

The Irish immigrant population in London quickly established its own subculture and support structures, often set up by the Catholic Church. The first hostel for Irish men newly arrived in London, the Residential House in Tollington Park, Holloway, was set up by the Church to induct young men into London life. But it was Irish clubs and dance halls that glued the community together. Dance halls like the Banba in Kilburn, the Buffalo in Camden Town, the Forum in Kentish Town and the Garrytown in Shepherd's Bush were the social centres of London Irish life. The Gresham on Holloway Road was conveniently close to the Whittington hospital in Archway where many Irish nurses worked. Not all were located in Irish communities; the Blarney and the Pride of Erin were on Tottenham Court Road.

The most famous dance hall — the Galtymore, or the Galty— was the core of Kilburn Irish life for over half a century. In the opinion of Donegal's popular singing star Margo, who often performed there in the 1950s:

It really saved lives. People from remote areas of Donegal, Mayo, Galway and Kerry lived for the weekend at the Galtymore.

Without that all-important Friday and Saturday night, many would have felt totally alone and would have fallen into depression. It was their home from home and kept the spirit high in difficult times.[26]

Although Kilburn, Cricklewood and Kentish Town were known for their "Little Ireland" atmosphere, with Irish social clubs and dancehalls, Sunday Mass and all Ireland's local newspapers on tap, it still made a difference that it was *not* Ireland. London was not a village. Kilburn and Camden were within walking distance of the West End. For many young Irish men and women who had only ever known a small town with a parish priest keeping watch on everyone in it, it was a kind of freedom, albeit a provisional one. The Catholic Church still presided over a lot of London Irish life. One reason for the multi-occupancy of many houses in London Irish communities was the preference of the Church that young Irish men live together in crowded and sometimes squalid conditions rather than take digs in English households where they might be prey to bad, i.e. non-Catholic, influences and temptations.[27]

Sometimes Irish labourers had literally no home to go to. For those, Arlington House in Camden Town became a haven. Opened in 1905 as the last "Rowton House", a series of hostels for London's homeless built by the Victorian philanthropist Lord Rowton, Arlington House sits like a red-brick monolith on Arlington Road off Parkway. Even today, and despite its usefulness as a quick through-route between Parkway and Camden Lock, Arlington Road gets relatively little footfall. George Orwell, Madness, the Pogues, David Thomson and Daniel Lux have all described Arlington House as the secret heart of Camden. The opening of Madness's "One Better Day" (1984) fixes a scene unaltered since the 1930s:

Arlington House, address: no fixed abode
An old man in a three-piece suit sits in the road

In the 1950s and 1960s Arlington House became an almost exclusively Irish preserve. In *Lovers and Strangers* (2017), her rich and moving history of immigration in post-war Britain, Clair Wills observed that writers such as Brendan Behan and Patrick Kavanagh also spent time in Arlington House,

> ...*suggesting that the line between Irish labourer and Irish bohemian was rather fine, at any rate when it came to where you slept.*[28]

According to data collected by the London Irish Centre, Arlington House "has been home to more Irishmen than any other building outside Ireland".[29] It not only housed them but disposed of them, after their deaths, in East Finchley Cemetery, a few stops up the Northern Line, where unless they had family to claim them, they were buried in unmarked graves. Offering a very different service, Kay's Irish Music Centre, next to Our Lady of Hal, the Catholic church at 161 Arlington Road, provided not only records but musical instruments, Irish newspapers, and tea and biscuits. The confluence of Arlington House, Kay's and Our Lady of Hal meant that Camden Town was second only to Kilburn as London's Little Ireland.

The Irish and Afro-Caribbeans were not the only ethnic groups carving out space for themselves in 1950s London. In 1939 there were about 8,000 Cypriots in London, based mostly in Soho. By 1966 there were 75,000.[30] Greek Cypriot immigrants mostly worked in the private sector, in the clothing, retail and restaurant business. Their tendency to live and congregate near to their workplaces, which unlike those of Irish labourers were fixed, meant they lived to an unusual degree in central London. The main focus of the post-war Greek Cypriot community in the 1950s was Camden Town and Westminster (with a notable presence in Fulham also) in rented accommodation that today would be beyond even a healthy middle class income.

Helen Evangelou's parents came to the UK from Cyprus in 1934. After the war her father got a job as a kitchen porter in a Greek restaurant in Goodge Street before becoming a chef at various restaurants in the West End. Her mother did seamstress work at home until she got a full-time job off Bond Street, hand finishing suits for Harvey Nichols, a position she held for the next forty years. Helen was born in 1951 and for the first twenty-five years of her life she lived in the family home at 57 Riding House Street, a dilapidated old Georgian house with no garden next to the Green Man pub, a hundred yards north of Oxford Street. Her family rented the basement and the first floor, with another family on the ground floor. There was one toilet in the backyard shared by four families, all Greek Cypriot. At night it was often freezing. Like Alan Johnson, Helen kept a chamber pot under her bed.

Riding House Street ran from Portland Place and All Saint's Church, next to BBC Broadcasting House, to Cleveland Street in Fitzrovia. As Helen recalled:

Perhaps the best thing about the house was its location and its proximity to, well, just about everything. Theatres, cinemas, restaurants and shops were all within easy walking distance, as well as music venues such as the 100 Club and the Marquee. Then again, if we felt lazy, there was not one but seven nearby tube stations to choose from. London was the world's greatest city, buzzing with energy and life, and I was living right in the centre of its beating heart.[31]

At the same time as Helen was discovering central London, Pip Granger was growing up in a small flat above the delicatessen at 61 Old Compton Street in Soho, next door to the 2i's Coffee Bar. She lived there with her father, who made a living smuggling brandy, tobacco and porn mags from France across the English Channel in a light aircraft. Her captivating social history *Up West: Voices from the Streets of Post-War London* (2009), is the only published account of the working class that lived in the heart of the West End in the post-war decades, in an area bordered by Regent Street, the Strand, Kingsway and High Holborn. Drawn from dozens of interviews, it tells the life stories of those who lived and worked within this unique area.

Although Pip's family life could be fraught she felt entirely safe within Soho's tight-knit working class community. Nearly all of Soho's and Covent Garden's narrow streets were safe for kids to play in, continuously watched over by shopkeepers and retailers. Pip also enjoyed the close proximity of central London's cultural attractions:

There was a lot to do. Although it wasn't laid on for you, it was there. We even used to go in the art gallery in the winter. We'd go for a walk, go in the National Gallery, to look at the paintings...I knew about Monet and Constable, because they were my sort of pictures. My brother would rather have been kicking a ball, but I learned about art.[32]

Many of the flats above shops or cafes were divided between flats and workrooms used for various legal and illegal businesses. Janet Vance grew up in a flat above 11 Frith Street on the corner of Bateman Street, opposite the Dog and Duck pub:

It was a café with flats above, and my dad had a gambling club in the basement. There were two flats on the first floor, two on our floor, and one at the top. Girls, prostitutes, lived in the other flat on our floor, but they didn't interfere with anybody, or work from there. Different girls worked from the two flats on the first floor.[33]

Following the slum clearances of the late nineteenth century, a number of LCC and Peabody Estates were built in the West End. The largest of these were the Peabody Estates at Wild Street, just off Drury Lane, and the Bedfordbury Buildings, which ran parallel to St Martin's Lane. Wild Street, with 347 tenants in thirteen blocks, had a higher density of tenants than any equivalent in the East End. The flats tended to be very small, with the "kitchen" also serving as a living room/second bedroom. They had no bathrooms, and all shared a toilet, a sink and a wash-house with the other flats on their landing.[34] But the location was priceless.

While Wild Street's kids tended to gravitate to Lincoln's Inn Fields for recreation, kids from the Bedfordbury or Soho headed down to St James's Park and Green Park, crossing Piccadilly on their way. All the boys went to the Gainsford Boys Club in Drury Lane, a sports club affiliated to the Inns of Court, which had facilities for football, boxing, table tennis and billiards. Olga Jackson recalled that she and her mates used to go every Sunday to the British Museum: *"Straight off to the mummies!"*. The museum was also a short-cut between school and home. Tricia Bryan lived in a council block on Tavistock Square, just around the corner from Burton Street where Joyce lived in Dickensian poverty, and went to school in St Giles:

> *We would walk home from St Giles, down Museum Street and into the main entrance of the museum, walk through, and come out the back for home. While we were in there we might say "Let's do the Egyptian Room today", and that would scare us a lot.*[35]

It wasn't only in their free time that young working class girls and boys who lived in central London had the chance to expand their horizons. The world of work, the various occupations of their extended families, did that also. In addition to her parents, most of Helen Evangelou's other relatives also worked in central London:

> *We were lucky that we had a few relatives who were tailors in Soho, and they made dad's suits, sports jackets and trousers. Cousins Kyriacos and Savvas Ktori worked at Sam Argus on Berwick Street, while George Evangelou, another cousin, had his own workshop on Meard Street.*[36]

Nothing in any British city rivalled Soho's range of food. Mike Hutton's history of the Windmill Theatre from the 1930s to the 1960s records his memories of the early morning street scene of the 1950s and the astonishing range of food available — Fratelli Camisa in Berwick Street and Parmigiani's of Old Compton Street displaying shelves of cheeses, freshly baked pizzas and a huge range of sausages swaying on hooks, as well as olives, anchovies, and raffia-clad bottles of Chianti; the smell of freshly ground coffee from the Algerian Coffee Shop on Old Compton Street, which had been serving customers since 1887; freshly baked bread from Grodzinski's in Brewer

Street; croissants from Maison Bertaux; and numerous shops specialising in Greek, Chinese and Indian food. For simpler fare, the Omelette Bar at 18 Lisle Street served up omelettes to order, prepared as the customer watched.[37] All were kept going by short order cooks, waiters, delivery men and counter staff.

The West End's power generator was its unique concentration of theatres, clubs and bars. With London's main theatres on the Haymarket, Shaftesbury Avenue and Cambridge Circus, Soho was perfectly placed to absorb not just their audiences but their entire support structure of stagehands, dressers, dancers and extras. Every Monday morning unemployed musicians lugging their instruments would congregate at the Musicians' Union HQ in Archer Street, seeking work in a theatre or club orchestra. The MU HQ was directly across the road from Sid Siger the Durex seller and just around the corner from the Windmill Theatre, famous for its "erotic" dancing girls and nude revues.[38] The dancers from the Windmill had to pass by crowds of mostly male musicians hanging about outside the MU, which led inevitably to propositions and trips to Soho's bars and cafes later on.

Pip Granger's account of the West End working class in the 1940s and 1950s paints the scene:

> *These shifting knots of people who came to Archer Street to check out the union's noticeboards, to gossip and to look for a gig. Anyone who already had an engagement for the coming week would go there to hire other musicians, usually looking for faces they knew. Mondays in Archer Street were often as much about putting old bands back together as they were about creating new alliances. At that time the average jobbing musician would not have had a phone, nor, most likely, a permanent home to put one in.*[39]

Soho in the 1950s saw an explosion of cafes, coffee bars and cheap restaurants. Jimmy's on Frith Street, which opened in 1949, set the template, being located in a small basement with whitewashed walls, small tables with gingham tablecloth, wine served with bread and a main dish of moussaka or salad and chips. Further down Frith Street was Bar Italia, one of the first espresso bars in London and the centre of Italian life in Soho from the 1950s to today. Many similar Italian cafes, with their signature Formica covered walls and chrome espresso machines, followed in its wake. The Torino on the corner of Dean Street and Old Compton Street doubled as a refuge for Spanish political exiles and down-at-heel artists and designers whilst also being a working man's café, albeit one in which they had to remove their overalls before sitting down. It also attracted drinkers from the nearby French Pub and gay couples seeking a safe space for a cup of coffee.[40]

Soho was a mecca for young working class men looking for excitement. Ted had been ejected from Sir William Collins School aged fourteen with his academic potential unfulfilled, the school's "Terminal Report" to his mum finding that despite forty-one days' absence during the last year he still managed to be ranked eighth out of twenty-eight pupils in the class and might have been top if he had made a "sustained effort". But Ted was keen to get out into the word, which he did in his first job as a messenger boy for the *Daily Sketch* on Gray's Inn Road. Part of his duties included assisting the *Sketch*'s press photographers which led in March 1953 to him accompanying a crime scene photographer to the recently uncovered scene of John Christie's multiple murders at 10 Rillington Place (the reporter was allowed in, he was not).

By 1956, when he was eighteen, Ted was working as a stockroom assistant for Ellis Leavy Jewelers in Poland Street, Soho, a fifteen-minute stroll from his flat on Russell Square, flogging off occasional bits of the firm's "seconds" (slightly damaged jewellery) and using the extra money to buy his first tailor-made suits. He took to the West End like a duck to water, making friends, acquaintances and contacts all over Soho and Fitzrovia. Turned down for National Service because of a slight heart murmur, he was one of the few 18-20 year-old males in his local area, a situation he found congenial. Working in Soho, he regularly dropped in to the Torino and other cafes such as the Moka and the Partisan. But in his world restaurants were for the middle class:

> *Eating out for me and my friends amounted to fish and chips or an all-night hot pie stall called Mrs Bills, located on a bomb site next to St Anne's Church off Shaftesbury Avenue. It used to be simply Bills, but when Bill died his wife took it over and renamed it. When the pubs turned out we would make our unsteady way to Mrs Bills for the most wonderful hot meat pies covered in brown sauce.*[41]

Anna Sullivan was equally seduced by Soho. Born in 1939 to a working class Jewish family in Hackney, she grew up on an LCC estate near the Marshes. Like many other flats, hers was freezing cold, the floors uncarpeted and icy, so everyone congregated in the kitchen because it was the warmest room. Her dad, who worked in a paint factory and was an active trade unionist, had joined the Communist Party in 1929 and was elected as a Communist councillor for the Ridley Road area. In the 1930s he helped organise the Unemployed Workers Movement and led anti-fascists against Mosley's Blackshirts at Cable Street in 1936. He left the Party in 1952 but his daughter absorbed his politics and would play a major role in the Anti-Nazi League in the 1970s.

By 1956 Anna had left school and was working as a dogsbody in Hackney Town Hall's legal department, fetching and carrying legal papers whilst dodging middle-aged men trying to grope her. She spent her free time dancing at the Tottenham Royal "with an ever-changing mix of young men, some in National Service uniform, some in Teddy Boy suits; we then went home on last buses, still sober and mostly virginal", and attending evening classes at St Martin's Art College in Charing Cross. It was while at St Martin's that she met her first boyfriend, who after classes took her to the cafes and bars of Soho, where she had her first Italian meal. A jazz lover, she often danced the night away at the 100 Club on Oxford Street, missing the last 22 bus back to Hackney; but it was worth it:

The bars I went to were full of writers and artists and I felt I was in bohemian heaven.[42]

The most famous coffee bar in Soho, the 2i's at 59 Old Compton Street, has a good claim to be the birthplace of British pop music. Named after its original owners Freddie and Sammy Irani, its small entrance led down to a deep basement with a tiny eighteen-inch stage made of milk crates with planks on top for the musicians to stand on. The 2i's attracted hundreds of teenagers every night, crammed into it to listen to new acts like Tommy Steele, Adam Faith, Joe Brown, Cliff Richard, and the Vipers Skiffle Group. For a few years in the middle of the decade it was skiffle, not rock n' roll, that forged an entirely new path for popular music.

The grime of its day, skiffle was a British slant on American folk and blues, produced by mostly working class teenagers working on their own. Their chief inspiration was the Lonnie Donegan Skiffle Group whose radical re-interpretation of Leadbelly's "Rock Island Line" (1955) is arguably the origin point of British rock and pop in all its variants. A lively synthesis of Deep South blues, trad and folk accompanied by a Zydeco-style washboard, between 1955 and 1957 skiffle was enormously popular with working class kids who were desperate to play R&B but could not afford the expensive instruments to do so.

In the late 1950s there were thousands of amateur skiffle bands across the country (one of which, formed in Liverpool in 1956, was John Lennon's the Quarrymen) but the focus of the craze was Soho. The Vipers, formed in the Breadbasket coffee shop in Cleveland Street, Fitzrovia in 1956, were led by Wally Whyton, a local lad who worked by day in a West End advertising agency but played Lonnie Donnigan-influenced skiffle at the Breadbasket at weekends. The Vipers soon became the resident skiffle band at the 2i's, from where they launched a series of hit singles especially "Don't You Rock Me Daddy-O" (1957) and their version of "Cumberland Gap" (1957).

Skiffle came and just as quickly went, but Soho was the centre of British jazz for decades to come. Dobell's record store in Charing Cross Road and the Soho Record Centre on the corner of Old Compton Street and Dean Street were the new churches for both modern and trad jazz, spreading the word to eager young recruits. Garth Cartwright's definitive history of the UK record shop, *Going for a Song* (2018), situates Dobell's at the heart of a new society starting to emerge, where working class kids had cultural opportunities denied their parents, providing "a democratic space where race, class and gender were ignored as everyone gathered to celebrate jazz".[43]

For the real thing they went to one of many jazz joints scattered throughout Soho such as the 100 Club, the Flamingo and the Marquee in Wardour Street, Club 11 on Windmill Street, the Mandrake in Meard Street and finally Ronnie Scott's Jazz Club, which opened in 1958 in Gerrard Street above a Chinese gambling den before moving in 1965 to its now famous Frith Street location. The impact and significance of Soho's burgeoning music scene, its jazz clubs and coffee bars, its skiffle merchants and aspiring rock singers, was so obvious that the British film industry latched on to it in hit films like *Expresso Bongo* (1959) and *Beat Girl* (1960), both of which cemented Soho's popular reputation in post-war Britain.

But the area was more than just London's centre of good food, good music and a good time. Since the seventeenth century Soho had been a centre of political, cultural and sexual radicalism. The first Greek Orthodox Church in the country was built there in 1677 by refugees from the Ottoman Empire, who gave their name to Greek Street. In the 1840s Marx and Engels drafted the *Communist Manifesto* in the upstairs room of the Red Lion pub on Great Windmill Street. The first British Marxist party, the Democratic Federation, was formed in 1881 at the Rose Street Club. In the 1950s Soho was the only space in the country where gay people could freely express themselves, a tradition continued from the 1770s when the French diplomat and spy the Chevalier d'Eon, who lived in Brewer Street for many years, was casually accepted as a woman after he changed gender identity at the age of forty-nine.

Soho was exceptional in an era when social attitudes were still rooted in the pre-war years and the "Butskellite" political consensus of the 1950s had frozen out radical alternatives (Nye

Bevan's career, for example, was effectively over from 1951). Only the Suez Crisis of 1956, and later the formation of the Campaign for Nuclear Disarmament (CND), threatened to disturb the peace. Ken Weller was born in Islington in 1935 to a working class family and in 1951 he joined the Young Communist League. In the later 1950s, as an engineering worker and a shop steward, he rejected the Communist Party's Stalinist politics and joined the Trotskyist Socialist Labour League (SLL), from which he was soon expelled for continuing to have thoughts of his own. After this he became active in CND's radical direct-action Committee of 100 and helped form the free-thinking Trotskyist group Solidarity.

But in 1956 Ken was still a naive twenty-one-year-old taking a moral stand against British Imperialism, shocked by the police's brutal response to a large anti-Suez demonstration in Trafalgar Square:

> *I saw one knocking over a middle-aged couple who clasped each other in their arms for fear...I looked in the gutter and there was a banner pole, like a broom handle, about five feet long, and I picked it up and the same policeman on a horse came charging at me and I hit him as hard as I could, broke the pole, and he turned and went back into Downing Street... Then there was a battle in Whitehall which turned quite nasty. The police would grab hold of someone and there would be a battle over their body. In one scuffle I ended up at the back of the crowd with a policeman's epaulette in my hand, minus the policeman. And then there were marches through the streets with linked arms.*[44]

The iconic landmarks of central London could alter depending on experience and perspective. For over a century the "Dilly", i.e. Piccadilly Circus and its environs, had been a focus for male street prostitution. By the 1950s the lower steps of the concourse outside the National Gallery on Trafalgar Square, popularly known as the Meat Rack, was well known for gay cruising and publicly available rent boys. The Dilly itself had its own Meat Rack, found under the arches at the end of Regent Street or on the concourse of Piccadilly Circus underground station. Less overt (but well known to sex workers, clients and police) was what Jeremy Reed's history of "rent" in the Piccadilly and Soho area from the early nineteenth century to the present day describes as

a fugitively coded typography of cafes, private membership clubs, pubs, urinals and clandestine meeting places, always ubiquitously policed, like the arcades of the County Fire Office in Piccadilly Circus, the Turkish Baths at Jermyn Street, Soho's Marshall Street public baths, the isolated streets of Bridge Place, Dove Mews, Falconberg Mews, Clareville Street, Leicester Square and Trafalgar Square, all serving as possible same-sex assignation zones.[45]

Since its opening in 1909, the first floor of the Lyons Corner House on the corner of Rupert Street and Coventry Street, between Piccadilly Circus and Leicester Square, had been an important meeting place for London's gay men. Known in the gay argot Polari as "the Lillypond", supposedly even its waiters were gay. The flagship store of the J.Lyons empire of stylish white and gold-fronted teashops (the other big stores were on the Strand and the corner of Tottenham Court Road and Oxford Street) the Coventry Street store was open 24 hours a day and employed over four hundred staff including cooks, waiters and the famous "Nippies", an army of elegantly uniformed waitresses.

The traditional London tea shop, like Lyons, Express Diary or the Aerated Bread Company (ABC), was entering its decline, although the big ABC building on Camden Road still supplied large amounts of bread and cakes to ABC shops all over the city. In 1954 Lyons' Coventry Street Corner House became the first ever Wimpy Bar, a brand invented and owned by J.Lyons. Luckily, its displaced gay customers had other options nearby. By the 1950s there were several gay pubs in Soho, including the Swiss Tavern in Old Compton Street, the Crown and Two Chairman in Dean Street, and the Golden Lion, also in Dean Street. The Rockingham Club on Archer Street was a more discreet gay club. These attracted the gay bourgeoisie but also functioned as an important part of the cultural education of young working class gay and bi-curious men in the 1950s and 1960s.

Soho was also a sanctuary and alternative for those black Londoners tired of the basement dens of Notting Hill and Bayswater. Aside from the lack of hostility shown to black men and women in Soho's coffee bars and pubs, there were specifically Afro-Caribbean drinking dens such as the Florence Mills Social Parlour on Carnaby Street, which played African-American and Caribbean music late into the night. Many other pubs and clubs hosted black music for a multi-ethnic audience, such as the Bag O'Nails on Kingley Street or the Caribbean Club on Denman Street, found on the second floor above the Argentina restaurant.

This vibrant mixture of class, ethnicity and sexuality has led Panikos Panayi, the author of *Migrant City* (2020), an important and game-changing new history of London, to suggest that

> *Within the West End, Soho became something of a model for the evolution of post-war London, in the sense that it contained a variety of groups living in close proximity from the end of the nineteenth century, meaning that it acted as a pioneer of cosmopolitanism.*[46]

It was a process that reached its apogee in the post-war decades, forming and sustaining a very particular type of working class. The working class that lived and moved in the West End was exceptionally exposed to art, culture and other lifestyles, whether as kids running through the British Museum, welders working on its railings, dancers in Soho or market traders in Covent Garden and Berwick Street. Writing of central London life at the time, the art critic Kenneth Coutts-Smith identified its unique quality:

> *The 1950s saw a social phenomenon that had never previously existed at any moment of the past, the appearance of a working class bohemia.*[47]

A working class bohemia is something to be, but it provides opportunities for good and for ill. Organised crime in Britain took root in the 1920s with the racetrack gangs led by Darby Sabini, the godfather of London's "Little Italy" in Clerkenwell. In the 1920s his gang ran protection rackets on all of England's major racetracks. They also controlled Soho's drinking and gambling clubs (one of their regular meeting spots in the 1930s was the Admiral Duncan pub in Old Compton Street). The only serious rivals to Sabini were the Islington-based White family, led by "Big Alf" White and his son Harry. In 1935 an informal truce gave the West End to Sabini and Islington/King's Cross to the Whites. After the war Sabini retired to Hove and his territory transferred to his rivals, but not everyone thought they deserved it. In one night of violence in July 1947, in which their key soldiers were brutally dispatched and Harry White "disappeared", the Whites were destroyed and replaced by Billy Hill and his lieutenant Jack Comer, aka Jack Spot.

From the 1950s to the 1970s Billy Hill was the West End's criminal kingpin. Born in 1911 in Seven Dials, one of twenty-one children, his family moved in 1914 to Netley Street, Euston, now part of the Regent's Park Estate. In the 1930s he established a niche for himself in the West End. During the war he offered forged documents to deserters, took over other protection rackets and organised smash-and-grab raids on jewellers. Renowned for his expert use of the "shiv" (knife) to carve up rivals, Hill was much smarter than his peers, bringing an unusual level of meticulous planning to several audacious armed robberies. Moving since his childhood in a world of criminal and semi-legal grifters, Billy took a brazen working class pleasure in defying conventional morality:

> After all, they told us all about Drake and Raleigh and Clive and Cook at school. And weren't they all gangsters? Weren't they nicking something that didn't belong to them? Only because it was on behalf of their government, that made it legal.[48]

In May 1952 Hill's men pulled off the UK's largest ever robbery to date on Eastcastle Street, just off Oxford Circus, when a Post Office van was expertly hemmed in by three cars, four men in each, its alarm swiftly cut and mail bags containing

£287,000 removed to secure sites in Spitalfields and Covent Garden. In 1954 Hill pulled off another coup when his men hijacked a lorry belonging to KLM Airlines on High Holborn and stole £46,000 in gold bullion. In neither case were the robbers or the cash ever found. These successful armed robberies forced the police to up their game, to focus on "project crime", i.e. highly organised one-off jobs with very large hauls.

Hill's dominance over Soho was challenged by his former friend and lieutenant Jack Spot, who grew jealous and tried to undermine him. In retaliation Hill leaked information that Spot was an informer. On 11th August 1955, in an effort to shore up his image, Spot picked a very public fight with Albert Dimes, one of Hill's new lieutenants. Unprovoked, Spot walked up to Dimes in Frith Street and stabbed him in the stomach and thigh. When Dimes sought refuge in the Continental Fruit Store on Old Compton Street, Spot followed him in only to be hit over the head with heavy weighing scales by the owner. Dimes then seized Spot's knife and slashed his face with it. Spot retreated, his reputation, and his face, in tatters.

Hill's reach was extensive but not absolute. In 1956 he was badly beaten up outside his flat by thugs hired by Spot, including "Mad" Frankie Fraser who went down for seven years for it. Nor did he control the West End's vice trade. The 1950s saw the beginnings of a change in how sex was sold. The old method, working girls soliciting on the street, thrived in the immediate post-war years and well into the 1950s. In the early 1950s the going rate for a quickie was £2 in Gerrard Street, £1 and ten shillings in Newport Court, and only a quid in Lisle Street.[49] The police estimated that in 1950 there were approximately three thousand prostitutes in the city, mostly in central London, with their operations expanding to take in mainline stations such as King's Cross, Victoria and Euston.[50]

The premier pimps in London were the Messina brothers, scions of a powerful crime family from Malta that controlled a network of brothels in Alexandria, Egypt. The brothers had arrived in the West End in the 1930s and maintained a vice empire there for nearly two decades. They paid their girls £50 a week but took far more from them through the various "ponces" that supervised them. The Messinas preferred their sex workers to be foreign with limited command of English as that made them easier to control and less likely to form bonds of friendship and solidarity with English prostitutes. All had to abide by the "ten-minute rule", i.e. no transaction lasting longer than ten minutes, in order to maximise profits. If a girl displeased or disobeyed them, Eugenio Messina would use an electric flex cord to beat her into submission.[51]

The fall of the Messinas began in 1950 when the *Sunday People*'s crime correspondent Duncan Webb (possibly in receipt of information from Hill, with whom he maintained friendly relations) exposed their operations, including the addresses of all their most profitable brothels in New Bond Street and Shepherd's Market. A clampdown followed. For a few years they tried to run their operations from Paris and Brussels but eventually others moved in and took over.

Barbara Tate's *Working Girls* (2009), an affectionate yet unsentimental memorial to the prostitutes of Soho in the late 1940s and early 1950s, describes the highs and lows of "Mae", one of Soho's busiest sex workers in that period. Tate was born in Uxbridge in 1927 to a father and mother who both abandoned her, her carpenter father when she was three and her mother when she was five. At age seventeen she secured a place in Ealing School of Art but yearned for more and so, in 1948 when she was twenty-one, she fled to central London. After a brief spell working tables at the Mousehole Club in Soho, Tate took up work as a "maid" (a general assistant and helper) for Mae, dealing with a wide variety of clients and Mae's Maltese ponce Tony. In the next three years Mae and the circle of prostitutes in which she moved became Barbara's closest friends:

> When I took up with Mae I had made the first true friend of my life, and it was in Soho and through Soho that I first came to feel a sense of belonging to a broader circle, a group of friends who included me among their number. I was still an outcast, perhaps, but if so I was an outcast among outcasts...in my crummy room and Mae's chaotic flat, I had found freedom. Freedom, friends and happiness.[52]

Mae's daily routine, shared by most of Soho's prostitutes, was described by Tate:

> *They rose late in the morning. Drank a few cups of tea or coffee, travelled to their flats in Soho, worked until about midnight, and then returned home to their bed-sits in Paddington, Brixton or Notting Hill.*

Mae's service was relatively straightforward and astonishingly quick, but there were others of more complexity such as Sadie the Sadist, for whom Tate occasionally worked as a Sunday stand-in maid. Sadie's flat was outfitted with stocks and pillories, and manacles fixed to the walls:

> *As well as these items of furniture she kept whips of every description —tawses, cat-o-nine tails, birches and a range of canes. The first time I saw Sadie's flat, I marvelled at the things men would pay for.*

Tate was under no illusions about Mae's lifestyle. She cautioned her about the danger to her sexual health from the large number of clients she saw. She particularly despised Tony, with whom Mae was besotted, because he simply lived off Mae. In regard to Tony, she summarised the crucial difference at that time between a pimp and a ponce:

> *In those days a pimp was a go-between who prowled the streets on the look-out for wandering customers. As such, he actually earned his living, which was something no self-respecting ponce would ever do.*[53]

The 1950s saw a level of public soliciting not experienced in central London since Regency times. Gilbert Kelland, who later rose to Assistant Commissioner but in 1955 was a junior police inspector assigned to the West End, recalled, "I remember one night walking along Shaftesbury Avenue after midnight and counting, between Piccadilly Circus and Charing Cross Rd, over 100 prostitutes".[54] The 1959 Street Offences Act put an end to this. Arising from the 1957 Wolfenden Report, which had revealed the full extent of prostitution in the West End, the Act stipulated that a prostitute found guilty of soliciting on the street would be subject to steep fines or imprisonment. This inevitably drove prostitution inside, with crude handwritten "Model" signs above or just inside doorways pointing up the stairs (to a surprising extent, these still exist in Soho). Out of sight of the public, the kind of intimidation used by the Messinas on their sex workers became, if anything, easier to apply.

The West End sold sex in other ways. The first genuine strip club in Soho, the Nell Gwynne in Meard Street, opened in 1957 and was soon followed by others such as Vicki's Studio in Old Compton Street and the Tropicana in Greek Street. In 1958 Paul Raymond took over a dilapidated building in Walkers Court — a seedy alleyway connecting Berwick Street and Brewer Street — and turned it into something new, something heralding the coming decade. The Raymond Theatre Revue Club did not hide sex away. It put it up in neon lights, quite literally with a neon "STRIPTEASE" sign above its door and a lavish Las Vegas-style décor within.

West End Central, the chief station of the St James's Division of the Metropolitan Police, was responsible for 24-7 policing of Mayfair and Soho. Over five hundred men, with twenty-four inspectors overseeing operations, worked out of its main building at 27 Saville Row. Some of them, such as desk sergeant Charles Hasler who lived in a council flat in Islington, travelled in to work, but most lived in the Sandringham Buildings on Charing Cross Road or the police section house in Broadwick Street, Soho. For young working class men living on their own, assigned mostly to mundane tasks such as arresting spivs and barrow boys, the temptations of Soho, on and off duty, were almost irresistible.

By the early 1950s West End Central was rife with corruption as policemen took the opportunity to top up their pay and enjoy a range of freebies (drinks, meals, women) as add-ons. In the 1950s Soho's pubs and restaurants routinely put out a Half Crown (two shillings and sixpence) with their rubbish as a "gift" to induce rubbish collectors to do a thorough job. It was accepted that before the collectors arrived in the early morning the nightly beat coppers would pocket the Half Crown and replace it with two bob (two shillings). In 1955 the *Daily Mail* reported that an unusually honest Detective Superintendent had sent a report to the Metropolitan Police Commissioner detailing systemic corruption at West End Central, involving "club proprietors, prostitutes, gaming house owners, brothel keepers and men living on immoral earnings", with some individual policemen receiving bribes of £60 a week. The day after the *Mail*'s story the Commissioner went to the station, stood on a table in the canteen and assured his men he did not believe a word of it.[55]

This dangerous and seductive world did not go unnoticed by Britain's film industry. The decade had been ushered in by two British films, *The Blue Lamp* (1950) and *Pool of London* (1951) that demonstrated uncanny prescience in dramatising social problems still in their infancy in the immediate post-war years. *The Blue Lamp*'s main narrative was drawn from an incident in 1947, when a seventeen-year-old armed robber shot dead an innocent bystander in Charlotte Street, Fitzrovia, a murder that prompted agonised public debate about post-war youth. The film inaugurates the new decade with the slaying of decent, old fashioned, unarmed police constable George Dixon, coldly gunned down by an amoral young thug.

Pool of London operates today on two levels. Firstly as a visually rich social document, a literal window into the past, with *cinema verité* shots of Shad Thames, Bermondsey, Rotherhithe and the City before the construction of Paternoster Square, levelled by bomb damage and eerily empty at night. Secondly, as an authentic glimpse of 1950s working class London life around the Pool of London and its interaction with transient foreign labour, as two sailors (one American, one Jamaican) are embroiled in a plot to smuggle stolen diamonds from London to Europe. It also contains the first, entirely unembarrassed, interracial romance in British film, between black sailor Johnny (Earl Cameron) and insurance clerk Pat (Susan Shaw).

1950s London, especially central London and Soho, went on to create its own literary subgenre, a retrospective bourgeois romanticism exemplified by Daniel Farson's evocative *Soho in the Fifties* (1987) and Nigel Richardson's semi-fictional *Dog Days in Soho* (2001). Both writers tend to ignore Soho's working class except as transient sex toys or colourful characters, like the peripatetic con man Iron Foot Jack. Farson's Colony Club crew — Muriel Belcher, Francis Bacon, John Deakin, Lucien Freud and various minor artists and alcoholics — were amusing in small doses but as incestuous as the establishment they despised.

Working class perspectives on Soho's well-guarded inner core such as the Colony Room and the Gargoyle Club are rare. The exceptions are Colin Wilson's *Adrift in Soho* (1960) and Terry Taylor's *Baron's Court, All Change* (1961). Both are classics of the "Soho genre" and yet receive less attention than the likes of Farson and Jeffrey Bernard. Wilson, in particular, has been slighted for his non-deferential view of a Soho he enjoyed but did not worship, and (a still worse crime) his publicly declared belief that his work was as important as that of his middle class contemporaries. After a period of dispiriting factory work Wilson had relocated from his native Leicester and famously spent the time writing his breakout non-fiction work *The Outsider* (1956) sleeping rough on Hampstead Heath.

Unlike Wilson, Taylor's hero did not aspire to a new existentialism, he simply worked in a hat shop in Soho and in his spare time hung around jazz clubs taking photos (as did Taylor himself). While Wilson's protagonist lived in a Notting Hill bedsit, Taylor's lived at home with his parents in Middlesex. Taylor's title came from Baron's Court tube station on the Piccadilly Line, the point at which the narrator, travelling into London, considered civilisation started. His break into the world he wants to inhabit comes from using money earned by dealing drugs to rent a small flat in central London. *Baron's Court, All Change* is a humorous and cutting depiction of a young working class hustler in late 1950s Soho finding that a life of funky jazz and sex with sophisticated older women is not as enjoyable as it sounds.

The only 1950s London novel that achieved for the capital what Alan Sillitoe's *Saturday Night and Sunday Morning* (1958) did for the North in terms of enduring influence is Colin MacInnes's *Absolute Beginners* (1959), a tale of an ambitious working class photographer (based on Terry Taylor) and his adventures in Soho and Notting Hill. *Absolute Beginners* has not aged well, but its enormous strength was to catch a specific moment, to identify the current of creative energy whizzing back and forth along the Central Line between Oxford Street, Marble Arch, Bayswater and Notting Hill, igniting sparks all around it.

Absolute Beginners presented 1950s Soho and the West End as a utopian dream:

The air was sweet as a cool bath, the stars were peeping nosily beyond the neons, and the citizens of the Queendom, in their jeans and separates, were floating down the Shaftesbury Avenue canals, like gondolas. Everyone had loot to spend, everyone had a bath with verbena salts behind them…The rubber plants in the espressos had been dusted, and the smooth white lights of the new Chinese restaurants – not the old Maj Jong categories, but the latest thing with broad glass fronts, and Dacron curtaining, and beige carpet over the interiors – were shining a dazzle, like some monster telly screens…in fact, the capital was a night-horse dream. And I thought, "My lord, one thing is certain, they'll make musicals one day about the glamour studded 1950s".[56]

For some working class youths, like Ted, this was an authentic reality. But it would have come as a surprise to Alan Johnson and Helen Evangelou that everyone had loot to spend and a bath with verbena salts behind them. Their family homes, like Joyce's, had no bath at all.

Don McCullin was born in St Pancras in 1935 but raised in Finsbury Park with an acute knowledge of North London working class street culture. With his dad disabled, his mum held the family together by working in a munitions factory. Even so, life in Finsbury Park was hard:

We lived in a two-room flat with no central heating or bathroom. Finsbury Park was a ghetto, full of violence, back then. Fights in the street; fights at school. I suffered and practised the violence myself—you couldn't let anyone walk all over you. It's amazing how I emerged with a totally different, liberal mindset.

The McCullins lived on Fonthill Road near the notorious Campbell Road just south of Finsbury Park station, which everyone knew as either "Campbell Bunk" or "the Bunk". Renamed Whadcoat Street by the local council in 1937 and *The Worst Street in North London* by a recent popular history, it was almost but not entirely demolished in the 1950s as part of slum clearance. Home to a *lumpenproletariat* of semi-employed grifters, thieves, drunks and prostitutes, the Bunk had no respect for any part of the state except the monarchy, the adults fiercely racist and the kids fighting running battles with the police and fire brigade. During the war Don went to primary school with kids from the Bunk and later played on the bombsites.

When Don left Tollington Park Secondary Modern at fifteen he worked in the dining car of British Rail's London-Liverpool train for a while before branching out:

I got a job in Mayfair as a messenger boy for an animation studio, delivering cans of film. One of my calling places was the Fine Arts Society, an art gallery that showed work from the turn of the century. It had a really huge influence on my imagination. When I was called up for National Service, I spun this yarn that I worked in the movie industry—they didn't know I was just a messenger boy. So I was put in the Air Force, renumbering old wartime film stock. Later, I spent time in photographic units in Kenya and Egypt, where we worked printing maps of the Suez Canal zone.[57]

After National Service Don dabbled in photography but it didn't become his career until his big break in 1959 when one of his photos, "The Guvnors", depicting a sharply suited Teddy Boy gang of that name — "the swaggering elite of Seven Sisters Road" according to Don's boyhood memory, who turned up in force every Saturday night at the Tottenham Royal — posing in the ruins of a bombed out building in Finsbury Park, was picked up by the *Observer*. McCullin snapped the right photo at the right time. The Teddy Boys were big news. They started out in the early 1950s as the first popular British youth cult, young working class men from the Elephant and Castle who took old-fashioned Edwardian suits and customised them for rough play, with long jackets, riverboat gambler ties, drainpipe trousers and brothel creeper shoes, all worn by a young man with a particular haircut that swept back on both sides to end at the back of the head in a parted triangle (the DA, or Duck's Arse).

"The Guvnors" presented the Teddy Boys in a glamorous light but they were essentially just street gangs protecting their territory. On 14th December 1958 Ronald Marwood, a twenty-five-year-old scaffolder and member of the Guvnors who lived in Huntingdon Street between Caledonian Road and Holloway Road, staggered out of the Spanish Patriots pub on Chapel Street after downing ten pints. With some mates he made his unsteady way to Gray's Dance Hall on Seven Sisters Road where a fight broke out between two rival gangs of Teddy Boys armed with knives, knuckle dusters, hammers, hacksaws and broken bottles. In the melee police constable Ray Summers grabbed one of Marwood's mates, whereupon Marwood stabbed Summers in the back with a ten-inch knife, leaving him to bleed to death on the pavement.

Marwood was not unusual in carrying and using a knife. Although it is rarely mentioned by those expressing horror about today's "black-on-black" knife crime, knives were used regularly in the 1950s by young white working class men. Pip Granger's dad was stabbed in the back by Frankie Fraser over a disputed bet. Ted was also stabbed in the back one New Year's Eve in Trafalgar Square after getting too friendly with another man's girlfriend (fortunately for my future existence, he survived). Marwood was convicted of murder and executed by hanging in May 1959. Between the murder and trial McCullin's photo was published and he was propelled into a career in photo-journalism.

From the start the Teddy Boys defined themselves as defenders of the old white working class and tooled up with knives and knuckle dusters to do so. Alan Johnson recalled that sometime in 1955, when he was seven and living with his sister and mother Lily at 107 Southam Street in Notting Hill, a young white woman hammered on their door pleading for refuge from pursuing Teddy Boys:

> *Lily went to the door and ushered her inside. Four or five Teds began to throw stones and junk from the street at our windows, shouting that the girl was a "fucking wog lover". We cowered inside, transfixed by terror, until eventually they gave up and went away.*[58]

Like Soho, Notting Hill's evolving culture was in great part a working class culture, but not a traditional one:

> *The dominant Trinidadian character of the migration to Notting Hill brought with it a passion for entertaining, food, music, drink and carnival. This combined well with a do-as-you-please local tradition among a shifting population that had never cared much for authority or property. The result endowed London with a new jewel, rivalling Chelsea, Fitzrovia and Soho for bohemianism, and Soho for its underworld and sex-commerce connections.*[59]

The jewel was still rough in the late 1950s. Most black families in Notting Hill lived in atrocious conditions, courtesy of landlords like Peter Rachman who built a property empire out of his use of the 1957 Rent Control Act. When the Act removed statutory rent controls from private landlords Rachman let out cramped, squalid housing and flats to black immigrant families, allowing the properties to go to seed, thus forcing out the previous sitting tenants. He then sold them at greatly increased prices. Any tenants who complained were visited by his thugs. Nonetheless, some black immigrants conceded that they would not have been able to rent anywhere else if not for Rachman.

It wasn't simply housing in which black immigrants congregated. Roy Stewart's basement gym at 32A Powis Square, also an unlicensed drinking club, was a popular gathering spot for young black men. Pubs like the Apollo on All Saints Road became known for a primarily black clientele. Off the streets, the numerous *Shibeens*— ad hoc, illegal clubs and music/dancing dens set up in flats and houses and just as quickly disbanded — provided refuge and relaxation for young black men and women, but often drove their white neighbours to distraction. This was fertile territory for Oswald Mosley's Union Movement and other far-right groups such as Keep Britain White and the White Defence League, all of whom leafleted and recruited in the area during 1958, especially among the local Teddy Boys. Tensions simmered throughout the summer. On Saturday 23rd August, after the pubs had shut, a gang of nine young white men armed with iron bars and knives drove around Shepherd's Bush, stopping to attack any black man they saw.

The touchpaper for what became known as the Notting Hill Riots was lit by an incident on 29th August 1958, when a Swedish woman, Majbritt Morrison, and her Jamaican husband Raymond had an argument outside Latimer Road tube station. It quickly escalated as white onlookers took Majbritt's side and Raymond's friends arrived. The next evening, when Majbritt returned home from a night out, she found the flat she shared with Raymond had been set alight. Majbritt, who was pregnant at the time, was herself attacked by Teddy Boys who called her a "black man's trollop". One smashed an iron bar across her back. An elderly white man intervened to protect her but by now white gangs were on the streets chanting "Kill the Niggers!".

Over the next four days, until 3rd September, bands of young white men roamed the district armed with knives, knuckle dusters, bicycle chains and dustbin lids, throwing petrol bombs, setting fire to houses and clubs. The trouble spread to Harrow Road and Paddington as well. The local hospitals began to fill up with wounded (by sheer luck, no one was killed). The police, taken by surprise, struggled to contain the violence, with some white gangs as large as two hundred men. The tide began to turn when a group of black men, who had barricaded themselves into the Totobag's Community Centre on Blenheim Crescent when it came under attack, fought back with Molotov cocktails. After throwing the cocktails at the white gang outside they emerged from the club brandishing meat cleavers, whereupon the racists retreated to Ladbroke Grove to find easier targets. On Wednesday 3rd September the heavens opened and it rained heavily for the next day. When the storm cleared the police finally regained control of the streets.

As Clair Wills has pointed out, echoing an admonition by the sociologist Ruth Glass at the time, the "Notting Hill Riots" were not confined to Notting Hill, and framing them in this way served to minimise them, implying they were unique, a violent eruption of thuggish Teddy Boys with no relation to the larger white community:

> Notting Hill then meant slums, and a criminal underworld where the "worst" types lived. In reality, the violence was spread over an area that stretched from Paddington to Kensal Rise, and there were isolated incidents in North London, in Liverpool Street and Southall throughout September.[60]

Whilst this is true, the implication – that the riots were the physical manifestation of a deeper white working class Id, that it acted out what less violent whites wanted — is contradicted by other evidence, not least that despite increased immigration to the area in the 1960s white riots did not recur. After the riots, Mosley, sensing an opportunity to reignite his political career, returned to Britain to stand in the 1959 general election for Kensington North, a constituency which covered Notting Hill and Kensal Town. His platform was unambiguously racist, calling for forced repatriation of Caribbean immigrants and a ban on mixed marriages. He received only 2,821 votes, 7.6% of the total, and lost his deposit.

Although Mosley's rejection and defeat were encouraging, the murder six months earlier of Antiguan migrant Kelso Cochrane in Notting Hill was its dark negative. Cochrane had arrived in the UK in 1954 and found work as a carpenter while he saved money to study Law. On 17th May 1959, returning from Paddington Hospital where he had attended A&E after a work accident, Kelso was attacked by a gang of white youths who killed him with a stiletto knife. Still scarred by the riots of the year before, the police were keen to deny a racial motive for what appeared from good evidence to be a racist murder instigated by members of Mosley's Union Movement.

On 27th May over five hundred people filled St Pancras Town Hall for a "We Mourn Cochrane" public meeting and the widespread revulsion at the murder was a factor in Mosley's defeat in Kensington North.

The Notting Hill Riots were a wake-up call. One of the most positive responses came from the black communist and civil rights activist Claudia Jones. Born in Trinidad and raised in New York's Harlem, Jones later became head of the American Young Communist League. Sentenced four times to jail terms for her political activities, in 1955 she was deported to London and settled in Notting Hill. There she joined the British Communist Party and launched the country's first black newspaper, the *West Indian Gazette*. After the riots, in an attempt to present the Afro-Caribbean community in London in a more positive light, she proposed an annual carnival to highlight West Indian music, food and dress.

As a result, the first Notting Hill Carnival, initially more like a town fete with music, was held in January 1959 in St Pancras Town Hall, and was televised by the BBC. It included a black beauty contest, a first for the entire country. It was such a success that the next year it was held in the much bigger Seymour Hall in Marble Arch and then moved to the Lyceum Ballroom on the Strand. Claudia Jones died relatively young in 1964 and was buried in Highgate Cemetery next to Karl Marx.

Although Mosley's defeat and the beginning of Notting Hill Carnival offered hope for the future, the riots and the murder of Kelso Cochrane made clear that the creation of a racially mixed working class in London would not be an easy process. Basil Dearden's *Sapphire* (1959), which won the 1959 BAFTA for Best Film, was an uncomfortable affirmation of that. On the surface a police procedural about the murder of a glamorous mixed-race dancer, *Sapphire* is a subtle dissection of racial, sexual and class attitudes in North London in the aftermath of the riots. Filmed on location in Earl's Court and Notting Hill, including Southam Street where the young Alan Johnson lived, it exudes a formidable authenticity.

The issue was further examined in *Flame in the Streets* (1961), a film based on Ted Willis's 1958 play *Hot Summer Night*. Willis, a working class playwright born in Turnpike Lane and active in the communist-led Labour League of Youth in the 1930s, later created the popular TV cop show *Dixon of Dock Green*. He wrote the play in direct response to the Notting Hill Riots. Set in what is clearly meant to be Notting Hill but actually filmed around the Grand Union Canal in Kensal Rise, the film examines racism through the prism of a mixed-race romance between Kathy (Sylvia Syms) and black teacher Peter (Johnny Sekka).

Flame in the Streets is unusual in highlighting race relations not just within industry but within the trade union movement. Kathy's father Jacko (John Mills), a trade union official, is genuinely anti-racist but he encounters it everywhere — in the factory, the union and in his own family. The factory is riven with racists who resent the promotion of competent black worker Gomez. Jacko condemns them for their bigotry but is less heroic when he discovers Kathy is to marry a black man and that his neglected wife Nell is seething with suppressed racism. Only a traumatic Guy Fawkes Night race riot forces the protagonists together. Racism is not defeated but there are some white people (Kathy, Jacko, some of Gomez's workmates) who reject it.

Majbritt Morrison's sensationalist memoir *Jungle West 11* (1964), given added notoriety by her involvement in the incident that sparked the riots, delved even deeper. Morrison recounted her role in the riots and how, abandoned and under terrible pressure in the 1960s, she later became an alcoholic and sex worker before dragging herself back from that life. Despite its obvious racist overtones, the nickname "Jungle West 11", created in the 1950s by the tabloid press and given a further boost by Morrison's bestseller, was commonly applied to the Paddington area until the 1970s.

Frank Norman's *Fings Ain't Wot They Used T'Be* (1959) eschewed politics and focused on the cultural changes to traditional working class life in the 1950s. Norman himself personified the radical nature of the times. Born in Bristol, he was abandoned in a Dr Barnado's home until he was a teenager, when he was sent to prison for three years for petty theft. Upon release he drifted, homeless, around London. His life changed when his prison memoir *Bang to Rights* (1957) became a minor publishing success. He then wrote a first draft of what would become the highly successful musical *Fings Ain't Wot They Used T'Be*, for which Lionel Bart wrote the tunes.

Norman's best work sees the London of the late 1950s and early 1960s, most especially Soho and the West End, through the eyes of an untutored working class interloper. On one level Norman revels in his new life — the theatres, clubs, booze and birds — but on another he recognises its superficiality. He was the template for the successful working class writer who would never for a moment give up his new lifestyle but cannot stop himself sentimentalising the culture he left behind:

> It used to be fun, dad and old mum,
> paddling down Southend.
> But now it ain't done, never mind son,
> Paris is where you'll spend your outings

But despite the efforts of writers like Taylor and Norman, not enough time had passed for the 1950s to become mythologised. In the 1950s and 1960s popular memory was still dominated by the Great Depression and the Second World War. Most working class people did not analyse their changing lives. They were too busy living them. Denise Haynes was born in 1942 and left school at fifteen to start work in C&A on Kensington High Street. As a 1950s London teenager she had a life undreamt of before the war:

> With my first week's wages I bought "Jail House Rock" and it went to Number 1 straight away. My dad went mad because I spent some of my wages on a bloody record. I was a big Elvis fan. I used to work all day until 6.00 and then go out dancing, but I'd still be wearing high heels. Hammersmith Palais we used to go to...There was a dress agency there, along by the Odeon, called Dinah Lee and they wanted a junior. Advertised in the window were pictures of black artists like Count Basie, Ella Fitzgerald, Lena Horne. I went in, got the job and it was £3 a week. I took a cut in money because I thought I was going to be working amongst the stars.[61]

Even outside the charmed circle of Soho, to which working class boys and girls were attracted like filings to a magnet, most working class families were beginning to see material improvements to their lives, of the kind that led Tory Prime Minister Harold MacMillan to claim they had "never had it so good". Even the young Alan Johnson, living in poverty in Notting Hill, encountered working class "affluence". His childhood friend Tony Cox lived at 318 Lancaster Road, where his family rented two floors of a four-storey house. Tony's dad Albert worked as an engineer on London Underground and his mum at a fish and chip shop on Shepherd's Bush Common.

The Cox's house had a large, light and airy living room, was heated by paraffin heaters on each landing and in the front room, and was carpeted throughout. Mr Cox's prize possession was a glass-fronted bookcase in which he kept the *Encyclopaedia Britannica*, the collected works of Charles Dickens and an assortment of second-hand classics. Johnson, an assiduous reader since his mother first took him to Latimer Road public library, looked on the bookcase as a religious icon and revered Mr Cox as the model of a working class father and provider he himself never had.

Jacky Hyams' family was not as interested in cultural improvement but they did want the latest consumer items. Of the late Fifties, she recalled:

> *Our flat began to show the material evidence of what was happening outside – the country's slowly emerging consumerism. My mum wasn't especially house proud, aspiring to a comfortable and carefully thought out home. She just went out and bought whatever big item we needed after my dad had handed over the money. First came the seventeen-inch TV set from Bardens on Kingsland High Street, bought on hire purchase...We acquired a fridge from the North Thames Gas Board showroom, also on the "never-never".*

In contrast to Mr Cox, Mr Hyams' most cherished possession was a new cocktail cabinet, kept in a corner of the living room:

It was an ugly, shiny edifice with a pull down handle that revealed the full works, the bottles of sherry, advocaat, gin, whisky, brandy and Babycham and the accompanying little cocktail glasses with plastic cocktail sticks, all lit up by an internal light.[62]

Ted also began to branch out. In the late 1950s he was working for Connolly Brothers doing maintenance work in central London, including in the Houses of Parliament and the Reading Room of the British Museum, where he was sent to wash down the brass and leather desk tops. Like the working class kids who daily ran through the museum, occasionally stopping to investigate the Egyptian collection, the proximity of the Reading Room's books had a transformative effect on him:

Try to imagine the effect this vast library had on me. The silence was like a church, with thousands of books stretching up to the ceiling and iron catwalks leading off to galleries of yet more books. For the first time I bitterly regretted my rudimentary education. It was because of this that I enrolled in the St Pancras Library and from that day to this I have always had a book on the go.[63]

After a period with Connolly Brothers, Ted ended up working in a small engineering factory still standing in the ruins of Aldersgate, but after the relative freedom of different jobs in central London the regimentation of factory work was not for him. Taking from the factory the one useful skill it offered him, proficiency in electric arc welding, he looked around for better employment, meanwhile preparing to marry his new girlfriend.

Like Ted, Joyce left school at fifteen, getting a job at Sprague's Bookbinders on City Road doing reception and general admin work. The eldest of five children, she continued to share a bedroom with her two sisters in the first two floors of the house on Burton Street, still cold, still unlit by electricity. To escape a cramped and uncomfortable home life, Joyce went every night to the Mary Ward youth club in Bloomsbury where she won prizes for her ballroom dancing skills, participating in competitions at the Royal Albert Hall. Although her family had barely enough to live on, she managed to secure decent ballgowns for the dances by sometimes accompanying her mum to the offices of the Crusade of Rescue Homes for Destitute Catholic Children at 27 Tavistock Place, where her mum cleaned the building, at 5.30 in the morning and nabbing some of the charity's stock of dresses, making off with them over her shoulder directly under the gaze of the police station opposite. At sixteen she was already an attractive young woman who had caused havoc with the local boys on trips back to Ireland, so much so that her stern "dad", Tom O'Connell, hired a slightly older man to escort her around to dance competitions, warning off possible boyfriends. This didn't prevent a brief tug of war over a local boy with budding young actress Barbara Windsor.

One night at the Mary Ward Joyce met a tall, black-haired young man who did not lack for ambition and who had begun to use his disposable cash to buy tailor-made suits from Sam Argus in Berwick Street. Somehow he blagged his way past her minder and her dad. Before long they were dancing at the Lyceum on Friday nights and going to the pictures on Saturday nights. After a couple of years' courtship, during which Ted had to formally promise Joyce's parish priest that any children resulting from a marriage would be raised as Catholics, Ted and Joyce were married in June 1959 at St Aloysius Catholic Church on Phoenix Road, Somers Town.[64]

The honeymoon was three days in Southend. Some fings were still wot they used to be.

THE 1960s

"What do you think about Society?"
"OK, as long as it don't bother me."

Chelsea Bridge Boys (1965)

On 6th May 1961 Tottenham Hotspur, one of North London's two iconic football clubs, won the Double. By defeating Leicester City in the FA Cup Final, after already coming top of the First Division, Spurs did what no other team had done in the twentieth century to that point and would not do again until their great rival Arsenal in 1971. Under its legendary manager Bill Nicholson, Spurs would go on to become the first British football team to win a European trophy when they beat Atletico Madrid 5-1 in the final of the 1963 European Cup Winners' Cup, but the Double was the achievement that put the club in the front rank of English and international football. It was celebrated by a huge parade that took six hours to travel from Edmonton Town Hall down the High Road and past the Royal to Tottenham Town Hall. Virtually all of Tottenham and adjacent areas came to celebrate, with shops and houses decorated in blue and white. It was a massive and spontaneous working class street party of a kind not seen since the Queen's Coronation in 1953.

A year before, a very different type of crowd had filled the streets of North London. On 4th January 1960 over two thousand council tenants in the borough of St Pancras (at the time a separate borough encompassing Highgate, Camden Town and King's Cross) went on a rent strike against its newly elected Tory council. Between 1956 and 1958, under the leadership of the radical socialist John Lawrence, St Pancras Labour Council had reduced council rents, applied a trade union closed shop for council employees and flown the Red Flag over the Town Hall on 1st May. In August 1958 Lawrence and thirteen other Labour councillors were expelled from the Labour Party for "views believed to be inimical to the best interests of the Labour Party and indistinguishable from those of known Communists".[1] The Labour council then raised rents. This did not prevent the Tories, after taking back the council in May 1959, from doubling the rent for tenants of the new, post-war council estates and trebling it for tenants of the pre-war estates.

The Tories badly misjudged the working class of St Pancras, described in 1960 by one national newspaper as "a lively, quick tongued population" who had "many of the East Ender's characteristics". The report qualified this with a warning that "the strong peppering of Greek, Irish and Latin residents gives St Pancras a peculiarly individual tang".[2] The Labour Party, however, noticed the changing social demographic of the borough and that marginal wards that contained a majority of this heterodox working class might cede Labour political control — as, after 1964, with the addition of a newly arrived liberal middle class, it almost perpetually did.

The "individual tang" and spirit of resistance of St Pancras was enflamed by the Tory rent increases. In response tenants formed the St Pancras Borough Council United Tenants Association (UTA) led by Don Cook, an ex-paratrooper and a member of the Communist Party (CP). On 1 September over four thousand tenants, half of the borough's council house tenants, marched from Kentish Town to St Pancras Town Hall on Euston Road to protest the rent increases. The Tories refused to back down and on 4 January 1960 the new rent scheme was imposed. Initially about 80% of the affected tenants withheld the increased rent but morale was badly dented when some local Labour Party leaders went publicly to the rent office to pay up in full.

After eviction notices were served the numbers refusing to pay dropped dramatically and the UTA decided to concentrate on two or three tenants whose flats would be defended by collective action. In June the three chosen tenants — Don Cook of Kennistoun House, Leighton Road, Kentish Town; Arthur

Rowe in Silverdale on the Regent's Park Estate; and Gladys Turner of Goldington Buildings, Somers Town — were told they were to be evicted. When Turner backed out, the battle over St Pancras's new rents came down to the evictions of Cook and Rowe.

Barricades went up at Kennistoun House and at Silverdale. Local trade unions declared they would support Cook and Rowe. Plans were made to fire rockets into the air to summon this support if bailiffs came to repossess. The CP's North London Area Organiser, Sam Aaronovitch, was responsible for coordinating much of this support. His son David, six at the time, recalled:

My memory of this event is composed of sounds and images. Of the serious hubbub of men and women coming in and out of our house with leaflets, placards, banners, loudhailers and excited faces. Of taking the bus down to Kentish Town with my mother, walking to a block of terraced flats and looking up and seeing a barricade and barbed wire on the top floor....Of Sam, in shirtsleeves on a step ladder, a loudhailer in his hand, regaling a small crowd of passers-by in a compelling voice.[3]

At 5am on the morning of 22nd September 1960 the bailiffs, supported by eight hundred police, moved to evict Cook and Rowe, and pitched battles occurred at both locations. The fire brigade put up ladders to reach Cook's flat but after he explained to the firefighters what was happening, they removed them. There followed a two-hour battle in Kennistoun House as oil was poured down the stairways to stop the advancing bailiffs, who eventually crashed in through the roof. The rockets were then fired. One local resident, primed to defend Cook, told reporters:

I heard the rockets. We all ran out in our pyjamas. Everywhere there were people running towards Kennistoun House. But when we turned into Leighton Road all we could see were police. There were hundreds of them. We could do nothing. We could not get near.[4]

Arthur Rowe's flat in Silverdale was also assaulted. After an hour of spirited resistance bailiffs had to smash through a brick wall to evict him. Irish labourers working on the Shell Centre in Waterloo, alerted by John Lawrence and their union secretary Brian Behan, left the site and marched up to Kentish Town to provide support, but were attacked by the police in Leighton Road. Vic Heath, by now an active member of the CP, was working at the time on the site and was one of nearly four hundred men who tried to come to Cook and Rowe's assistance. Other promised union support failed to turn out.

In the evening, once word of what had taken place had circulated, a crowd of four thousand angry tenants surged down Kentish Town to St Pancras Town Hall. They clashed with a ring of police around the Town Hall and fighting broke out along Euston Road. Vic and a few ex-army mates tried to get in round the back but were ambushed and arrested. By midnight the violence had subsided but police stayed around the Town Hall, Kennistoun House and Silverdale all night. When the UTA called on tenants to withhold all their rent as a protest, the council sent bailiffs around the estates to intimidate those thinking of doing so. Faced with a ban on public demonstrations, the campaign wound down. In May 1962 Labour retook the council from the Tories and although Cook and Rowe were rehoused the new rent scheme, the focus of the struggle, remained.

The St Pancras Rent Strike laid bare the attitudes of some in local government towards the capital's council housing tenants. All agreed there was an urgent need for new housing for London's working class, although not all agreed these needed to be in London and some actively preferred their tenants relocate to the "New Towns" of the south-east. Many working class Londoners felt the same, yearning to escape to what they saw as better-quality suburban living. This was hardly surprising given that in 1961 30% of all London's houses still had no bath and many, like Joyce's in Burton Street, only had an outside toilet.[5]

Not all felt this way. George Skeggs, who came up to Soho from the East End as a teenager in the 1950s, instantly fell in love with the area and made it the centre of his life (as it still is). Hanging out at the 2i's and the Nucleus coffee bar on Seven Dials, he drove around on a 150 Vespa wearing French and Italian clothes. In 1963 he and his new wife — local girl Helen McKenzie, born and raised on the Wild Street Peabody Estate and who worked in a shoemakers in Drury Lane — moved into a flat in the Bedfordbury Peabody Estate next to Covent Garden, known as the Bury. The flat had three rooms with no bath, toilet or running water. Of life there, George remembered:

> Living on the Bury, we had to wash the landing on a rota, and also arrange our bath days too. The bath was situated in the washroom on each landing, with a thin partition around it for the sake of one's dignity, as others on the landing might need, or be doing their weekly washing at the same time while you were having a bath! The only modern convenience in the washhouse in those old Victorian buildings was a gas water heater which was activated by placing a sixpenny coin in a slot. You would always make sure you took enough sixpences in with you, or you might end up sitting in a bath of lukewarm water, with a tide mark around your waist and that's no joke![6]

For all its privations, George and Helen enjoyed life in the Bury and made many friends there. In 1966 they were moved to a modernised flat on the Wild Street Estate. Their two daughters were born at nearby Charing Cross Hospital in the late 1960s and George often took them for walks in St James's Park and across to Whitehall to see the Changing of the Guard. By the 1980s, when they left, both the Bury and Wild Street were much improved from the 1960s, although both estates were still a thriving oasis of social housing in the beating heart of London.

Those born further out had fewer social compensations. Amanda Millhouse, born in 1961 in Hackney, lived in part of a three-storey Victorian mid-terrace house. Her dad was a furniture salesman, her mum a nurse:

> We had the basement and 1st floor and a spinster lived in the flat above. The house had large sash windows that let in the draft and the glass was so thin that it easily smashed. There was no

heating in the house and we had rising damp. We had paraffin heaters in the kitchen and hallway and a two-bar electric heater in the front room. The bedrooms had no heating, so in the winter we would dress under the duvet. There was no bathroom in the house, so washing was mostly done in the kitchen sink. We did have a metal bath as well, but it took forever to fill up and got cold really quickly.

Like many working class families in London, Amanda found solace in the public baths:

Mum would take us to Hackney Baths where we could have a proper bath. You were given lovely big towels with LB Hackney sewn into them and ladies wearing white coats and rubber shoes would allocate a cubicle made of wood with a huge bath inside it and a bench. She would run the bath from outside the cubicle and you could shout "more hot water in number 6!" and she would oblige. The pipework was copper and always polished to a high shine. We finally got a bathroom in 1968. A big white, cold enamel bath. Still no heating though. Our dining room was turned into a kitchen and was always cosy. We heated it using the gas cooker oven.[7]

The atmosphere of early 1960s Hackney saturates Alexander Baron's *The Lowlife* (1963). Born in 1917 to a Jewish-immigrant Hackney family, in the 1930s Baron fought Mosley's Blackshirts as part of the Labour League of Youth with his friend Ted Willis, and went on to become a prolific novelist. He never romanticised Hackney and he knew exactly where it stood in relation to London:

Hackney isn't the East End — that's the mark of an outsider, when you hear someone call Hackney the East End. The East End starts two miles down the road, across the border of Bethnal Green.[8]

Baron's cult masterpiece takes its hero Harryboy Boas, a gambler and hopeless dreamer living in a Hackney bedsit, from betting shop to dog track to brothel by way of Ridley Road

Market in a futile search for meaning and success, ending where he began in the arse-end of nowhere. *The Lowlife* is set in a dying world, amongst a white working class about to be eclipsed and transformed by new tower blocks and the provision of social housing to incoming Afro-Caribbean families.

A few miles west, things were not so different. Gary Kemp, born in 1959, was brought home from the hospital to an early-nineteenth-century terraced house in Islington that did not have electricity until a year later. His family rented most of the rooms in the house, although it had no bathroom and the only toilet was outside in a small walled yard. As well as his own immediate family, the house also contained his uncle's family as well as an older cousin, her Turkish-Cypriot husband and their son. While the three families kept to separate floors, the children formed a group and colonised the doorsteps, the backyard and the basement as play areas.[9]

Another working class boy who would also go on to fame and success in music, Steve Jones, grew up at the same time in Hammersmith, an area on the brink of incorporation into the ever-expanding ambit of central London. In 1960-61 the Hammersmith Flyover was built to relieve congested traffic on Hammersmith Broadway and to link the Talgarth Road to the start of the Great West Road. Effective in funnelling traffic to and from Heathrow, the flyover simply blighted the area in a different way than had traffic congestion.

Steve lived in a third-floor flat in the Riverside Gardens Peabody Estate near Hammersmith Bridge with his mother, his two uncles, his nan Edith and grandad Fred. His father, a boxer from Fulham, was not interested in family or fatherhood and his mother had a hard time getting money out of him. As so often, the women — his mum and his nan — carried the load. His granddad, like my own on my mum's side, was a "lazy cunt" and professional skiver, while his nan, the main carer, cleaned other people's houses as well as their own. For all that, Steve's early memories were happy ones. The flat was crowded but not uncomfortable:

There were no lifts so you had to walk up the stairs to get there, but this was nobody's shithole. It was a proper Victorian housing estate — decent accommodation for decent working class people who were getting by OK....There was a real sense of community on that estate. There was a boozer on the corner with an off-license next to it, and when we'd take back the R.White's lemonade bottles to get the deposits, I'd sit outside the pub listening to the guy who played the piano.[10]

Steve's life took a darker turn when he was sexually assaulted by a man who hung about in the underpass beneath the flyover and, when he was ten, by his own step-father, a man his mother had married when he was six. After the marriage they had moved out of the Peabody Estate to a one-bedroom basement flat in Benbow Road, Shepherd's Bush, lacking a bathroom or an inside toilet, and the safety and warmth of the Riverside Gardens Estate was ripped away.

Richard Gregory, born in 1955, also grew up and went to school in the Shepherd's Bush and Hammersmith area. His father worked in the Osram Lamps factory on Brook Green and Richard lived in Shepherd's Bush Road until he was twenty-five (and continued to live in the area for the rest of his life). In the 1960s Shepherd's Bush Green was his playground. He recalled that, well into the 1960s, lacking any supermarkets or franchise shops except Woolworths, the working class of Shepherd's Bush bought all their food from local butchers, greengrocers, bakers and fishmongers.

Unlike Steve, Richard had a childhood free of adult abuse, roving freely about the area with his friends:

I remember going to infant school alone, getting the bus to Hammersmith Broadway and buying sherbet flying saucers (8 for a penny) at a kiosk in Butterwick. During my primary school years I went out with friends all the time, playing football, going swimming, exploring the parks, bomb sites and derelict houses.... We went to Shepherd's Bush Market a lot without necessarily buying anything — Ellis's Pet Stores was a particular source of fascination, with exotic fish in the aquarium and a talking macaw. We earned additional pocket money by running errands for our parents — the local shopkeepers knew them, and the tobacconists and off licences turned a blind eye. Children's television ended at the six o'clock news, and our evenings were free — we would be out in the streets of Shepherd's Bush until it got dark.

Like Pip Grainger and the kids of Wild Street, Richard gained much from his proximity to London's great cultural institutions:

We would take a bus to the Natural History Museum, Science Museum or Commonwealth Institute, all of which offered free entry; or go to one of the many local cinemas — the Saturday morning shows at Hammersmith Odeon were always packed with children.[11]

It was all on the cusp of a new era. The political governance of London underwent a fundamental change when the London Government Act 1963 abolished the LCC and created a new body, the Greater London Council (GLC). It also amalgamated and created new London boroughs. From 1965 Greater London encompassed thirty-two individual boroughs, some of which were defined as "Inner London" and some as "Outer London". The GLC's powers were not as extensive as the LCC's and so the quantity and quality of social housing varied depending on the politics of individual councils. Changes to government subsidies for social housing first introduced in 1956 had provided London's boroughs with more funding the higher they built. Although the 1964 Labour government abolished this subsidy the damage had been done and the momentum was hard to reverse. Tower blocks — tall, inelegant, ugly, alienating — became the norm of new London council housing in the 1950s, through the 1960s and even into the 1970s, until their unpopularity and intrinsic flaws become impossible to ignore.

Between 1965 and 1975 the GLC alone built 384 tower blocks in London, and most of the boroughs continued the trend begun in the 1950s. Estates such as Camden's Chalcot Estate appeared incongruously in the late 1960s. The Chalcots, four twenty-three-storey tower blocks on Adelaide Road between Chalk Farm and Swiss Cottage, were constructed by Eton College

Estates between 1965 and 1968 as high-rise luxury living. But just as they were finished the Ronan Point disaster made tower blocks unattractive, prompting Camden Council to buy up the four blocks, add a fifth for good measure, and rebrand them the Chalcot Estate (the name taken from the seventeenth-century Chalcot Farm which had been corrupted into Chalk Farm). Initially they were popular because of their incredible views but deep-seated structural flaws soon began to appear.

Jerry White's history of London in the twentieth century estimates that during the peak period of council tower block construction in the 1960s and 1970s approximately 68,000 flats in blocks of ten or more floors were built in the capital. These included Balfron Tower in Poplar, opened in 1967, and Trellick Tower in Westbourne Grove, opened in 1972, the grandest expressions of Brutalist architecture designed by the modernist architect Erno Goldfinger. Today, nearly all of Balfron Tower's working class residents have been ejected, "art-washed" out, and most of its apartments are privately owned. Even Soho was saddled with a seventeen-storey tower block, Kemp House on Berwick Street, built by Westminster Council in the 1960s. In 2017 Westminster gave the rights to redevelop the block to private contractors PMB, reserving only four flats for "affordable housing". In 2020, a one-bedroom flat in Kemp House could be had for £625,000.

Although there were genuine exceptions that became much cherished by their residents, such as the Churchill Gardens and Golden Lane Estates, most working class council tenants did not want to live in tower blocks. They didn't want to live in slums either, and were mostly glad to see them go, but they would have preferred to be relocated to other, better houses or low-level flats that formed part of a tangible and connected community. Their views were seldom canvassed by planners or architects.

Other mega-structures drove their way through North London working class life, quite literally in the case of the Westway, a 2.5-mile-long elevated dual carriageway running from North Kensington in the west to the Marylebone flyover in the east. The Westway, initially intended as one element of a massive new ring road around central London (a plan discontinued after the Westway provoked intense popular opposition) was built between 1962 and 1970, leading to the almost complete annihilation of a particular working class community in Notting Dale and Kensal Town. Within a few years Norland Market and Norland Gardens (seen in the opening credits of the 1962 pilot of *Steptoe and Son*, where an old Trotters Yard was used for exterior shots of 25 Oil Drum Lane), Hunt Street, Poynter Street, Stebbing Street, Hume Road, Boxmoor Street and all their cafes, pubs, schools, shops and dance halls were razed to the ground, to be replaced by the huge Edward Woods Estate. The estate's tower blocks bore the names of the streets they had replaced.

Beginning in 1962, compulsory purchases of houses and properties, some of which were slums but some of which were not, meant that nearly 3,500 residents needed to be rehoused. Not all of this was passively accepted. After the Westway opened, residents of houses in Acklam Road in North Kensington, past which the dual carriageway funnelled twenty-four-hour traffic mere feet from their windows, displayed banners saying "Get Us Out Of This Hell" and staged disruptive protests to the traffic of up to eighty people at a time. But escape was relative. New tower blocks built on the Warwick Estate at the eastern end of the Westway approaching Edgware Road simply loomed over it, their residents consigned to never-ending views of bleak Ballardian dystopia. Between 1973 and 1980 Mick Jones of the Clash lived in his grandmother's flat on the eighteenth floor of Wilmcote House, an experience which soaked into several of the band's songs, especially "London's Burning".

Not everyone involved in providing new council housing agreed with the philosophy of building tower blocks or that modern social housing had to be Brutalist. Camden Council, in particular, offered a progressive alternative. Formed out of the former boroughs of St Pancras, Holborn and Hampstead, the new Borough of Camden had more affluent areas, more highly rateable properties and therefore more financial resources than boroughs such as Newham. Under the leadership of the Camden Borough Architect Sydney Cook and his gifted protégé Neave

Brown, Camden Council (mainly Labour during this period) commissioned and built a series of innovative "low-rise, high-density" council estates that stand to this day as an example of what imaginative municipal socialism can achieve.

The Branch Hill Estate on the fringes of Hampstead Heath was the living embodiment of what John Boughton called

Camden Council's determination that there should be no no-go areas for council housing and that its residents were as entitled to live in leafy Hampstead as its traditionally more privileged denizens.[12]

Branch Hill and similar examples of game-changing council estates, such as the now iconic Alexandra Road Estate, would be constructed in the 1970s, but others such as the Dunboyne Estate between Belsize Park and Hampstead Heath were constructed and opened in the 1960s. Dunboyne, designed by Neave Brown, was an exercise in chic white modernist design. Its seventy-one flats were arranged in parallel terraced rows, in groups of eight or sixteen, each with a large terrace overlooking lush communal gardens. It was five minutes' walk from Hampstead Heath.

Dunboyne was part of a vision followed by the Camden Architect's Department that saw similar estates dotted throughout the borough. In the 1960s Cook and his team were responsible for nearly all of the best, high quality developments in neglected and now fashionable parts of the borough such as High Holborn, where they inserted new council blocks off Red Lion Square and many other sites within a ten-minute walk of the West End. Ted's close mate Ronnie Garrett and his family, who we often visited when I was a kid, lived in the Red Lion Square Estate for many years. It was extremely handy for Ronnie as he worked as a postman in the Holborn sorting office just around the corner.

Other estates in Camden, constructed before Cook and Brown's time, were not so favoured. The Ampthill Square Estate at the northern edge of Somers Town was a product of the 1950s. It consisted of eight six-storey blocks on its eastern side and, on its western side and its most distinctive feature, three twenty-one-storey tower blocks that to this day cast shadows over Mornington Crescent. The local GP's surgery is nestled in the concrete plaza between the blocks, dwarfed by its titanic neighbours. It was only while I was researching this book that I discovered that the family GP who practised out of the NHS surgery on the Ampthill Square Estate, Dr Linehan, a large, grizzled Irishmen known to everyone as "Paddy", was very probably my mum's half-brother and therefore my uncle. Although my mum's real father was a family secret, it is possible that every time I went to see Dr Linehan as a child he was aware he was seeing his nephew.[13]

Ampthill Square did not reflect Camden's approach to council housing in the 1960s and 1970s. Nor was Camden the only borough trying to provide high quality social housing that avoided the mistakes of the tower blocks. The Lillington Gardens Estate in Pimlico was constructed in phases by the City of Westminster between 1961 and 1970, and decisively rejected the tower block template. Presented in rich red brick, Lillington Gardens provided high-density, three-to-five-storey flats of great individuality, designed around roof-level "planted gardens" that provide a canopy of greenery to adorn and support the estate. The estate also includes the Lord High Admiral pub in Vauxhall Bridge Road as an integral part of its design, a structure now Grade II listed.

From 2002 to 2019 Lillington Gardens was owned and managed by City West Homes, an arms-length management organisation of Westminster Council created in 2002 to manage its housing stock. But in 2019, following the disaster at Grenfell Tower, Westminster took back management control of all its council estates. In 2020 Lillington Gardens still provides high quality social housing, an estate described by the architectural critic Rowan Moore as "ruggedly romantic", a stones' throw from the river and the Tate. It is just one of a large number of attractive and well-maintained council estates threaded throughout central and North London.

The ethnic composition of London's working class changed rapidly in the 1960s. One of the key elements of this transformation was a second wave of Afro-Caribbean immigrants arriving in the UK in the early 1960s in order to avoid the restrictions of the 1962 Commonwealth Immigration Act, which essentially repealed the right of free movement of subjects of the British Commonwealth to the "mother country". By 1961 there were already over 100,000 West Indians living in London. The 1962 Act limited new immigrants to those holding vouchers for work or study or to dependents of those already in the country. As a result, mass unskilled migration from Commonwealth countries was cut to a trickle but not before a last rush, mostly from India and Pakistan. Ultimately, it made little difference. During the 1950s and 1960s the racial and cultural profile of London's working class was rewritten to such an extent that from the early 1970s there was no longer a homogeneous "white English" working class in Inner London.

The Nigerian writer Buchi Emecheta was one of the new black working class making a home for itself in North London. Her father was a railway worker who died when she was young. She arrived in London in 1962 as an eighteen-year-old with her new husband, a brutal man who beat her and burned the handwritten manuscript of her first novel, *The Bride Price* (eventually re-written and published in 1976). Buchi found work in Chalk Farm Library and in 1966, pregnant with her fifth child, she left her husband and took her children to live in a series of dreary rented flats in Camden.

In 1969 Camden Council rehoused her and her children in Rothay, a small block of flats on the Regent's Park Estate in Albany Street, immediately adjacent to Christ Church Primary School which I attended from 1967. She later wrote:

The June day on which we moved was mercifully dry. I left the bigger children at the new flat with the Gas Board engineer whilst he fixed in our old cooker. Before I arrived with the removal van, however, my eldest son Ik, who was then eight had explored the whole of Regent's Park and its environs. He told me in no uncertain terms "These are really, really posh nosh flats, mum". I could not help agreeing with him.[14]

Buchi maintained her family through her work as a library assistant at the British Museum while she studied at night for a Sociology degree. Her first published novel *In the Ditch* (1972) presented for the first time the travails of young black female immigrants to London, struggling not just with the racism of white society but the ingrained sexism of their male relations and partners. Her powerful autobiography *Head Above Water* (1986) dispenses with fictional cover and tells her story with unflinching honesty.

Not all immigrants overcame economic and cultural barriers as well as Buchi Emecheta. Clair Wills explained the difficulties of those new arrivals, mainly from India and Pakistan, who did not speak English very well or at all (West Indians tended to speak excellent English). Inevitably they had to rely on those who could translate for them. This could produce a segregated labour force, with Asians heavily dependent on piece work and overtime:

> What was incontestable was that large groups of Indian and Pakistani men were engaged in working class jobs, at the heart of Britain's industrial recovery. Yet they did not behave like the white working class men alongside whom they worked. They tended (at this stage) not to join unions, to work unbelievably long hours, to sacrifice family life for higher wages, to spend nothing on leisure, and to refuse to integrate into the communities in which they lived.[15]

The birth-pangs of a multi-ethnic society in London provided opportunity to racists and fascists. Mosley's Union Movement was in decline but other fascist groups such as the National Socialist Movement (NSM) sought to fill the gap, switching their attention from Jews to Caribbean and Asian immigrants. The resurgence of domestic fascism in the early 1960s led to the creation of the 62 Group, successor of the old 43 Group, by Harry Bidney, a Soho nightclub manager, and the Jewish Communist Gerry Gable (who in the 1970s would edit the anti-fascist magazine *Searchlight*). When fascists led by Mosley himself held a rally in Ridley Road, Hackney, on July 31st 1962, a large opposition mobilized by the 62 Group gave them a thorough pasting, a running street battle in which Mosley was pushed to the ground and kicked in the head. He never again tried to bring fascism back to London's streets.

Despite this resistance, integration was advancing quickly in the 1960s. One of its drivers was the spread of non-English food and restaurants. Even though the first Indian-run restaurant in the country, the Hindoostane Coffee House, had opened in London on Portman Place as far back as 1809, Indian food did not become truly popular until the 1970s. But there were outliers to that trend. In 1961 Ted and Joyce were living in a small basement flat in Mecklenburgh Square, Bloomsbury, after Ted's mum's flat on Bernard Street, where they had been staying, was demolished in 1960 along with other houses on the street to make way for the new Brunswick Estate. One evening Ted and a few mates were drinking in the Perseverance pub on Lamb's Conduit Street when they bumped into an acquaintance, an Egyptian taxi driver named Charlie, who suggested they go for an Indian meal at a new restaurant in nearby Tavistock Place, at the time one of the few Indian restaurants in London.

Ted was an immediate convert to Indian food and later took Joyce along to try it. She too loved the food, particularly the Vindaloo, for which she had an unusual tolerance. From then on they went there regularly until one night they took a cousin of Joyce's who could not contain his seething racism. When the Indian waiter took the order for coffee and asked "black or white?", Joyce's cousin snapped back, "Yes, I'm white and you're fucking black". A fight then broke out that spilled out on to the street. After that Ted and Joyce had to find another Indian restaurant in which to enjoy a curry.

Chinese restaurants had been part of London life since the 1880s. By the 1930s there was a proto-Chinatown in Limehouse based around Pennyfields and Limehouse Causeway consisting of Chinese restaurants, laundries, grocery stores and seaman's hostels. It was a primarily male community which led to marriages with white English women and mixed-race families that mostly adopted Christianity. But the East End's Chinatown sustained so much bomb damage in the war that in the late

1940s and 1950s it relocated to the West End. The 1950s saw a big increase in London's Chinese population, fuelled by refugees from the Chinese Civil War, an increase which peaked in the early 1960s as immigrants from Hong Kong arrived to beat the new restrictions of the Commonwealth Immigration Act. The act allowed for immigration if employers could prove a need for them, so male agricultural workers from Hong Kong continued to move to London throughout the 1960s, settling mainly in Soho and Bayswater. The natural place for them to work was in the catering trade.

In the 1950s Gerrard Street and Leigh Street were two unregarded backstreets wedged between Shaftesbury Avenue and Leicester Square, known for seedy brothels, dingy nightclubs and porn shops. In the early 1960s it only had two restaurants, Boulougne at number 27 and Peter Mario's at number 46, the latter a favourite of Billy Hill. By 1967 number 44 had become "Happening 44", a psychedelic nightclub that used slide projectors for primitive light shows, and the Loon Fung Supermarket had opened in the old Tailor and Cutter building to supply new Chinese restaurants made out of run-down properties sold on cheap short leases. By 1970 Gerrard Street was home to seven Chinese restaurants plus Chinese gambling clubs, travel agencies, beauty salons and two supermarkets, and was the heart of London's new Chinatown.

The city's Greek Cypriot population also began to put down permanent roots in North London following the peak of its post-war immigration, 1960-1961, when 25,000 Cypriots entered Britain, after which levels fell back to an average of 4,000 a year. During the 1950s and 1960s many Greek Cypriot families migrated north from the West End, where they were clustered in the clothing and catering trades, to Cypriot communities in Camden Town and Green Lanes where they could buy food from Greek Cypriot grocers and eat out in local Greek restaurants. The majestic All Saints Cathedral in Pratt Street just off Camden High Street, which became a Greek Orthodox church in 1948, was the centre of Greek Cypriot life in London. That community was primarily working class, the men mostly working as tailors or waiters or on the buses, the women as seamstresses and dressmakers.[16]

During the 1960s Helen Evangelou visited All Saints every Sunday with her father (her mother stayed at home cooking the Sunday roast) and recalled how the weekly services were as much a social occasion as a religious ceremony:

We would take the bus from Howland Street or Tottenham Court Road up along Hampstead Road and past the art-deco cigarette factory with its statuesque black cats — always a source of childhood fascination. Inevitably we would bump into other friends and family at the bus stop...After the church service was over we would file outside and be greeted by more friends and family. This would take forever: cheeks were kissed, extended family were asked after. How was the business going? Was there any news from Cyprus? When was young Maria getting married?...Before finally heading off people would queue to buy the Greek savouries on sale in the church ground".[17]

London's Greek Cypriot community, though thriving, was not as large as its Irish. By 1961 the Irish-born population of London was 174,000, 5.4% of the total. Most of these lived in Kilburn, Queen's Park, Cricklewood and Harlesden. Like the Afro-Caribbean and Greek Cypriot communities, it was a solid working class enclave. Its religious centre, the Sacred Heart Catholic Church on Quex Road in Kilburn, was famous for the large number of Irish Londoners who went there every Sunday, so many that it had to perform twelve Masses throughout the day.

Many institutions kept this community afloat, particularly the dance halls and pubs of the area, foremost of which were the Galtymore and the Crown pub in Cricklewood. There were many Irish dance halls threaded throughout North and North-West London— the Blarney, the Gresham, the Estate — but none was as dear to its users as the Galty. It reached the peak of its success in 1967 when Larry Cunningham played there to a crowd of 6,850 locals. Cunningham, still working full-time as a builder, notched up a massive chart hit with "A Tribute to Jim

Reeves" and his cover of "Lovely Leitrim" displaced the Beatles from the No 1 slot in Ireland. When he and his band the Mighty Avons played the Galty the crowd backed up down Cricklewood High Street.

Other Irish pubs frequently descended into Saturday night chaos. Phyllis Izzard, a young Irish woman who migrated from Mooncoin in County Kilkenny to London in the late 1950s, lived in Barnet with her sister but travelled down to Kilburn and Camden for nights out. She recalled a night in the early 1960s in the Round Tower on Holloway Road when the police were called to break up a fight:

> But they just stood back and let the Irish fellas flog each other to death. They were probably quite wise; they used to do that a lot. They just moved in and picked up the pieces when it was all over. But these fellas decided that nobody was taking their mates away. They'd been killing them five minutes previously but now they weren't going to let them be taken away, so they pulled the doors clean off the Black Maria.[18]

Sean McGlinchey was born in 1958 in Ladbrook Grove, "second-generation" London Catholic Irish, to a mother from Donegal and a father from Belfast. In 2020 he recalled:

> We had a basement flat. As with all the other kids in the area, we had a great deal of freedom and were allowed to play out in the streets completely unsupervised until dinnertime. Dad bought a car to learn how to drive but the local kids were always letting down the tyres and sitting on the bonnet and even the roof. Looking back, it must have been quite rough and ready, although as kids we didn't really notice it as everyone was in the same boat.

In 1965 life for the family changed dramatically:

> At the age of seven I was hospitalised with Rheumatic Fever which is associated with poor, damp living conditions. I was in hospital for months and missed a whole year at school.

After being discharged from hospital, I was sent to a rehabilitation centre in the country for many weeks which I really enjoyed. My condition meant that our family got enough points to qualify us for council housing and we moved into Huxley Street, Queen's Park in 1966. I vividly remember going to see the empty house and being amazed at how spacious and beautiful it was. There were three bedrooms, a front room and a back room, an indoor bath and toilet and a proper garden!...There was a great community spirit here and we quickly made friends with the local kids...This was the place we regarded as our first true home and mum lived there for fifty years until she died.

There was far more to the London Irish community than a bunch of raucous builders enjoying the "craic" in the Crown on Saturday night. Like many, Sean's parents did not conform to the stereotype:

My dad was acutely aware of the importance of education to get his children a better quality of life and moving up the social ladder and he encouraged us to do well at school. I imagine that dad's job, serving affluent people in hotels, gave him a clear picture of the class system in England. He was passionate that gaining a good education was the key to his children getting their foot on the ladder and climbing out of poverty.[19]

Tony Kilshaw arrived in London from Dublin in 1963 aged seven with his parents and brothers and sisters. His dad was a merchant seaman, a bus conductor and truck driver, his mum a cleaner and home help. After staying with his aunt in Hammersmith for a while the Kilshaw family moved to Hackney where they lived in hostels and temporary accommodation. Eventually they found a couple of rooms in Paddington where they lived for two years before finally securing a three-bedroom council house off the Harrow Road in Queen's Park. As a teenager he drank in the Irish pubs of Kilburn, Biddy Mulligan's, the Bell, the Rifle Volunteer, the Duke of Cambridge and in a drinking club called the Flamingo located under a West Indian restaurant on Shirland Road.

Tony recalled that even in the late 1960s the experience of London for a child or teenager was more akin to the immediate post-war years than to the redeveloped city it would become in the 1980s:

> *Evidence of the war was still all around and we played on bomb sites. We had a camp in a bomb site in Aybrook street just off Paddington Street in Marylebone. I grew up playing in Central London. We used to regularly bunk into cinemas in the West End and then go to the Wimpy bar in Oxford Street to discuss the films.*[20]

Kilburn was the geographical core of Irish settlement in London but its public voice came out of the Irish Centre on Camden Square. Formed by the Catholic Oblate Order in 1955, by the 1960s the Irish Centre was vital to Irish life in London. Originally a place where new arrivals from Ireland, fresh from the Holyhead train at Euston, could find cheap lodgings, welfare advice and job opportunities, it expanded to provide a wider range of social activities to Irish immigrants far from home. In 1969, 2,299 Irish Londoners came to the Irish Centre for help with housing, employment and welfare issues, but even before that it had become a locus of Irish social life in London.[21] Clair Wills's history of immigration in post-war Britain found that in a single month in 1964 the Irish Centre held

> *a ceilidh, a Corkman's Social, a Mayoman's Bacon and Cabbage Supper, the Roscommon Association dance, the Galway Association Bacon and Cabbage Supper, as well as Derry and Waterford events and a meeting of the Gramophone and Recording Club.*[22]

The Irish pubs of Camden Town, like the Dublin Castle, the Camden Stores on Parkway, the Mother Red Cap opposite the tube station and the Bedford Arms on Arlington Street, dominated the area's social life in the 1960s and 1970s. In 1963 Ted and Joyce with their one-year-old son (me) migrated to Camden, moving from their small flat in Mecklenburgh Square to a two-bedroom council flat provided by St Pancras Borough Council on the eighth floor of the Rydal Water tower block on the Regent's Park Estate. At the time Ted was working for Turner and Cooper, a small building firm with offices at the end of Long Yard, a cobblestone mews running off Lamb's Conduit Street near Coram's Fields.

Ted stayed with Turner and Cooper for most of the 1960s, one of a colourful gang of highly skilled tradesmen including Silent Lou, a carpenter whose prize possession was an immaculate toolbox he had made himself full of his polished tools carefully laid out, Enoch, the firm's unflappable drain blockage expert, and Little Billy, whose talents were legendary, as Ted recalled forty years later:

> I saw him once, presented with a set of architects' drawings by a cocky young site agent, take a woodbine cigarette packet from his pocket and with a pencil stub copy one or two measurements from the drawing on to the fag packet. With that skimpy information and a lifetime's experience he then fit a timber spiral staircase into position whilst the young site agent looked on in disbelief.[23]

Despite naming its six central blocks on Robert Street after lakes in the Lake District, the Regent's Park Estate was not the most beautiful of Camden's council estates. Built in the 1950s, most of its blocks were blank stone slabs with tiny balconies and not much landscaping between them, although in comparison to many later tower blocks they were safe and robust. Rydal Water and its neighbours contained narrow, dark and cold internal stairways accessed from a door in the living room that could be used as a fire escape if necessary, which they never were as the blocks were virtually indestructible. Later blocks of flats built in the 1960s like Rothay and Troutbeck on Albany Street were done in a different style, less sturdy brick and more pale grey concrete and panelling, and have not weathered the years well.

But the estate contained hidden gems that its residents prized, most particularly the Cumberland Adventure

Playground. Opened in 1965 in the middle of the estate, the Cumberland was a literal toy town with its own roads and small cars which kids could drive about, stopping at zebra crossings and traffic lights. Later it would mutate into a different kind of adventure playground with climbing frames, wooden castles, rope swings and tunnels. When I was seven or eight, I impaled my foot on a rusty nail there and had to be taken immediately to A&E at nearby University College Hospital.[24]

The Cumberland was named after Cumberland Market, London's hay and straw market from the early nineteenth century until the 1920s, home to its own school of artists and a now-defunct arm of the Regents Canal which fed goods for the market to Cumberland Basin. In 1938 the Basin was dammed off and drained, and after the war it was covered over and turned into allotments in the middle of the Cumberland Market Estate. Unlike the surrounding area, which the Crown Estate had sold to the local council to build the Regents Park Estate, the Cumberland Estate had been retained and kept its grand Victorian buildings as social housing, very much like a Peabody Estate. For the kids of the adjacent council estate, though, the Cumberland Estate was part of our own and we used to run through it regularly.

The Regent's Park Estate was a pleasant place to raise a young family. In 1964 we got a phone, something still not that common for working class families, and in 1965 a fridge. Sadly, though, there would be only one set of grandparents for me and my younger brother Jamie. In October 1968 Ted's mum Edith, who had been abandoned by her husband after the war and who raised two sons on her own in post-war King's Cross, and who was still living there in a flat in 35 Argyle Square, died suddenly of a heart attack whilst out shopping in Camden Town's Inverness Street Market. I was six at the time and aside from a vague memory of "Nanny Pat", called after her daughter from her first marriage and to differentiate her from "Nanny Grandad", my mum's mum, I am sorry to say I do not recall her.

The influx of Irish and Greek Cypriot immigrants into Camden Town in the 1960s began to fundamentally alter the social make-up of its working class. It was a population kept fed by the market stalls of Inverness Street and Queen's Crescent and a big Marks & Spencer on the High Street. But the area's small industries were beginning to falter and its largest employers were closing or relocating. In just a few years Camden lost all its industrial icons. The Carreras Cigarette Factory closed in 1961 and moved to Basildon. In 1963 Gilbey's merged with other major alcohol manufacturers like Smirnoff and Hennessy to form International Distillers and Vintners, closing its massive site at the Camden Goods Yard and relocating to Harlow. The specialist engineering firm Airmed in Parkway followed it a few years later. For two decades much of Camden was a post-industrial desert, especially the massive, abandoned and rusting Goods Yard.

Retail began to take over. Parkway, running between the High Street and Regent's Park, had always been an eclectic byway of pubs, cafes, shops and small warehouses, including Baloney's Bottle factory, Harvey Johns toy shop and Palmer's Pet Shop, established before the war and still selling pet animals — not only dogs and cats but monkeys, snakes, tarantulas, frogs, iguanas and parrots — to customers in the 1980s. Camden High Street was a solid working class thoroughfare with four shoe shops, a Woolworth's, clothes shops of varying quality and Bowman's department store that mostly sold furniture and china. The Brighton pub, a traditional North London working class boozer, was its social centre, while Castle's Pie n' Mash on Camden Road was one of the best in London. The High Street was always incredibly resistant to gentrification and through the repellent power of some mysterious urban force field it still is.

Derek Jarman was born in UCH in 1945 and grew up in a flat in Kentish Town with his bus driver dad and factory worker mum. He didn't see the River Thames until he was six when he was taken to the Festival of Britain on the South Bank. Leaving school at fifteen, he started work with Kendon Bodies on Fortress Grove, a small firm that made furniture, delivery vans and lorries. But his main interest was politics. In 1960 he got involved in the St Pancras Rent Strike and although a young teenager he went down to Kennistoun House to help defend

Don Cook from eviction. In 1971, upon being elected a Camden Labour Councillor, he finally got a telephone.

Even in the 1950s and 1960s Camden Town already had its parallel life, its intimate flirtation with artists and actors, as Derek recalled:

> Lucian Freud lived in the flat above us, which was used for the purposes of entertaining, and art. It had two big mirrors on the walls (we still have one in our living room, and the other went to Imelda Staunton and Jim Carter) and the wallpaper was just brown wrapping paper. There were a lot of women going up and down the stairs. We used the same staircase as the models.[25]

Other parts of North London near to Camden Town, such as St John's Wood on the other side of Primrose Hill, had a similar social mix. Stewart Goddard (later to become Adam Ant), born in 1954, spent the 1960s growing up in the dilapidated De Walden building on Allitsen Road between St John's Wood High Street and Primrose Hill, and later a new Camden Council development around the corner. The De Walden flat had two rooms with no electricity or gas. The only water supply came from an ancient brown-stone sink on the landing shared by eight other families. Electricity and a cold-water sink were eventually installed but otherwise it was little different from a Victorian slum. Stewart recalled:

> However, by far the biggest worry for the families on our floor was the community "crapper", aptly named and situated at the darkest and coldest end of the landing....Until I was twelve, we would have to use buckets of water to flush it out every morning.[26]

Not all of the De Walden building was this Dickensian nor all memories of it so grim. Lynn Becks, born there in 1958, lived at number 44 on the first floor with her parents and her younger sister and brother:

> So 5 of us living in that tiny place overlooking Charles Lane at the back. The front door opened onto a small living room

which had a door into a little kitchen with a toilet at the end. A tin bath hung on the wall. We had one bedroom between us. It was small but great growing up there. My grandfather, Jack Cording lived at the end of the balcony with his wife Daisy and my other grandmother Maud Thomas lived further down Allitsen Road in Opie House. As children we loved playing in the courtyard.

In similar vein, Tracy Dumbleton's memories of De Walden were brighter than Stewart's:

Mum had grown up with most of the people there so once all the children were born it was like one big family. Our neighbours were the Lake family at number 2 and the Goddard family at number 3. We had 2 rooms, a living room/kitchen and a bedroom, the shared toilet was on the landing with the big grey tin bath hanging on the back of the door, I can remember mum boiling bucket after bucket of water just to fill the bath, it was bliss when Dad fitted a geezer in the kitchen, hard to believe that running hot water could cause so much excitement.[27]

Like Steve Jones, Stewart's father was an unreliable alcoholic and had little to do with his upbringing, the care of which fell to his waitress mother, his grandmother Nanny Smith and two of his mum's colleagues, Joan and Kathleen. After his mum and dad divorced in 1963 his mother got a job as a domestic cleaner for Paul McCartney, who in the late 1960s lived nearby with his girlfriend Jane Asher. In 1965 Stewart started at St Marylebone Grammar School, a state grammar school which accepted working class boys who passed the 11-plus examination. Eight years later I also started at St Marylebone and I recall some of the same teachers. In 1976 John Barnes, who would go on to play for Liverpool FC and England, also began to attend St Marylebone, and remembered:

St Marylebone wasn't a typical grammar school, elitist and full of middle class children. All my friends were working class kids from council estates in Great Portland Street and Camden Town, but they bought into the ethos of the school in terms of education and discipline.[28]

By 2020 a one-bedroom flat in the renovated De Walden Building was selling for over half a million pounds, but in the 1960s those parts of North London were still available to working class families. Jobs, though, were getting harder to just walk into after school or after throwing over a previous one. Many of the older craft skills, as practiced in the small manufacturing firms dotted throughout Camden, Holloway, Clerkenwell, King's Cross and Paddington, were being rendered obsolete by new technology, by new developments in computers or miniaturisation, or else confined to niche markets. Larger manufacturing and engineering firms, going global if successful and nowhere if not, were restructuring to accommodate leaner production methods. As Roy Porter observed in his social history of London, during the 1960s the full impact of this process was masked

> *since general prosperity afforded work in various fields — retailing, tourism, construction. Men who lost work making buses became mini-cab drivers, opened betting shops, repaired TVs, or sold used cars and double glazing.*[29]

It was the beginning of a historic shift in the economic life of working class London, apparent first in North London, which had always contained less heavy industry than East, West and South, from manufacturing to "light industry", sometimes so light it made nothing at all. It was for this very reason that the nature of working class employment in central London did not metamorphose quite as much. Factories didn't close there because they had never really opened. It had *always* been an eclectic mixture of leisure industry, market trading and colourful retail, an urban kaleidoscope of unusual jobs and unclassifiable pastimes, and so it remained.

One of the more traditional working class occupations, building and construction, continued to provide a steady stream of jobs. In the early 1960s a major new building project began in the Cripplegate area of London, which until its almost complete destruction in the Blitz had been the centre of the city's rag trade. On its ruins there was to be a new Brutalist mega-structure called the Barbican Estate, consisting of fourteen terraced blocks of flats and three forty-two-storey residential towers surrounding a major new arts centre, the Museum of London and an artificial lake. Initially there were only three toilets for the entire site for two hundred builders, which had to be emptied by hand at the end of every day. Most of the workers therefore had to walk to the public toilets at St Paul's every time they needed to go.

Vic Heath was working on the Barbican site where he helped organise a series of protests against the lack of basic facilities that soon brought the site to a stop. After this the company in charge, Turriff, built some extra toilets and a canteen. But when workers supported a carpenter who had been sacked for arguing with a supervisor, Turriff decided to sack the entire workforce and bus in scab labour to replace them. This was met by determined mass pickets, as Vic recalled:

> They tried to break the strike, but when they brought in the coach carrying the scabs through the big car park that led to the gates, we launched a volley of bricks at it. We smashed the windows, dented the bodywork and absolutely wrecked the coach. We didn't think it was right, but we needed to get our message across. Meanwhile, the police were battling us as they tried to get the site gate open…They finally managed to get the coach on site but when they did, all the men on it left immediately.[30]

After seven weeks Turriff capitulated and re-employed the builders who had taken action. Vic continued to work on the site until 1968, constantly holding the employer to account for the provision of good health and safety and to abide by the strictest residential building regulations to ensure the Barbican's towers were built well and to last. Until the construction of Saffron Square in Croydon and St George Wharf Tower in Vauxhall, both gigantic and high-priced blocks of private flats, the Barbican's three towers were for many years London's tallest residential buildings.

The construction boom in 1960s London provided employment for builders and the related trades of the construction industry, but it also transformed the capital with an excess of unlovely office blocks whose only rationale was to generate profit for developers. As a result, Victoria Street, London Wall and Upper Thames Street were turned into charmless wind tunnels. The most iconic new building in central London, the thirty-four-storey Centre Point at the junction of Oxford Street and Tottenham Court Road, built between 1963 and 1966, at least had a distinctive look even if it had no tenants until the late 1970s (tenants were unnecessary when the value of the building simply increased in line with London land prices). Constructed for £3.5m but already worth £11m upon completion, on windy days its fountains sent a fine spray of water clean across Charing Cross Road.

Another iconic skyscraper, Euston Tower, opened in 1970 at the other end of Tottenham Court Road, part of a massive redevelopment to widen Euston Road and build an underpass on its junction with Hampstead Road. Aware of the plans, the canny property developer Joe Levy secretly bought up houses and factories on the north side of Euston Road. When the LCC declared its proposals for Euston Road he offered it his properties on the road, without which the redevelopment could not proceed, in return for permission for lucrative office planning permission on the rest of the land. Permission secured, Levy garlanded Euston Square and Euston Road with new office blocks, including the thirty-six-storey Euston Tower. The development erased a vibrant working class community in the area north of Euston Square including Seaton Place Market which used to be open seven days a week selling food to local residents.

Tottenham Court Road itself, with its riot of small electrical goods shops wedged tightly between Goodge Street Underground station and the Dominion Theatre, was stubbornly resistant to redevelopment and continued on its ramshackle way until the early 2000s. It wasn't the only hold-out. Printing, bookbinding and their related industries exerted a particular centrifugal force in central London. In the 1960s and 1970s

Clerkenwell (not remotely part of East London, with the Angel to its north and Farringdon to its south) was the centre of London's printing and ancillary services, typesetting, suppliers etc., all wrapped around a still-extant Little Italy. It was an area whose working class demographic was boosted further in 1965 by the opening of the modernist tower blocks of the Finsbury Estate, a community sustained through the next half-century by the network of council estates surrounding Old Street and St Luke's Square.

Colin Miller was born in 1951 and moved to London from Longhoughton, near Alnwick, Northumberland in 1964 when he was thirteen. His father was in "private service", i.e. a servant, and in London he worked a chauffeur/butler to the Duke of Northumberland at Syon House. Despite this, Colin went to a comprehensive in Hounslow and encountered a racial and ethnic mix which dissolved the lazy racism instilled into him by his parents. After leaving school with only two CSE's, Colin became an Apprentice Bookbinder for Orrin and Geer in Farringdon Road near Clerkenwell Green. Orrin and Geer specialised in Bibles and related material but also high-end products for the likes of Smythson's, the Bond Street stationers run by Samantha Cameron's family. Colin found it an eye-opener:

> Being an apprentice, I was always being sent on errands to collect or deliver stuff. It was a great excuse to wander and take as much time as I dared all over central London.

He was also introduced to the world of the print unions, in which bookbinders belonged to the Society of Graphical and Allied Trades (SOGAT). Those at Orrin and Geer belonged to SOGAT's London Central Branch which covered Fleet Street. It was a mini-society in itself. The Branch — known as the Chapel, with the Branch Chair referred to as the Father of the Chapel —not only acted as a traditional union but as an employment exchange. If employees wanted a move to another job or printers they went to the union, and there had to be a very good reason for an employer to refuse to employ someone sent to them by the union. The union also organised casual work in Fleet Street, principally Saturday nights working on the Sunday papers as stringers (tying bundles of papers) or buckers (loading and unloading the delivery vans).

Of the culture of the printers, Colin remembered:

We socialised, but only on the annual beano or for the Christmas drinks. But there was a thriving collective culture, such as cooking lunch, or betting on the horses and dogs. The monthly Chapel meetings were always attended by every member and issues such as discipline were dealt with through the Chapel. Despite the relatively small size of the company, we didn't have much connection with the boss. This tended to be the case in every Chapel I worked in (we didn't call them firms). Stuff was done through the Chapel...It was very male, very white. We had a single black bookbinder who came over after joining the air force during the war. He was also the most skilled, getting the special one-off jobs. Women did the folding and sowing work, men the forwarding and finishing. Women and men worked on different floors and rarely mixed, even in works outings.[31]

The old London working class maxim — that a man either worked as a cabby, on the markets, in the print or became a criminal — ignored not just the building trade but a whole range of idiosyncratic occupations, not least those supporting the leisure and entertainment industries of the West End. But it did reflect the informal, non-industrial flavour of much London working class life. Taking one of the traditional routes, Gil Jackson was an apprentice compositor working in Covent Garden from 1962 to 1967.

Gil was from Tooting, but like many others his horizons were greatly expanded by working in central London. Eased into the profession by his brother, who worked as a letterpress machine minder and a trade union representative for the National Graphical Association, Gil started with Odhams Press in July 1962. He gives a flavour of what it was like for a sixteen-year-old working class boy to start work in central London, crossing Waterloo Bridge with his brother, walking past the Royal Festival Hall where he had only recently seen Thelonious Monk play:

Across Waterloo Bridge we reached the Strand and the Aldwych. To the east in the distance was Trafalgar Square where I had been employed on a school summer holiday job working for the Navy league at Admiralty House...The excitement of going to work that first morning in London, with all its possibilities, was a dream come true.

Gil threw himself into the life of central London. When not in the West End's pubs Gil would wander around Soho on his lunch break investigating bookshops. Working in Covent Garden and arriving early to work, he frequented pubs like the Nag's Head that catered to the porters and the Opera Tavern that saw trade from actors working matinée performances on St Martin's Lane and Shaftesbury Avenue. The market pubs, open from midnight all through the night, were meant to be for market traders only but rules were routinely flouted and they saw many other customers, including print workers from the *Daily Herald* night shift, ad-setting journeymen and off-duty police from Bow Street.

From 4am the traders disappeared into the pubs for sustenance and some off-book dealing. As Gil recalled:

Here a trader can while away the hours discussing business with other like-minded traders with a pint, a bacon sandwich, and a smoke before finishing their work for the day. This is what is known as the Dracula Hours, where from midnight porters, buyers and sellers transacted their business, moving the ware of whatever market they specialised in...Nevertheless, anywhere that the police exercised what they saw as their entitlement while at the same time using it as an excuse to keep an eye on things, others were bound to follow. Villains and printers...came into this category of being able to pop in for a swift half.[32]

Jacky Hyams, after leaving school at sixteen impatient to enter the adult world, worked in a variety of temping and secretarial jobs in the West End, desperately seeking the social and sexual freedom the capital in the 1960s seemed to offer a young woman:

I was a rebel, in that I wanted to throw off my East End background and didn't accept the general status quo: that a young girl best sit tight and hang on for Mr Right. Yet I wasn't in any way political in my thinking. My ideas about freedom and free love weren't feminist as such. I didn't go on marches or protest on the streets.

Jacky's mum Molly worked at the Berketex Bride shop in Oxford Street where she enjoyed the work environment and the camaraderie of the shop assistants, but her daughter was more restless, constantly in search of better opportunities. Jacky used the full employment of the time to flit from job to job, leaving quickly if she got bored, buying clothes at Biba and eating Chinese in Soho. In 1967, after a one-night stand resulted in pregnancy, she had an abortion which left her depressed for a short while. But for a resilient young woman the excitements of central London were too tempting to resist. Earning good money from regular temping work with Office Overload, Jacky moved into a flat share in Muswell Hill with two other women. Discovering *Sergeant Pepper* and softcore drugs, Jacky's life in the late 1960s was a conscious rejection of the Dalston she grew up in:

We laughed a lot, drank and smoked too much, slept too little and lived, mostly, for the next party or holiday in the sun.[33]

Helen Evangelou had a similar experience. In 1967, aged sixteen, she joined the sales and marketing department of the publisher Collier MacMillan in Mayfair:

My walk from Riding House Street took about 20 minutes. I went through the back streets and into Bond Street, where I usually stopped to buy a pack of Sullivan Powell Turkish cigarettes... Then it was up Brook Street, through Grosvenor Square and into South Audely Street.

By seventeen, Helen's social and political horizons had expanded. She went on CND and anti-Vietnam War marches but also enjoyed the social life of the West End:

Friday nights were drinking nights and they were always a bit extreme. Our little group would leave work to go the pub, the Red Lion near Curzon Street. We thought it was really nice, but we were so young we never fully appreciated just how classy it was — it was very popular with actors and I remember seeing Stewart Granger and Richard Burton there. We would gather in one of the little booths and get completely pissed. [34]

Ted also enjoyed working in the centre of London. By now he was highly skilled in the use of "Oxy Cutters" (oxygen acetylene cutting equipment) which led to work assignments in the West End with his unskilled mate, a younger man nicknamed Razzle Basil who had a knack for finding private jobs for them to do out of hours. Although Turner & Cooper did not provide sick or holiday pay, Ted managed to take his young family on a break to Cornwall every summer with a fresh wad of cash gleaned from selling lead he nicked from the office roofs of Holborn to the scrap metal dealers working under King's Cross railway arches.

Like Gil Jackson, Ted would often end up in the pubs of Covent Garden, made easier for him as his brother-in-law Frank, a sharp working class lad from Waterloo married to Joyce's sister Kate, worked as a garden porter, a job secured for him by his father. Joyce's younger brother Danny worked nearby as a stagehand at the Royal Opera House and often met Ted and Frank in the West End for drinks. Frank worked long and hard hours and on the proceeds relocated his family to Sidcup where he opened two greengrocer shops which were extremely successful, enabling his sons, my cousins Steven and Stewart, to escape the poverty in which he and Kate had been raised. A collector of beautiful antique clocks which hung on the walls of his large house, in later years Frank kept a Jaguar parked outside the house even though he had no license and didn't drive. He just liked the look of it.

In the 1960s Danny started work with Connelly Brothers, as Ted had in the 1950s, while his attractive young girlfriend Josie Rowley worked as a hairdresser in Penton Street off the northern end of Pentonville Road near the Angel. Chapel Market remained the heart of working class Islington, although it too moved with the times. In 1965 its Marks & Spencer store, located at 47 Chapel St since 1930, was enlarged to provide a new Food Hall, with two entrances, one on Chapel Street and one on Upper Street. At the same time the new Public Carriage Office, used for the inspection and licensing of London's iconic black cabs, opened on Penton Street.

Josie's family, the Rowleys, were well known in their little slice of North London, where they were the landlords of a network of popular pubs in Somers Town and the Angel. Josie's uncle on her dad's side was landlord of the Lord Wolseley in White Lion Street adjacent to Chapel Street Market while her aunt ran the Spanish Patriots at 14 White Conduit Street (out of which a paralytic Ronald Marwood had staggered in December 1958 to murder PC Summers). Her mum's family ran the Cock Tavern on Chalton Street, the social hub of Somers Town then as it is today. The Rowleys, like Ted and Frank and many other working class grafters, did a lot of their transactions off-book and cash-in-hand, and saw nothing wrong with that at all.

Cash-in-hand work greased the wheels of the West End's micro-economy. One of that economy's engines was organised vice — prostitution, strip clubs and porn outlets. After the fall of the Messina brothers, their vice empire was inherited by their former subordinate Bernie Silver and his henchman, former Maltese traffic cop "Big Frank" Mifsud. Silver, born in 1922 in Stoke Newington, had moved west after the war to work for the Messinas, but he always had bigger ambitions. From the late 1950s Silver and Mifsud built up an organised crime group known as "the Syndicate". By the mid-1960s it controlled nineteen of Soho's twenty-four strip clubs and had nearly all the Metropolitan Police's Obscene Publications Squad in its pocket including its head, Detective Chief Inspector Bill Moody.

Together with Billy Hill, still the West End's Gangster No1, Silver and Mifsud were unassailable in the 1960s, despite attempts by lesser criminal gangs such as the Nash Family, based on the Bourne Estate next to Leather Lane in Clerkenwell, to expand into London's clubland. In February 1960 Jimmy Nash, one of six Nash brothers, had an altercation with one of Billy Hill's lieutenants in the Pen Club in Spitalfields and shot him in the head. Despite this the Nash family stayed mainly within Islington and Shoreditch, although they eventually gained control of the Bagatelle and Embassy Clubs in the West End. Later in the decade they provided muscle to the Kray Twins in their own moves on the West End.[35]

Clubs, whether strip, drinking or private, were the essence of Soho life in the 1960s. The Colony Room was proudly eclectic and would take anyone of any race, class, sexuality and profession as long as they were interesting, but many of the others catered to a specific customer base — the Kismet for "resting" actors; Le Duce, the Flamingo and the Alphabet for gay men; the Paint Box Club for Dilly rent boys (who also did a brisk trade at the Kismet) and clients; the Careless Stork and the Festival for lesbians; the Roaring 20's and the African Club for black men and women, although they were welcome in the others too; the Bees for gamblers and card sharks; the New Cabinet Club and the Mazurka for "Faces" (big-time criminals).

The Premier and the Hogarth were reserved for meets between police, lawyers and crime bosses to agree payouts and other arrangements. A Flying Squad officer of the time recalled:

There were those clubs like the Premier where a lot of business was done with Old Bill. In those days the police took their money like they was receiving their wages. They didn't seem to care who knew because it went right to the top, into the Commissioner's office.[36]

Most other clubs were straightforward drinking dens with a bit of sex work thrown in. If heterosexual, this was tolerated by the Vice Squad, as long as they had received a bung to do so. If gay, less so. On nights when Trafalgar Square's Meat Rack was being heavily policed, rent boys would congregate elsewhere, at coffee stalls and snack bars like the Little Hut in Dean Street, the Bar-B-Q in Frith Street and at Billy's Snack Bar in an alleyway off Wardour Street. Ham Yard off Great Windmill Street, today bustling with wine bars but at the time a discreet byway, was popular for quick blowjobs.

The precarity and vulnerability of the gay scene in Soho led to the emergence in the 1960s of an unofficial "gay village" in Earl's Court, a community of pubs, clubs, hotels, saunas, shops and cafes. The village revolved around the Coleherne Arms on Old Brompton Road, an extremely popular pub renowned for its leather scene with blacked-out windows to protect privacy. Camden Town also had its own small but vibrant slice of gay nightlife, The Black Cap pub on Camden High Street, a discreet gay venue since 1963. In the later 1960s it dropped the discretion and became known for lively and outrageous drag shows.

Amber was a young gay man who throughout the 1960s worked as a waiter and cook's assistant at the Londoner's Club in Earlham Street, Seven Dials. When the club closed at 1am he would sometimes stroll down to Piccadilly, pick up a boy and take him back to his small flat above the Polar Bear pub on Lisle Street for sex, heightened by the amphetamine-like effect of a few diamond-shaped purple hearts, ten of which could be bought for £2 in most Soho clubs. Amber was a nocturnal animal who got the most out of what was on offer through the night and early morning in the West End:

> on a typical buccaneering night he would do trade at the Dilly, go to an all-night café called the Snake Pit in Meard Street run by a butch ex-policewoman, Big Edna, where gangsters, bohemians and Soho working girls sat under green and blue lights, then go to the Leicester Square toilets to freshen up, as they had private dressing rooms and a towel for twopence, get washed up, then go on to Covent Garden for a breakfast of rum and toast.[37]

The tawdry glamour of 1960s Soho was captured on film by Arnold Miller's sexploitation documentary *London in the Raw* (1964) and his associate Peter Davis's shorter film *Strip* (1966).

London in the Raw sought to capitalise on the success of the Italian "Mondo" films which presented sexual material under the guise of serious documentary, but in doing so it offered genuine vignettes of the sex industry hidden behind the doors of Soho's clubs where most dancers were topless and most hostesses for hire. Filming in several clubs including Churchill's, the Blue Angel and Billy Hill's 21 Club, Miller exposed how both sex workers and clients were ruthlessly exploited by club owners. *Strip*, less concerned with getting bare flesh on screen, was filmed entirely inside the Phoenix Strip Club and was even more revealing about the lives and working conditions of its hostesses and dancers, many of whom were recent migrants from the Caribbean and Poland.

London in the Raw and *Strip* were recently re-released on Blue-ray by the BFI, with the added mini-features *Chelsea Bridge Boys* (1965) about a rockers' biker gang roaring around Chelsea and the Kings Road, and *Pub* (1962), fifteen minutes of roving camera in a Hackney pub. All of these provide a compelling time corridor into places now entirely vanished. Although parts of Miller's work were straightforward and obvious fiction designed to titillate, it nonetheless reflected the era's constant mingling of sleaze, crime, entertainment and opportunistic working class chancers, an intersection seen at its sharpest in the careers of David Litvinoff and John Bindon.

Litvinoff, born like Bernie Silver to an old East London Jewish family and gone west in search of fortune, had a finger in many pies — crime, film, art, sex — and survived by linking them all up. His friend Mim Scala described him as someone who could *"talk the birds out of the trees, money out of pockets, boys into bed and gangsters out of killing him".*[38] Intimate with the Kray twins, he used his connections to gain entry to London's celebrity and criminal worlds, providing personal services to both. He ended up as "dialogue coach and technical adviser" on Nic Roeg's era-defining film *Performance* (1969), for which he recruited notorious London gangster John Bindon in a small role. When Keith Richards was arrested for drug possession, Litvinoff and Bindon, keen to stay in with their famous friend, found the man who had grassed him up and gave him a severe beating.

Like Litvinoff, Bindon utilised charm and bullshit to get what he wanted — he gabbed his way into a lead role in Ken Loach's *Poor Cow* (1967), from which he entered the acting world — but unlike Litvinoff he was a genuine criminal. Son of a Fulham taxi driver, he was a violent gangster who imposed a ruthless protection racket on the pubs of Fulham and Hammersmith and broke the jaw of anyone who defied him. He also freelanced for both the Krays and the Richardsons. Joyce's brother Danny, who could be a bit of a naughty boy, knew Bindon to chat to. One day in the late 1960s in a Fulham pub Danny was having a drink with his cousin Patsy, recently over from Ireland, and saw Bindon at the bar. When Danny told his cousin who he was and that he was known to always carry a gun on him, Patsy asked for proof. At Danny's request Bindon opened his jacket to reveal a handgun on his belt.

Bindon's good looks and humour gained him access to exalted circles. His sexual relationship with Princess Margaret — he was invited to Mustique where Margaret asked to see his celebrated party trick of hanging five empty half-pint beer mugs on his erect penis — was alluded to in *The Bank Job* (2008), in which David Suchet plays a fictional version of Bernie Silver, concerned to get his hands on the explicit photographic evidence of their liaison. After supporting roles in *Get Carter* (1971) and *No Sex Please, We're British* (1973), Bindon could have moved into acting full-time, but he was a street thug at heart. In 1978 he stabbed gangster Johnny Darke to death outside a Fulham night club but got off on a technicality.

It is often crime fiction, rather than its "literary" equivalent, which nails this milieu best. Joe Thomas's addictive novel *Bent* (2020) re-tells in gripping style the career of the deeply compromised West End detective Harry Challenor, a man so lost in Soho's vice world and his own paranoid schizophrenia that he was discarded by his even more corrupt bosses. Jake Arnott's dazzling postmodernist examination of a successful 1960s working class criminal, *The Long Firm* (2005), significantly sites its Kray-analogue Harry Starks in Soho, not Bethnal Green.

Fictional creations like Harry Starks orbit and reflect the giant meta-cultural Black Hole of 1960s working class criminality, Ronnie and Reggie Kray. Born in Haggerston and based in Bethnal Green, the Kray's criminal empire did not much concern the British state until they moved into Soho and the West End. They took their first step west in 1960 when they acquired the high-class gambling club Esmeralda's Barn in Knightsbridge. Bored with the East End, they used the Barn and the Le Monde club in Chelsea to expand into the more lucrative and glamorous West End. They also bought the El Morocco nightclub on Gerrard Street and liked to hang out there with Barbara Windsor and Ronnie Knight. But their fame and lifestyle led to disrespect in their old manor. Ronnie's shooting of George Cornell in the Blind Beggar pub in Whitechapel in 1966 after Cornell had publicly called him a "fat poof", and Reggie's carving up and dismemberment of Jack "the Hat" McVitie in a flat in Stoke Newington one year later, demonstrated how little they had learnt from Billy Hill.

After the Krays were arrested and sentenced to life, crime in the West End returned to its semi-legal, semi-tolerated normality. The twins had never really fitted in and certainly never played for the Soho Ramblers, a "charity" football team for the area that included some of London's better-known gangsters such as "Mad" Frankie Fraser and Eddie Richardson, one of the Richardson Brothers. The Ramblers were organised out of Atlantic Machines at 28 Windmill Street, the West End offices of the South London-based Richardsons, from where Fraser and others ran their lucrative fruit machine business.

The casual corruption and off-grid lifestyles of men like Bindon and Litvinoff mirrored the more systemic corruption of the Metropolitan Police, especially within its elite teams — Vice Squad, Obscene Publications Squad, Flying Squad — based in central London. Although some senior officers at Scotland Yard had achieved their rank through accelerated promotion schemes out of Hendon Police College, most police officers from Constable to Chief Inspector came from working class backgrounds and had come up the hard way. For many of them taking bribes, looking the other way for favours, fitting people up, was simply pragmatic working class adaptation to a world run by the rich and powerful.

When called upon to pursue real detective work, to "solve" crime, the Met were notably unsuccessful. In 1964 and 1965 six (perhaps more) female sex workers, all of whom worked the Bayswater, Notting Hill and Shepherds Bush areas, were murdered and their bodies left naked on the banks of the Thames or in other public spaces. The media dubbed the killer "Jack the Stripper" but they also became known as the Hammersmith Nude Murders. The sensationalism reflected the hypocrisy of the era, simultaneously wallowing in salacious details while skirting over the large number of working class women forced to engage in sex work. The river footpath between Fulham and Hammersmith became notorious for the trade.

The hunt for Jack the Stripper was run out of Shepherd's Bush Police Station but despite an enormous outlay of men and resources the killer was never caught. Some investigators on the case thought the killer was a policeman, although this has never been definitively proven. The most recent and thorough examination of the case concluded that the reason for the failure of the police's massive operation to catch the killer, including using Women Police Officers as bait and entire decoy operations to entrap him, was that he knew from the inside what was happening and simply laid low during those times. The entire forensic evidence on the case has since been lost or destroyed.[39]

The Met couldn't even protect itself. On 12th August 1966 three officers from Shepherd's Bush station, Detective Sergeant Head, Detective Constable Wombwell and Constable Fox, who were on plain clothes patrol in an unmarked police car, sighted a van with three men in it parked in Braybrook Street near Wormwood Scrubs. The three men were career criminals who had just left the Clay Pigeon pub on Harrow Road and were out to steal a vehicle. When Head and Wombwell approached the van to investigate, Head was shot in the face through the open window. Wombwell was shot dead as he ran back to the police car. Fox was killed by gunfire as he tried to reverse the police car to escape. After a massive manhunt the killers were arrested and given life sentences.

The "Massacre of Braybrook Street" generated national headlines. The funeral procession for the three policemen, which trailed past Shepherd's Bush Police Station on Uxbridge Road, was lined by six hundred serving officers of the Met. The shooting led to the formation in December 1966 of the Met's D6 Firearms Wing, designed to improve the training of the force's armed officers. A small force of five constables, three sergeants, two inspectors, three superintendents and one chief superintendent, D6 was initially based in rooms above the garage at the back of Old Street Police Station, from where it conducted firearms training of Met and Special Branch armed officers. In 1967 it became a separate department known as D11 which soon expanded to become a key part of the Met.

After the creation of the Greater London Council in 1965, the London Fire Brigade (LFB) was enlarged, absorbing the Middlesex Fire Brigade, parts of the fire brigades of West Kent, North Surrey and South West Essex, as well as the smaller borough brigades of Croydon, East Ham and West Ham. The LFB became a significant London employer and one of the great working class occupations of the capital, maintained by a network of fire stations in the heart of the city. I remember when I was five or six my mum took me to an "open day" for local kids held at Somers Town Fire Station on Euston Road and I was allowed to sit in the driving seat of a fire engine.

In 1962, Dave Wilson, born in 1940 in a Fulham slum, started his LFB basic training at Southwark Training School, after which he was assigned to Camden Town Fire Station. Although he still lived in Fulham, he journeyed back and forth by underground when not staying at the station overnight:

Breakfast at the fire station was served at eight o'clock. They could be very subdued affairs or very lively depending on the events of the previous night duty or which firemen were on duty. They were invariably a full English breakfast. Fried egg, bacon or sausage, fried potatoes, fried bread, black sausage, baked beans, toast, any combination of the former, depending on the state of the mess funds.

After brief stints at Brompton and Chelsea, Dave was transferred to Soho Fire Station in Shaftesbury Avenue in 1965. Soho was a more relaxed and informal environment, with some firemen taking other work when off-duty, arranged by the station's general fixer, Eric:

> *Off duty, Eric was a theatre fireman, and he worked for at least two theatres...He ran a kind of mini employment agency, and firemen in the division wanting part-time work as a theatre fireman would only need to telephone Eric, who would know of or locate suitable employment, all at no charge to the fireman.*[40]

Dave later moved on to Reading, outside London, but the pull of the capital was too strong and in 1969 he returned for a spell as part of Paddington Red Watch, back where he had started in Jack the Stripper land.

The police force and fire brigade were traditional occupations for the white working class, but during the 1960s new life choices and career options were beginning to open up for the capital's growing BAME population. London Transport and British Railways led the way in the 1950s and they continued to expand and diversify in the 1960s. Not all existing staff were happy about this. In 1966 a Dominican immigrant, Xavier Asquith, who worked as a guard at Marylebone mainline station, applied for a post on promotion at Euston station. His application was rejected because of an informal colour bar maintained at Euston between British Rail (BR) management and National Union of Railwayman (NUR) shop stewards, which stipulated that while BAME staff could work there as cleaners or labourers they could not fill public-facing roles such as guard or ticket collector.

Xavier's Irish workmate Tony Donaghey had applied for the same post and got the job, even though Xavier had more seniority than him. As an Irishman who had experienced discrimination himself, Tony refused to take up the position and compelled the Marylebone branch of the NUR to oppose the colour bar being run at Euston. With the national union getting behind the campaign and the intervention of the Labour government's Secretary of State for Transport, Barbara Castle, BR had to give way, and on August 15th 1966 Xavier became the first non-white guard to be employed at Euston Station.

The trade union movement's experience of mobilising people was a useful asset when widespread opposition arose to the 1963 Beeching Report's proposed closure of the North London Line to passenger services. While there was opposition amongst all of its users, it was at Willesden Junction and Hackney, hubs of transport union activity, that the campaign got seriously organised and a petition signed by 57,000 people was presented to Parliament. Despite this, the service cuts continued in 1965 with Sunday closures at Canonbury, Caledonian Road, Kentish Town West and South Acton, designed to eliminate paying staff time-and-a-half for Sunday working. With the planned running down of Broad Street station and a policy of providing only "absolute minimal facilities" on the North London Line until its future was decided, the existence of the line and the unique service it provided to working class North Londoners hung by a thread for several decades.[41]

Most politically active working class people continued to work within the given trade union and Labour Party structures but some tried to create new spaces. The Labourist ice began to melt in 1960 when the TUC Annual Congress passed Resolution 42, put to it by the working class playwright Arnold Wesker, on the importance of organising arts activities for working class people. As a result, in 1964 Wesker, born in Stepney and raised in Hackney, launched Centre 42 at the former train repair shed known as the Roundhouse on Chalk Farm Road, abandoned by Gilbeys in 1963 after using it for nearly a hundred years as a secure bonded warehouse for wines and spirits. Centre 42 never had the funds it needed to fulfil its ambitions and in 1970 Wesker left as he felt the Roundhouse had become another middle class art venue, but for a few years in the 1960s it was the focus of a genuine attempt to introduce working class audiences to new forms of modern culture.

Not all initiatives were as well-intentioned as Wesker's. By the end of the decade, after the demolition of much of its older uninhabitable housing and the construction of the Westway, Notting Hill had transformed from a slum for dirt-poor blacks and whites to a cultural nexus for a new and assertive black London politics. One of its leaders was Michael de Frietas, also known as Michael X, who after his arrival in the UK from Trinidad and Tobago in 1957 became an enforcer for Peter Rachman and a part-time pimp. As the 1960s progressed he appeared to reform himself to become a spokesperson for black working class liberation.

In 1966, with the help of community activists and residents' associations, Michael set up the London Free School (LFS) on Elgin Avenue, which provided free education to local people as well as legal advice, a playgroup for children and other community work. De Frietas ran English classes for older Irish and African people and was by all accounts a good teacher, bringing out the oral histories and memories of people who had never before been given a voice. The LFS went on to become a centre of cultural radicalism in the Notting Hill and Ladbroke Gove area and was instrumental in building up the annual Notting Hill Fair, which by the 1970s became Notting Hill Carnival.

Like John Bindon, De Frietas managed for a time to blag his way into "respectable" circles, even creating a political persona that many took seriously. In 1969 he set up a Black Power commune, the Black House, on Holloway Road, used as a base for political organising, but in the end, like Bindon, he fell back into criminal activity. Forced to flee the country after charges of extortion were brought against him, he created another commune in Trinidad and Tobago which he ran with iron discipline. In 1974 he brutally murdered two visitors, one the daughter of a British Conservative MP, and in 1975 was executed for the crime.

Most black Londoners just tried to get by. When Len Dyke came to Britain from Jamaica in 1955, he started work as an electrician with British Rail. In the mid-1960s he set up Britain's first Credit Union in Finsbury Park, a savings and loan facility used mainly by London's Afro-Caribbean population. But it was the creation, with his business partner Dudley Dryden, of the Dyke & Dryden franchise that changed the face of black business in London. Dyke & Dryden began by selling Jamaican records but branched out into hair and beauty products, a specific and valued service to black women in particular.

The first Dyke & Dryden shop opened in 1965 in West Green Road in South Tottenham, a lively and still industrialised area on either side of the New River between Seven Sisters Road and Green Lanes. The "Harringay Warehouse District" between Eade Road and Hermitage Road was a sprawl of big factories and businesses including Maynards the confectionary manufacturers and Courtney Pope the furniture makers. Social life in South Tottenham depended on this vibrant economy, which also included Hetchin's Bike Shop, Tottenham Lido on Lordship Lane, the Batsford chip shop and the Ever Ready factory on St Ann's Road, the Corner Cinema on the junction of Seven Sisters Road and the High Road next to Wards Store, and Greenways stationers with its huge toy department. Harringay Arena on Green Lanes north of Finsbury Park, the host of professional boxing, ice hockey, roller speedway, and from 1947 to 1957 the annual Harringay Circus, had closed in 1958 but its abandoned site was used until the mid-1980s for Sunday markets. In the mid-1950s stock car racing started in the adjacent Harringay Stadium and continued to be put on until 1979, appearing in several films of North London life right up to its final appearance in the violent climax of *The Long Good Friday* (1980).

Dyke and Dryden's shop sold hair and beauty products on the ground floor level while its top floor served as a travel and shipping business that also assisted with citizenship issues such as passport applications and renewals. By the 1970s Dyke & Dryden had six shops and warehouses and had become a crucial element of the London Afro-Caribbean community's self-identity and support structure, the prototype and inspiration for every barber shop, hairdressing salon and nail bar that caters for the city's BAME population.

That population was beginning to branch out. Gail Lewis was born in 1951 to a black Guyanese man who arrived in London in 1947 and a young white woman. The relationship soon failed and her mum was disowned by her father and grandfather, white working class men who felt she had "betrayed" them. Her mum's father, a militant socialist, threw her out of the family home and left her to live in a Salvation Army hostel. Eventually Gail's mum ended up in a room in a large house in Kilburn where she met the man who would raise Gail, who had arrived from Jamaica in 1949. Gail recalled that her adoptive dad "smelt of rubber all the time" from his work in a car tyre factory.

Gail grew up in Kilburn and Queen's Park, where she was the only black kid in her class. As a result she spent a lot of time with her best friend in Harlesden and hanging out on Paddington Recreation Ground. After leaving school she worked for a few years in a factory and as a cleaner until she reached a turning point in her life:

> *Finally I got a job working as a library assistant at University College London when I was 20. I spent my time looking at all these books, but more importantly, seeing exactly what a student was. I remember thinking, "If they can do it, maybe I can".*[42]

As a teenager Gail had joined the Young Communist League but later put more time and energy into anti-colonial and anti-racist work. After UCL she went to the LSE where she joined the Brixton Black Women's Group, seeking to link up black women's groups across London in the Organisation for Women of African and Asian Descent (OWAAD). Her political and anti-racist activity in OWAAD were the first steps in a career as one of Britain's leading feminist and LGBT academics.

Perhaps the greatest opportunities afforded young working class men and women in the 1960s were those provided by the music industry. The Beatles had demonstrated it wasn't necessary to come from London to achieve huge success, but the Rolling Stones came out of Dartford on the far fringes of London and played their first professional gig in 1962 at the Marquee Club in Wardour Street. Unlike the Beatles, the Stones launched themselves out of a specific London scene. The centre of that scene was "Tin Pan Alley" — Denmark Street between Charing Cross Road and St Giles.

Since the 1920s Denmark Street had been the centre of Britain's music publishing industry, with *Melody Maker* and the *NME* originally located there before both moving to Long Acre. By the 1960s publishing was giving way to recording studios and musical equipment. In 1961 Regent Sound Studio, where the Stones recorded their first album, was founded in the street, based above the offices of Essex Music. In 1964 the Kinks recorded "You Really Got Me" in a basement studio on the street. 1969 saw its first guitar store, Top Gear Music, which quickly became a social hub for guitarists. The close proximity of recording studios, publishing houses and music equipment shops meant that many musicians socialised in the street, particularly at the Giaconda café. The Small Faces were formed after its original members met at the Giaconda.

The Who were a product of the North-West London working class with no desire to emulate the Beatles. Pete Townshend came from a family of peripatetic working class musicians and grew up in Acton, later attending Ealing Art College where he joined the Young Communist League. In 1964, with Roger Daltrey (born in Hammersmith) and John Entwistle and Keith Moon (born in Acton and Perivale) he formed the Who. The creative tension between Townshend, the introverted Art College graduate, and Daltry, the Hammersmith boy who worked on a building site, gave the Who a crackling energy that at their height made them Britain's most exciting and unpredictable rock band. "My Generation", released in 1965, was the anthem of the decade's rebellious working class youth.

In the space of a few years the Who moved on from the hard rock of their debut album *My Generation* (1965) to the rock opera *Tommy* (1969). They also provided a soundtrack for the Mods, a sub-cult formed in the late 1950s by fashion-obsessed working class Londoners called "Modernists" because they liked modern jazz. Its key components were tailor-made suits, a musical backbeat of jazz, soul and R&B, and the recreational use of motor scooters such as a Lambretta or a Vespa. The Mod social scene revolved around all-night dance clubs, its energy sustained by amphetamines and purple hearts. The Flamingo Club at 33 Wardour Street was a mecca for Mods because of its high-end jazz, R&B and soul, and the three-year residency at the club of Georgie Fame and the Blue Flames in the mid-1960s.

By the late 1960s Mod was splintering. Peacock Mods, based mainly in North London, inclined to Pop Art psychedelia with a definite gay influence. They were kept supplied by the first overtly gay menswear shops in London, in the Newburgh quarter of Soho off Regent Street, a den of alleys worked by prostitutes and small tailors which became the centre of Mod fashion, a look described by Jeremy Reed as "confrontationally liberated bisexual".[43] Hard Mods, based mainly in South and West London and soon to morph into the first Skinheads, preferred Ben Shermans, Doc Martens, ska and rocksteady.

Steve Jones — who by the late 1960s was a prolific petty thief around the Shepherd's Bush and Hammersmith area as well as occasionally nicking from big department stores like Selfridges in Oxford Street — recalled how important it was on the Mod and Skinhead scene to dress the part and look good:

For me, having the proper sheepskin coat or the genuine cashmere Crombie was a way to feel good about myself. It was your own little thing that marked out a space you could be successful in. The two tone suits were the perfect example of that. Not many of us were heading for the kind of job where you'd need a whistle, but we could go down to a place called Stewart's on Uxbridge Road — he was this little Jewish tailor who saw an opportunity — and get him to make us one for £10. Every skinhead kid from my area had to go through that rite of passage.

In the 1960s, at least, as Jones remembered it, "there was none of that Nazi shit going on". Shepherd's Bush and White City was a racially mixed area, old white working class mingling with immigrant Irish and new Afro-Caribbean and Asian families. Whatever background the Skinheads came from, "what brought us together was that we all loved Jamaican and black American music".[44]

It was a moment in London working class culture caught in all its social awkwardness by the Leyton Buzzards' "Saturday Night Beneath the Plastic Palm Trees", which spent five weeks in the charts in 1979 and led to an appearance on *Top of the Pops*, its chorus recreating life for a London working class teenage Suedehead at the end of the 1960s:

Saturday night beneath the plastic palm trees
Dancing to the rhythm of The Guns of Navarone
Found my Mecca near Tottenham Hale Station
I discovered heaven in the Seven Sisters Road

Rod Stewart, born in 1945 in Archway Road in Highgate, was the son of a Scottish Master Builder who had moved to London and opened a newsagents. After leaving William Gresham Secondary Modern in Muswell Hill in 1961, Rod worked for a couple of years as a labourer in Highgate Cemetery before detouring into music. A keen supporter of CND and participant in the annual Aldermaston marches, in 1963 he moved into a bed-sit in Muswell Hill whilst occasionally busking in Leicester Square. Over the next few years he established himself on the London R&B scene as "Rod the Mod". After two years with the Jeff Beck Group, in 1969 Stewart released his debut album *An Old Raincoat Won't Ever Let You Down*. Though not yet twenty-five, his covers of "Dirty Old Town" and "Handbags and Gladbags" combined rock and folk with a deep vein of working class melancholia. He was on the way to enormous success.

Across London in Stoke Newington, Mark Feld, born in Hackney General Hospital in 1947, was also searching for a cultural identity. By 1955 Mark regularly took the number 73 bus from Hackney down to Berwick Street Market in Soho where his mum worked a grocery stall (his dad also worked a stall on Petticoat Lane). When not helping his mum, he would nip around the corner to the 2i's to buy coffee. On his ninth birthday his parents gave him a guitar that cost twice what his dad earned per week.[45] Ten years later Feld, now calling himself Marc Bolan, was drinking coffee with his mate David Bowie in the Giaconda in Denmark Street, dreaming of rock stardom. In 1967 Bolan formed T. Rex. Success was not immediate but, like

Rod Stewart, it would arrive suddenly at the point the 1960s became the 1970s, kickstarting glam rock in the UK.

Unlike Stewart and Bolan, who reached the height of their fame and influence in the 1970s, the Kinks, formed in 1964 by brothers Ray and Dave Davies, are indissolubly linked to the 1960s. After the war the Davies family had moved from Holloway Road to East Finchley where the Davies boys were born, and later moved again to Fortis Green near Muswell Hill, where in the 1960s the working class swam in the same sea as a vaguely cosmopolitan middle class. Ray and Dave's dad was a slaughterhouse man who had moved from the Welsh valleys to the capital and married a London girl. He worked at the cattle markets of Smithfields and Caledonian Park, supplementing the family's food with occasional cuts of meat nicked from work. The Davies boys were the youngest and only boys of the family's eight children. In 1962 they formed a band, the Ray Davies Quartet, and went through a series of lead vocalists, one of whom was Rod Stewart, who like them had attended William Grimshaw Secondary Modern.

Not entirely comfortable in the lower-middle class milieu of Muswell Hill, the social life of the Davies family centred south of Fortis Green, on Holloway and Seven Sisters Road, and even further south in central London. Ray later recalled that in 1959, when he was fifteen, he rode the bus from Muswell Hill down to Leicester Square to explore Soho:

> *This was my first solo venture into the dark, seedy world of sleaze...a new world, a dark world of neon lights and nightclubs, cafes, streetwalkers, small-time underworld crime characters. I spoke to no-one, I just walked and observed.*[46]

After a year at Hornsey College of Art Ray formed the Kinks and achieved early success with their volcanic breakthrough hit single "You Really Got Me" (1964). Between 1964 and 1971 the Kinks produced a series of pop singles that, for power of endurance and appeal, matched those of the Beatles and the Stones. But while the two mega-groups mutated into global phenomena, the Kinks remained rooted in their time and place. Their fidelity to the society that formed them, to their experience of London in the 1960s, produced small masterpieces such as "Tired of Waiting for You", "Dead End Street", "Sunny Afternoon", "Dedicated Follower of Fashion", "All Day and All of The Night", "Lola" and "Waterloo Sunset".

In these years Davies overflowed with creative juice, from the sheer boldness of "Lola", years ahead of its time for its positive depiction of a trans woman or crossdresser who "walks like a woman and talks like a man" and is no less alluring for it, to "Waterloo Sunset", possibly the greatest song ever penned about London:

> *Millions of people*
> *Swarming like flies 'round*
> *Waterloo underground.*
> *But Terry and Julie*
> *Cross over the river*
> *Where they feel safe and sound.*
> *And they don't*
> *need no friends.*
> *As long as they gaze on Waterloo sunset*
> *They are in paradise*

The Kinks most anti-modernistic and challenging albums, *The Kinks Are the Village Green Preservation Society* (1968) and *Muswell Hillbillies* (1971) were not commercially successful when released but have endured while flashier products of the period have disappeared. They reflect a quiet but proud working class sensibility not easily swayed by contemporary fashion. The cover of *Muswell Hillbillies* is a grainy photo taken inside the Archway Tavern at the north end of Holloway Road. The largest and most iconic pub of the area (as it still was in the early 1990s when I worked opposite it in Archway Job Centre) there is little of the "Swinging 60s" about it, welcoming young working class dropouts and fag-shrouded old men alike. It was neither an East End boozer nor a new multicultural hub but a lively communal centre for North London's working class.

Despite intoxicating stories of how Michael Caine and David Bailey conquered the West End and became national icons, working class Londoners did not experience the decade in the manner of successful film stars and models. Gary Kemp, who grew up in Islington, remembered, *"The revolution never came to our street, although we heard the Beatles singing about it on the new Radio 1 station"*.[47] Beyond a few famous names, working class interlopers of the 1960s London "scene" were a relatively small number who happened to live, work or socialise in central London and its bastard offshoots like Chelsea or Ladbroke Grove. King's Road, running west from Sloane Square to Fulham, was for a while the totem and heart of Swinging London, throbbing with new style and fashion in venues like Salon 33, Chelsea Girl, the World's End, 4.30, Kween's Mini-Store and the Great Gear Trading Company. The iconic Chelsea Drugstore, a three-floor, chome and neon mini-mall containing a chemist, clothes shops, drinking fountains and places to eat, employed purple catsuit clad girls on motorbikes to make its deliveries. For some this was a work environment, and it led inevitably to other things.

The "alternative" working class of London tended to congregate in music shops, when they did not actually work in them. The Musicland shops in Kilburn, Ladbroke Grove and Berwick Street were famous for stocking imported American albums from psychedelic music to ska, blues and soul. R&B Records in Stamford Hill was a locus for Rude Boys and Mods, stacked to the gills with Jamaican music, ska and blues of every kind. R&B Records stood not for Rhythm & Blues but for Rita and Benny Isen, the Jewish working class owners of the shop who renamed themselves Benny and Rita King and began to produce records of their own under the R&B record label, including Bob Marley and the Wailers' "Simmer Down" in 1965, which established them in the UK.

There *were* working class hippies, of course, alive to the counter-cultural undercurrents and philosophies of the era. In the late 1960s and early 1970s many of them gravitated to Notting Hill and Portobello Road, which for a couple of decades fizzed with anarchic creativity and political dissent.

The demolition of old houses to make way for the Westway left a literal gap in the area that was quickly filled. Barry Miles' *London Calling: A Countercultural History of London since 1945* (2012) records:

> *The cleared land looked like a bombsite and quickly filled with rubbish. Sometimes, on a warm night, Dave Tomlin, playing the saxophone, would lead a procession of people there to build a bonfire. People would sit around and take acid, smoke pot, play music and improvise poems as the smoke drifted in clouds around them.*[48]

In the late 1960s and early 1970s Hawkwind and the Pink Fairies played free gigs under the Westway on Saturdays as cars shot by overhead. Pash's Music Shop on Elgin Crescent was open all hours and in permanent session while the London Free School jostled with the Mangrove restaurant on All Saints Road as the nucleus of a new and assertive black civil rights movement.

Born in 1952, Andy Coates grew up in Bounds Green. His dad worked for the Co-op and his mum was a typist. Bounds Green in the 1960s was a diverse place:

> *Growing up in Bounds Green, N11, there was a great mixture of skilled working class people who worked in the Lea Valley factories, clerical workers, and bohemian members of the intelligentsia (the family of Dexter Fletcher lived two doors down). My friends were from all these backgrounds, often Jewish (the Brownlow Road Synagogue was nearby), and there were others, from the New Southgate area from much less well-off working class families.*

Leaving school at sixteen, Andy started work as a labourer in Barnet but he ended up arguing with teenage Skinheads who idolised Enoch Powell. Before long he had drifted south to a squat in Kentish Town and entered London's counter-cultural scene, hanging out at the Roundhouse and the Scala:

My own friends were from left-wing families like my parents who liked rock music and smoking cannabis, and my most abiding memories are of going to Camden Town to the Roundhouse for Implosion on Sunday, taking part at around 15 years old in demonstrations to defend Oz magazine, and similar causes, and going to the first rock festivals. I began work at 16 in manual jobs, then completed my O levels at Barnet College and did some clerical jobs, and lived as a 'Head' in my first flat in Kentish Town. At around that time I began to go to more demos and got involved in left politics, initially anarchist.[49]

Steven Georgiou, born in 1948 in Marylebone to a Greek Cypriot father and a Swedish mother, floated on the currents of this counter-culture but did not join it. He grew up in a flat above his family's restaurant, the Stavros, at the north end of Shaftesbury Avenue. Interested in music from an early age, at age fifteen his father bought him a £200 guitar on hire purchase. Because it was difficult to practice in the crowded family flat, he would go up to the roof and listen to the music drifting across from the studios of Denmark Street. After a year at Hammersmith School of Art in 1966 he began performing solo in various bars and cafes and adopted the name Cat Stevens.

Stevens had almost instant success when the title song of his debut album *Matthew and Son* (1967) reached number two in the charts. Over the next ten years he expanded his musical range and achieved massive international success with albums like *Tea for the Tillerman* (1970), *Teaser and the Firecat* (1971) and *Catch Bull at Four* (1972). Helen Evangelou, a huge fan, spotted him once in the late 1960s in an art materials shop on New Oxford Street but was too overawed to approach him. Ted kept his LPs and played them on Sunday mornings along with his other favourites, Johnny Cash and Hoyt Axton.

Cat Stevens' ethos and music, derived from his warm and supportive family and a Greek Orthodox spirituality that would later take other forms, was essentially positive. But despite their personal success not many of London's working class artists and songwriters felt there was a Peace Train coming or that Morning Had Broken. Ray Davies later said explicitly, "The 60s were a lie". By 1971 the Kinks were complaining:

Unionists tell you when to strike
Generals tell you when to fight
Preachers tell you wrong from right
They'll feed you when you're born
and use you all your life

In similar vein, the Who disparaged lazy talk of revolution — "Meet the new boss, same as the old boss" — and assured the world the working class Won't Get Fooled Again.

John Bird, born in 1945 in Notting Hill to an Irish working class family, experienced grinding poverty in his childhood, his entire family living in two ground-floor rooms in a house in St Stephens' Gardens. After leaving school early he spent time as a butcher's boy while, like Steve Jones, indulging in petty theft to top up his income. Later he worked in the store room of an art shop and used the time to read poetry he barely understood. Eventually he drifted into homelessness and learnt to survive on the streets of central London, sleeping rough in mainline stations or behind the Empire Cinema in Leicester Square.

After three years in jail for breaking bail, during which he passed the time with intense reading, John drifted into the margins of London's counter-cultural scene. He worked for a while as a warehouseman then chucked it on a whim to sign on, cadging money and drugs off gullible Americans keen to experience "swinging London". In 1967, having blagged his way into delivery work, he was delivering a consignment of beads to Harrods when he bumped into his friend George and three other American guys on the Kings Road. Immediately abandoning his job, he joined them on an impromptu trip to Woburn Abbey for a pop festival where *"I met girls and listened to the Small Faces, high on the endless supply of grass"*. But he sensed that he had let his friends down:

London was full of people looking for a good time. But everywhere was awash with fakes and frauds. London was no more swinging than it ever had been. And George was right: I wasn't a part of it. I didn't know anyone who was meeting Terence Stamp or Michael Caine.

A year later, after encountering someone selling a left-wing paper in North End Road Market in Fulham, John went to a meeting of the Socialist Labour League (SLL) in St Pancras Town Hall and for a while joined the SLL. Genuinely interested in Marxism and the reading list provided by the SLL, John went on anti-Vietnam War demos and got a job at the AEC factory in Acton in order to raise the class consciousness of London's working class. This phase passed quickly, shattered by the reality of working class life:

I had a problem. I never seemed to meet revolutionary workers. I came from the working classes and they seemed to me very unheroic, very un-revolutionary...I was getting pissed off with what seemed to me like a revolutionary religion.

Bird jumped from job to job. In 1969 he worked at another factory in North Acton that made Vaseline and baby products:

I drove a truck cleaning the lines of broken glass and boxes. The factory was full of women. The pay was good and the girls and women spent most of the time being sexually rude. I loved it.[50]

Unable to settle down, in 1970 Bird worked briefly as a dishwasher at the Houses of Parliament, an institution he would return to in 2015 as a Life Peer, elevated for his creation in the 1990s of *The Big Issue* initiative for London's homeless. Despite his membership of the SLL and the Workers Revolutionary Party in the 1970s, he eventually discarded revolutionary ideology, instead channelling his energy into a project of immense use and value to the poorest street people that, in true North London fashion, made some money as well.

Between the 1950s and the 1970s mass immigration into the capital fundamentally altered its social and cultural dynamic. Encouraged by central and local government and entranced by visions of suburban living, significant numbers of London's old working class moved out of London to New Towns such as Harlow, Basildon, Stevenage and Crawley. Firms like Gilbey's relocated there and sometimes took their workforce with them. In the 1960s Greater London's overall population declined by half a million people, 7% of the total. This was not unprecedented. Between 1850 and 1910 over 180,000 East Londoners moved further east, over the River Lea to West Ham and beyond, to escape the overcrowded slums of Mile End, Bethnal Green and Stepney, leaving those areas with a net loss of population.[51]

The 1960s saw similar movements. By 1971 two thirds of Islington's residents in 1961 had either died or moved away. In 1961 about 41% of Islington's workforce was employed in manufacturing industries such as engineering, printing, clothing and brewing. By 1971 this had dropped to 32%, still a significant amount of its population. This led to an increase in the number of unemployed in Islington at a time when unemployment levels nationally were decreasing.[52]

There *was* a white working class diaspora during these years, as there had been in the late nineteenth century, but it was not a complete and irreversible exodus, even for those who participated in it. Some of the transplanted working class, particularly mothers not working outside the home, did not enjoy the relative isolation of the New Towns in comparison to their old communities. Many of the men who moved out continued to work in London, often in central London, in public transport, as self-employed plumbers and electricians and builders, working in Covent Garden, Smithfields and Billingsgate Markets, or in a variety of service industries. They sometimes hung out there after work and continued to regard their old manor with sentimental affection. Some of their children, once grown, hankered to return. Some did.

Chip Hamer's family, like many white working class Londoners, moved from London (in their case from Lordship

Road, Stoke Newington, where Chip was born and spent his first years) to Essex in the 1960s. But, again like many who did so, Chip did not approve of his parents' decision. He was, in his own words, *"back into London for sport and music as soon as I was old enough"*. As a teenager in the 1970s he spent a lot of time at the Marquee, the 100 Club, the Music Machine in Camden Town and the Sundown Club on Tottenham Court Road. In the 1980s he moved back into London and pursued his musical and political activity.[53]

But those who now neither lived nor worked in London ceased to be London working class. Those that remained, that intermingled and sometimes intermarried with a new, incoming working class, experienced a new and different London, one that offered social, cultural and sexual freedoms unavailable to the older, pre-war working class. For the most part that new life centered on North London.

Even at the time British filmmakers knew they were living through an extraordinary and transformative period and they wanted to tell stories that reflected it. The prevailing view of London at the start of the decade as a sleazy urban wasteland, seen in films like Michael Winner's *West 11* (1963) in which Diana Dors burned hot in Rachman's Notting Hill, had shifted dramatically by the time England won the World Cup in 1966. *West 11* was filmed on location in Notting Hill, the Troubadour coffee house in Earl's Court, the new Wimpy on the Strand and Ken Colyer's Studio 51 jazz club in Great Newport Street, and intimated a London shortly to arrive. When it did it was immortalised in a string of "Swinging London" films such as *Alfie, Georgy Girl, The Italian Job* and *Performance*, presenting different aspects of the era in contrasting styles.

The so-called "kitchen sink" films of working class life — *Saturday Night and Sunday Morning, Billy Liar, This Sporting Life, Kes*— tended to focus on the working class of northern England. Those set in London were located either in the East End (*Sparrows Can't Sing*) or South London (*Up the Junction, Poor Cow*). Only later did authors and filmmakers see the potential of North London to provide a more complex environment for stories of modern working class life. *Withnail and I* (1986) acknowledged that Camden Town in the late 1960s contained as much squalid tragedy as Notting Hill, astutely using failed actors as examples of a bohemian working class drowning in debt and drugs.

One of the most authentic cinematic depictions of London's working class in the 1960s, *Quadrophenia* (1979) was created by artists who themselves came from a working class background — Pete Townshend, Sting, Phil Daniels, Ray Winstone, Phil Davis, Timothy Spall, and even John Bindon in a small role. Based on the Who's 1973 rock opera, *Quadrophenia* caught the aspiration of working class youngsters in the mid-1960s, their will to assert themselves through clothes and music, their underlying naivety. The inside knowledge of the world portrayed is apparent from the details of Mod fashion to the use of A. Cooke's Pie and Mash Shop in Shepherd's Bush (Cooke's was a local landmark, used by Steve Jones and Paul Cook before the Sex Pistols, and one of the first venues where the Who performed).

The final scenes of *Quadrophenia* show a defeated working class, the protagonist Jimmy lost and disillusioned, his hero Ace Face revealed as a servile bellboy in a Brighton hotel. Yet that was not the whole story, or anywhere near it. The lives of those who made the film attested to that. Pete Townshend had not been defeated, nor had Ray Davies, nor had Steven Georgiou, nor had Buchi Emecheta, nor had Gail Lewis, nor had Ted and Joyce, nor had countless young working class men and women who discovered and enjoyed the new opportunities and lifestyles available in London in the 1960s.

Working class North Londoners were often ambivalent about the changes in their lives and the city around them. Eddie Mence was born in 1948 in Islington and left school at fifteen. From 1963 to 1983 he worked in a small workshop off Upper Street restoring old barometers. It was a typical London working class occupation, skilled manual labour but personal and intimate:

What I loved about my job was... the pay wasn't terrific... but there was a lot of job satisfaction in it. I mean these barometers had been in someone's attic or basement for years and years...

*And when it would come in it would be in a very poor state...
I would strip it all down and then it would go down to the wood
mill and the wood mill would repair any parts of the frame that
were missing. Then it would go to the French polishers and the
French polishers would obviously restore its case. Then it would
come back to me again. I'd already stripped it down and so
I had all the brass parts there and so I'd restore all the brass work
and reseal all the dials. Also, I had to replace missing parts as well
if necessary. And so, it was a pretty hands-on job in a way.*

On the one hand he enjoyed his life as a young man in 1960s
London, a life he could not have lived if the city had not evolved
and changed. He liked Mod clothes and bought *Melody Maker*
and the *NME* every week to keep up with the charts and new
records. But it was *working class* Islington he enjoyed, the cafes
and shops of pre-gentrification Upper Street. In later years,
with inevitable nostalgia, he lamented the loss of that world:

*Upper Street was a great street to work in in a way... a nice area
not like it is now. Now it's all coffee bars and bistros and that. But
then it was a working class area very much really.*[54]

Working class children, especially, were pushing at the
boundaries their parents had accepted. In Hackney Amanda
Millhouse and her friends often played in Victoria Park, but
were very aware of the many attractions to their west and how
easy it was to get there:

*Regent's Canal runs through the park and it was a favourite walk.
There were always children pushing each other in, or fishing or
riding bikes along the towpath. My friends and I liked to walk
from there up to London Zoo. You can see the aviary from the
towpath and watch the birds flying around. I loved the shape of
the aviary — it seemed so futuristic and exciting.*[55]

Central London would always attract the adventurous
working class. Ted spent many of his off-work hours, and some
of his in-work hours, at the Alexandria café in Rathbone Place,

Fitzrovia, an establishment immortalised by Frank Norman in his play *A Kayf Up West* (1964). Other Turner and Cooper workers, such as veteran CP activist John Bowles and Ted's assistant Razzle Basil, joined him, and the café resounded to passionate arguments about books, films, capitalism, Vietnam and Enoch Powell. For Ted, who by now was reading H.G. Wells, Bertrand Russell, Jack London and John Steinbeck, it was a substitute for the academic education he had missed out on as a teenager:

> *The Alexandria was like an informal working class university. I would sit there over endless cups of stewed tea with a rag-bag collection of well-read and politically minded builders, postmen, cab drivers, anarchists, tortured intellectuals and general layabouts.*[56]

While Ted was expanding his social and intellectual horizons, Joyce was looking after their young sons (me and my younger brother Jamie, born in 1965), taking us up Robert Street and through Chester Gate to Regent's Park every day to play. Needing part-time work to fit around primary school and childcare, in the late 1960s Joyce took a job as a domestic cleaner for Shirley Conran, who lived in a large house adjacent to Regent's Park. She shared the job with the young mother who lived across the landing from us in Rydal Water. Joyce remembered that Shirley's writing of *Superwoman* (1975) was greatly assisted by the author not getting out of bed until midday while her two cleaners, who also fed her sons Jasper and Sebastian and cleaned up the food they flung about the kitchen, did the housework.

When I was five years old I started at Christ Church Primary School on Redhill Street, a small byway between Albany Street and the Cumberland Estate. At the time our block of flats sat next to a long row of dilapidated terraced houses at the end of which, at the junction with Stanhope Street, was an old-fashioned barbers. When I was six or seven I was sent, by myself as was usual then, to get a haircut. With no instructions to go by the barber gave me a severe "pudding bowl" and sent me away.

I arrived home not at all happy which made it even funnier for my mum, dad and brother.

Shortly after, all the houses and the barber shop on the south side of Robert Street were demolished and replaced with the long, linear, seven-storey blue-grey Woodhall council block, the first stage of the "Tolmers Square Area One: Netley Street" redevelopment project (Area Two of the project, Tolmer's Square itself, would prove to be a lot more contentious). Woodhall consisted of two maisonettes on the two lower floors and enclosed access decks on the front on the first, third, fourth and fifth floors. All units had south-facing gardens. It ran half the length of Robert Street. When it was finished the entire street, from Hampstead Road to Regent's Park, looked like a clean, modern council estate, primed and ready for the 1970s.

THE 1970s

"Even growing up poor in a metropolis, you can still see the possibilities, because of the proximities... Out in the country, or in smaller towns, there are fewer opportunities to witness other ways, but bunk the fare on a number 52 or a southbound Northern Line train and a few stops later you hit a city bristling with alternatives. It hit me between the eyes, and opened them too."

Robert Elms

Alfred Hitchcock's *Frenzy* (1972) is an eccentric and unpleasant film but it provides a tantalising glimpse of Covent Garden Market in the early 1970s. Hitchcock's late-period oddity is based on Arthur Le Bern's novel *Goodbye Piccadilly, Farewell Leicester Square* (1966), a noirish thriller set in the immediate post-war years but with a plot inspired by the unsolved Jack the Stripper murders of the mid-1960s. La Bern, who grew up in Darby Sabini's Clerkenwell, knew London's underworld, razor gangs and bent coppers from the inside out. Hitchcock was the son of a Covent Garden porter, and on his return to London for the first time in forty years he wanted to tell a story that captured the sights and sounds of the old market before it was gone. If nothing else, he did so, for *Frenzy* exudes the atmosphere of working life in the market.

Hitchcock's desire to catch the old market on film arose from its imminent departure, in 1974, to a new location in Battersea. In 1961 the market, plus Jubilee Hall and adjacent buildings containing 4,000 workers and 340 separate companies, had been placed under a public body called the Covent Garden Market Authority (CGMA). In 1964 the CGMA decided that the old market was poorly situated to handle a continuous stream of lorries in and out of central London every day except Christmas Day, and it chose vacant land in Nine Elms as the location of New Covent Garden Market.

The market's fate had been decided, but there remained a massive struggle to preserve some of its old environment, not least its working class housing. In 1968 the GLC bought all the properties owned by the CGMA and produced an ambitious plan for the rebuilding of the area. The proposed redevelopment would have turned Holborn and the Strand into dual carriageways and demolished 60% of the area's buildings and 82% of its housing, creating between Shaftesbury Avenue and Kingsway a mini-Manhattan of private residential and office blocks, hotels and elevated walkways. The plan would have eradicated the existing Covent Garden and displaced 3,500 people who still lived there.

In December 1970 a meeting of members of the local community, including prominent working class families such as the Toomeys and the Driscolls, met in the White Hart pub on Drury Lane to organise a fight back. On 1 April 1971 six hundred people, which the history of the campaign describes as "housewives, market porters, students, artists, pensioners and businessmen", crammed into the Methodist Kingsway Hall.[1] John Toomey told the meeting how rising rents had forced him and his young family to move outside Covent Garden while his parents and brothers remained. John had been raised in a two-room top-floor flat in Neal Street, Seven Dials, in the 1920s. In the war he had worked as a carpenter helping to repair bombed houses in central London, later becoming a printer. He was also an active member of the St Aloysius Catholic Parish in Somers Town and the Somers Town Housing Association set up by the Christian socialist priest Basil Jellicoe. In the 1970s Toomey turned his energies to defending the residents of Covent Garden and went on to become a Camden Labour Councillor.

The White Hart meeting led to the formation of the Covent Garden Community Association (CGCA), a voice for the remnants of central London's working class of market traders, printers, stagehands, publicans, café owners and small retailers.

The CGCA campaigned for a new home for every displaced resident and protection for those retailers nestling around the Piazza who would be removed. The size and strength of the opposition convinced Camden Council, which had recently switched control from Tory to Labour, to abandon its support for the plan. The redevelopment was given the death blow when Tory Environment Secretary Geoffrey Rippon declared that 250 buildings in the area had listed status and could not be demolished. In 1973 the GLC dropped the plan entirely.

As part of its campaign the CGCA organised street festivities to draw local people together. One party involved 1,500 people in the courtyard of the Wild Street Peabody Estate. Sarah Smith, born in the late 1950s and the daughter of a market stall holder, grew up in a flat on Wild Street without running water or an indoor toilet. As a child she played around Covent Garden and went on exploratory walks around the West End. She remembered that Holborn and its surroundings "*was like a ghost town on weekends... so we were safe*". After getting married in the 1970s in St Clement Danes Church in the Strand she and her husband lived in a flat on Charing Cross Road but later moved back to the Odhams Walk council estate on Long Acre.[2]

Odhams Walk was built in the late 1970s as part of the alternative social housing for those displaced by the redevelopment. After the initial GLC plan had been defeated, a public enquiry threw out its subsequent plan in favour of the CGCA's alternative which included a substantial increase in social housing provision to cater for local families in poor housing, their children, and residents who had been forced out of the area but wanted to return. The new housing would utilise the area's main and genuine redevelopment opportunity, the space left over after the demolition of the old Odhams print works.

Overcoming initial scepticism, the CGCA secured a radical design scheme from the GLC that provided an intricate rampart of seventy-three low-level, L-shaped patio flats built in a burnished brown brick cascading around open stairways for the first two storeys and rising to an upper-level walkway serving a further twenty-nine flats, all sitting above a small enclosed plaza of shops and resident parking. Its location, directly opposite Covent Garden tube station, made it one of the most anomalous and attractive council estates in London. The majority of people allocated to the new flats, like Sarah Smith, were from local families who had grown up in the Covent Garden area. In 2021 60% of the flats in Odhams Walk were still occupied by council tenants although those that were purchased under the Right to Buy scheme had sky-rocketed in value. In 2016 one of them, bought for £170,000 in 1995, was sold for £1.3m, making it at the time the most expensive ex-council flat ever sold.

The fall-out of the battle over Covent Garden left the working class residents of the area even more entrenched, at least for a while. Eileen Kelly, who grew up in the area and whose husband moved with the market to Nine Elms in 1974, initially did not want to stay. Like many locals she was distressed by the proliferation of strip clubs and porn shops in nearby Soho and the generally seedy tone of the West End in the 1970s (even the highly public corner of Regent Street and Piccadilly was disfigured by the Eros Cinema which during the long heatwave of 1976 showed *Clockwork Nympho* and *Sextet* continuously). But over time Eileen came to appreciate the redevelopment of the Piazza and the surrounding area as an improvement on what had come before and was glad she had stayed.[3]

A vision of gargantuan modernism entirely antithetical to the spirit of central London, hostile to any notion of humane daily living for those who still lived in it, had been defeated, primarily because of a grassroots campaign to defend housing and workspace rooted in the centre of the city. In the years that followed, despite an inevitable process of commercial gentrification, the resident population went up and none of the promised council flat demolitions, against which John Toomey and others had campaigned, took place.

The continuing provision of good quality social housing at affordable rents to Britain's working class was something the Conservative government was determined to prevent. The 1972 Housing Finance Act replaced the requirement for "fair rents" for council tenancies with that of "reasonable rents", i.e. rents in line with private sector rent, and phased out government subsidies to local authorities for their upkeep, requiring them to make a profit on their housing stock. To ensure compliance it mandated that if councils did not implement the Act they would be denied all subsidies and councillors would be surcharged and debarred from office. On top of this, the 1973 Land Compensation Act required councils to rehouse those made homeless by redevelopment, meaning that large numbers of BAME residents of sub-standard housing owned by London councils were eligible for rehousing in new housing estates as soon as they were displaced.

With substantial numbers of white working class families already moving to Outer London and the New Towns, the racial profile of Inner London estates underwent a major transformation in very short time. The demographic of estates like Holly Street in Hackney and Broadwater Farm in Tottenham altered rapidly, literally in the space of a few years. In the early 1970s 63% of people allocated a flat in Holly Street were white. By the end of the decade 77% of those allocated were black. By the mid-1970s at least half of the flats on Broadwater Farm were held by black tenants. To add to this, by 1980, in line with new legislation mandating provision for the homeless, most incomers tended to be families and individuals who had previously been homeless or transient.[4] The long-term consequences of these policies were seldom considered; the ground was not prepared.

The Marquess Estate in Canonbury at the north end of Essex Road epitomised unintended outcomes. Opened in 1975, the Marquess was designed by the same team that had created Lillington Gardens and its innovative, intricate scheme of streets and alleyways weaving about the estate's houses, green squares and play areas – dubbed a "village within a village" — was praised for providing a community atmosphere lacking in the tower blocks. It was opened by Labour Prime Minister Harold Wilson who called it a "magnificent showpiece". But its layout and situation, with only two entrances on the same street and no clear throughway, meant that very few people strolled through it. The low flat roofs leaked and the estate's labyrinthine pedestrian paths made it difficult for postmen to navigate and impenetrable for the police. Adrift from the world around it, it soon had twice the level of vandalism and crime as estates nearby.

These estates were not fated to become "sink estates". Many that declined in the 1970s and 1980s, such as the Marquess, were redesigned and improved in the 1990s and 2000s. The construction of small, sensitively designed council estates such as Odhams Walk demonstrated that lessons had been learnt from the era of the tower blocks. Westminster Council's Harewood Avenue flats, just off the western end of Marylebone Road near the Lisson Grove Estate, were built in the early 1970s to provide decent low-level homes for working class residents (today the Lisson Grove Estate continues as was but the Harewood Avenue flats are privately owned).

Keeley Hawes, daughter of London cabbie Tony Hawes, was born in 1976 in Paddington and grew up in a three-bedroom council flat on Harewood Avenue overlooking the trains going in and out of Marylebone mainline station. She recalled her youth as a "safe, cosy childhood" in the centre of London, riding her brother's Chopper bike around the estate until her mum called her in with a loud shout of "Dinner!". Later she worked a number of part-time jobs in Sainsbury's on Saturday, McDonalds after school in the evenings and a stall in an antiques market at weekends, before going to drama school.[5]

One of the most impressive new council estates of the decade, the World's End Estate in Chelsea that opened in 1977, defied the new anti-tower block trend to incorporate four imposing tall blocks at its core. Conceived and built by Conservative-led Kensington and Chelsea Council (a different entity from the twenty-first-century body that callously washed its hands of the tenants of Grenfell Tower), the estate challenges those who decry Brutalist architecture by offering a beautiful setting for mass social housing overlooking the River Thames. The World's End was high-rise and high density but it offered 750 homes to over 2,500 people, with seven tower blocks and nine four-storey walkway blocks bound together by tree-lined courtyards.

Its rich gold brick façade is actually cladding but despite its size it adapts perfectly to its setting, a soft bronze edifice that compliments the smooth curve of the river where it sits (and does so even more today when expensive private apartment blocks dot the entire riverside from Chelsea to Wandsworth). John Boughton rightly concludes, "*The estate looks and feels good and those courts provide a haven to the many who live in and love World's End*".[6]

Boughton also draws attention to a neglected strand of local housing policy during this period, the "municipalisation" of housing stock by local councils, i.e. the purchase by local councils of previously private flats and houses and their subsequent use as homes for council tenants. Some Inner London boroughs such as Camden and Islington applied this policy proactively, as a means to secure and offer good quality housing to working class tenants before they could be bought up and boosted out of their price range by middle class incomers. By 1975 Islington Council had municipalised 3,000 properties that might otherwise have gone on the property market. Under the leadership of Housing Committee Chair Margaret Hodge, Islington embarked on an ambitious new programme of council house-building and by the end of the 1970s the number of council-owned homes in Islington had doubled from 1971. These amounted to half of the borough's entire housing. Camden's council-owned housing stock also increased to about 30,000, an historic high.[7]

London councils also had to maintain their existing stock of social housing, some of which had been neglected for decades. The first twenty-three blocks of the massive White City estate near Shepherd's Bush opened in 1939 but the war delayed its completion. By 1953 the finished estate consisted of thirty-five low-level brick blocks (a mixture of balcony and staircase access) containing 2,000 homes for nearly 9,000 people. The blocks surrounded semi-enclosed courtyards. For their time they offered a good standard of housing with separate bathrooms with tiled floors and a wash basin (some even had separate toilets), and balconies to all flats. The estate also provided fourteen shops, a medical centre and several playgrounds.

White City was a traditional LCC estate, but a good one. During the 1960s there were attempts to improve and diversify it with the building of the new Malabar Court as sheltered housing for elderly people. During the 1970s it entered a difficult period, damaged by unsympathetic local government, too many "problem families" given flats in one enclosed location, crime, vandalism and a loss of social cohesion. It acquired a reputation, became a byword, as indelibly associated with social dysfunction as the nearby White City Stadium was with greyhound racing until its eventual closure in 1984.

Robert Elms, whose family moved in the late 1950s from a Notting Hill slum to the new Watling Estate in Burnt Oak at the end of the Northern Line, visited the White City estate every Saturday and during school holidays because his aunts, uncles and cousins still lived there. On his visits back he met up with friends and family and went to see Queen's Park Rangers (QPR) play at home at Loftus Road:

> These weekend trips back "home" were a feature of estate life for most Burnt Oak families, who maintained their ties to their old Inner London communities in Islington, King's Cross, Paddington and Notting Hill.

Although it involved a long bus journey from Cricklewood bus garage down to Shepherd's Bush, Robert never minded the time out of his life, "*For somehow I knew, even then I knew, that we had been banished from what I thought of as* real *London,* proper *London,* our *London*". Of visiting the White City Estate in the 1970s, he remembers, "*I always felt perfectly safe walking through the flats to football and stopping for a pint, felt most of its inhabitants were decent people living in tough conditions*".[8]

Trellick Tower went to seed much quicker than White City. Opened in 1972, its prison-like environment, its skyways to nowhere, bred crime and vandalism like mould spores. The residents went through its first Christmas without any water, heat or electricity after vandals smashed a fire hydrant, sending gallons of water down lift shafts and corridors, blowing fuses and plunging the block into darkness. Not long after this a young mother, crushed by the experience of living in the block, threw herself off one of its balconies. In later years Trellick would be taken back by residents and made habitable, but it would be a hard struggle.[9]

Once again, it was Camden that attempted to chart a different and better course for its tenants. The architectural philosophy set out by Sydney Cook and his disciples in the 1960s was fully applied in the 1970s, producing council estates that are now acknowledged as amongst the best public housing provision in the world. The programme's finest product, the Alexandra and Ainsworth Estate (commonly called the Alexandra Road Estate) in Swiss Cottage, constructed between 1972 and 1979, has been called "a magical moment for English housing".[10] The architect of Alexandra Road, Neave Brown, rejected the tower block as a means of providing housing units. Alexandra Road comprised two parallel pedestrianised streets and three three-hundred-metre-long terraces. The largest of these, seven storeys high, backs on to the railway and is built ziggurat-style, rising at the rear, to block the noise of passing trains. It combined radical modernism and a return to terraced housing, rejecting the "streets in the sky" concept of the tower blocks.

Alexandra Road provided 520 homes for 1,660 people, each unit with a front door to the street and each living room having a balcony with glazed sliding doors, for whatever its residents wished to do with it. An astonishingly original design, Alexandra Road's semi-brutalist stained white radiance was softened by a profusion of greenery. Criticism of it as the "hanging gardens of Camden" by one Tory councillor missed the point that this was exactly what Brown wanted to give Camden's working class families to live in. With the central redbrick thoroughfare of Rowley Way resplendent in both summer and winter sunshine, Alexandra Road stands as a testament to what ambitious, generous and humane social housing can provide for working class Londoners. Listed Grade II in 1994, even now over 80% of the estate's flats are council-owned and occupied.

Alexandra Road was matched by other new estates built by Camden Council in the 1970s. The Whittingdon Estate, sited between Dartmouth Park Hill and Highgate Cemetery, was built on land owned by Camden Council after the demolition of older working class terraced housing in Highgate New Town, most of which had lacked bathrooms. The new estate avoided the design mistakes that plagued the Marquess. All of the Whittingdon's homes had south-facing outdoor space and good natural light, its pedestrian throughways were staggered and organic but not overly complex, its green spaces merged into each other and the wall of green to its west provided by the cemetery, which some flats overlooked. The Whittingdon went significantly over budget but its financial indiscipline was insignificant in comparison to the misuse of public funds of later Private Finance Initiative (PFI) projects that received far less criticism.

This ambitious construction programme was helped by the fact that, after the City and Westminster, Camden was the richest borough in London. But new estates such as Branch Hill on Hampstead's West Heath also emerged from an idealistic socialism that saw no reason not to provide working class Londoners with high quality homes in areas traditionally assumed to be the exclusive province of the middle class. Branch Hill was built between 1971 and 1978 and was controversial throughout (the Tory opposition on Camden Council was viscerally opposed to council tenants having pleasant living space in the heart of Hampstead). But in the end the estate provided twenty-one pairs of two-storey houses in three rows, all done in the signature Camden style of stepped terraces, smooth white concrete walls and dark-stained timber joinery.

Like many others, the working class boys who would go on to form Madness were born and raised in this network of Camden council estates. To get about they and others would jump on and off the North London Line, the "Magic Line" as it was known to working class kids who used it to travel back and forth between Hackney and Kilburn. In the early 1970s Lee Thompson lived on the Holly Lodge Estate in Highgate. But although his mum was an extremely honest person, his dad was not:

Dad was into warehouses and safe-cracking and "parcels", as they call it. Finding the keys to a lorry, normally round about Christmas, with all the electrical goods and cigarettes and alcohol on. Which is normally an inside job, half the time...I didn't really see much of him. I can count on my fingers the sort of things he taught us. "Do it at night and do it alone". That was one of his things.

Lee's mate Mike Barson was born in Edinburgh but the family soon moved to London, living in Robert Street on the Regent's Park Estate before moving to a house in Kentish Town when his mother was left money by her mum. Because they were new to the estate he and his brother were bullied by local kids, one time his brother being chased by a gang: *"He went and hid in a big bin container under all this cardboard. One of the kids found him and started pissing on the cardboard"*. I recall a similar incident when I was about ten, when a bigger kid chased me through Clarence Gardens on the estate and I hid unsuccessfully behind some bins. He didn't piss on me, though, instead he forced me to sit on a rickety plank with wheels and then propelled it down a concrete underpass.

Mark Bedford, whose dad worked a printing machine in Fleet Street, lived in part of a maisonette on an estate in Holloway with his parents. His entire family worked in the print, his grandfather on the *News of the World* in Bouverie Street for forty years, his uncle on the *Evening Standard* and the *Evening News* as a driver, delivering the papers. Of his boyhood, he recalled:

In the summer you'd be up really early and you just literally went out into the street. All the kids did the same, and we'd play football or cricket...It was down to the older kids to look after the younger kids. I have memories of the streets being very empty.

Mark recalls a particular North London working class attitude that shaped him and his mates growing up:

I was surrounded by a lot of people of my age who had a bit of hustle about them. A bit of "I want to be someone". Even if they were just local kids who were great at football, or they just dressed well. They'd have really good clothes, or they wore some piece of 70s fashion that you wanted. There was a culture of that. You were on the street, you were maybe working class, but you were looking good or being good at something or other.[11]

Camden Council also established a striking modernistic estate in the heart of Bloomsbury, although more by accident than design. The Brunswick Centre, opened in 1972, was originally a private development but after its finances collapsed it was bought by Camden Council and used as social housing. A multi-tiered mega-structure with stepped ranks of heavily windowed apartments and a pedestrian shopping concourse in the middle, its exterior was originally intended to be painted cream but Camden could not afford to do so and so it was left as simple white concrete, a form which has weathered the years very well.

Catherine Tate, born in 1969, grew up on the Brunswick. When she was five her dad left and she was raised by her florist mum and her grandmother (she later channelled her upbringing into classic TV comedy characters like Lauren and Nan). On most Saturdays during the later 1970s and early 1980s, after popping in to see my own nan in the old LCC Hunter House next to the Brunswick, I crossed through the Brunswick Centre on my way to the bookshops of Charing Cross Road. It was less well-heeled than it is now, many of its shops shuttered up and its pub an uninviting dive, although even then it contained the Renoir Cinema overlooking Brunswick Square. In 2006 the centre was given a lick of paint and sleek metallic water pools which lit up at night were added to its concourse. The improvement has been remarkable. One hundred of its four hundred apartments are now privately owned, but the block itself is still owned and managed by Camden Council.

The scale of council housing throughout the capital in the 1970s demonstrates that it was still a working class city, although invisible economic forces were steadily producing a "melancholy, long, withdrawing roar" of its established white working class culture. The last remnants of some of North London's more traditional working class employment, such as Challen's Piano Manufacturers on Hermitage Road next to Finsbury Park, gave up the ghost in the early 1970s. At the same time, new home ownership in Inner London was being driven out of the reach of working class people, even of those in permanent and decently paid employment. The average value of a Georgian house in Islington, of the kind that Gary Kemp's family lived in, increased from £6,000 in the mid-1960s to £130,000 in the mid-1970s.

The building of new estates by Camden and other London boroughs barely offset this. Although by the late 1970s the GLC was the largest public landlord in the country with a total of 222,000 homes, there were still not enough affordable council properties for London's working class. The chronic lack of accessible social housing in London produced an estimated 30,000 squatters in the capital in 1975, a mass movement given a voice by the Family Squatters Advisory Service (FSAS) based in Elgin Avenue and the All London Squatters movement (ALS). The most symbolic and high-profile squatters' action was the two-day occupation of the still empty Centre Point in January 1974 by activists from the Housing Action Group.

The second stage of the Tolmers Square Redevelopment Project, Tolmers Square itself, led to the most significant squatters action of the period. Joe Levy's front company Stock Conversion had already bought and sold most of the land adjacent to Euston Square, resulting in the demolition of old working class housing, the erasure of Seaton Street Market and the construction of Euston Tower. Stock Conversion also bought about a quarter of Camden High Street with a view to demolition and more office development (it was to be disappointed there). One of the last hold-outs was Tolmers Square or "Tolmers Village", a circle of dilapidated Victorian housing east of Euston Tower over Hampstead Road, which

Stock Conversion had deliberately let go to seed. Squatters had inevitably moved in and by 1975 the square had forty-nine separate squats housing over 180 people.

The squatters were mainly students and middle class dissenters, but they were animated by a genuine communal self-help philosophy and they forged real links with the local community. The spine of that community was Drummond Street, known for its cheap "all you can eat" Indian restaurants and the iconic Laurence Corner army surplus store, providers of the best and most extensive range of ex-military kit in London, which fronted Drummond Street and Hampstead Road. Local residents, having seen Levy buy up property and then leave it to rot, were mostly sympathetic to the squatters, who treated the occupied houses and their gardens with great care. John and Ethel Vine, who ran the corner grocery store, gave squatters food from their shop, as did Jayant Patel, owner of London's first vegetarian restaurant on Drummond Street.

The communal squat lasted until 1979 when it was finally dispersed. But while it didn't save the original houses, which if left *in situ* would in time have eventually been bought and gentrified, it did prevent the proposed office development and led to a compromise solution that followed the ideas of the 1978 *Tolmers People's Plan*, whereby Camden Council compulsorily purchased the site and constructed a new, low-level social housing estate built around a garden and community pub.

Similar squats cropped up in Gospel Oak, situated between Kentish Town and Hampstead with Parliament Hill Fields to its immediate north. Kentish Town was divided into Kentish Town East, where entire streets of terraced housing were waiting for the gentrification that would in time raise their value enormously, and Kentish Town West around Queen's Crescent, where large council estates had been built in the 1950s and 1960s, some good, some not so good.

Since 1865 Kentish Town High Street had been dominated by the antiquated Daniels department store, but it closed down in the early 1960s, leaving only Woolworth's for general shopping. By the 1970s there was little of interest on the High Street except Chamberlain's bicycle shop, Blustons Coats and

Gowns (known locally as "the nan shop"), the Jolly Anglers pub and the Forum Dance Hall on Highgate Road north of the tube station. The Grafton pub on Prince of Wales Road and the Pineapple on Leverton Road sustained social life in the area, friendly and welcoming in a way the darker, more functional Jolly Anglers was not.

Nearby Gospel Oak was a largely forgotten area that had been left derelict since the war, with whole streets full of empty properties marked for demolition by Camden Council. The old houses, as subsequent gentrification has demonstrated, merely needed some TLC and during the 1970s the area became home to the largest squatting community in North London, driven there by need and poverty. The squatters renovated the houses and set up communal facilities including a bakery, a nursery and an arts centre. At the very centre of Gospel Oak, on Lissenden Gardens off Highgate Road, sat a beautiful series of three five-storey redbrick Edwardian buildings built in Arts and Crafts style, with stained glass windows in their entrances and common parts and perfect views of Parliament Hill Fields.

The long-time owners of Lissenden Gardens, the Armstrong family, were benevolent paternalists who kept rents low but were lax about repairs. In 1972 they decided to sell the buildings to a property firm, prompting the tenants to set up a Tenants Association and petition Camden Council to buy the buildings and turn it into a council estate. Their petition failed and the estate was bought by a property company who immediately raised the rents. But the company had not reckoned with the residents of Lissenden Gardens, a typical North London mixture of bourgeois bohemian and working class dissident.

Initially the Tenants Association asked the council to buy the estate and then sell it back to the tenants to run as a housing association. However, the more left-leaning of the tenants felt this would not work and would lessen the estate's social diversity, so the campaign refocused to get Camden to buy and run the estate itself. When Camden issued a Compulsory Purchase Order on Lissenden Gardens in July 1973, the

Conservative government rejected it out of hand. But Camden Council, under its new leader Frank Dobson, got creative and started to issue "Dangerous Structure" notices around the estate, requiring the new owners to repair all such designated areas. It also bought up any empty flats. Feeling the pressure, the new owners backed down and in October 1973 Dobson, later to be Labour MP for Holborn and St Pancras, announced that the council had bought the estate for £2.8m.

Camden's Labour councillors and Lissenden Gardens tenants headed back to the estate to celebrate. Frank Dobson remembered:

> *The bath in the bathroom —it was one of the big, big ones — was entirely full of ice and expensive champagne. The owner said to me "Once we've cleared out the champagne, now we're council tenants, we'll obviously have to keep coal in the bath."*[12]

Ironically, in November 1973 squatters occupied the empty flats in Lissenden Gardens, leading to complaints from some tenants that they were jumping the queue for council flats. Squatters usually took over empty properties owned by local councils, sometimes coalescing together to form larger communities such as those in Elgin Avenue in Maida Vale, Talacre Gardens in Kentish Town and Tolmers Square. In 1974 hundreds of homeless and semi-homeless people moved into vacant flats in Goldie House, Welby House and Ritchie House on the Hornsey Rise Estate between Archway and Crouch End. They formed a proto-community, the disparate social elements of which were described by one of the squatters as

> *students, intellectuals, a group of Italians who, it strikes me now, may have been part of the Red Brigades, ex-soldiers, junkies, anarchists from Paris, acid heads, families, rent boys, a few professional people, older teenagers who were past the age of foster care, a former professional boxer. Of course, there were conflicts but I have never known another place where spontaneous events, friendships and romance occurred so naturally.*[13]

Many council tenants did not welcome squatters, either because they disliked their lifestyle or because they saw them as queue-jumpers, grabbing vacant council properties for which their friends and family were patiently waiting. This wasn't always fair. Many vacant properties were not council-owned and were deliberately kept empty by their owners to accrue value and be easy to rent later. Many squatters were not drop-outs but working class men and women, some with kids, with nowhere else to go. But it was a widespread perception, not dispelled in 1975 when the Hornsey Rise squatters were evicted and the three blocks were once again used to house council tenants.

Sometimes local councils inherited housing problems which they then had to solve. Charles Rowan House, a striking Expressionist-style redbrick building wedged between Amwell Street and Wilmington Square in Clerkenwell, had been built in the 1920s for the families of Metropolitan Police officers, but by the 1970s it had gone to seed. In 1974 Islington Council purchased the building to become council housing but the building continued to decline, becoming one of Islington's "hard to let" properties. With many flats empty, squatters moved in. In an effort to defend their interests the residents set up the Charles Rowan Housing Co-operative, which lobbied the council for much needed improvements. These would eventually come, but not for many years. In the meantime, the social life of the area in the 1970s and 1980s centred on the New Merlin's Cave pub on Margery St, famous for its jazz, played in a room at the back, where on Sunday afternoons British jazz giants like George Melly and Bruce Turner played live to locals and their kids, who were allowed to tear about the pub as they liked

On the other side of King's Cross, the Hillview Estate, between Argyle Street and Cromer Street, had been built in the 1890s by the East End Dwellings Company for the "industrious working classes". A traditional estate of seven four-storey mansion blocks built around a central courtyard with staircase and balcony access, it extended almost to Euston Road and St Pancras station. Some of its buildings backed on to the long "Plum Pudding Steps" on Argyle Walk, where on Sundays in the early 1950s Ted and other teenagers played illegal dice games until the police arrived to disperse them. By 1974, when Camden Council bought the buildings, the Hillview had become the slum it was meant to replace.

At first Camden Council moved established tenants out but this simply freed up flats for drug dealers, prostitutes and vagrants, turning life for the remaining tenants into a nightmare. Camden effectively gave up running Hillview and turned it over to the charity Shortlife Community Housing (SCH), who in the late 1970s managed the estate on behalf of the council. SCH and Hillview Residents Association worked together to clean out the estate and rid it of its brothels and drug dens. The antagonism between squatters and tenants threatened to turn violent until a report in the *Camden Journal* in 1979 exposed the situation and demanded immediate action. Finally, tenants and those squatters interested in making the estate a decent place to live joined forces in the Save Hillview campaign and local Labour councillors began to listen to them.

In the end it was tenants themselves who cleaned up the estate, forced the pimps and dealers to leave, held communal parties in the courtyard and even welcomed referrals from groups such as the Terence Higgins Trust and African Refugees Housing Action, so much so that in the 2020s the Hillview has a thriving Ethopian community. Camden Council agreed to refurbish and improve the estate and hand it over to a tenant-led Community Housing Association, with those short-life tenants who had worked to turn the estate around given assured tenancies. John Mason, who in 1978 became Hillview's first short-life tenant and who was still living there forty years later, told a local researcher:

Hillview has settled into a diverse and tolerant community. Short-life housing is full of oddballs; its long-term legacy is an estate where very different people live relatively harmoniously together.[14]

The Hillview Housing Association followed in the footsteps of the Stephen & Matilda Estate in Wapping, adjacent to St Katherine's Dock and Tower Bridge, which in 1978 became the Stephen & Matilda Tenants Co-operative, the first local authority estate to be established under tenants' control in Britain. By 1974 the estate, old LCC housing consisting of two five-storey tenement blocks built round two courtyards, was fully occupied by well-organised squatters who after years of campaigning succeeded in establishing it as a new housing co-operative. One of its prime organisers was tenants' rights activist Peter Kemp, a fifty-year old social worker and mature student at Queen Mary College, University of London between 1981 and 1984, one of the most intelligent and modest men I ever met. He was proud of his small flat there and the values of the new co-operative.

The paucity of social housing and the cost of private housing was not the only existential problem facing London's working class. Although manufacturing industry had never been a huge part of North London's economy, the engineering and electrical factories of Acton, Ealing and Hounslow had provided jobs for *all* Londoners. In 1971 the Park Royal industrial estate still contained five hundred firms employing 39,000 workers. Further out, one of the biggest industrial firms in London, the Eastman Kodak plant in Harrow and Wealdstone, employed more than 6,000 people at its peak in the 1970s and was heavily unionised by the TGWU. The backstreets of North Kensington were also full of firms such as Fidelity Radio. Fidelity employed over five hundred workers at two sites in Olaf Street and Blechynden Street making stereos, tape recorders and radios.

Fidelity was owned by a vicious bully named Jack Dickman who paid low wages and refused to recognise the AEUW union. In April 1974 a strike broke out to recognise the union, supported by most of the women workers, including its young "quality control inspector" Myra Scales. Myra had worked briefly at Marks & Spencer and the Heinz factory at Park Royal before securing her job at Fidelity, a job she put at risk by supporting the strike:

We all went outside at Olaf Street on one particular day, to make it clear that we wanted a union at the firm. Jack Dickman came out of the factory and shouted at us "Get back inside, you bastards!" Some people went to move back inside, but we said to them "No, you've got to stay! He's got no right to talk to you like that!". They did stay, and the union was allowed to negotiate with the Dickmans. After that a union was established at Fidelity. We were all put on an hourly rate. We still got a bonus, but it wasn't our wages.[15]

From the mid-1970s these bastions of London's remaining industry began to close or relocate. Lucas Aerospace in Acton shed 1,500 jobs and the General Electric Company in Willesden lost 6,000 over the course of the decade. Leading firms like ICI, Thorn EMI and Rank Xerox moved entirely out of London to more convenient sites near the M4 at Reading, Swindon and Bristol. Large furniture manufacturers in Tottenham Hale like Harris Lebus and Bambergers, located since the 1900s near Ferry Lane Wharf on the River Lea because it offered a quick route to transport wood to and from the Thames, closed down in the late 1960s and early 1970s.

At its zenith in the 1950s and 1960s Gestetner's, the world-famous manufacturer of the stencil duplicator, had employed over 6,000 people at its factory in Broad Lane, South Tottenham. In the 1970s, in a huge blow to North London's economy, it closed and relocated to Northampton. By 1980 Acton's massive laundry sector had mostly closed, shedding 5,000 jobs with it. A seven-week postal strike in 1971, when for the first time postal workers and mail delivery workers in London went on strike simultaneously, opened up delivery of mail and small packages to private motorcycle couriers. New firms like Mercury Despatch adapted mini-cab radios for use by motorbikes. Soon their orange Suzuki GT250s were delivering messages and packages all across London, especially in its busy centre.

The nature of working class employment in London now began to tilt decisively towards the welfare services, the NHS, London Transport, local authorities, retail, catering and leisure services, self-employment, market trading and a variety of cash-in-hand illegalities; and for an increasing number, structural and semi-permanent unemployment. Fred Rooke personified this process. From 1950 to 1975 he had worked as a crane driver at British Rail's King's Cross Goods Yard (now Granary Square). He did the job to bring home the bacon to his family, not because he loved it or the employer, both of which he loathed:

> And when they closed that goods yard (in 1975) we all, including me, all walked off — no pension, no nothing. We was treated terribly. I wish I'd never seen the place.

From 1975 Fred worked as a driver for Islington Council and found it a very different working environment. Unlike the Goods Yard he enjoyed a clean restroom, shower facilities, decent pay and an on-site trade union representative to whom he could take any concerns. From the security of his new job he took immense pride in his two children going on to Grammar School and, eventually, becoming a head teacher and a local authority finance manager.[16]

In the early 1970s Vic Heath found himself on a construction industry blacklist for his trade union activities on various building sites, including the Barbican and the huge Thamesmead development. Turning to the public sector, he applied for a scaffolding job at LT's Acton Works, where the union convenor was Don Cook, his old CP comrade who in 1960 had fought with Arthur Rowe against the St Pancras rent increases. But even though it was a public body and the work was not on building sites, LT management still used the blacklist and tried to sack Vic after a few days. The move failed when Don Cook informed them he would bring the Acton Works to a standstill if they proceeded with it.

The job involved joining the National Union of Railwaymen and after nine months in post Vic was elected shop steward. He later transferred to Golders Green, much nearer to his home in Camden Town, and was promoted to Safety Officer for the Northern Line. Unwisely moving back to the private sector, he was again subject to the blacklist, forcing him in the mid-1970s to take up a lowly labouring job with Camden Council. However Vic's professional and union expertise was by now acknowledged and he soon became a full-time union convenor with his own office, a position he held for the next twenty years.[17]

As late as 1975 a horse-drawn coal merchant's cart still regularly trudged up Tottenham High Road and Brown's Bakeries in Philip Lane, Tottenham, sold bread and pastries on a hand-held cart, but such sights were getting rarer. In the 1970s London's street markets appeared to be thriving but their future health was not assured. Inverness Street Market in Camden Town had been bustling from 9.00-5.00 Monday to Saturday since 1860, with fruit and veg stalls, good quality cheap clothes and household items. In the 1970s it was still busy, known for its first-rate cheese stall that offered continental cheeses for less than delicatessen prices. Not officially part of the market, Haral's Greek Food Centre on the street had been going since the 1940s, selling a wide range of European and Oriental foods. Stall holders and customers frequented the Good Mixer pub on the corner of Inverness Street and Aldrington Street, an old working class boozer that got a new lease of life in the 1990s from *arriviste* pop stars and their hangers-on.

Church Street Market, running from Edgware Road to Lisson Grove, was open Tuesday to Saturday and its over two hundred stalls provided an eclectic range of merchandise including fruit and veg, antiques, carpets and general bric-a-brac. Its western end, providing mostly fruit and veg and household hardware, was alive with a mixture of Irish and West Indian working class and seedier elements staggering in from Paddington. After shopping at the market many of its customers went to the Regent Snack Bar on Edgware Road for pie and mash, the Lord High Admiral pub on the market or the Sea Shell on Lisson Grove for London's finest fish and chips. On Sundays and Mondays, stripped of its stalls, Church Street was a dead zone where kids played on the empty road.

Over in King's Cross, Chapel Street Market continued as the social hub of working class Islington, larger and more popular than it had ever been (the iconic opening credits of *Only Fools and Horses* used Chapel Street Market to establish its milieu and shots of Del Boy walking through "Peckham market" are actually of Chapel Street). But the writing was on the wall for some of the traditional street markets. Contrary to urban mythology it wasn't always "gentrification" that killed them. By the late 1970s Exmouth Market was virtually empty, reduced to a few struggling stalls. Most of its pitches and half its shops were vacant despite large potential custom from nearby Mount Pleasant Sorting Office and the *Guardian* offices in Farringdon. Only the intervention of Islington Council's Planning and Conservation Departments kept it going and spruced it up, a life-support that in the 1990s led to a very necessary regeneration.

Berwick Street Market in Soho, dating from the 1840s when the area first became densely populated, was still untouched by modernity and attracted a mixed crowd of actors, strippers, prostitutes, locals and tourists, although since the war it had lost its millinery trade to Oxford Street and now concentrated mainly on exotic food. Portobello Road was still going strong in the 1970s, held together by its two thousand antique stalls, and would for a couple more decades yet. Other traditional North London markets such as Queen's Crescent off Kentish Town, Whitecross Street in Clerkenwell, Leather Lane in High Holborn and North End Road in Fulham, continued to provide local residents with a wide range of goods and food, as they do today.

Earl's Court lacked a large street market but was sustained by a colourful assortment of shops, cafes, bars and eateries full of customers from the area's squats and bed-sits, leavened by a good number of builders and cleaners from the local Polish community. The Hot Pot on the intersection of Hogarth Road and Hogarth Passage sustained many of the poorest and underpaid, offering French bread and butter for 7p, soup for 9p, spaghetti bolognese or chicken-rice and vegetable for 30p, and tea or coffee for 10p. The Hot Pot was surrounded by a dense collection of pubs and bars, including the Tournamant pub and the Pontevecchio Italian restaurant on Old Brompton Road, the two quality stand-outs on a stretch of old-style cafes and bars, all of which provided employment to cooks, table staff and cleaners. At the end of Hogarth Passage on Stratford Road sat the Singing Bamboo, a restaurant/club that offered a wide range of pan-Asian food cooked by both Indian and Chinese chefs. At night the basement of the Singing Bamboo transformed into a live music venue where customers ate at tables whilst enjoying the music.[18]

In 1976 the UK's first American-style shopping mall opened in Brent Cross, having taken nineteen years to build. Upon completion it had seventy-five stores, indoor fountains, air conditioning (unheard of in London at the time) and was open late every weekday. It was the future of working class shopping whether you liked it or not. My one and only trip to Brent Cross, four stops up the Northern Line from Chalk Farm, was with my mum shortly after it opened. I must have been there to carry the shopping. We never went back, mum preferring Camden Town and Oxford Street. At almost the same time the second branch of McDonalds to ever open in London (the first, bizarrely, was in Woolwich) appeared on Seven Sisters Road. Inside its plastic hall customers could get a Big Mac, fries and a coke for 49p.

Cultural changes reflected social demographics. Between 1971 and 1981 a further 750,000 people, nearly 10% of the total population of Greater London, moved out of the capital. Most of these were the white working class seeking a new life in Essex, Kent and Sussex. But although white working class individuals and families left London for what they perceived as a better quality of life (whether they and especially their children saw things that way twenty years later is not clear), the working class as a collective entity did not leave London. By the early 1970s London's working class was already multicultural. By 1971, 55% of the UK's entire West Indian population lived in London. In 1951 the total Indian and Pakistani population of Tower Hamlets had been less than a thousand. Forty years later the total Bangladeshi population of the borough was 36,000 and by 2011 it was 81,000, sustaining a vibrant "Banglatown" in Spitalfields. In the early 1960s there were only a few hundred Indian restaurants in the entire country. By 1980 there were 7,500 of which nearly 1,500 were in London.[19]

In 1971 Robert Elms started school in Edgware and remembers:

On my first day at Orange Hill School in 1971, I would estimate that "indigenous" white English was a minority in my class. There were a large group of Jewish boys, a pair of brilliant Nigerian twins, an Italian whose dad ran the local café, some Indians, Greek Cypriots, a Maltese lad, a Polish kid from RAF stock, a Grenadian and just the one Irish boy, Patrick.[20]

But Elms made a point of mentioning that the Catholic school on the same road had hundreds of first and second generation Irish kids, the Irish strain being easily the strongest in their patch of North London, just north of Kilburn and Cricklewood.

Graham McPherson, later to become famous as Suggs of Madness, started at Quintin Kynaston Comprehensive on the St John's Wood end of Finchley Road in 1972 and had much the same experience. A large school for 1,700 boys from the council estates of Camden, Kilburn and Maida Vale, Quintin Kynaston was a Comprehensive in the true sense of the term, taking, in Suggs' words,

Kids of every ability from the top to the very bottom. Every cultural background: West Indian, African, Pakistani, Indian, Chinese, Greek, Turkish and, given the school's proximity to Kilburn, a huge proportion of second generation Irish.[21]

Many of Suggs's friends lived on the Regent's Park Estate, setting off across Regent's Park every morning to walk past the Zoo and across St John's Wood to arrive at Quintin Kynaston by 9am. I had the same experience at the same time, but while I walked south over Regent's Park to Marylebone, many of my friends went off to Quintin Kynaston. Suggs's time at the school was the basis for "Baggy Trousers", Madness's most popular song and an enduring anthem of working class schooldays ("Off to fight the next-door school, every term that is the rule", a rule followed by Rutherford Comprehensive on Penfold Street, Lisson Grove, which at the beginning of each term trooped around to St Marylebone Grammar to give us a kicking as we emerged at the end of the day).

Schools inevitably reflect population movements. In the post-war years the large concentration of working class Jews in Hackney continued to disperse north-west towards Hendon and Golders Green, becoming middle class as they did so, although in the 1970s 15% of Hackney's population were still Jewish (mostly the Orthodox Jewish community of Stamford Hill). In similar fashion Greek Cypriot families in the 1970s began to gravitate north from Camden Town to Finsbury Park, Wood Green and Palmer's Green, a two-way traffic between generations sustained by the number 29 bus. Greek Cypriots congregated on the northern end of Green Lanes near Harringay Stadium while Turkish Cypriots, who began arriving in London in greater numbers after Cyprus became independent in 1960, coalesced on the southern end near Stoke Newington, an enclave that became known as "Famagusta N16". The entire thoroughfare was dotted with Greek and Turkish Cypriot cafes, restaurants, greengrocers, banks and newspapers, and still is.

Greek restaurants became popular in North London in the 1960s and 1970s, especially in Camden Town and Mornington Crescent. Greek Cypriots also established a thriving rag and clothing trade in Finsbury Park, on the street-front showrooms and backstairs factories of Fonthill Road and Blackstock Road, which dominate and define the area to this day. Turkish restaurants were rare in the 1970s but the Turkish community did introduce one important dish into London's street life. The Doner Kebab made its first appearance in Britain in 1966 with the opening of the Hodja Nasreddin Kebab House in Newington Green. In the 1970s a rapidly expanding number of kebab houses, Turkish and Greek, made the Doner available to those needing cheap, filling fast food before or after an evening in the pub. Robert Elms' first kebab was bought from a Greek restaurant in Edgware run by George Michael's dad.

Greek restaurants and Turkish kebab houses were appearing all over North London, but were nowhere near as plentiful as Irish pubs. Nearly half the pubs in London were Irish-run during the 1970s, and in Cricklewood, Kilburn, Queen's Park, Camden

Town, Kentish Town and Holloway Road that percentage was considerably higher. Some were large affairs with live music; some were cramped, unadorned and unwelcoming to any but hardened drinkers. Some of them, especially those in Kilburn and Camden Town, would pass round the bucket to collect for the IRA as the evening wore on, ringing out with renditions of "Bold Fenian Men" and "Off to Dublin in the Green". Pubs like Biddy Mulligan's in Kilburn, Mooney's in the Strand and the Favourite in Hornsey Road functioned simultaneously as drinking dens, collection points to raise money for Republican prisoners' families and employment exchanges for men seeking work on the sites.

A teenager at the time, Sean McGlinchey remembered

...feeling differently about Ireland than many of my more Irish second-generation friends. A couple of them had developed an Irish lilt in the way they spoke especially after returning from spending the whole of the summer holidays there. Almost all of the plentiful pubs in our area were Irish. There was one on almost every corner. Most of them would have Irish music blaring out, either records or a live band, on a Saturday and Sunday afternoon and evening catering for the nostalgia for the "old country" that many Irish immigrants craved. It was as though time had stood still and a little piece of Ireland had been recreated in the Harrow Road.[22]

Biddy Mulligan's, on the corner of Kilburn High Road and Willesden Lane next to Brondesbury Mews, was the unofficial meeting place of both the Official and the Provisional IRA in London. Sinn Féin claimed to collect about £17,000 a year for the IRA in Kilburn, a lot of it in Biddy Mulligan's. It was so well known as a gathering spot for IRA sympathisers that in December 1975 the Ulster Defence Association (UDA) bombed it, the first time the UDA had launched an attack outside Ireland.

Irish Londoners had already produced Camden's first Irish-born mayor, Paddy O'Connor, in 1966-1967. Michael O'Halloran, who had arrived in London aged fifteen in 1948 from County Clare to work on the railways, became Chairman of Islington North Labour Party in the 1960s and in 1969 was elected Labour MP for the constituency (succeeded in 1983 by Jeremy Corbyn). Called "the least coherent man to ever come to the House of Commons" by veteran left-winger Tam Dayell, O'Halloran admitted that he had been selected as Labour candidate by the "Irish Mafia" and was surprised to be there.[23] As a staunch Catholic he strongly opposed the legalisation of abortion and in 1981 was one of twenty-eight Labour MPs who defected to the Social Democratic Party.

The resumption of the Troubles in Northern Ireland from 1969 and the IRA's bombing campaign in London in 1973-74, particularly the Birmingham and Guildford pub bombings, caused problems for London's Irish community, but not as much as many feared. They were simply too many, too much a part of London's social fabric, especially in areas like Kilburn and Camden, to be isolated and intimidated. Despite the occasional show of public support for Irish Republicanism — in June 1974 a funeral cortege of 5,000 people for IRA hunger-striker Michael Gaughan marched through Kilburn to Sacred Heart Church on Quex Road — the fact that 85% of Irish immigrants to London came from the Republic meant the Troubles were not central to their lives.

Irish Londoners had so much more to keep them occupied. By the 1970s there were frequent Irish cultural festivals in Roundwood Park in Harlesden and Queen's Park in Kensal Rise. Camden Town was an exciting alternative to Kilburn, with pubs like the Dublin Castle, the Bedford Arms, the Rat and Parrot, the Devonshire Arms, Mother Red Cap and the Buffalo Bar (later to become the Electric Ballroom) renowned for live Irish music. But although Irish identity and affinity was strong in the London Irish community — Irish festivals, Irish pubs and dance halls, regular trips back to Ireland for second- and third-generation London Irish — it was still a *London* Irish identity. Patrick, born in the early 1950s in Kilburn, married another first-generation Irish woman and his children went to Catholic schools. In spite of that he still felt:

Growing up in north London we had exposure to other cultures.

Going to school, the number of Italians there were! You went to the restaurants of the Italians in the class, I had a job waiting in one. So you learned how they did things differently, like they got married on Sunday, which we didn't, all the little cultural differences, so you were much more open to people doing things in a different way.[24]

In Shepherd's Bush, Richard Gregory experienced the same immersion in other cultures:

But in the 1970s Shepherd's Bush Market became popular with new arrivals from the Middle East, and began to transform into the cosmopolitan and multicultural district that we know today. I am very much in favour of the change (and the food has improved immeasurably). It took time, certainly, but I like to think that Shepherd's Bush is now a place where people of all ethnicities generally get along rather well. In the Brexit referendum the constituency voted overwhelmingly to remain in the European Union, though the national vote narrowly favoured xenophobia.[25]

Sean McGlinchey, after taking his O Levels at St Aloysius Catholic School in Archway, a long trek from his home in Queen's Park, transferred to Kilburn Polytechnic to take his A Levels:

The Poly could not be more different from St Aloysius. It was multicultural and had women as students and teachers. It was a liberating feeling but five years of a single sex education had made me self-conscious and tongue tied around women. The teaching itself was liberal and respectful. I enjoyed the freedom too much and found it difficult to have the self-discipline to both study and have a good time. I chose solely to have a good time and failed 2 of my 3 A levels. I knuckled down, re-sitting and passing them by myself and got through clearing into Lancaster University.[26]

By the 1970s other North London boroughs were also undergoing rapid transformation. Hackney was no longer Alexander Baron's half-forgotten post-war landscape. On Mare

Street and Dalston Kingsland shoppers could drop into Marks & Spencers, Woolworths, Percy Ingle Bakers, John Colliers and, a local favourite, the Cottage Kitchen deli. It was only a short walk up Stoke Newington High Street to Sam Stoller the Fish Specialist and The Egg Stores, London's finest Kosher delicatessen. But Hackney's side streets were full of shop fronts covered in corrugated iron, shabby mini-marts and dodgy pavement car dealers, and many of the borough's Victorian houses were so neglected and decayed that even squatters avoided them. The Hackney Empire, next to the Town Hall on Mare Street, was still open but it had declined from its glorious Music Hall heyday, which would return in the late 1980s, and until 1984 was used as a Mecca Bingo Hall.

London's oldest community-run cinema, the Rio on Dalston Kingsland, offered the only local cinema to an area once full of them. The Hackney Picture Palace and Hackney Pavilion, once massively popular, had closed in the 1960s. By 1970 only the ABC on Mare Street and the Coliseum on Stoke Newington Road remained. The Rio had been running since 1909 and gone through several iterations as a silent and cartoon cinema, a short-lived art house venue and finally a burlesque joint. When it was threatened with closure in 1976 a group of locals took over the lease and turned it into a thriving independent cinema that also acted as a community and advice centre, as did the Centerprise bookshop/café on the other side of the road. Like Centerprise, the Rio offered facilities to the many socialist, tenants and squatters' rights groups active in Hackney in the 1970s, such as the Tape/Slide project, an initiative to teach unemployed young people the basics of street photography and how to construct a social history of their community.

Hackney was now home to a fast-growing Afro-Caribbean population, not welcomed by all of the white working class and never welcomed by the local police who harassed them at every turn. In response to growing need, new estates appeared in the 1960s and 1970s, most notably the Holly Street complex constructed between 1966 and 1971. The Holly Street Estate was the opposite of Sydney Cook's projects, with four nineteen-storey blocks slammed down on Queensbridge Road without much thought. But the estate's main problem were the nine low-rise five-storey blocks ranged in quadrangles around them, in themselves not badly designed but all connected by a mile-long internal corridor known as "the snake". The snake had no natural light at all, no air filters, no way to soften smells and noise that reverberated up and down it and into all its connected flats. Dark, dank and sealed off, it was a magnet for vandalism, muggings and drug dealing, and would have been no matter which borough it was in.

The old LCC Pembury Estate on Pembury Road had been a Hackney landmark since it was built in the 1930s. Patricia Daley arrived in the UK from Jamaica aged twelve to re-unite with her divorced mother. After first living together in a shared house in Dalston, in the early 1970s they moved into a flat on the Pembury:

We spent a year in a two bedroom 3rd floor flat in one of the 1930s blocks. The estate's residents were primarily white working class. Often, someone would daub "nigger" or "NF" on the stairwell and we would have to sidestep dog shit to get to our front door. I was thrilled when we moved into a newly-built three-bedroom house on the edge of the estate. Finally, I had a room of my own, though there was only space for a bed and a dressing table...Homework was done on my bed or in the public library. Hackney Library on Mare Street was a sanctuary and haven for me.

Patricia had a talent for languages and an interest in music and the wider world, and luckily encountered teachers who helped her along:

I got the opportunity to go the opera, ballet and musicals in Central London. My trips out of Hackney were dependent on these organised activities. For a year or two, we travelled on the 22 bus every Sunday to our black church at World's End in Chelsea, but we could not afford to break the journey. I would spend the journey familiarizing myself with London landmarks from the top deck of a double-decker bus.[27]

After school she took a course at Middlesex Polytechnic, supporting herself with a small grant from the Inner London Education Authority (ILEA) and by working part-time at Brent Cross. Janet later became an Oxford Don and a Fellow of Jesus College, but unlike most of her colleagues who theorised about the working class in academic journals, she knew of what she spoke, regularly visiting her old manor to take care of her ailing mother who still lived there.

Growing up in Hackney in the 1960s and 1970s, Amanda Millhouse experienced the borough's social transition. Although her working class Tory dad nodded along in agreement with the views of Alf Garnett on *Till Death Us Do Part* and casually used racist epitaphs at home, none of this passed on to his daughter:

> *When we were studying Othello, my A level English group were taken to the BFI on the South Bank to see the Laurence Olivier film. My class was 50/50 white and BAME girls. Larry appeared blacked up and rolling his eyes. We were outraged and couldn't stop laughing and started heckling. Our teacher was horrified at us, not the portrayal on the screen. We watched to the end and when we complained about the performance to our teacher, she could not understand why we were so disgusted.*[28]

The widening of horizons and attitudes was partly a result of the "gentrification" now routinely condemned. But the phenomenon was more complex than rocket-boosted house prices and social cleansing of council estates. In some ways, gentrification was a radical movement. As Jerry White observed of its pioneers:

> *They chose to widen their life experience among working class neighbours rather than the sort of people they had met at school. They took a risk rather than playing it safe. Through gentrification they rejected consumerism and the mass product of suburb or luxury flat or New Town house. Their energies went into reviving, with individual flair, the beauty of neglected old buildings.*[29]

In the mid-70s, when she was fourteen, Amanda first encountered the real people behind it when a middle class couple who lived across the street asked her parents if she would like to babysit for them:

It was my first contact with middle class people. He was an architect and she was a lawyer. Their house had bare brick walls in the kitchen, a rough farmhouse refectory table and we were given freshly ground coffee in a cafetiere. They also put out unsalted nuts even though it wasn't Christmas. The living room and bedrooms had huge paper lampshades and every wall was painted white. It was the start of gentrification in the street and I loved it. They were everything I wanted to be and when I came to buy my first flat, it was decorated just like their house.[30]

No area of London experienced this phenomenon more than Camden. Areas of serene middle class affluence such as Hampstead and Highgate and the Nash terraces around Regent's Park sat in close proximity to working class estates and a fair degree of hidden poverty, whether it was found on the estates or in squalid bedsits on quiet back streets. In 1970 when Nick Kimberly arrived in Camden Town to begin work at Compendium bookshop, he was shocked that for the first time in London, at Camden Town tube station, he saw people openly begging.[31]

There was another side to working class life in Camden and Islington. The municipalisation policy, i.e. the buying-up of disused properties by London councils, ensured that not all of their council tenants were housed on large estates. In 1975 Gary Kemp's family were relocated to a modernised terraced house in Elmore Street, off Essex Road, which as he recalled was a major step up:

My room was small, but at least after a hot bath I had my privacy. Mum got her avocado suite, and Dad finally had a garden to play in. To us, it was a mansion.[32]

In 1976 Islington Council bought from the GLC land and houses in the slum clearance area adjacent to King's Cross station, including Balfe Street and Keystone Crescent. Balfe Street was so derelict that it had been slated for demolition even before World War Two. In the post-war decades many of the flats on the street were owned by a shady outfit called York Way Motors who in 1970 sold them to Joe Levy's even shadier Stock Conversion. For a while their future seemed bleak but in 1975 numbers 5-35 were listed, protecting them from demolition. In the 1980s an alliance of the King's Cross Community Association and the Chair of Islington's Housing Committee, Margaret Hodge, ensured that they became part of the Keystone Crescent Conservation Area. The properties owned by Stock Conversion were then subject to a CPO from Islington Council.

Ted and Joyce were among the beneficiaries of munipalisation. In the early 1970s Rydal Water had begun to go downhill, with graffiti around the entrance and urine in the lifts, so Ted asked Camden Council if they had any alternatives. As luck would have it, they did, and in 1974 the Council moved our family to one of its properties on Haverstock Hill just up the road from Chalk Farm tube station, the top two stories of a slim Victorian house that came with two bathrooms and a view down the hill to the Roundhouse.

By the early 1970s Ted had moved on from Turner & Cooper to a builders firm called Howard & Co based in Floral Street, Covent Garden. It proved to be a turning point in his life when the firm's General Manager, Bruce, asked him to do some office work, manning the phones and keeping routine records, and then made him site manager on a few jobs. After working in the office and accompanying Bruce to various West End clubs, Ted, who had always appreciated a nice suit, begun to accrue other symbols of male status and style such as a Rolex watch and a gold Dunhill lighter, both of which he managed to get cheaply through various contacts. He also opened his first bank account.

When Howard's went into administration Ted's experience with the firm led to him running a small team of self-employed tradesmen for a landlord named John Grosman, who ran a "property management" business out of a few rooms above a dry cleaners shop in Praed Street, Paddington. Grosman was not entirely legit but he paid well, if in brown envelopes, and the work was unmonitored and informal, as Ted preferred. In 1972, when the police started to investigate Grosman, Ted moved on to a job as building manager for a property company called Associated Development Holdings (ADH), initially based in Belgravia but later moving to Dover Street off Piccadilly.

Very quickly Ted became a general fixer and chauffer for ADH's self-made millionaire Director, Mike Carlton. He earned a place in Carlton's inner circle during the power blackouts of 1973 by using a contact of his, a cash-only general dealer on Goodge Street called Morrie, so dodgy he was actually known as Dodgy Morrie, to obtain a number of high-wattage Tilly Lamps and three car batteries to provide light and power to ADH's Dover Street office. In order to drive Carlton's Rolls-Royce Silver Shadow, Ted had to pass a rigorous course at the Rolls-Royce Works on Scrubs Lane in Willesden, which he duly did with a first class certificate. Carlton, a contradictory individual with no social airs, liked to sit in the front passenger seat and chat about politics. On one journey he confided to Ted that he had begun his working life as a typewriter salesman and after bullshitting his way into property in the 1960s he now developed his portfolio more for fun than profit.

Most days started in the coffee bar of the Park Lane Hilton where Carlton and his inner team, including Ted, would plan the day's activities. Outside the boardroom these were often very direct. On one occasion Ted was tasked to take some of Carlton's men up to a compound on the freezing Norfolk Broads in the middle of the night and use a large pair of Stillson bolt cutters to remove the chains on the gates, whereupon Carlton's security team moved in and took over the property. Another job involved a quick flight to Jersey to pick up a packet of diamonds, return and deliver them to his boss. The work met the two essential criteria for an ambitious working class hustler — it paid well and it was never boring.

Ted's life on Haverstock Hill complimented his work for Carlton. In the 1970s Hampstead and its environs were not as wealthy as they later became and there was a large working class presence in the area. The Maitland Park, Dunboyne and Queen's Crescent estates were only a few minutes' walk from the Heath and the older LCC South End Close Estate sat right at the Heath's southern tip, directly across South End Green from the Hampstead Classic cinema. The Classic was the nearest cinema to Haverstock Hill and during the 1970s and 1980s I probably saw as many films there as in the West End or, the other favourites, the Parkway Cinema and Swiss Cottage Odeon. The cinema sat directly across the road from the second-hand bookshop where George Orwell had worked in the 1930s (since replaced by a Gail's Artisan Bakery with a strange non-Blue Plaque to commemorate Orwell's time there). Saturday nights saw large crowds milling around the Green for a film and a kebab across the road. The Classic is gone now, replaced by an M&S Food Hall, but South End Close Estate is still there as are the Dunboyne and other nearby estates.

Chalk Farm and the Hill had a distinct if unflashy cosmopolitan air even before the Roundhouse opened as the Centre 42 arts venue in the 1960s. In 1947 Mansi's Café, run by the Italian Mansi family since 1931, transformed into Marine Ices, purveyors of a wonderful range of Italian ice cream. Directly opposite Chalk Farm tube station, it quickly became a London landmark. In 2013 Gerry Slater, who like me enjoyed ice creams from Marine Ices regularly as a kid and teenager, recalled:

My Dad used to be a black cab driver, and he told all his punters that Marine Ices sold the best ice cream in London. As a child he used to take me up there in the cab. My only experience of ice cream was a "Toni Bell" or "De Marco's" whipped cornet. They were great but this was a whole new ball game. The colours, textures and smells blew my mind. It was heaven for a kid.[33]

Ted quickly found that the Hill offered the same level of stimulation as the West End's pubs and clubs. In particular our local pub, The Load of Hay, up the Hill towards Belsize Park, was home to a rich collection of artists, printers, painters and decorators, working class grafters and middle class eccentrics. As Ted experienced it:

> ...it was an amazing place, full of characters like Mick the Brick and Little Dave, self-employed builders who might be seen deep in conversation with a boozy accountant named Leslie. Mick and Dave's clientele consisted for the most part of fellow boozers in various Hampstead pubs and it was understood that they only worked mornings, afternoons being spent in the Load, most time in the company of those who employed them...
>
> At various times in the Load you could find Mickey the Fish, Brian the Buddhist or Mick the Murderer in earnest conversation with Hilary Mullin, a chubby left-wing QC with a deep and abiding love of vodka; Chris Berry, a tall, bearded Welsh computer wizard exchanging esoteric thoughts with Howard, an intellectual window cleaner. Drinks were served by two barmen, Flanagan, a black-bearded 6ft 2in Irish Guardsman and Tommy Cafferty, a card carrying member of the Czech Communist Party and editor of a Marxist magazine. The whole scene was presided over by landlord Michael Woodison and his Irish wife Sligo Lil.[34]

One of Ted's best mates on the Hill was genial Fleet Street printer Dave Noys, known as Big Dave to differentiate him from Little Dave, who every couple of years gave the front of our house a free lick of paint. The culture of the printers was notorious for "Spanish practices" that had evolved over decades and didn't seem to interfere much with the regular production of either tabloid or broadsheet newspapers. As pay was doled out in cash from the on-site cashier, one of the dodges was to sign on for a night shift, give a transparently false name, collect a pay packet, and then either go back home or down the pub. Big Dave's favourite alias was "Mr W. Woodpecker, 1 Upper Tree, Ealing Common".

Maurice Chittenden worked for News International, first the *Sun* and then the *Sunday Times*, for forty years. He recalled the Fleet Street of the 1970s, where huge low-loaders navigated down narrow Bouverie Street where the *Sun* and *News of the World* were based, to deliver reels of newsprint to cavernous press halls. The working culture, for journalists as much as printers, was relaxed:

> *After lunch — that was any time after 3pm — you were more in danger of being bowled over by a reporter returning to the office or intoxicated yourself from the alcohol on their breath. Returning to his desk the reporter would either hammer out a thousand words of purple prose or fall asleep over his typewriter, often both. When I had finished my first shift at The Sun I was handed a signed green chit to collect my pay from the cashiers on the ground floor. A printer was ahead of me in the queue. 'Name?' the cashier asked him. "Mickey Mouse," said the printer. "Address?" the cashier said. "77 Sunset Strip," he replied.[35]*

The two main print unions, the National Graphical Association (NGA) and the Society of Graphical and Allied Trades (SOGAT), maintained a closed shop in the main newspapers and did not make any serious attempts to discourage the printers' working practices. These were steeped in a culture of skilled working class artisanship with its attendant jokes, rituals and ceremonies. James, a young printer in the late 1970s, recalled the traditional end of a trainee compositor's apprenticeship:

> *In broad daylight, around midday, a van pulled up in Fleet Street outside the art deco Daily Express building and two men bundled another young guy out of it. He was naked and painted purple from head to foot. They then tied him to a piece of street furniture on a central reservation in the middle of this busy road and drove off. He wasn't there for too long before he was covered and helped away though.[36]*

Jacky Hyams saw another side of Fleet Street as a news desk secretary in the *Sunday Mirror* building on Holborn Circus. In 1974, after years of temping with various disreputable companies in the West End she started with the *Mirror* and quickly sussed the nature of the workplace. Long liquid lunches in the pubs around Fleet Street were the norm. Many journalists banked their salaries and simply lived off their generous expenses, which were rarely if ever checked. Like nearly all young women working in an office environment in the 1970s she was routinely sexually harassed and propositioned. "You just dealt with it, no big deal," she recalled. In any event, with its culture of constant boozing and flirtation in nearby pubs, working at the *Mirror* was "...just the right job for a girl who loved partying, men, laughter and gossip".

Union meetings and procedures were a different matter. Jacky was apolitical, living for sex and her next holiday, and so was astonished when one day a deputation of three NGA representatives, all older men in dark suits, stood by her desk while one of them informed her that she had been overheard referring to one of their members as a Messenger when he was in fact a Tape Room Assistant, and unless she ceased using this term forthwith, "serious action" would be taken. She was not attracted to this culture or to trade unions in general:

This union stuff was way over my head. I'd had to be part of it to get myself here, but I really didn't want to get caught up in it in any way beyond that. It was just too...arcane.[37]

In 1976, after a series of disastrous flings and affairs, and thoroughly fed up with Britain, Jacky decided to emigrate to Australia, where she found the culture and lifestyle she was looking for and began a new life.

Contrary to left-wing folklore the culture of the print unions and their restrictive practices was not a primitive form of anarcho-syndicalism (on the contrary, many printers were conservative-minded working class men saving up to retire to the south coast). Nor was it any great crime. It was simply the working class equivalent of routine and far more extensive middle class professional fiddling, nepotism, generous expenses, liquid lunches, career leg-ups and other systemic privileges.

The fiddles of the printers were mirrored in the employment practices of certain London councils. Usually, the more continuous one party's hold on power in a borough the more relaxed and unaccountable became its internal working practices. Suggs recalled that in the 1970s, "*Working on the council was the cushiest number you could get: everyone was skiving or chipping off early, even the supervisors*".[38] In the late 1970s Tony Kilshaw got work as a maintenance carpenter for Camden Council:

> *I got the job by going to the union office in Camden. They rang the general foreman and told him they had a Chippy for them. That was it, no interview or qualification checks. Sadly, though, there was terrible corruption. When the wages van arrived on Thursday morning two black cab drivers would turn up to collect their wages. They were on the books as carpenters. This was just in one depot. Often, materials would disappear straight after being delivered to the depot.*

By virtue of the size of their membership, formal agreements with employers and established legal freedoms, trade unions in the 1970s had status and leverage since lost to them. Printers had a closed shop and they exploited it. Others *were* exploited and the union was the only defence. Tony remembered the industrial relations of the construction industry:

> *Work was easy to come by in the early and mid-70s in London. The* Evening News *and later the* Evening Standard *would have 5 or 6 pages of building jobs. I worked on building sites as both a labourer and a carpenter. I remember one site in Victoria where we were building a leisure centre. We decided to try to unionise the site and contacted UCATT for help. The union rep turned up, went straight into the site agent's office and got his permission before even talking to us.*[39]

The power of the unions, although providing better pay and conditions to working class people who worked in unionised sectors, tended to operate for the benefit of male workers who made up the bulk of their members. *Nightcleaners* (1974), a powerful and politically incendiary film produced by the Berwick Street Film Collective of radical and feminist film-makers, told the stories of low-paid female workers cleaning office buildings at night in central London and the campaign to unionise this precarious and exploited workforce. At one point, one of the filmmakers asked an older Irish cleaner, Ann, what she understood by the word "socialism". Ann said that for her it meant *"a better life for working class people, but that couldn't be, could it?"*, adding *"It's like asking for the Moon, isn't it?"*

Sheila Rowbotham, involved in making the film, remembered:

Most of the women we approached were middle aged and looked older. The accumulated exhaustion of working at night and looking after their families in the day, had marked their faces. Moreover a sizable minority were immigrants from the Caribbean and exceedingly nervous. They needed the money, little as it was, most desperately, moreover they were contending with racism in working class communities as well as in the job market.[40]

The opportunities, or lack of them, afforded working class Londoners tended to reflect which part of the city they moved within. In the 1970s Holloway was still a solidly working class area full of rough Irish pubs, although house prices were beginning to rise steeply. Seven Sisters Road south of Finsbury Park was alive with a variety of shops like Matthew and Dewhurst butchers which bought its meat direct from Smithfield, Gibber's Greengrocers, and Richards the fishmonger which sold flying fish and shark as well as the standard fare. A new Argos opened in 1974 which quickly saw a lot of local custom. Holloway Road was bedevilled by constant loud traffic but it did possess the massive, ornate flagship of Jones Brothers directly opposite the old LCC Lorraine Estate. The store was the heart of the area and massively popular with its working class customers. The Lorraine Estate is still there today, suitably improved, but Jones Bros closed its doors in 1990.[41]

Camden was an area with more opportunity than most but in the early 1970s it was not the vibrant cultural hub it would soon become. Years of uncertainty about the proposed ring road around central London (which if built would have turned Camden Town into a massive motorway junction and levelled half the shops and homes in the area) had blighted any possible redevelopment. As a result, the Lock and the warehouses of the Goods Yard remained empty after W. & A. Gilbey departed, a stasis symbolised by the "Great Wall of Camden" separating the old Goods Depot from Chalk Farm Road. The Wall, more than six-feet thick, had been built in the 1850s to contain the spoil deposited after the building of the railway. In the 1970s it was a massive, forbidding barrier blackened by 130 years of coal dust, running two thousand feet from the North Yard stables to the Roundhouse.

Ray Picton, born in 1962, lived on the "Borrowdale" block of the Regent's Park Estate with his older brother, his postman dad Ernie and secretary mum Joyce. Ray and I went to the same primary school and became best friends. As a London postman Ray's dad received invites to Post Office socials held at the enormous Mount Pleasant Sorting Office in Farringdon, to which he took his wife and occasional guests, including sometimes my mum and dad, who were also taken there by Ted's mate Ronnie Garrett. Unlike mine, Ray's parents stayed on the Regent's Park Estate into the new century. After his dad died his mum continued to live in Borrowdale until 2018 when Camden Council moved her to comfortable sheltered accommodation just up the road, on Albany Street next to the Army Barracks.

Ray went on to become a primary school teacher in Hackney and eventually Head of a school in Wiltshire. His memories of Camden are not as bright as mine:

London was a bit of a shithole. Camden Town was certainly downtrodden with the Bingo Hall the main attraction (now an Odeon). Camden Lock was a flea market and everyone strived to move to Hampstead. Regent's Park was a solace and a world apart from everyday life. Living six floors up was isolating but with great views of the expensive houses in the distance.[42]

Like my own, my brother Jamie's perspective had moved north of Camden Town:

I travelled on my own on the tube from a young age, going to primary school on the underground after we moved to Haverstock Hill. I certainly don't recall any sense of danger or worry about travelling around London as a child. I remember walking from Haverstock Hill on a Sunday into Camden Town to play Space Invaders at an arcade (that would make it about 1978) and the place being deserted except for a few Irish boozers open.[43]

But the ground was shifting. In 1974 a new flea market opened on the land between the canal and Commercial Place which specialised in selling Mod, Rocker and Skinhead gear. The West Yard, where the old stables could be easily transformed into small craft workshops and cafes, was cheap to rent and so attracted a range of craftspeople such as jewellers, wood carvers, potters, glass workers and antique repairers. Within a year Camden Lock was buzzing at the weekends, a mecca for adventurous young people and bohemians of all types. Some of the new micro-businesses that opened in the 1970s, like Roger Stone's jewellers workshop in the West Yard, were still going in 2000. The Lock's success spread outward and new shops began to open between the canal and Camden Town tube station.

With fashion and food came music. The new market, which initially only opened at weekends, appeared at the same time as Dingwalls Dance Hall, opened in 1973 on the site of the old Dingwalls warehouse. Dingwalls was as much an instant success as the market, partly because it was possible to get alcohol there all day from 11 to 11, as long as you had food as well (usually a bag of chips). Like the market, the success of Dingwalls had a knock-on effect. In 1977 the Music

Machine opened at the Mornington Crescent end of Camden Town, followed shortly after by the Electric Ballroom directly opposite Inverness Street in 1978. The Caernarvon Castle pub, perfectly situated under the now iconic Camden Lock railway bridge at the corner with Castlehaven Road, crackled with live blues and jazz.

A critical mass was quickly reached and by the late 1970s Camden Town was generating the same kind of energy and youth culture as had 1950s Soho and 1960s Chelsea. Mark Bedford recalled:

> We used to go to Camden Lock a lot, because we were chasing girls. A lot of girls from Camden School for Girls used to work at Camden Lock on a Saturday, on the food stalls there. So we'd hang around the food stall and they'd give us tea and we might be lucky to get a burger or something, and when it got too cold we would move inside and watch the band at Dingwalls.[44]

Camden Town was inheriting the mantle of Ladbroke Grove and taking it to a new level. One of the Grove's most influential music shops, Rock On, began life as a record stall opened at an indoor flea market at 93 Golborne Road, near Trellick Tower, by Irishman Ted Carroll in 1971. Carroll, who was also managing a new London-based Irish band called Thin Lizzy, recalled the Grove of the time:

> The local population was predominantly black along with a few older bohemian types, some poor white families and lots of hippies living in squats. Everyone appeared to get on well on a "live and let live" basis.[45]

Rock On soon became famous for the quality and rarity of its 45s and 78s and was such a success that in 1974 Carroll opened another stall in Soho Market, renowned for sourcing and selling obscure records from America. In 1975 the operation expanded to 3 Kentish Town Road directly opposite Camden Town tube station. At the time rents in Camden were cheap and Carroll lived in a flat above the shop. Rock On, in tandem with Dingwalls, the Music Machine and the Electric Ballroom, established Camden as the new centre of London's pop culture. Not having much ready cash at the time, Graham McPherson nicked the 45 of John Lennon's "Imagine" from the shop.[46]

Whether it was the painters and decorators of Haverstock Hill or the stallholders of Soho and Camden, the kind of self-employment found there, with its relaxed attitude to convention and legality, was common in working class London. It was an attitude captured in two of the most acute portrayals in popular culture of North London working class men surviving on the fringes of the law in the 1970s: Adam Faith's Budgie in the ITV drama of the same name, and Norman Stanley Fletcher, the lead character of the immensely popular BBC comedy series *Porridge* (1974-1977).

Porridge, in particular, avoided cliché. Its protagonist appears a typical working class man from Muswell Hill, a *Sun* reader and passionate Spurs fan, but there is more to Fletcher. He doesn't blink when put in close confinement with ethnic minorities and gay men, in fact they become his close friends. Despite his oft-declared "looking after Number 1" philosophy, Fletcher is a mentor and protector of younger and more vulnerable inmates. His cynical commentary on 1970s society in *Porridge*'s underrated sequel *Going Straight* (1978) caught a flavour of life in the capital for the older working class male as his traditional employment opportunities dried up.

Despite this, decent employment could still be found in the public services. In 1974 St Pancras Hospital on St Pancras Way next to the station (expanded in the 1920s out of the old St Pancras Workhouse, an institution that in the 1870s saw over 20% of children admitted to it die within a year) was renovated and re-organised to focus on geriatric and psychiatric patients. I recall my great-grandmother Phoebe being taken in for a brief stay there in the early 1970s and visiting her in its very old-fashioned main building. From its opening in 1978 the largest employer in Hampstead was the NHS Royal Free Hospital on Pond Street, a mega-hospital that grew out of the closure of the Royal Free Hospital in Liverpool Road, Holloway, which had a long record of serving the area's working class since its establishment in 1850 as the London Fever Hospital, becoming part of the NHS in 1948 after amalgamation with the Holborn Royal Free.

The Liverpool Road Royal Free was noted for its large number of women's wards and a sympathetic approach to abortions. About one thousand babies were born there every year, including me in 1962. When it was slated for closure, Islington's working class mums staged a campaign to keep it open but in the end its work transferred to Hampstead. University College Hospital (UCH) on Gower Street also provided a wide range of jobs, including ambulance crews, porters and cleaners. In the 1960s and 1970s UCH employed over nine hundred nurses, of which about five hundred were student nurses. Most of these boarded nearby and made their own contribution to central London's nightlife.

In 1976 Joe Kerr, a callow eighteen-year-old from a small rural village, arrived in London looking for work and quickly secured a job on the buses. After training at London Buses Chiswick Works, which offered every kind of staff amenity including football teams, snooker rooms and staff excursions to Brighton or Calais, he was assigned to Stamford Hill Garage as a conductor on the 149. His first shift was a jaunt up to White Hart Lane on a Saturday afternoon as the ground emptied:

> *I grew up rapidly in the next few minutes as I tried to load my bus properly, and then collect the fares, largely failing in both tasks in the face of a full-blooded football crowd of 1970s vintage.*

Joe was dismayed to find that despite the multi-ethnic nature of London's schools and the devotion of its white kids to black music, many of their fathers, even in the public sector, had not quite caught up:

> *The canteen was a convivial and lively place, but of the three rows of tables that organised the space, those on the left were where white crews sat, those on the right were occupied by black and Asian crews, whilst the middle row was a neutral zone. There was little overt hostility, and mostly we were all happy to work*

*and talk together, but there were also supporters of the National
Front to be found.*

Of all the buses he worked on, Joe enjoyed the 243 the most
because it provided a rich panorama of North London working
class culture, its evening run taking it from Wood Green past
Tottenham's black Caribbean pubs to the Jewish Hasidic
community on Stamford Hill who caught the bus down to
Hatton Garden, then through old, pre-gentrification Shoreditch
and along Old Street, before turning south to drop off postmen
at Mount Pleasant Sorting Office and printers on Fleet Street
and, last of all, the "exclusively white and often racist" meat
porters of Smithfield at Holborn Circus, picking them up again
in the morning, frequently plastered after visiting the early-
opening Smithfield pubs.[47]

In 1974 the London Fire Brigade, required to adapt to
a change from a fifty-six-hour week to a forty-eight-hour
week, launched its most extensive recruitment drive since
the war. The newly enlarged force faced serious fires such as
the conflagration in December 1974 of the Horsley Hotel in
Maida Vale, a rickety and byzantine structure used by the hotel
industry to house cleaning and catering staff, a large number
of whom were migrants. Although firefighters from Paddington
Red Watch got the residents safely out of the building, they
were themselves trapped when a roof collapsed and three floors
came down on them, killing a twenty-six-year-old probationer
fireman. The Horsley Hotel fire resulted in the largest number
of LRB bravery commendations from a single incident.

Despite the dangers and tragedies, the LFB was a cohesive
and mostly contented workforce. When the Fire Brigades Union
(FBU) balloted for a national strike in 1977 for higher wages,
the men of the London Fire Brigade voted overwhelmingly
against taking industrial action. Come the strike, though, they
accepted the majority vote, heeded the call of the union and
came out, although by informal agreement the most serious
threats to life were attended to. The LFB's "brother" service,
the Met Police, had more serious problems. In 1972 Robert
Mark was appointed Commissioner of a force whose non-

uniformed branches, it was increasingly acknowledged, were riddled with corruption.

When Mark was Deputy Commissioner he had created A10, a unit within the Met tasked with rooting out corrupt officers. As Commissioner, Mark was given a remit to extend this work by the Home Secretary, politically embarrassed by the revelation in the *Sunday Times* that the head of the Flying Squad, Commander Ken Drury, had taken a holiday in Cyprus with a major Soho pornographer and associate of Bernie Silver, Jimmy Humphries, all paid for by Humphries. The story alleged widespread corruption in the Flying Squad and the Obscene Publications Squad linked to the Soho porn trade, one reason that trade had mushroomed during the late 1960s. In his autobiography, Mark explained that while he had encountered corruption in his career outside London, *"I had never experienced institutionalised wrong-doing, blindness, arrogance, and prejudice on anything like the scale accepted as routine at the Met"*.[48]

It was well known within West End Central that the Albion pub on Ludgate Circus and the Premier Club in New Compton Street were venues where police and criminals could meet, have a drink, suppress evidence and divvy up various criminal takes. Following the *Sunday Times* story, Ken Drury was suspended from duty and then resigned. But the writing was on the wall for Bernie Silver's Syndicate and the corrupt officers on its payroll. A raid on Jimmy Humphries' home found diaries with the names, dates and amounts of the Syndicate's payoffs, which led to a major investigation led by Superintendent Gilbert Kelland and A10. In 1974 Bernie Silver was sentenced to six years in prison for living off immoral earnings. Big Frank Mifsud got away.

A10's unravelling of massive corruption at the heart of the Met lasted five years, from 1971 to 1976, and led to the dismissal or "early retirement" of 478 bent coppers and the arrest of fifty of the worst offenders, including the head of the Obscene Publications Squad, Detective Chief Superintendent Bill Moody, and the head of CID, Commander Wally Virgo. But the underlying culture of the Met was hardly addressed. Despite Mark's reforms and the purging of West End Central, the force remained institutionally racist, and in some ways became even more so with the deployment of Special Patrol Group (SPG) vans in Inner London's black communities in the 1970s and 1980s.

The Met had still not come to terms with the fact that large and thriving black communities now existed in Brixton and Notting Hill. It especially distrusted any attempt by those communities to organise politically. In Notting Hill, the focus of black culture was the Mangrove restaurant and community centre at 8 All Saints Road. The Mangrove was opened in 1968 by Frank Crichlow, who arrived in the UK from Trinidad in 1953. Living in Paddington, in the 1950s he worked for British Rail but in the 1960s turned to music and politics. The Mangrove quickly became the heart of the area's Caribbean community, a meeting place for black radical activists and white allies, as well as the office for a local newspaper and an organizing centre for the Notting Hill Carnival.

The Mangrove was an affront to the Met's conception of how black people should behave and it was subject to continuous police harassment, being raided twelve times between January 1969 and July 1970. In August 1970 a protest march of 150 people headlined "Hands off the Mangrove" marched to Notting Hill Police Station, where it was attacked by two hundred police officers. This led to the arrest of nine people accused of riot, including Crichlow, the black activist Darcus Howe and the leader of the British Black Panthers, Altheia Jones-LeCointe.

In 2021 Steve McQueen, raised on the White City Estate, made the BBC film *Mangrove*, a powerful and compelling slice of history which brought the subject to a mass audience for the first time. It told the story of how the police attempted first to shut down the Mangrove and then to frame and imprison its most active supporters. The attempt failed, with the Mangrove Nine acquitted of all charges. The judge found there was "evidence of racial hatred on both sides", the first official acknowledgement of the Met's institutionalised racism. The opening of a new, revamped Metropolitan Police Training College at Hendon in 1974 seemed to do nothing to alleviate this.

The Met was reacting to a growing Afro-Caribbean culture in London. In 1966 London's first black publishing house and bookshop, New Beacon Books, opened in Stroud Green Road off Finsbury Park. Specialist reggae shops like Peckings in Askew Road, Shepherds Bush, were becoming popular with a large number of black and white Londoners. So, too, was the former gay club Crackers at the north end of Dean Street in Soho, taken over in 1972 by a new DJ and transformed into the soul music and dance hotspot of central London. Its Friday lunchtime slot, based on the assumption that not much work was done on Friday afternoon and kids would bunk off school then, quickly became essential, especially to black kids desperate to show off their sharp clothes and dance floor technique.

Harlesden in north-west London was also forging a new identity centered on black music and dance. By the mid-1970s there were dozens of record shops and record labels along Church Road, Craven Park Road and the High Street between Neasden and Harlesden. Harlesden was also the centre of a network of pirate and community radio stations that supported the black music scene. In 1968 Trojan Records opened at 12 Neasden Lane in a large warehouse called Music House and before long had launched reggae across the UK and the world via artists such as Jimmy Cliff, Bob and Marcia, Desmond Dekker, Lee "Scratch" Perry's Upsetters, the Maytals and Nicky Thomas. By 1975 Trojan was the biggest and most successful black music label in Europe.

Trojan reflected a British-Jamaican cultural fusion already well underway by the 1970s, a hybrid culture on full display at the revived Tottenham Royal which had evolved from a cradle of 1950s rock n' roll to hosting soul and reggae nights featuring Desmond Dekker, Gregory Issacs and others driving the British disco and Southern Soul dance scene. Eddy Grant, born in British Guiana, arrived in the UK in 1960 and lived with his parents in Kentish Town, attending Ackland Burleigh school in Tufnell Park before forming the Equals in 1965, the first racially integrated pop group in Britain. The Equals had a number of chart hits, including the 1968 number one "Baby Come Back" before Grant left the band in the 1970s to set up Coach House

Studio and Ice Records, based out of the grounds of his large house in Stamford Hill. His studio and record company built up and promoted an Afro-funk music that fused reggae, calypso, steel drum and electronic pop.

From 1974 the BBC Radio London show *Black Londoners*, fronted by Alex Pascall, gave a voice to the city's growing black community. Pascall had arrived in Britain in 1959 as a twenty-two-year-old from Grenada and eventually found a house in Crouch Hill, where he has lived ever since, meanwhile helping to organise the Notting Hill Carnival and other black cultural and musical events. *Black Londoners*, broadcast from Radio London's offices on Marylebone Road, was part phone-in and part news programme interspersed with music, providing a platform for many black artists and politicians. It started as a monthly show but was so popular it quickly went weekly and, from 1978 daily, became a mainstay of BBC Radio's output.

The Metropolitan Police's animosity towards this increasingly public culture was on full display at the 1976 Notting Hill Carnival. In 1975, for the first time, the Carnival fully utilised static and roving sound systems, dotted throughout the route, blasting out reggae and steel drum beats. Visitors loved the music, colour and rhythm and to the organisers' amazement it attracted half a million revellers who for two days held a street party across Ladbroke Grove and Notting Hill. Although there was relatively little trouble, it was a frontal challenge to the Met's racism, one it was determined to stamp on next time around. In 1976 Kensington and Chelsea Council tried to site the Carnival in Chelsea Football Club's ground at Stamford Bridge or on Wormwood Scrubs. The attempt failed, and it went ahead in its usual locale.

This time, the police were ready. On the first day up to twenty-five police officers surrounded each band even before they started playing. On the second day 1,600 police officers flooded the area of the march and surrounded and harassed bands and dancers. Robert Elms and his girlfriend tried to get into the area to join the street party but were stopped by an SPG patrol lined across Harrow Road, one of whom asked him, "*Why do you want to go in there with all the niggers?*".[49] Provoked by constant surveillance and needless arrests, black youths fought back and pitched battles took place across Notting Hill and Ladbroke Grove, resulting in the injury of three hundred police officers. For the rest of the decade the Met policed the Carnival with massive numbers, sometimes up to 10,000 officers at a time.

Few novelists considered the new black London working class worth writing about. The prime inheritor of Samuel Selvon's mantle was Andrea Levy, whose father arrived on the *Windrush* in 1948. Despite their middle class backgrounds her mother took in sewing and her father worked at the Post Office. Levy grew up in Twyford House on the Blackstock Estate, Elwood Road, between the old Arsenal stadium and Blackstock Road. After leaving Highbury Hill Grammar in the early 1970s Levy worked for a while in the wardrobe departments of the BBC in White City and the Royal Opera House in Covent Garden, devouring as many books as she could get her hands on in preparation for writing about the reality of her and her parents' lives.

Her first two novels, *Every Light in the House Burnin'* (1994) and *Never Far from Nowhere* (1996) are bracing accounts of growing up in North London's black working class in the 1970s and 1980s. Her debut novel is directly autobiographical, telling the story of growing up on a Highbury council estate, the subtle nuances of working class family life, and tending her father and mother as they pass through the NHS to their inevitable ends. In *Never Far from Nowhere*, Levy expands the story to the interlocking relationships of two sisters and the young men they encounter but grounds all of them in a specific working class milieu — *"Not within the sound of Bow Bells, wherever they were, but in Islington, North London".*[50]

While London's black culture thrived, its traditional centre of bohemian energy, Soho, had been overtaken by the porn industry. By the mid-1970s Soho contained up to 185 sex industry establishments of some kind of another, from strip clubs to porn shops and cinemas. In certain streets and alleyways this could be oppressive, especially to local residents. Despite, or more likely because of, this Robert Elms and many other working class teenagers were drawn irresistibly to the area and were not disappointed:

Carnaby Street was mods and skinheads kicking off, Wardour Street was rockers in the Ship before recording in heavy metal alley, Greek Street was "retired" actresses fallen on hard times, Meard Street was brothels, Walker's Court was clippers, Dean Street was funky knitting and twelve-inchers. This was a scrappy, scruffy, but neon-bright tenderloin with "models" available up every stairway, dancers in every cabaret and chancers in every boozer: sex, sex, sex; sell, sell, sell.[51]

The sex wasn't always sleazy. The first Ann Summers in the UK opened in September 1970 at Marble Arch, providing a variety of outfits, equipment and advice to men and women who didn't want to drop into backstreet porn shops. The shop was named after Annice Summers, the secretary of the original owner Kim Caborn-Waterfield. Annice fronted the shop and acted as *"an agony aunt for dozens of customers who came into the shop seeking advice on how to spice up their sex lives"*.[52] In 1971 Ann Summers was bought by David Gold, an imaginative East End entrepreneur, and it expanded into a franchise that in the 1980s was run by his daughter Jacqueline as the first "respectable" chain of sex shops.

Soho catered for other emerging subcultures. In 1969 an unusual shop called Dark They Were, and Golden Eyed (after a Ray Bradbury short story) opened in Bedfordbury Street near Covent Garden before moving to Berwick Street and finally to St Anne's Court, a narrow alley connecting Wardour Street and Dean Street. Dark They Were became the largest SF and comic book retailer in Europe, specialising not just in SF books but in American and British underground comics, fanzines, the occult and other esoterica. In its way it opened the minds of curious working class teenagers just as much as the sex shops and clubs that surrounded it. While Robert Elms was cutting a rug in Crackers up the road, I was exploring whatever Dark They Were had to offer.

Both of us, and many others gravitating to Oxford Street between 1968 and 1993, would have encountered Stanley Green, "the Protein Man", who walked the street every day with a large black placard with the stark message LESS LUST BY LESS PROTEIN. Stanley, born in Tottenham in 1915, travelled daily from his council flat in Ealing to Oxford Street to spread his message that too much protein led to sexual excess. Unfortunately for Stanley, many of those making their way to central London were quite keen on sexual excess and he was good-naturedly ignored by nearly everyone, and strangely missed when he died in 1993.

Addictive though it could be, Soho and the West End were only a part of working class life in North London. Saturday football and everything that went with it was a far bigger feature of that life, revolving around its four iconic football teams — Tottenham Hotspur (Spurs), Arsenal, Chelsea and QPR. The great rivalry was between Arsenal and Spurs whose matches constitute the "North London Derby". The rivalry was wound tighter by the result of May 1971's Derby when Arsenal beat Spurs 1-0 in the final minutes of the final match of that years' League contest to take the First Division. A week later Arsenal beat Liverpool 2-1 to win the FA Cup and thus the Double, the decisive goal scored at the end of extra time by popular Arsenal hero Charlie George, a local boy from the Holloway Road who famously lay on the turf with his arms in the air to celebrate.

By the mid-1970s Spurs had a team with iconic players such as Pat Jennings, Martin Peters, Martin Chivers, Steve Perryman and Glenn Hoddle. This didn't prevent a brief demotion to the Second Division in 1977, a humiliation reversed the following year. Despite this, the club was moving with the times. In February 1975 it opened the Spurs Shop on the corner of Tottenham High Road and Park Lane, selling a variety of club-related merchandise such as football kits, pens (55p a set), mugs (55p for one) and key rings (45p). Shortly after Spurs opened the Hotspur Club at the Chanticleer restaurant in Paxton Road adjacent to the ground, offering dining and ordinary membership. Relatively swish compared to the burger vans surrounding it, the club attracted players as well and was such a success that by 1978 there was a waiting list to join.

The nature of the support base for Spurs and Arsenal, whilst overlapping, reflected the clubs' historical and social roots. Spurs, based at their ground in White Hart Lane, was hardcore North London, a mélange of white working class, Afro-Caribbeans from Hackney and Tottenham, a large proportion of the Jewish population of Stamford Hill and North-East London, and assorted supporters from Edmonton to Golders Green. Brian Dennis, born in 1947 in West Green Road between Turnpike Lane and South Tottenham, spent most of his childhood around and, literally, *under* White Hart Lane, where a number of workshops and small factories were located:

> *For years and years you could see Thermos flasks being made under the ground — that was in one factory. There was another factory that made KiteKat, which is cat food...then, if you came up into the middle tier of the ground, almost at eye level, there was underground car parking. We kids used to be able to bunk in and play all our football underneath the pitch but above the factories. We used to play all our five-a-side football underneath the ground itself.*[53]

North of Finsbury Park support for Spurs came with the territory, so much so that the club entered the fabric of everyday life for many working class families in the north of North London. In their popular signature song Chas and Dave (not, as often assumed, East Enders, but from Edmonton just north of White Hart Lane) ensure that amongst the many things to elicit an angry cry of "Gertcha!" from their dyspeptic dad is *"Tottenham Hotspur, couldn't put one in"*. Spurs fans were always proficient with communal songs and chants. These ranged from "Nice One Cyril" —bastardised from a TV advert in 1972 for use on Spurs' full back Cyril Knowles, hence *"Nice one Cyril, nice one son, nice one Cyril, let's 'ave another one"* — to the joyous "We are the Yids!" chant flung back at rival fans who tried (but failed) to taunt the club for its unusually high level of Jewish supporters.

The hatred for Spurs amongst the more feral of its rival clubs' supporters was caught by John King's *The Football Factory* (1996), recording the fierce social tribalism that animated some of Chelsea's less sophisticated fans:

> *Tottenham have always had a reputation for being flash. Silver Town yids. They're the rich spivs to West Ham's poor dockers...You go through Stamford Hill and Tottenham and you wouldn't think you're in the same city as Hammersmith and Acton. We've got our Paddies down in West London, but none of these yid ghettoes.*[54]

Arsenal was different. After it moved to Highbury in 1913 it threw off its East London origins and attracted a greater amount of North London middle class support, epitomised in later years by Islington North MP Jeremy Corbyn. It also had a large base in the Irish and Greek Cypriot communities of Camden and Holloway — hence Harry Enfield's café owner Stavros's regular Saturday outings "up the Arse" — and throughout the Camden and Islington working class. Gary Kemp remembered, when he was twelve, the use to which he put his old turntable, amp and moveable mono speaker:

> *In 1971, when Arsenal won the Double and the outside of our house became decorated like a battleship, in red and white bunting, my brother and I placed the speaker on the window ledge to blare out the raucous "Good Old Arsenal" to the entire street.*[55]

Arsenal had a policy, going back to the turn of the century, of recruiting Irish players. From the 1970s to the 1990s many of the club's key players were Irish, including Liam Brady, David O'Leary, Pat Jennings, Frank Stapleton and Pat Rice. Brady, in particular, defined the team in the 1970s. Son of a Dublin docker, he became an Arsenal apprentice in 1971 and moved to lodgings in the capital. From 1973 to the end of the decade he was the crucial mid-field lynchpin of the team. Under the management of another Irishman, Terry Neill, Arsenal reached three FA Cup Finals in a row in between 1978 and 1980.

London Irish football support went two ways. QPR had an especially deep and passionate support base in the Irish working class of Kilburn, Kensal Rise, Hammersmith and Shepherd's Bush. From 1952 until 1967 QPR was a lowly Third Division team, even in 1967 when the club won the League Cup 3-2 against West Bromwich Albion thanks mainly to the mercurial talents of Rodney Marsh (raised in poverty in Stoke Newington but lifted out of it by apprenticeships with West Ham and Fulham before moving on to QPR). It remains the only major trophy the club has ever won. QPR's very lack of success, its relative nearness to the lives of its working class supporters, built intense fan loyalty. Sean McGlinchey recalls:

> I remember getting the QPR kit for my 10th birthday and the joy of wearing the iconic blue and white hoops of QPR with Rodney's Number 10 on my back down to the local Park for the first time. I remember going around the streets cutting peoples hedges at the age of 10 trying to get the 2 shillings and six pence (12 and half pence) that I needed to get into a game at the theatre of dreams, Loftus Road...QPR have been a constant in my life. I went there with mates, new girlfriends, and younger family members in the hope that I could convert them and get them to feel the magic that I felt.[56]

Steve McQueen recalled his first immersion in the world of Saturday football:

> The first game I ever went to was QPR v Liverpool at Loftus Road...I was seven years old so it must have been 1977. I went with my uncle Bertie. Stan Bowles was playing and that was a big deal. I can't actually remember the result, but I do remember that I had a packet of Wrigley's spearmint gum and I chewed the whole lot.[57]

By contrast, Chelsea were an eclectic mixture of West London working class and Kings Road style. Under manager Tommy Docherty the team had a good 1960s. It lost to Spurs in the FA Cup Final of 1967 but worked up to winning the UEFA Cup Winners Cup in 1971. But they had a terrible 1970s, only enlivened by the surprising chart success of their 1972 League Cup Final song "Blue Is the Colour", which reached number five in the charts and became indelibly associated with Chelsea's fans. Like QPR's, failure didn't matter to their hardcore fans. Suggs, a rare Chelsea fan in Camden Town, admitted:

As shit as Chelsea were in the mid-seventies, I loved going to the football. It was the highlight of my week. Squashed in the Shed with thousands of other kids just like me, singing, chanting and clapping in unison.[58]

Violence between competing football fans, always a part of the game going back to the nineteenth century, began to escalate in the 1960s. In 1967, on the evening of a "friendly" match between Arsenal and QPR, police intercepted hordes of QPR fans armed with swords and bayonets at Highbury and Islington tube station. The 1967 FA Cup Final, which saw vicious clashes between Spurs and Chelsea fans, seemed to mark a turning point and liberate sections of the main fan base to organise for regular rucks, but it was in the 1970s that it truly took off. Ray Picton remembered:

I was an Arsenal fan but most of my friends were Tottenham. I did spend a lot of time at White Hart Lane but Highbury was my spiritual home. At the height of fan violence I was once at Highbury for a Man United game. The usual banter between the two sides carried on until we all stopped in our tracks when a group of fans suddenly started chanting for Millwall! The inevitable terrace fight ensued.

One Boxing Day in the mid-1970s, when Ray was a teenager, he went with his dad to see Arsenal v Chelsea:

It was fairly uneventful until a group behind me and my dad started to fight each other. My dad turned round and said "do you mind?" at which point the fighting stopped. We walked to a safer place on the terrace and once we were away from them the fighting continued.[59]

Ray's experience was similar to that of QPR fan Robert Elms, which was that while gangs of hardcore hooligans could be terrifying to encounter, it was not that hard to avoid physical violence if you were not in an opposing gang looking for a rumble and if you kept your wits about you:

At Loftus Road, I regularly witnessed huge firms of hundreds of lads, from bigger, tougher teams, try and "take" the Loft, our humble home section; routinely saw pitch battles occurring while the game continued unaffected on the pitch. Watching Cold Blow Lane's finest clad in butchers' coats, tooled up, pissed up and riled up, coming your way, can certainly put the fear of SE1 into you...But it was also true that unless you specifically wanted to get involved, the violence had a remarkable way of dancing neatly around you.[60]

The survival skills needed to evade hassle at big matches transferred to other areas of life. Most of North London's working class, like most working class people anywhere, usually preferred to ignore politics. Sometimes that couldn't be done. Ted came up against the ruling class directly and personally when, in 1975, Mike Carlton temporarily wound up his property empire. Searching around for another job, Ted became the Security and Maintenance Supervisor of Eaton Square in Belgravia, a position he held for the next three years.

Amongst the tenants of Eaton Square were the Duke of Westminster, Lord Boothby, Lord Howard De Walden, Sarah Churchill, Roger Moore and Rex Harrison. Ted's office was a converted mews stable out of which he managed forty-eight porters and assorted contractors. He came to know a fair number of residents and contractors and occasionally met some of them socially in the Star Tavern, a pub in Belgrave Mews that attracted a mix of actors, racing drivers, police officers from West End Central and crime bosses like Billy Hill. On one occasion, when Sarah Churchill was once again blind drunk, Ted had to carry her back to her flat and dump her on her bed. On another, as the pub emptied after a long liquid lunch, he was left alone chatting to Christine Keeler about her glory years.

Each block in Eaton Square was attended to by a live-in porter who was expected to be available to the residents twenty-four hours a day, fixing boilers and cleaning the common parts. Many were afraid to go out in the evening in case residents complained. They could be easily exploited as they had no employment contract, a situation that one of the porters, Derek Lumley, a TGWU shop steward, was attempting to rectify by asking Ted, each time he requested a particular task be done, point to where it said that was part of the porter's job description. Ted greatly respected Lumley who reminded him of his old friend and CP activist John Bowles, and so he suggested to the Grosvenor Estate, who owned the Square, that it was time to create a proper employment contract for the porters.

Eventually the Estate conceded and a twining system was created that provided porters with a specific amount of time off, a great improvement to their lives. As Ted later put it:

> It was all brought about by a resident porter and part-time shop steward not prepared to knuckle under to what was a left-over from the days of the Lord of the Manor's word being law.[61]

This was low-level class war, almost invisible in a mega-city like London. Its public version could be seen at Crosfield Electronics in Archway, a firm which processed imaging devices for the print industry. In 1974 Crosfield was taken over by the multinational De La Rue Group which assured its workers they were in no danger of redundancy. However, at the end of the work shift on 6th March 1975, with no prior warning, Crosfield's three hundred workers were informed their work was being moved to Peterborough and they were redundant as of that moment. The sheer brutality of the employer's tactics persuaded some to take the redundancy money and leave but a number of other workers, angered at their summary dismissal, started an occupation of the factory that lasted for two months.

The workers, mostly female, were given a small amount of strike pay by their union but otherwise were dependant on the solidarity of the London labour movement, which initially appeared effective as electricians refused to disconnect the factory's electrical supply. But in May a Possession Order was granted to De La Rue and the occupying workers decided they had little option but to accept the company's new offer of increased redundancy whilst retaining a small number of those previously slated for dismissal. The protestors had used all they had and squeezed out a few concessions but the legal and economic power of their employer had steamrollered them.[62]

A more brutal example of overt class struggle exploded between 1976 and 1978 at the Grunwick photo processing plant in Chapter Road, west Cricklewood. It was an area where many firms like Walls, Nestle, Heinz, Hoover, Grunwick and Kodak employed so-called "unskilled" workers, most of them BAME women. Nearly 80% of the workers at the large United Biscuits factory in Harlesden were drawn from the local black population. Grunwick was one of the worst employers, devoid of the benefits provided by firms like United Biscuits and Esso where trade union influence had helped create decent terms and conditions (Heinz, an American firm, had a social club and a sports facility next to the factory). Grunwick employed mainly BAME women on long hours and low pay in what was essentially a high-tech sweatshop.

On 20th August 1976, when the temperature was in the 90s and the air conditioning had broken down, one of the female workers was summarily sacked for not working fast enough, whereupon 137 of her outraged colleagues walked out, led by a small (4ft 10in) Indian woman named Jayaben Desai. On the day of the walkout Jayaben squared up to her 6ft tall manager Malcolm Alden and told him:

What you are running is not a factory, it is a zoo. But in a zoo there are many types of animals. Some are monkeys who dance on your fingertips. Others are lions who can bite your head off. We are the lions, Mr Manager.

All the women who walked out were sacked. The women were not in a trade union so they contacted the TUC and the young Secretary of Brent Trades Council, Jack Dromey, born in Kilburn to Irish parents and educated at Holland Park Grammar School. Dromey had previously worked on legal cases for squatters and was making a name for himself in the local TGWU. The TUC advised them to join the Association of Professional, Executive, Clerical and Computer Staff (APEX) and seek recognition from the employer. When the employer refused this and remained intransigent Dromey offered to help organise their strike committee and drum up solidarity from other unions.

This solidarity almost won the dispute early on. Members of the Union of Post Office Workers (UPW) refused to cross the picket line to deliver mail but allowed the firm to collect it from the Cricklewood sorting office. The UPW was a well organised and assertive union. Arthur Chaplin, who worked at the St John's Wood sorting office from 1953 to 1987, remembered the power and leverage the union possessed at the time:

> *It was a very strong union there, actually the union ran the office. I became assistant secretary. The union did everything, they did the leave, they did the re-sign and all that. All the holidays, and it goes by seniority. That's how it was and you were doing it for other people. It was a real beautiful office. I was doing a lot of overtime because the wages were terrible really.*[63]

In November 1976 the UPW went further and refused to allow Grunwick staff to collect mail from the sorting office. As Grunwick's business revolved around processing holiday photos sent to them, this would have crippled the firm. But the owner of Grunwick, George Ward, had powerful allies, like the right-wing National Association for Freedom and new Tory leader Margaret Thatcher. Faced with a legal challenge, the blacking of the sorting office was called off and the Grunwick strikers appeared defeated. In the meantime, the strike had attracted national attention. ACAS recommended the firm recognise the union but Ward simply refused to do so. Jayaben Desai and Jack Dromey worked furiously to resource the picket lines and fight back against lines of aggressive police, sent there to ensure that buses carrying strike-breakers got safely into the plant. On one day, 13th June 1977, police arrested eighty-four of one hundred pickets outside Grunwick.

In response the strike committee called a national demonstration outside the plant for 22nd June and asked for aid from other trade unions and political groups. Tony Kilshaw, who in the late 1970s was working on building sites as a chippie before going to Queen Mary College, London University, in the 1980s to study History and Politics, was in the Communist Party at the time and went down to Grunwick on 22nd June to offer support. He and a mate arrived early and decided to take the initiative by chaining the gates shut. This obstacle to the buses carrying the scab workers did not last long:

The chains were cut and the police held us back to let the scab workers in. My mate soon got arrested. More and more people were joining the demonstration throughout the day and word filtered through that the Miners were coming. We heard them before we saw them. They came down the road led by a brass band. In my memory it's like the arrival of the cavalry in a cowboy film.[64]

The NUM contingent stood in front of Jayaben Desai and her fellow strikers and dared the police to attack. Violent clashes followed. Wayne Minter, one of the organisers of Rock Against Racism and a frequent attender at Grunwick, remembered:

Two hundred miners pushed straight through all the police and set up in front of the gates...You'd go off for a cup of tea and there'd be Yorkshire miners, who are probably not the most politically sophisticated people, sat in cafes with Asian women in saris talking politics. The next day the police were bashing everybody to pieces again but it was an incredibly uplifting moment.[65]

On 11th July 20,000 trade unionists and other supporters marched to the factory. In spite of the legal ban postmen at Cricklewood sorting office, nearly all of whom were white, once again blacked mail for Grunwick, resulting in them being suspended for three weeks. In early 1978 the TUC and APEX started to back off from the dispute and by July 1978 it was called off, but although the specific battle at Grunwick was ultimately lost certain advances had been made. For the first time white male Yorkshire miners and white Irish postal workers had stood toe to toe with North London female Asian workers against a common enemy. None of them forgot the experience, even if they had to return to work and get on with their lives. Urmilaben Patel, one of the women who stood with Jayaben Desai from start to finish at Grunwick, remembered that after the final defeat of the strike

> we all went to the Job Centre. I went to a rehabilitation centre in Acton. The company, Remploy, were doing so many things, they were a big company. I was packing dresses. The clothes were all on rails. We took them and folded them, put them in a bag and put a label on. I really enjoyed that. I miss that factory. The people were so nice.[66]

Further west, the Southall Black Sisters formed in 1979 specifically to address the needs of working class black and Asian women. This new, racially attuned politics was best demonstrated in the late 1970s by the activities of the Anti-Nazi League (ANL). Created to confront the rise of the National Front (NF), the ANL was set up by the Socialist Workers Party's London Organiser, Paul Holborrow, and trade union officials Ernie Roberts and Peter Hain, both of whom later became Labour MPs. The ANL was run from its office in Finsbury Park and sent its forces to where the NF were strongest. Hoxton NF, led by the virulent racist thug Derrick Day who lived on an old LCC estate in Shoreditch, was a particularly violent branch of the party, leading to regular street battles on Brick Lane between fascists and anti-fascists. From 1978 to the early 1980s the NF's headquarters was at Excalibur House, 73 Great Eastern Street between Old Street and Shoreditch. Excalibur House's trusted nightwatchman, "Simon", was in fact an anarchist activist who had infiltrated the NF and who passed on useful details of the building to the ANL.[67]

The NF were also active further north, where every Saturday its members sold their paper *Bulldog* outside Wood Green Shopping Centre. When the NF attempted to expand its reach into North London in a march through Wood Green on 23rd April 1977, they were confronted for the first time by determined physical resistance. In the lead up to the march ANL members tested out red smoke flares on Tottenham Marshes and went round the Greek and Turkish cafes of Green Lanes to drum up support. On 23rd April nearly 3,000 anti-racists —young BAME people, trade unionists and activists from Haringey Labour Party, the SWP, Rock Against Racism and the Indian Workers Association — attacked the NF as it marched from Duckett's Common down Wood Green High Road.

The march was harassed every inch of the way with bricks, bottles, flares and smoke bombs. As it neared its end fighting broke out between racists and anti-racists in Broomfield Park and Alderman's Hill, Palmer's Green. The *Socialist Worker* journalist and Hackney GP David Widgery later wrote:

> *Conventional anti-fascist politicos had been augmented by North London gangs, rockabillies, soul girls and tracksuited Rastas... a squad of black kids accurately hurling training shoes borrowed from Freeman, Hardy and Willis.*[68]

Three years before, in 1974, the NF had won 8% of the vote in Wood Green in the General Election. By 1979 it secured 2.8%.

Wood Green was not the only battleground in North London. By 1975 Anna Sullivan, born to Hackney working class parents in 1939, had moved on from a tumultuous youth in which she had three children to whom she was a single mother, and had started a career as a full-time teacher. She became active in the National Union of Teachers (NUT), whose London-based left-wing activists held their lively and fractious meetings at the General Picton pub in King's Cross. Her friend Susie Burrows (who like her sister Saffron was born in St Pancras and grew up in Stoke Newington, their parents teachers and trade union activists in Hackney) described the difference Anna made to kids by her teaching methods:

> Children sometimes arrived in her class unable to read aged 9 or 10, and hating school. Some of their parents were in the National Front. Anna was a wonderful teacher and her world view was crucial. She taught them all to draw and paint, to read and love writing. Some won national art and poetry competitions. She had no time for bullying. If there was any racism, sexism, homophobia, disablism or class prejudice, she would stop the class, challenge the perpetrator and have a full discussion.[69]

Anna also joined the SWP and ANL. As she was already selling *Socialist Worker* in Chapel Street Market, where the NF were especially active, she was asked to take charge of the ANL's fight against the fascists in the area. In the late 1970s South Islington ANL became one of the main bastions of anti-fascist activity in London and Anna, its primary organiser, was one of the NF's main targets. They began to produce leaflets exhorting supporters to come to Chapel Street at the weekend and "smash in the face of Red Anna". From 1976 to 1979 Chapel Street saw regular Saturday confrontations between ANL and NF activists, with the NF usually leading off with a physical assault on ANL paper-sellers. The Met sent SPG vans to police the battles but the SPG, heavily prone to a bit of racism themselves, arrested only ANL activists.

Communal anti-racist organising was one of the most significant developments in London's working class culture during the 1970s. Its only real equivalent was the emergence of punk. Punk did not explode from a vacuum. Amongst other influences it traced back to working class London pop stars such as Rod Stewart and T. Rex. With *Gasoline Alley* (1971) Stewart had carved out a niche for himself at the heart of early 1970s pop as the raspy-voiced proletarian alternative to Bowie's classless pan-sexual aesthete. Steve Jones was inspired:

I used to find out where Rod had got all the gear he was wearing on the album covers and head up over Chelsea bridge to nick it from the shops on the Kings Road where he'd bought it...Later, when people were thinking about who influenced the Sex Pistols, they would never really say The Faces, because it wouldn't be considered cool enough, but we took a lot from them, not just at the beginning when we were trying to find our way, but all the way through the band.[70]

Glam had more influence on punk than punk PR merchants cared to admit. Slade, Sweet and Mud were raucous working class bands stomping out loud, anthemic chants for excited crowds to feed back. Its leading figures inspired the King's Road fashion and music scene of the early 1970s. Even in the middle of the decade it was still a fulcrum of the capital's street fashion, as Robert Elms remembered:

Every weekend in, say, 1975 or 76, Teddy Boys, soul boys, proto punks, Bowie freaks, mods, rockers, surfers, queer pioneers and the generally overdressed but unaligned, all paraded along what was then a still shabby-chic street that reeked of the stale end of the 1960s.[71]

The pub rock scene was primarily a North London affair that, like glam, had its heyday between 1972 and 1975. Its heart was the Hope and Anchor pub on Upper Street in Islington. When the Tally Ho in Kentish Town switched from rock bands to Irish music, the Hope and Anchor picked up many its customers and started to host bands that would kick-start punk. Other venues, usually large old Victorian pubs such as the Sir George Robey in Finsbury Park, the Dublin Castle in Camden Town, the Pied Bull at the Angel, the Nashville in West Kensington, the Mean Fiddler in Harlesden, the Pegasus on Green Lanes and the Bull and Gate in Kentish Town, were also important. The Dagenham Roundhouse and Admiral Jellicoe on Canvey Island were notable pub rock venues on London's neglected outskirts.

Pub rock bands practised and developed their sound in the small and challenging live venues these pubs provided — a raucous mixture of huge bars, high ceilings, flowing booze, sawdust, decrepit urinals, bands playing six feet away from seated customers and barely controlled mayhem. Their aim was not to polish that vibe but to capture it on vinyl. By 1974 it was a thriving sub-genre boasting bands like Dr Feelgood, Kilburn and the High Roads, Eddie and the Hotrods and the Stranglers. Many who would go on to build careers out of punk and post-punk, like Joe Strummer, Ian Drury and Elvis Costello, came up through pub rock.

Punk as a genre would be taken up and exploited by ambitious bourgeois hustlers like Sex Pistols manager Malcolm McLaren, but at its core it was a white working class response to the power and confidence of black street music. From 1975 it began to spread out across the city and the country, most obviously in the rise and impact of the Sex Pistols. The Pistols were formed in 1975 by Paul Cook, Glen Matlock and Steve Jones, all of whom were born and grew up in Hammersmith, Shepherd's Bush and Paddington and coalesced around McLaren's eclectic fashion shop, SEX, on the King's Road, Matlock because he worked there and Cook and Jones because they drifted in and out nicking stuff. McLaren saw the potential of their new band and drew in two other, less manageable boys who would go on to define the band, the talented and mercurial John Lydon (Johnny Rotten) and, after Matlock left, the unpredictably violent Simon Ritchie (Sid Vicious). Excepting Ritchie, who had no particular talent of his own, the Pistols were North London working class boys bursting with untapped potential. McLaren's genius was to shape a look and iconography around them that ensured maximum impact.

John Lydon was born in 1956 to a dirt-poor Irish London family in Benwell Road next to Arsenal's Highbury stadium. Later the family moved to the newly built Six Acres Estate between Finsbury Park and Holloway Road. Often ill and with his father away on building sites or oil rigs, Lydon played on the streets of Holloway and got into youth gangs. Kicked out of school at fifteen, he fitfully attended Hackney Technical College where he met Ritchie, and later worked on building sites. Lydon and Ritchie lived in squats in Hampstead for a while before drifting into the ambit of McLaren and the Sex Pistols. The volcanic relationship between Lydon and McLaren— Lydon considered McLaren and his partner Vivienne Westwood *"a pair of shysters who would sell anything to any trend they could grab on to"* — turbo-charged the band.[72]

In 1975, after McLaren secured rehearsal space on the second floor of 6-7 Denmark Street, the Pistols started playing together daily and firming up a sound. They even occasionally stayed above the studio in a tiny flat with an Ascot water heater, a put-up bed and a small black-and-white TV, especially Steve Jones, who relished the experience:

> *I fucking loved being in Denmark Street. It's probably my favourite place I've ever lived. It was right up the West End, in the middle of all the action. You only had to walk out the front door and all the brasses would be there – I was living the dream![73]*

They weren't the only working class lads to need a jolt from central London to fire up their creative juices. Paul Weller was a Woking boy drawn twenty minutes by train to the capital for his fix. On 16th October 1976, six months before the release of their debut single "In the City", the Jam drove down from Woking to Rock On in Berwick Street, Soho, plugged their gear into the music stall's light socket and performed live on the pavement. A year later Weller used a photo of the band posing underneath the Westway for the cover of their second album, *This is the Modern World* (1977).

After their first gig, in October 1975 at St Martin's Art College on Charing Cross Road, the Sex Pistols began to tour extensively. Their big breakthrough was on 29th August 1976 when they headlined a punk mini-festival at the Screen on the Green on Upper Street, near the Angel, which included the London debuts of the Clash and the Buzzcocks. The impact on audience and media was immediate and electric. Punk had taken off as quickly and successfully as had Rock Against Racism and the ANL, with whom it shared a lot of energy and followers.

The Pistols were punk's ice-breaker but it consisted of many bands in and outside London —the Stranglers, the Clash, the

Damned, UK Subs, X-Ray Spex, the Buzzcocks, Cockney Rejects, Sham 69 and hundreds of others. The Slits were the female Sex Pistols, gouging out fresh territory for themselves within a male-dominated music industry and a male-dominated punk movement. Their guitarist, Viv Albertine, raised by her mum in genteel poverty in Muswell Hill where her only recreation as a kid was to wander Hampstead Heath because it was free, remembered seeing the Pistols at Chelsea School of Art in 1975. They had an immediate life-changing impact on her, in particular their lead singer:

> He looks ordinary...he's just a bloke from Finsbury Park, London, England, who's pissed off. Johnny sneers at us in his ordinary North London accent, his voice isn't trained and tuneful, it's a whiny cynical drawl, every song delivered unemotionally...I've always thought that my particular set of circumstances — poor, North London, comprehensive school, council flat, girl — hadn't equipped me for success. As I watch the Sex Pistols I realise that this is the first time I've seen a band and felt there are no barriers between me and them.[74]

The whole point of punk was that it came from below, it did not follow an ideology, it was DIY, it enabled working class teenagers to buy tat in a charity shop, tear it up and customise it with images and words culled from anywhere, to express themselves as they liked. Some formed bands in pubs and backrooms and bedrooms. Some, like the Finchley Boys, a group of lads from the Grange Estate in East Finchley, after seeing the Stranglers play at the Torrington pub in Finchley in 1976, organised around supporting the band as if they were a football team.

Not all who followed punk bands were even punks, some just followed the excitement. Cathal Smyth, who grew up in Muswell Hill and hooked up in the late 1970s with Lee Thompson and Suggs to form Madness, remembers in 1977:

> I wasn't into Punk. Me and Lee went to see The Damned at the Hope and Anchor, came out and got bottled. It just caught me on

*the side of my head. It was about ten smoothies who thought we
were punks. But we weren't, y'know? Lee picked up one of those
metal advertising signs outside a newsagents and walloped a guy
with it. He went down. Stopped in his tracks.*[75]

Punk only had two years of really deep impact, 1976-1978.
In its aftermath a new kind of working class youth began to
emerge in North London, not as angry and nihilistic as the
original punks but dashing, experimental, self-confident
and multi-cultural. Punk itself morphed into post-punk very
quickly, almost literally with John Lydon's Public Image Ltd
(PiL), formed in 1978 after he left the Sex Pistols and the band
collapsed. Duncan Lloyd, a regular in the punk clubs of West
and North London in those years, vividly remembered PiL's
debut:

*I went to see Johnny Rotten and his new band...in their first ever
gig at the Rainbow in Finsbury Park on Christmas day, 1978.
The night was just one big punch up between skinheads and
punks with PiL stopping several times as it all got out of hand
and bouncers were lining the stage.*[76]

Given a boost by Rough Trade Records, a label created in
1978 out of the Rough Trade record shop on Ladbroke Grove,
bands like PiL, the Fall, Siouxsie and the Banshees, Joy Division
and the Cure took punk to its next and arguably purest level,
while others veered off in new directions.

Working class punks were just as keen to exploit the
opportunities presented to them as ruthlessly as entrepreneurs
like McLaren. North London, in particular, offered rich pickings
for a bright working class lad on the make. Danny Wright, AKA
Danny Lux, was born in 1958 to a poor Anglo-Irish family in
Islington. Left to fend for himself by his alcoholic father after
his mum left, he learnt quickly to duck and dive. By the early
1970s he was trawling Carnaby Street and the Kings Road to
steal suitable clothes. He took the same approach to getting
into gigs:

Naturally no financial transactions were forthcoming with even the fares bunked. We dressed for the occasion, wearing Biba's finest...I found gigs easy meat, bearing a strong resemblance to bunking into the cinema, flashing bits of paper masquerading as tickets, sneaking through exits...we discovered methods to get backstage...Once backstage, we mingled. No reserve was shown in tucking into big spreads.

Danny blagged his way into Kingsway Higher Education College, chose only arts-based courses — *"everything I guessed to be a doddle, with minimum written work"* — and settled down to exploit it, charming his way into the homes and beds of the middle class girls he encountered and taking them for all he could. Eventually he confined his academic work to Film Studies, and not much of that, existing from what he pilfered from the Hampstead and Highgate homes of his fellow students. Finally, the college noticed his almost total lack of work and booted him out, forcing him to survive by other means:

Stan had a job working for an agency, cleaning houses in Golders Green. I took a couple on. These were nothing like the big houses in nearby Hampstead, more like large suburban numbers. The interiors were always spotlessly clean when I arrived, so I spent most of the time gazing at the mismatched kitsch. I sprayed furniture polish into the rooms, making it smell like I'd be working furiously on the woodwork...the places were stacked with plentiful Valium so I'd help myself.[77]

A fifteen-year-old Suggs, though still a schoolboy and nowhere near the professional hustler Danny was, had a similar experience, as did many of his friends:

I was about 14 or 15 and still at school when I first met Lee, Chris and Mike. They were all pretty local to where I was living at the time in North London. The bonding took place in Hampstead because that's where the girls and the parties were. The Duke of Hamilton let in underage drinkers like me and also had a happy hour for girls. So there was a real 'scene' – you had all these yobbos from Kentish Town and Highgate with all these girls who had big houses and parents away for the weekend. Like, Peter O'Toole's daughter would have a party and there'd be 150 people in her house for a weekend.[78]

In 1976, still only eighteen, Danny ended up in a new council flat in Archway with his dad and working as a general handyman in a plush Green Park hotel, which enabled him to continue his lifestyle.

Creating a lifestyle had been the essence of punk. By the end of the decade it had spun off into a new pop-cultural movement which, like punk, was an explosion of working class creativity polished and assisted by strategically placed art colleges. The New Romantics bounded out of the Blitz Club in what was left of Covent Garden after the evacuation of the old market. After a short period as a special Tuesday night event called Blitz held at Billy's Club in Meard Street, Soho, above a brothel called the Golden Girls Club, the actual Blitz Club opened on 6th February 1979 in Great Queen Street, between Kingsway and Long Acre in Covent Garden. Tuesday night at Billy's and *every* night at the Blitz was a riot of fashion and personal reinvention, a kaleidoscope of cloaks, kilts, Turkish pants, kimonos, hats, veils, design-conscious cosplay and creative use of slap.

Blitz soon rivalled and outpaced the Roxy as *the* place for new bands and style statements. It was created by two working class boys, one from South Wales and one from London, Steve Strange and Rusty Egan, at that point the mainstays of the electronic synthpop band Visage. Strange ran the club and, famously, controlled the door, while Egan worked as the DJ. Eighteen-year-old George O'Dowd (Boy George) worked the cloakroom and his own dazzling image. Between 1979 and 1981 Strange and Egan injected German and Japanese electronica into London's clubland, forging an entirely new pop/fashion aesthetic out of nothing but the unfettered imagination of those who came to the club.

The seeds of the Blitz Kids had been laid by new bands like Tubeway Army and Adam and the Ants. Like Lydon's PiL, Tubeway Army, fronted by Gary Webb (Gary Numan), a bus driver's son from Hammersmith, had staked their claim to post-punk significance just as punk was fading away. They released their debut album in 1978, but it was their second, *Replicas* in 1979, including the hit single "Are Friends Electric?" with its innovative use of Minimoog and Polymoog synthesisers that established them as an important New Wave band.

Adam and the Ants, whose debut album *Dirk Wears White Sox* was released only two months later, did the same, although their style was more pantomime retro than futuristic SF. In the early 1970s Stuart Goddard (Adam Ant) had gone from the De Walden Estate in St John's Wood to Hornsey College of Art, and from there to the Kings Road and Malcolm McLaren, although by the end of the decade he had developed ideas of his own about the style he wanted to adopt:

> *I concentrated on a new look for the stage, deciding that I would go for an apache/gypsy warrior look, with knee bells to make my moves percussive, kilt flying, and a white stripe across my nose. Malcolm tried to get me to model Vivienne's new pirate clothes, but I preferred my own look.*[79]

These were the precursors of New Romanticism. As the 1980s unfolded they would be replaced by even bigger bands such as Spandau Ballet, born from North London's working class as surely as were the Sex Pistols, and perhaps more representative of it.

Not for the first time, Covent Garden acted as a strange attractor for the most colourful elements of London working class life, uniquely placed to nurture, protect and influence that life. At the start of the 1970s its old market, an integral part of London's culture for centuries, was in its golden twilight. At the end of the decade the Piazza and its adjacent streets were quiet, almost deserted, but about to experience a new dawn. Just as an old working class had departed, fighting a gallant rear-guard action, a new working class arrived with panache and style.

THE 1980s

Are you a pub man, or a club man?
Maybe a jet-black guy with a hip hi-fi
A white cool cat with a trilby hat
Maybe leather and studs is where you're at.
Make the most of every day, don't let hard times stand in your way
Give a wham, give a bam, but don't give a damn
Cos the Benefit Gang are gonna pay!

Wham!, "Wham Rap", 1984

In December 1979 a West End club that would become as iconic as the Blitz, hidden in the arches under Charing Cross mainline station, opened its doors for the first time. There were already gay nightclubs in London — the first was the Copacabana in Earl's Court which opened in the 1970s, above which sat Harpoon Louis, a venue famous for its drag shows — but Heaven was the UK's first gay "superclub" and it extended London's gay nightlife from small and mostly discreet clubs to an entirely indiscreet, large-scale high-tech venue. Middle class gay men in the capital had always had relatively safe spaces in which to meet. Now, in the heart of London, at a club shouting its identity as loudly as it could, young working class gay and bisexual men had somewhere to dance and flirt as freely as they liked. The first song played on the opening night was Dan Hartman's "Relight my Fire".

A few hundred yards up the road, two clubs of a different type were also thriving, although not for long. Rodo's and El Heuco, together known as the Spanish Rooms, were two adjoining unlicensed clubs on the top floors of 18 Denmark Place, a narrow alley off Charing Cross Road near Tottenham Court Road tube station. The clubs were frequented by an eclectic mix of customers, many from London's Spanish working class community, the *barrio espanol* that since the 1940s had coalesced around Ladbroke Grove, the women working mostly as domestic servants or hotel chambermaids, the men as waiters or chefs in restaurants or as porters and cooks in NHS hospitals; other migrant workers from Latin America also drawn to the clubs' lively salsa music; and workers from Soho's clubs and sex shops who went there for a drink after their shift.

The only way into the Spanish Rooms was through a locked, steel-lined front door. Visitors had to shout up for a key. The two bars were hidden from the outside world by boarded-up windows and the door that led to the fire escape was bolted shut. For these reasons the clubs had been declared an illegal fire hazard and were due to shut for good on Monday 18th August 1980. At 2:30am on Saturday 16th August, when both clubs were packed, John Thompson, a minor drug dealer, accused a barman of overcharging him and after a brief scuffle was thrown out. Thompson then took a taxi to a twenty-four-hour petrol station in Camden Town, returned to Denmark Place with a can of petrol, poured it through the letterbox and lit a match. The fireball ignited the timber-framed staircase and shot upwards into the crowded Spanish Rooms where many customers were incinerated as they stood at the bar clutching drinks. In the panic and chaos some tore the boards off the windows and jumped. A few managed to escape through a music shop on Denmark Street that backed on to one of the clubs, but the blaze still killed thirty-seven people.

At 3.33am Green Watch of Soho Fire Station on Shaftesbury Avenue, who had been on shift since 6pm the previous day, received a call about the fire. Upon arrival at Denmark Place they found a conflagration. Supported by additional engines from Paddington, a crew led by Sub Officer Ron Morris broke down the front door and slowly advanced up to the club rooms, methodically attacking the fire as they went. But it was already too late. Green Watch fought the fire for the rest of the night and eventually returned to the station, leaving Red Watch spending most of Saturday 16th August removing what remained of the dead. The incinerated mass of bodies were unrecognisable, burnt to a crisp and fused together. Some fell apart when being moved out of the windows, bits of burnt corpses slipping out of water-proof sheets to land heavily on the pavement of Denmark Street. Many on Red Watch, who had seen their share of dead bodies, needed trauma counselling for years to come.

Yet the fire was barely reported and is now virtually forgotten. This reflected a widespread indifference to the victims, disregarded because of their outsider status. Reporting on the fire, the *Daily Mail* told its readers that the Spanish Rooms attracted "*not just minority groups and tired prostitutes, but all kinds of folk intent on slumming*". At Thompson's trial for murder the *Mail* reported that the mass murderer had "*felt at ease amongst the pimps, lesbian prostitutes, screeching homosexual queens, hash dealers and drooping addicts*" of Denmark Place, making it clear they deserved no sympathy.[1]

Denmark Place, really just a squalid alleyway, survived for decades after the fire. I used to take a shortcut through it, jumping over puddles of urine, every Saturday on my way to Batista's Café and Collet's bookshop on Charing Cross Road. In 2019 it was demolished to make way for Crossrail and other redevelopment around Centre Point. There is no memorial there to the mostly foreign and immigrant victims of the fire, even though the number of deaths was higher than those of the King's Cross Underground fire of 1987.

The obliteration of the Spanish Rooms and the consignment of its victims to historical oblivion mirrors a process of social cleansing that began in the 1980s and accelerated through the next four decades. It was kickstarted by the Thatcher government's introduction, in the 1980 Housing Act, of the Right to Buy, whereby council tenants who had rented for more than three years could purchase their flats or houses at less than its actual market value (usually a discount of between a third and a half). The discount was based on the length of tenancy, with the proviso that if the buyer sold the property within a set period they would have to pay back some of the discount.

The scheme was immediately popular. In 1982 200,000 council houses were sold to their tenants. That figure doubled in two years, over 11% of the total available. By 1987 more than one million council houses in the UK had been bought and by 1997 local councils had lost a quarter of their total stock of social housing. The effect of the policy need not have been disastrous if councils had been able to use the proceeds from the sales to build more and better social housing, but this was forbidden. Although it would take decades for the full effect of the policy on the availability of good quality social housing in the UK to work through, the seed had been planted.

In 1981 a third of all Londoners still lived in council houses, although their living conditions had vastly improved from the 1950s.[2] Councils such as Camden continued to build where and when they could, finishing ambitious projects already begun and hoping for a reversal of Tory policy by a future Labour government. The last completed flats on the award-winning Whittingdon Estate, most of which had opened in 1979, became available in 1981 on the quiet backstreets of Dartmouth Park Road overlooking Highgate Cemetery, the entire estate providing 271 dwellings for 1,100 people, ranging from one-bedroom flats to six-bedroom houses.

At the other end of Camden, on York Way just north of King's Cross, the Maiden Lane Estate opened in 1982. Maiden Lane exemplified the new era and its challenges. The estate was not badly designed or constructed. On the contrary, it was an elegant low-level build with space and dignity, its white pre-cast concrete softened by green lawns and imaginative landscaping. But it was plagued by social policy and economic recession. The 1977 Housing (Homeless Persons) Act did not foresee the results of prioritising "needs-based allocation" of council housing. Maiden Lane was one of its first victims, as Camden Social Services allocated many of the new flats to homeless or "problem" families. If done too quickly or without consideration this could fundamentally alter the social dynamic of an estate, replacing a majority of working class families where one or both parents were in secure employment with families or individuals who were mainly unemployed. Some of these, especially male adolescents for whom there was little prospect of employment, felt no connection to the community and proceeded to trash it.

That these systemic problems could be addressed and resolved is proven by Maiden Lane itself. In the new century it became a much cleaner and safer estate than in the 1980s and 1990s, finally achieving what its idealistic architects had wished. It was not their fault that in 2020 Camden Council was so hobbled by austerity economics that it could only afford to build an extra 273 flats on the estate of which 149 were for sale on the open market, 53 for shared ownership and only 71 as new council flats.

Across London, Trellick Tower began to be reclaimed by its residents. In 1984 they established a Resident's Association which managed to secure an intercom system and a concierge on the ground floor. Later the lifts and corridors of the building were modernised and improved. Today it is still a Kensington and Chelsea Council block with social tenants, although individual flats have been bought and sold for up to £1m. One of its adjacent attractions, the Meanwhile Wildlife Park, was not part of Trellick's original design but was built from the waste ground up by locals in the late 1970s and early 1980s. It still skirts one side of the tower and the Grand Union Canal, a fringe of protected ecology around a forbidding monolith that appears to be rotting from the ground up, supermarket trolleys abandoned in the dead space that rings its graffiti-covered base.

By the 1980s North Kensington, a self-contained area bordered by the Grand Union Canal to its north and Notting Hill to its south, had visibly transformed as a result of the mass slum clearance that accompanied the building of the Westway in the 1960s, but only from one form of working class community to another. From Harrow Road to the Westway, Ladbroke Grove was still peppered with betting shops, cafes, off-licenses, mini-marts and laundrettes. Even in the late 1980s Portobello Road and All Saints Road had an air of dereliction similar to that of Harrow Road. The area's major employer was the Unigate Dairies factory on the south side of the Westway, where milk was pasteurised and bottled on massive production lines until the factory's closure in the early 2000s. The old slums had been replaced by large modern council estates like the Brunel, built in the early 1970s on disused railway land north of Westbourne

Park Road and dominated by the twenty-storey Keyham House. These were charmless blocks that Westminster City Council did not much care about, and their residents knew it.

Not all London's working class lived on council estates. There was a diversity of rented housing available throughout the city, including multi-occupancy houses, small flats and bedsits. Tariq Goddard's mother was an Uzbek immigrant working as a nurse, while his father's family were engaged in a variety of "relocation" and security work in the City and the East End. Born in 1975, Tariq grew up in a tiny mews flat in Connaught Street off the Edgware Road, owned by the Church Commissioners, who had also owned many down-at-heel properties in Paddington back when it was known as Jungle West 11, many of which were turned into brothels.

Tariq's flat was above an old stables, surrounded by tenants who were either sliding down the social scale, such as disinherited aristocrats, or on the way up such as successful furniture dealers from Church Street Market, professional drivers, high-end bodyguards and a number of actors, all of whom, in Tariq's memory, seemed to be in 'Allo! Allo! and who fitted perfectly into the louche environment around the south end of Edgware Road. At the north end, Church Street Market was still packed with a cosmopolitan mixture of local shoppers and visitors, described in Alec Forshaw's *The Markets of London* (1989) as

> *Hooray Henrys from Little Venice and Maida Vale, Irish housewives from Kilburn, West Indians from Kensal Green, nurses from St Mary's Paddington, and dossers who've tottered along from the station.*[3]

The market perfectly complemented the long metropolitan thoroughfare of Edgware Road, remembered by Tariq as a fusion of Middle Eastern ethnicities and old London working class:

> *There was a strong smell of coffee, as a pioneering coffee shop stood at the corner and sacks of the stuff were kept in the*

basements. Our street had florists, fishmongers and butchers, and lots of small restaurants. The only signs of globalisation were the Safeways and McDonalds that had opened on the Edgware Road. Hyde Park, just across Bayswater Road, was our garden.[4]

Eventually, in the 1990s, the landlord evicted most of its variegated range of tenants and gentrified the mews, but for a while it had been a true cross-class London bohemia on the very edge of Hyde Park.

Kilburn was no bohemia but the 1980s saw it begin to change from the heartland of London's Irish working class to something more diverse. Kilburn High Road, a long and unfashionable trail of old boozers, newsagents, greengrocers, curtain fabric shops, electrical repair shops and Joe's Used Ballbearing Emporium and Cycleworks, ran south from Brondesbury to Maida Vale. Its most famous landmark was the Gaumont State Cinema with its art deco tower and iconic STATE sign, although when the cinema closed in 1981 the Grade II listed Gaumont became a Bingo Hall. Brondesbury Mews, built in 1885, was entirely given over to a sports car repair business (and still is, the only London mews I've ever encountered that hasn't renovated itself to become a property gold mine). But Kilburn Market was already starting to sell "middle-eastern" clothes and ethnic food shops were appearing. Kilburn would never be Camden or even Hackney, but it was attracting students and squatters who couldn't find a space elsewhere in North London.

Chris Scott, who worked throughout the 1980s as a motorcycle courier in central London, found himself in 1980 stuck in a bedsit in Streatham. After being introduced by a mate to a squat in Muswell Hill near Alexandra Palace, he learnt the ropes quickly, specifically that if you had to break into a vacant property it was important to immediately change the locks and then claim that the door had been open and you had simply entered. This conferred "squatters rights", eviction being illegal without due process. Most of all, it was important to pick an empty council property in a Labour-run borough, which owned the largest number of empty council flats and could absorb some being taken off them for a while. Chris's flat in Muswell Hill was a good example:

> *Once the iron was prised off the windows, I could see that the place was bare but in good order. Some councils sabotaged empties by smashing up or blocking toilets to discourage squatters, but not here. The taps flowed, the electricity worked, the toilet flushed, and only the copper immersion tank was missing a heating element. As we were to learn in future years, the utility companies rarely completely disconnected a property, and even dirtbag squatters had the legal right to these essential services.*

The temporary right of possession having been established, the place could be spruced up:

> *Living off pot noodles and kebab soon lost its sparkle, so I set about scavenging the essentials to make the place habitable; kitchenware from charity shops or whatever my mum had going spare. An uncannily comfortable double mattress was dragged home from an alleyway in nearby Crouch End. I dragged that bed from squat to squat for years.[5]*

In 1983 Chris managed to get into a more desirable squat in Gower Street in Bloomsbury. Unlike the Muswell Hill squat, rife with drug dealers and anarchist cliques, this one was populated by the employed working class, women working in shops or hospitals, men in despatch or as medical students. The location made it possible for Chris and his mates to walk most nights to the nightclubs of the West End where they danced, drank and took copious amounts of speed. But Chris found he couldn't afford the 4am comedown as he had to be up early and over to Victoria for his job with Superbear motorcycle couriers.

In 1980 Danny Wright also found a place in the centre of London. After living in various squats in Hampstead and Kentish Town he fetched up in one in Riding House Street just off Oxford Circus, where Helen Evangelou had grown up in the 1950s. The squat had electricity but no running water, meaning that all the residents kept large containers of water in their rooms, fed by hosepipe from a derelict building next door. Toilet functions were done in the backyard. Danny had a room at the top of the house, his only furniture a mattress and a chair:

> *I still claimed the dole but the money wasn't enough to meet my needs for a day. Luckily I could earn some cash by scoring for people in the house who were all into gear. I also scored blow for nurses in a nurses' home around the corner, which I'd visited for creature comforts. For a quid, I ate well at the canteen, using the shower units and swimming pool.[6]*

Squats were not the only accommodation without basic amenities. On 20th November 1984, a fire broke out in a cheap bed and breakfast hostel at 46 Gloucester Place in Westminster, south of Marylebone Road. The address was being used by Camden Council to out-house some of their homeless residents in another borough. 46 Gloucester Place, run by an agency called London Lets, was a death-trap, with fire extinguishers empty, the fire alarm inactive and the fire exits blocked. Once the fire took hold, there was hardly any way out. It resulted in the deaths of twenty-seven-year old Shamim Karim and her two children, aged five and three. The *Camden New Journal* reported:

> *The family who died were among more than 20 people trapped after a rear staircase in the building collapsed. The bodies huddled in a third floor bedsit were found by firemen wearing breathing apparatus. Mrs Karim's husband was out at work at the time.*

Later investigation found that nineteen families, all Bengali, were living at the hostel. They told investigators that the daily breakfast Camden Council paid London Lets to provide was never forthcoming, that the entire building contained only two cookers and that hot water and central heating had been available for just two hours a day, one in the morning and one in the evening. After the report was published some of the seven hundred families consigned by Camden Council to outsourced bedsits stormed a meeting at Camden Town Hall and occupied the Council Chamber in protest.

The occupation lasted for almost a month and garnered national media attention. The *Camden New Journal* interviewed one of the protestors, Soowa Miah, bunking down in Town Hall Committee Room 3 with his family, and reported:

> *They share it with several other homeless families, sleeping with his wife and four children on makeshift beds and mattresses. But Soowa says his present conditions are infinitely better than the one he has left behind. For the first time in eighteen months his family have space, heat, light and clean toilet facilities.*[7]

Eventually, after an emotional meeting with Camden's Labour Leader Phil Turner, during which Turner broke down upon hearing of the living conditions the protestors had endured, Camden Council agreed to move them from their temporary accommodation into council housing stock within the borough. One of the occupation's supporters, a fifteen-year-old boy named Nasim Ali who was at that time living on the Regent's Park Estate, smuggled food into the council chamber to help the protest. Nineteen years later he would become Mayor of Camden, the youngest mayor in the UK as well as its first Muslim and Bangladeshi mayor.

Where Camden led the way in provision of high-quality council estates, Hackney trailed. It had a few pockets of decent quality provision such as the Burma Court Estate on Clissold Crescent, built immediately after the war on land cleared from bomb damage. But the quality of its old LCC estates was epitomised by the Kingsmead in Homerton, built in 1937 on twenty-two acres of land taken from Hackney Marshes and consisting of seventeen five-storey blocks laid out grid fashion. The Kingsmead was meant to replace older slum housing but it declined after the war as Hackney's local industry moved out. By the 1980s the main employer in the area was Homerton Hospital. The Kingsmead went into a rapid decline that led to gang culture on the estate and, its absolute nadir, the use of one of its flats by a gang of paedophiles who were arrested and convicted in 1985 for the rape and murder of several teenage boys.

Hackney's new build was meant to offer a new beginning, but many of its modern estates — Holly Street, New Kingshold, Trowbridge, the Nightingale — were blighted from the start by bad design and poor management. They added to Hackney's problems instead of relieving them. In 1979 nearly 10% of Hackney's 46,000 council owned houses and flats were unfit for human habitation and 19% of them needed substantial renovation and repair.[8] By 1982 the amount of people waiting for a council flat from Hackney Council was so large that unless the need was literally critical, they could expect to wait decades.

Hackney, like all London boroughs, was crippled by the Right to Buy and cuts to its government grant. It was obliged to sell its council houses but not allowed to use the proceeds to build new ones. This was a social disaster. In the early 1980s Hackney had the second highest male unemployment rate in London (22%), the second highest proportion of overcrowded households and the second highest proportion of children in care. Only Tower Hamlets beat them on these indicators and Hackney had higher rates even than Tower Hamlets for female unemployment and street crime. In 1983 a government study found that Hackney was the most deprived area in England.[9]

In the 1980s and 1990s Holly Street and the Nightingale became almost unmanageable by the local authority, so much so that in the 1990s most of Holly Street had to be demolished. But Hackney was much more than just large estates. Shoreditch and Hoxton were still the white working class redoubts where my dad's family had lived for several generations, full of second-hand furniture shops, old tailors, scrap metal merchants and greasy spoon cafes. Further north, in Dalston Kingsland, Ridley Road Market throbbed with colour, food and clothes every week from Tuesday to Saturday. In the 1980s the clothing industry provided one in eight of Hackney's jobs, with nearly every main road and many side-streets festooned with shops selling dresses, coats, shoes, suits and slacks, with every kind of tailoring, repair and cleaning shop to compliment them.

Much of the merchandise circulated in and out of Ridley Road Market, the beating heart of the borough:

On Friday and Saturday stalls line the street between the permanent booths, and between the stalls is a crush of people: Asian women with their nylon saris trailing the wet pavement, West Indians pushing double buggies dozing or staring out of plastic greenhouse rain covers, squeezing past knots of dark-eyed Turkish Cypriot ladies exchanging gossip. A giant Pakistani with a spade bear, skull cap and flapping kunta stands by a blazing pile of boxes and crates. Three teenage black boys nudge each other as they notice two helmeted white policemen peering out in a gap between the racks of cheap skirts. Behind, a Bengali man staggers down the steps of a clothing factory clutching a huge batch of cut cloth for machining at home.[10]

Hackney's social life revolved around old pubs such as the Penshurst on Penshurst Road, the Queen's Head on Victoria Park Road, the Alexandra on Lauriston Road, the Pembury Tavern on Pembury Road and the Amhurst on Amhurst Road.

In 1980 Amanda Millhouse left home and got a job in a local clothing factory. The pay was low, £1ph. The factory had a clocking in and out system and workers did not get paid for tea breaks. As Amanda worked as a "cotton cleaner", removing the loose strands from finished garments, she was not allowed to sit down. On one occasion, when severe period cramps forced her to take a seat, she was immediately told off for doing so by the factory owner. In 1983, having had enough of the clothing factory, Amanda started work in Hackney Unemployment Benefit Office (UBO) in Spurstowe Terrace and was immediately plunged into the world of civil service trade unionism:

After my first week in the office I joined the CPSA union. It was my first experience of left wing politics. My home and school were conservative, so this was new territory for me. I quickly got involved and was encouraged to stand for a role on the sub-committee, which I did and duly became Chair. I was out of my depth and was guided by my new Guardian *reading colleagues. I had found my political home.*

A key feature of life at the UBO was after-work drinking at the Amhurst. The life was literally intoxicating, as Amanda admitted:

I did drink to excess frequently and would have to be half carried home on some evenings. Living alone made the pub an attractive prospect – lots of people I knew and lots of rounds to be bought. I liked playing pool and listening to people's stories.

The Amhurst could be a volatile place:

One evening in the Amhurst the landlord was getting agitated by a man who had got quite drunk, wasn't bothering anyone, but wasn't a regular. The landlord asked the guy to leave. As the man gently remonstrated, the landlord swung a punch so hard that the man's front teeth were embedded in his knuckles. We all looked on in horror, but no-one said anything. Many of us left just before the police arrived so we didn't have to be a witness.[11]

The Amhurst's customers were the employed working class but the surrounding estates were full of the unemployed who signed on at Spurstowe Terrace and went for emergency payments to the DHSS office on Sylvester Road. In the early 1980s the number of London's jobless began to rise steeply as the Thatcher government applied its monetarist experiment to British society. The subsequent de-industrialisation was rapid, chaotic and uncushioned except by the barest safety net. Some of London's working class avoided the worst of it and even managed to thrive within it, but for many it was a story of increasing precarity and long-term unemployment.

This was not solely due to Thatcherism. Between 1966 and 1996 over three quarters of London's manufacturing jobs disappeared. Between 1981 and 1991 the number of skilled manual workers in Islington more than halved from 29.6% of the workforce to just under 13%. In 1983 Tom Durkin of Brent

Trades Council, a senior union activist in North-West London, described the irretrievable loss of industrial jobs in the area he covered as "gone like the snow in summer", a loss symbolised by the demolition that year of the iconic Ebonite Tower in Park Vale. But while this was certainly true of the big employers of Park Royal and Acton, alternative forms of work *had* appeared. When the large ABC works on Camden Road shut down in 1982 it was demolished and replaced by an aggressively modernistic new Sainsbury's. The building was new but the business was not. After the first Sainsbury's had opened in Drury Lane in 1882 its next three stores were all based in the Kentish Town area, so in a sense it was merely coming home.

Jobs were lost but also transformed and transported, most particularly in the enormous increase of work at and around Heathrow Airport. In the 1970s major air-frame and aero-engine manufacturers such as Napiers in Acton Vale and Handley-Page in Willesden had closed or relocated, with the growing mega-complex of Heathrow absorbing some of those made redundant. The TUC's history of employment in west London between 1945 and 1995 concedes:

> *Heathrow underlines the switch in West London from a national production centre for aircraft parts to a massive complex for aircraft servicing and the associated passenger services required to run the UK's biggest airport.*[12]

Inevitably, for reasons of proximity, most of these jobs were taken by the Asian immigrant population of Hounslow and Southall. The extension of the Piccadilly Line to the airport in the 1970s also provided new jobs in construction.

The decline of industrial employment at Park Royal was not only a story of loss. The area began to change into a different kind of industrial park, full of smaller enterprises and a new network of cafes and bars. Today Park Royal is a mixture of corporate HQs like Diageo, modern flats like Regency Heights (half with affordable rents as a condition of the build), large Ocado and Mash warehouses, smaller engineering and car repair units, furniture manufacturers, Gowing and Pursey Construction, the Willesden National Grid Substation, Middlesex Hospital and a centre alive with nightclubs and Lebanese cafes.[13] Its transformation was a process akin to the long-term decline in employment in London's docks that started in the 1880s when the major docks suffered falling demand for their services, a decline offset by other jobs clearing East End slum housing and building the London Underground.

The employed working class responded to change in a variety of ways. In June 1981 staff at St Mary's NHS hospital on Harrow Road, a large complex serving the Paddington and Kilburn areas, occupied parts of the hospital to protest plans to cut one hundred beds and eventually close the entire hospital and transfer services to a new St Mary's in Praed Street near Paddington Station. The action arose from a long history of trade unionism at St Mary's and nearby hospitals such as the Middlesex, Charing Cross and Hammersmith, which during the 1970s had been compelled by powerful health service unions to phase out their private "pay beds". In 1981 NHS management, emboldened by the new Tory government, began to push back. Union activists were targeted and dismissed. When health unions declared a work-in at St Mary's in June 1981, the police were called in to evict the occupiers. A TGWU steward was sacked and a nurse was suspended for attempting to prevent the forcible removal of patients from a ward by untrained security guards. By October over four hundred staff were working-in and the struggle spilled over to large demonstrations on Queensway and Westbourne Grove.

Despite a lack of appreciation from its management, London's health, welfare and transport services were kept going by their low-level workers, people like David Lammy's mother. David was born in Archway in 1972, the son of Guyanan parents (his father arrived in London in 1956 and stayed initially in a dosshouse in Stoke Newington, while his mother arrived in 1970) and lived in Tottenham. In 1974 his father left the family and David and his four siblings were raised solely by their mother, who took on multiple jobs to do so, including working for London Underground, as a home help, a care assistant and later a housing officer. David remembers meeting her as she emerged into the daylight from Camden Town tube station after a long shift, before feeding him and going off to her next job.[14]

The 1980s saw a major increase in jobs in London in finance and the media, jobs that occasionally offered opportunities to working class men and women looking for something different but mostly went to those with the right academic or social background. The erosion of "traditional" working class employment meant a doubling down on those corners of the private sector in which the skilled working class had always carved out a living, such as the jewellery and diamond business of Hatton Garden. "The Garden" was, and is, a wider area running from Clerkenwell to Holborn and from Saffron Hill to Leather Lane, fringed on the west by the old LCC Bourne Estate. Like the nearby Whitecross Street Market in Clerkenwell, Leather Lane Market has been in existence for hundreds of years. It now runs on weekdays and is continuously busy selling food, clothing and shoes, a favourite with the tenants of the Bourne and other LCC estates on Rosebery Avenue.

The centre of the area is Hatton Garden, with its nearly thirty separate jewellery businesses and over fifty-five shops. In the 1980s, despite the value of the product and the wealth of the larger merchants, the trade was kept going by the craftmanship of an army of silversmiths and goldsmiths. By 2012 only one workshop was left but thirty years earlier the north end of Greville Street contained dozens of workshops full of cutters and mounters. Many of the shops still had *schleppers* standing outside practising the ancient arts of hustle and charm, trying their best to entice the public inside. Some still do.

Rachel Lichtenstein recalled when her father, an antiques dealer and market trader before moving to Lawrence Collins jewellery store where his brother worked, opened a new jewellery shop in 1989 on the Garden. He purchased it from an Italian immigrant who had come to London after the war and started a tailors shop on Leather Lane and who later branched out into jewellery. After a period running a hybrid tailors/jewellery store the Italian owner eventually bought a full-time jewellery store on Greville Road, which Rachel's father purchased with borrowed funds. The entire family helped it get started:

> We all worked long hours, cleaning out the dusty display cabinets, rushing round to different suppliers, fetching boxes, bags, labels, stands, tickets, and all the jewellery needed to fill the large windows. The stock was mainly on approval from suppliers, meaning we did not need to pay for it up front — but if it sold the suppliers took a bigger cut of the profit. Many people helped us out. They trusted my dad, they knew him from the street, knew his father and brothers.[15]

Working class Londoners who worked in and around central London continued to mine their opportunities. By the mid-1980s Joyce had been working for a while as a catering manager at the Gallaher's Cigarettes building on Kingsway. While she never indulged in any fiddles herself, she recalled that the amount of unrecorded product that made its way out of the premises or fell off the back of various lorries was prodigious. In 1985 she moved on from Gallaher's to do in-house catering for Herbert Smith, a large legal firm in the City, where she stayed long enough to accrue a small occupational pension. In 1987 her younger sister-in-law, my aunt Josie, gave up hairdressing and started a new job on the check-out till at the large Marks & Spencer on Camden High Street, a job she held until she was seventy-one in 2020. Marks were generous with employee benefits such as cheap and sometimes free provision to its staff of M&S food past the sell-by (but not use-by) date. Josie had so much of this that she and my uncle Danny had to put an extra freezer in the hall of their council flat in Kentish Town to store it all.

Less secure employment, such as motorcycle courier work or second-hand bookselling, saw a resurgence in 1980s London before bigger corporate rivals cleaned up the field and reduced its anarchic diversity. In 1984 Chris Scott, after hearing that a typesetter in Holborn needed an in-house rider, popped into Sunshine Typographic off Leather Lane to enquire about the job. The manager, a working class Thatcherite named Bernie, immediately hired him, with the friendly warning:

Now look, son. We're not taskmasters 'ere. Just turn up on time and do the job wivaht killing yerself. We don't wanna be scraping yer brains off the Gray's Inn Road, all right? Start Mundy, 8.00am sharp. See Mo about a bleeper.

Chris liked the work and the environment of central London, but Bernie himself was a puzzle:

I never worked out if he was a former criminal, or if he just had connections in those circles. It was said he kept a shooter under the spare wheel of his Rover SD1, and there was always a steady stream of knocked off goods coming through the office. For a lot less than they cost at Argos, I got my mum one of those fancy TVs with a built-in VHS slot, and a new-fangled microwave oven.[16]

For the rest of the decade Chris worked at Sunshine and a number of other motorbike despatch firms while flitting around different squats in King's Cross, Kentish Town and Hackney.

Those involved in the capital's second-hand book trade could be as peripatetic as squatters and motorcycle couriers. Iain Sinclair, at that time earning a precarious living through a mixture of private gardening in Finchley and Golders Green, basic maintenance work at Liverpool Street station and second-hand book dealing in Camden Passage, encountered a rich collection of eccentrics, market traders and déclassé bohemians all chasing bargains around the city from the great scrum of Farringdon Road second-hand book market to Camden Passage and Dalston Kingsland:

An old Scotsman called Jock would come here (Farringdon Road) every day and scavenge off the stock on the bottom of the pile that had been rejected by the Saturday people, and take the books back on the bus to Hackney to sell at his stall on Kingsland Waste market. I sometimes bought books off him which I would take back to Camden Passage, where they would be picked up by mid-range dealers in Islington. By the end of the week they would be back in Saville Row and fancy West End shops...From Saturday to the following Friday the books would just flow like a tide or a river across London.[17]

In the 1990s the Farringdon Road book market, which had been in sharp decline since the 1970s, was killed off by lack of custom and rising rents. Sinclair's hypnotic debut novel *White Chappell, Scarlet Traces* (1987) is a dark, dazzling memorial (intertwined with occult reflections on London's hidden history and the Jack the Ripper murders) to a time and place where desperate booksellers, unemployed poets and street-grafters met in greasy spoons over a bacon sarnie to discuss book scams and hunt down rare editions of T.S. Eliot and Arthur Conan-Doyle.

I saw some of this culture myself in the mid-1980s when running a second-hand bookstall in Villiers Street Collectors Market in the disused stables underneath Charing Cross station. After securing a good stock of books from my mum's cousin in Cardiff, a librarian given a load of remaindered and second-hand books to dispose of, I worked Villiers Street every Saturday for nearly two years. At the time I was living in a "hard-to-let" Tower Hamlets council flat next to the River Lea, so early on Saturday mornings I caught the 15 bus from Poplar along Commercial Road and through the City to Charing Cross to meet my dad who arrived with the stock in his car. For the rest of the day I sold books near the entrance to the market, sustained by a thermos and sandwiches prepared by my mum. An insular, eccentric community, the public face of Villiers Street was mainly stalls of books, magazines, stamps, coins and postcards, but further in, through the arches and inside the stables it contained a large display of militaria such as real and replica guns, swords, knifes, flags, SS badges and once, I distinctly recall, a black marble bust of Adolf Hitler.

These kinds of markets were sometimes worked, on and off, by those claiming the dole. I did exactly the same by pocketing the cash from our book sales whilst signing on and declaring I had done no work in the previous two weeks. But while

London Transport, the NHS, local councils and frontline public services such as UBOs and DHSS offices provided much-needed employment in the capital, unemployment as a whole continued to grow. In response the government tightened the rules for "being available" for work, without proof of which benefit could be suspended. Voluntary groups began to organise to assist and advise the jobless, especially the long-term, i.e. those signing on for more than six months, who after that period were called in for special interviews.

Experience of unemployment varied enormously depending on circumstances. Some signed on for a short while before finding work. Some did bits of work here and there while signing on. Some never found proper work and were lost and desperate. There were a growing number of advice bodies such as the network of Citizens Advice Bureau, which themselves provided part-time and full-time employment, to assist tenants and claimants. In 1984-1985, whilst still signing on, I worked for two days a week as an unpaid volunteer at Choice, a combined advice centre and charity shop on Holloway Road that provided information and assistance to people dealing with Archway Tower DHSS or Camden Council about Housing Benefit.

In 1981 a coalescence of groups and individuals fighting for the rights of the unemployed in North London came together to form Islington Action Group of the Unwaged (IAGOU). To start with they issued a series of demands which they put to the manager of Finsbury Park UBO in Medina Road, including that notices be put up in Urdu, Greek and Turkish; that childcare facilities be available at the office; that toilets be made available to waiting claimants; that if Giros were not received then replacement Giros be handed out over the counter rather than re-posted; and that the local UBO and DHSS office work in tandem and not in separate silos.

These were moderate demands that the IAGOU struggled to get heard. It also sought, with the assistance of Islington Council and the GLC, to set up a permanent centre for the unemployed. Eventually the council agreed to contribute funding and a centre was due to be opened at 355 Holloway Road. But the plans were scuppered when many of Islington's Labour councillors defected to the newly formed Social Democratic Party and Islington suddenly became an SDP stronghold. One of the first things the new SDP councillors did was to cut grants to groups like IAGOU. As an ex-Labour, now SDP, councillor explained: "*A centre for the unemployed in Islington would only encourage people to stay on the dole*".[18]

After Labour regained the council in 1982 IAGOU were given the keys to the new centre. As well as refocusing their activity to assist unemployed people who didn't sign on, the IAGOU also targeted the activities of the ES's Specialist Claims Control Unit (SCCU), special investigators who subjected the unemployed to stringent tests to ferret out any who were doing work on the side or otherwise not abiding by the rules, and to drive down the number of officially registered unemployed. When the SCCU were sent into Archway Tower in 1982 the IAGOU responded with public demonstrations. SCCU investigators were photographed and their pictures and car numbers were flyposted around the area. IAGOU also helped activists in Hackney set up a similar group.

In 1985, like Amanda a few years earlier, I took up a full-time job at Hackney UBO in Spurstowe Terrace, Dalston. At that time the UBO network of the Department for Employment (DE) was a fraying, under-staffed bureaucracy under enormous strain by a weight of numbers it was never designed to cope with, an army of unemployed who were compelled to demonstrate a daily search for jobs that were mostly not there and who occasionally verbally and physically attacked the staff, and was kept going only by the efforts of a handful of dedicated people who somehow managed to do a professional job in an environment of deep disaffection and cynicism. Frontline benefit staff were represented by the Civil and Public Services Association (CPSA), a white-collar trade union that since the 1970s had become one of the most militant in the country. The two most organised and active offices of CPSA's notoriously obstreperous DE Central London Branch were King's Cross UBO on Penton Street, Barnsbury, and Hackney UBO on Spurstowe Terrace. Union activists in these offices often met up during Branch meetings, national disputes and demos or at CPSA socials. It was at one of these that I first met my future wife.

During the 1980s King's Cross UBO had a unique sense of camaraderie both in and out of the office, forged by mutual adversity and after-hours drinking. The Chair of the CPSA DE Central London Branch and the leading union rep at King's Cross, Martin John, lived in Midhope House on the Hillview Estate, a short walk down Pentonville Road. Often on strike, its picket lines were large and energetic, followed by breakfasts at the Alpino café on Chapel Street Market. Social life revolved around the Lord Wolseley pub on White Lion Street and, once a month on pay day, a trip to Serendipity cocktail bar in Camden Passage to enjoy its 5-7pm "two for one" deal. One of its supervisors, a large and friendly woman named Sue Tilley, frequented London's bohemian art world and was a great friend, and later biographer, of the performance artist Leigh Bowery. She was later immortalised by Lucien Freud in the now iconic painting *Benefits Supervisor Sleeping* (1995).

Hackney UBO had a rougher edge. Its office parties usually ended badly with the attendance of the police or an ambulance, sometimes both. When the SCCU visited the office for a blitz on the area's unemployed, staff acting on CPSA's instructions refused to work with them, feeling they were conducting a political campaign to victimise the claimants and artificially drive down the jobless total. These actions were seldom appreciated by those signing on. The only face of the system they ever saw were the frontline staff and they saw them through unwashed plexiglass screens. King's Cross UBO had no screens, allowing for more civilised interaction between claimants and staff. Sometimes, though, none of this made any difference. In 1987 Palmer's Green UBO was burnt down in an arson attack, almost certainly by a claimant pushed too far by a welfare bureaucracy that didn't seem to care.

The entrance to Spurstowe Terrace was down a long concrete alleyway with high brick walls and rubbish bins, from where claimants entered a main hall lit by fluorescent lights suspended on chains. There were only a few seats in the hall. Here, from Monday to Wednesday, claimants queued and signed on to receive their bi-weekly cheque sent in the post. Thursday was PI (Personal Issue) Day, when those who had no fixed address or an address that was judged unsafe to send cheques came in to receive their Giro personally. As this group contained a large number of the homeless, the alcoholic and the mentally unstable, it was a lively day. Some PI claim files had **PV** written in red capital letters on the top right-hand corner, to covertly inform staff taking it out of the box that the person they were about to see was Potentially Violent.

Amongst the beleaguered staff at Hackney were its CPSA rep George, a Greek Cypriot Trotskyist and one of the nicest and most tolerant men I've ever known; Sonya, a flame-haired young union activist inevitably christened Red Sonya, who in time took over from George; Linda, a well-read alcoholic who worked with another alcoholic named Lou, with whom she had screaming rows and the occasional knife fight, and who eventually resigned to become a street cleaner; Colin, a tall, blond bisexual scandalmonger who was a hit at London's clubs and who found any hint of seriousness at the UBO, especially its political militancy, hilarious and ridiculous; April, a stunningly attractive black girl from the Pembury Estate who only had to appear at the counter to get immediate compliance from the male unemployed; Carl, a likely lad who sold football shirts inside the office to claimants, hanging them up with price tags on the signing-on counter; Fabian, a saintly Franciscan monk on retreat to the UBO who attended work every day in his robe; Ian, a young substance abuser who spent his lunchtimes in the middle of the Pembury Estate inhaling glue from a paper bag, and who was later found dead of an overdose; Bill, an immensely scruffy, soft-spoken ex-hippie who loathed his job as the office fraud investigator and survived it by being gently but permanently stoned; and Eric, a highly promiscuous and bitingly witty gay man whose stories of what and who he'd done at the weekend left everyone amazed that such feats were possible.[19]

About a year after I started at Hackney A (Hackney B was directly across the road but they functioned as one entity) its manager suffered a total nervous breakdown and for six or seven weeks went wandering around Hackney Marshes every day rather than go into work. His absence went unnoticed by both his superiors and his staff, who simply carried on getting the Giros out, closing the doors at 3.30pm and heading down the Amhurst as soon as possible. Eventually, the Department of Employment HQ at Caxton House, Victoria, noticed that one of its London offices no longer had a manager and temporarily promoted a supervisor to fill the role.

London's benefit system was dysfunctional but not actively corrupt. The same could not be said of its police force. In 1978, in response to allegations by a Supergrass of wide-spread corruption in the Met, the Hampshire and Dorset force was tasked with conducting an investigation named "Operation Countryman" which ran from 1978 to 1982. Initially Assistant Chief Constable Leonard Burt's team were given accommodation in a Portakabin in the back yard of a South London police station that was wide open to other officers. When they were refused better office space they moved to a secure location in Godalming, Surrey. After uncovering evidence of widespread corruption in the Met Burt's team were actively obstructed, with files going missing, surveillance equipment not delivered and officers refusing to be interviewed. In 1982 Burt was called back to Dorset and his investigation fizzled out.

Countryman failed because the problem was not a few "bad apples" but a system of unaccountable and racist policing that felt no pressure to reform itself. In January 1983 Colin Roach, a twenty-one-year-old black man, after having been arrested and taken to Stoke Newington Police Station, died of gunshot wounds received *inside* the station. The police claimed that he had shot himself, but as he was shot twice in the head that strained credulity. A pathologist considered that the body's position did not indicate suicide. Despite this evidence, and mass protests by Hackney's black community, there was no public enquiry.

Outright murder inside a police station was unusual but harassment of young black men and teenagers was not. In 1984, a twelve-year old David Lammy was walking through an industrial park off West Green Road when three uniformed police officers suddenly jumped him without warning and aggressively frisked him. He recalled:

> *They claimed it was because I matched the description of a black mugger, but in reality it was because they could not tell one black man from another.[20]*

Lammy went on to become the Labour MP for Tottenham and, in 2020, Shadow Foreign Secretary.

The Met was a deeply compromised police force and yet there were many examples of organised crime for it to tackle, most notably North London's premier criminal gang the Adams Family, AKA the Clerkenwell Crime Syndicate. The Syndicate was created in 1980 by its "godfather" Terry Adams, the eldest of eleven children born to a dirt-poor Irish family in Barnsbury, Islington in the 1950s, with the help of his brothers Patrick and Tommy. The brothers' firm started in the 1960s with petty crime and extortion on Chapel Street Market and by the 1980s had become a vast racketeering and drug trafficking empire, resting on a disciplined but ruthless application of violence, with its base in Clerkenwell and Hatton Garden. One of the Garden's premier jewellery dealers, Solly Nahome, acted as their financial advisor and helped to launder the millions they made out of London's illegal drugs trade.

By the end of the decade the Adams family were in charge of most of the cannabis, ecstasy and cocaine coming into the city, owned clubs and discos across North London and were silent partners in several clubs in Soho and the West End. Their money was difficult to trace but they were also protected in other ways. In 2002 a classified report into police corruption revealed that at least three Met detectives were working for the brothers and had sabotaged an investigation into a murder they were strongly suspected of ordering.

Crime in London, especially in the more glamorous precincts of central London, had long been a staple of British cinema, but it was seldom presented as the result of poor schooling, unemployment and poverty, carried out by fairly stupid men usually caught and sent to prison. More often than not it focused on professional career criminals, club owners, gang leaders and implausibly articulate mockney caricatures. The greatest London crime film ever made, *The Long Good Friday* (1980), bucked this trend by saying something about the eclipse of working class communities and the arrival of a new Docklands, at the same time reducing its ambitious "hero" (Bob Hoskins) to a man whose sense of power and control is shown to be an utter delusion, easily destroyed.

Television, on the whole, did better. In the 1970s and 1980s Euston Films, an independent subsidiary of ITV formed by the socialist writer/director team Trevor Preston and Jim Goddard, produced a string of classic TV series such as *The Sweeney, Out, The Nation's Health, The Knowledge, Fox, Minder, Widows* and *The Fear* that, taken together, form a dramatised social document of London working class life at the time. Its creative apex was the thirteen-part *Fox* (1980), a complex saga of London's white working class on the cusp of the new decade.

Fox centered on a working class family from Clapham but its scope, characters and setting encompassed the entire capital. The first few episodes are dominated by head of the family and father of five sons Billy Fox (Peter Vaughan), an ex-Covent Garden porter and lord of his Manor. His two sons from his first marriage, a successful self-employed builder (Bernard Hill) and a cynical Soho club manager (Derrick O'Connor), epitomise two strands of London working class life in the post-war decades. His middle son (Larry Lamb, channelling his own London upbringing in Edmonton) is a taxi driver, negotiating between older and younger brothers. The youngest and only "political" son, a twenty-something left-wing student, laments the loss of a vibrant working class culture in the heart of London when the old market moved, concerns his family find naïve and pointless. When Billy dies his widow and extended family must move out from his shadow to a new and different future.

If *Fox* was Euston's *Bleak House*, then *Minder* was its *Pickwick Papers*, replete with an immortal fictional creation, a modern Falstaff or Fagin, in used-car dealer and "independent businessman" Arthur Daley. Forever skirting the edges of the law, a receiver and seller of stolen goods who sees himself as a pillar of the community, always smartly suited and yet indisputably a spiv, Arthur has endless ambition mistakenly applied, in the dream that one day, as he memorably put it to his general gofer Terry McCann, "the world is your lobster".

Because it is such an enjoyable show, its fluid, witty dialogue trotted out by a rich collection of superbly drawn characters, *Minder*'s sociological significance can be overlooked. Like all Euston productions it was made entirely on film, a radical departure for the time, and was filmed on location all over North London, capturing the reality of its backstreets, industrial parks, allotments, railway arches and lockups as well as its pubs and clubs. It also reflected, in exquisite detail heightened for comic effect, an essential and enduring part of London's working class life — the cash economy, the off-book black market, the "little bit of business", the "nice little earner", shifting things that might have fallen off the back of a lorry; the importance, in this world, of "holding folding".

As importantly, Arthur and Terry are categorically not "East Enders" or "Sarf Londoners". They are working class North Londoners at home in the centre of the city. *Minder*'s end credits, a black-and-white montage of Arthur and Terry at various locations run with Denis Waterman's iconic theme song "I Could Be So Good For You", delineate their world — the Blue Anchor pub next to Hammersmith Bridge; on the bridge itself; on the steps of the Royal Albert Hall; walking through Leicester Square; leaving the New Rockingham Club, Soho; by the wonky lamp post on Newman Passage north of Oxford Street; and standing outside the "Winchester Club", which aside from the name change was actually the Eton Club on Adelaide Road next to Chalk Farm tube station.

Minder's creator and primary scriptwriter, Leon Griffiths, knew his territory. Named after Leon Trotsky by his communist parents, in the 1950s he was the *Daily Worker*'s drama critic and later wrote scripts for *The Racing Game* and *Play for Today*.

Originally from Sheffield, he immersed himself in London culture. Before he came up with the idea for *Minder*, and during its first few seasons, he was often to be found in the members-only drinking clubs of North London, most especially the Eton Club, where he discovered a rich seam of comedic gold, recorded it and recycled it. Of the characters he used as source material, he later admitted:

> *They lived on their wits and were great storytellers. I don't suppose half of what they said was true but it didn't matter. They were alive, they crackled with a sort of crazy energy.*[21]

Griffiths took his inspirations from many different characters, including the regular boozers at the Load of Hay and Sir Richard Steele on Haverstock Hill, but they could be found all over. Richard Cracknell, who during the late 1980s helped his father behind the bar of the Bull pub on Seven Sisters Road when it was the centre of everything slightly dodgy in Tottenham, remembers characters that could have been written for *Minder*:

> *There was Johnny Castles the car dealer, and his dealership was on the one-way system behind the Robert E. Lee pub. His office was a caravan on the site…He was always buying and selling stuff. He bought a great big batch of cowboy boots, must have been worth a fortune, but at the time they just weren't the fashion. He tried to convince my Dad to have a country and western night at the pub so he could flog all these boots he'd bought unseen.*[22]

By this time, the early 1980s, Ted was a regular at all the pubs on Haverstock Hill and around Hampstead. He was also a member of the Eton Club, it being two minutes' walk down the hill from our flat. Inevitably, he too fed into *Minder*, Griffiths taking a harmless scam Ted had running (whereby he diverted some of the toilet rolls and tiny milk and jam cartons from Mike Carlton's properties and sold them to Dodgy Morrie to use in a small hotel he owned in Gower Street) and having Arthur do the same in the season four episode "Willesden Suite". On one occasion Ted's mate Big Dave, also a member, entered the club, saw him at the bar and loudly greeted him with "Ah, the bold Edward", this being jotted down by Griffiths to resurface as Sergeant Chisholm's sarcastic "Ah, the bold Arthur" to his maddening nemesis.

Ted was now back working for Carlton, who had re-started his property business from a new office in Holland Park and reassembled his old team — his second in command, his PA, and his driver and general fixer — to carry on as before. Joyce was also roped in to organise the catering for dinners at Holland Park for Carlton's business and property contacts, all paid cash in hand. The inner team continued to enjoy additional benefits such as free use of his villas in Florida and Spain. But when Carlton was killed in 1986 in a mysterious plane crash in Botswana the game was up and Ted was suddenly catapulted back into self-employment.

For a few years in the late 1980s Ted survived by doing any driving, courier and maintenance work that came along, and using a garage/lockup he had on the nearby Queen's Crescent Estate to store stuff that might be useful or sold on (including the books we sold at Villiers Street). Initially taking any work going, including sweeping out the bottom of an empty swimming pool in Hendon, for a while Ted became a self-employed "services agent", utilising his wide range of professional contacts to make introductions for people that needed informal labour and pocketing a commission fee as middle-man. It was hand-to-mouth and, for a man now turning fifty, much closer to *Minder* than he really wanted to be.

Minder took the social experience of that part of North London's working class that lived on the fine line between legality and illegality and brilliantly mythologised it for a 1980s audience. But it was a twilight performance. In the 1980s a newer and younger working class was looking for nice little earners of their own in very different bars and clubs than their fathers frequented. By 1980 the New Romantics were at their peak, laying down connecting tissue between 1970s punk and 1990s club culture. As with punk, and later with house and grime, the new movement was driven by the innate creativity of working class kids using whatever came to hand to break out of pre-ordained lives. It started with the Blitz and its denizens, a scene Robert Elms succinctly characterised as:

All young, nearly all working class and skint, it was incestuous and fabulous. Most of them fucked each other and chucked each other, but above all, despite the bitching and the backbiting, helped each other.[23]

It was easy to underestimate the Blitz crowd, but they could scent opportunity when it arose. When the Covent Garden theatrical costumier Charles Fox held its closing down sale, they all descended on it and snapped up every glamorous costume and uniform available at bargain prices, all later to be used in music videos, promotions, fashion shows and gigs.

As the Sex Pistols had done for punk, Spandau Ballet did for Blitz. Initially called the Gentry, the band was formed in 1976 by Gary Kemp and his friend Steve Norman after they saw the Sex Pistols at the Screen on the Green on Upper Street. After a couple of years, they were joined by Gary's brother Martin and new lead singer Tony Hadley. Like the Kemp brothers, Hadley came from an Islington working class family. His dad was an electrical engineer and his mum a council worker, and like Gary he had attended Dame Alice Owen's Grammar School on Goswell Road near the Angel, one of the best performing state schools in the country.

The rest of the band were cut from the same cloth. Steve Norman grew up on the nearby Bourne Estate in Clerkenwell. Their "manager" Steve Dagger came from the Tybalds Estate in Holborn, the son of a Fleet Street printer and Father of the Chapel. He also attended the Dame Alice Owens School before going on to the London School of Economics (LSE) where he met Robert Elms, who personified the offspring of working class parents who moved out of Inner London in the 1950s and 1960s and who now wanted to move right back in (Elms did, living with his then-girlfriend Sade Adu in a squat in a disused fire station in South Tottenham).

In 1978 the Gentry became Spandau Ballet after Steve Dagger arranged a special session for them at a rehearsal studio called Halligans at 95 Holloway Road near Highbury Corner (in the 1960s the site of Michael X's Black House) to which he dragged Bob Elms and club promoters Steve Strange and Chris Sullivan one Saturday morning. They were good enough to get everyone involved in promoting them, with Elms suggesting they change their name to Spandau Ballet, a piece of graffiti he had seen on a wall in Berlin. From there on it was rapid success as Spandau played Blitz on 5 December 1979 and other venues such as the Scala Cinema and the deck of *HMS Belfast* moored in the Thames.

Spandau didn't send demo tapes or invite record companies to shows, they did gigs at unusual locations and didn't let music critics in if they weren't dressed stylishly enough. It all paid off in November 1980 when their debut single "To Cut a Long Story Short" reached number five and, a year later, the pulsating "Chant Number 1 (I Don't Need This Pressure On)" propelled them to the top of the charts. By 1983 and the stunning success of "True", Spandau Ballet were enormous. They were also a challenge to the po-faced music press, as Gary Kemp later explained:

> We didn't talk to the music press, as we had no interest in trying to persuade them that what we were doing was good. They didn't believe we were working class and tried to paint us as middle class Tories. The music papers at the time were full of middle class white boys who didn't like the fact that we were from council estates. They wanted to believe we were right-wing, but we were anything but. We all came from the Essex Road in Islington and we had no sympathies with anything remotely Thatcherite.[24]

The other major bands of the early to mid-1980s, Wham! and Culture Club, were similarly treated by the gatekeepers of music cred. Yet, like Spandau, they didn't emerge from privilege and they didn't make it through social connections. George Michael and Boy George were young, gay working class men who emerged from far-North London (Michael) and far-South London (George) and who fled to Camden Town and Soho at the first opportunity in order to chase their dreams.

Born in East Finchley in 1963 as Georgios Kyriacos Panayiotou, Michael was the son of a Greek Cypriot father and an English mother. His dad, a former farm worker, arrived in England in 1953 and through family connections found work in a restaurant. Spending his free time in North London dance halls like the Tottenham Royal, he met and married George's mum, a working class girl from Highgate, in 1957. Initially living in a flat above a launderette in Finchley, in 1969 the family moved to Burnt Oak, Edgware, so that George's dad was nearer to the restaurant, the Angus Pride, that he opened there in 1960.

In 1978-1979 George and a mate regularly bunked off school on Friday afternoons to travel down the Northern Line to do some busking, either at Camden Town or Green Park tube stations. By 1980 George and another school mate, Andrew Ridgeley, had formed the duo that would become Wham!, although George did most of the songwriting. Signed by new label Innervision Records in 1981 they made an immediate impact in June 1982 with "Wham Rap!", which declared, as a nineteen-year-old George swaggered down the street in his jeans and leather jacket:

> *Hey, everybody, take a look at me*
> *I've got street credibility,*
> *I may not have a job, but I have a good time*
> *With the boys that I meet down on the line.*
> *I said, D-H-S-S*
> *Man the rhythm that they're givin' is the very best*

In the context of the mass unemployment of the time this was flippant and naïve but it made a point. In the summer of 1981 the Specials' "Ghost Town" and Spandau's "Chant Number 1", dark songs about urban dysfunction, performed in very different registers, dominated the charts as riots tore up Britain's inner cities. In its cavalier way "Wham Rap!" was part of that rebellion. It was a "rejection of work" demand decades before that philosophy found a name, framed in a way that Michael's peers from Burnt Oak would understand.

It was also, as Michael admitted, a piss-take of rap songs. Following it up with "Young Guns" (September 1982) "Bad Boys" (July 1983) and "Club Tropicana" (July 1983), Wham! became a pop phenomenon.

These were early effusions, playful fireworks thrown off the Catherine Wheel of George Michael's immense talent. When he wrote "Wham Rap" he was still a teenager himself. After Wham! he would mature into a far more thoughtful person and songwriter, as albums like *Listen Without Prejudice* (1990) and *Older* (1996) attested. In the meantime, 1984 was the year of Wham! with "Wake Me Up Before You Go-Go", "Careless Whisper" and "Freedom" all hitting number one, followed by their best and most infectious single "I'm Your Man" in 1985 also at number one.

For the arbiters of pop music status, excepting a few like Neil Tennant and Robert Elms, who by then was writing for *The Face* and making a splash of his own, Spandau and Wham! were the wrong kind of working class. They should have been Boys from the Blackstuff drowning in Northern bathos, but instead they were a young, assertive London working class playing to their own tunes. In fact, George Michael voted Labour throughout the 1980s and had great regard for Tony Benn. In September 1984 Wham! did a benefit gig for striking miners at the Royal Festival Hall. As Micheal said later, *"To call us Thatcherite was so simplistic, basically saying that if you've got a deep enough tan and made a bit of money then you've got to be a Thatcherite"*. It never seemed to occur to Wham!'s critics that the young unemployed and semi-employed, rather than be further depressed by Joy Division telling them how shit everything was, might prefer a brief excursion from it all in Club Tropicana.

Club culture had of course been around for decades, but it was in the 1980s that it became a core element of the city's economic infrastructure, providing not only entertainment but employment in sound and light system maintenance, cleaning and delivery work, security inside and outside the club, and taxi cabs and fast-food services to support them. Clubs also boosted tourism and its related services in hotels, restaurants and pubs.

In 1984, in direct response to the growth of London's clubs, London Transport increased the number of its Night Buses from twenty-one to thirty-two (there are now over sixty).

Club culture in the modern sense began in Soho with Blitz, Le Beat Route and Gossips in the early 1980s from where it spread rapidly, particularly to Camden Town. When Steve Strange's and Rusty Egan's Barracuda Club in Baker Street closed in 1981 they needed a new venue, settling on the old Music Machine at the southern end of Camden High Street opposite the Cobden statue and next to Mornington Crescent tube station. In 1982 they reopened it as the Camden Palace and it immediately became an essential part of London's nightlife. George Michael and Andrew Ridgeley were often to be seen there, dancing the night away. In July 1983 the *Evening Standard*'s "Young Londoners" column, in a piece on the Camden Palace, reported:

The glossy magazines are eagerly reporting that London nightlife is reverberating to the same boom which signalled the Swinging Sixties. And the pace, they note, is set by the street kids who flock to the new clubs hosted by entrepreneurs young enough to be children of the wrinklies running Annabel's and Tramps.[25]

My brother Jamie was often down the Palace in the mid-1980s, part of a local sub-cult called the Camden Stylists, passionate devotees of Paul Weller's new band the Style Council, who closely emulated the band's personal style and fashion statements (a mix of Peacock Mod and continental chic) and strutted their stuff through Camden's bars and clubs. At that time the Palace held a 1960s Night every Wednesday, which Jamie and the Stylists often attended. Of those particularly, Jamie recalls:

Many a great night...One outstanding memory is of the last track of the night, at 3:00am, being the Hawaii Five-O *theme and everyone in the club joining up in a long line and pretending to do the surfing seen in the opening titles, out the front of the club and up Camden High Street with everyone humming the tune out loud!*[26]

Camden's most famous musical sons, Madness, didn't fit neatly into any category. They were never much into punk. They didn't rate the music and they didn't like the spitting and the screaming, a touch of North London fastidiousness that translated to their musical style and personal fashion sense. Nor were they Blitz Kids, having honed their music and built their image in the pubs of Camden Town and Kentish Town, most especially the Dublin Castle on Parkway. They were not really skinheads either, although initially, as a ska band with a white Rude Boy look, they had a skinhead following. Suggs later admitted:

> For those first six months, we were happy to see 20 people in the audience — even if they were just 20 of our mates. None of us had any great academic aspirations or opportunities. We were doing nothing all day and nothing all night, so the band was our only real outlet...It was a heavy time. Margaret Thatcher was talking about the demise of "society" and the white working class were divided between left and right. At some early gigs our audience were Sieg Heil-ing.[27]

This was not what Madness were about and they soon moved away from it. They became part of the first wave of 2 Tone, a heady mixture of ska, reggae and rocksteady that came out of the Midlands in the late 1970s, led by racially mixed bands such as the Specials and the Selecter from Coventry and the Beat and UB40 from Birmingham. In 1979/80 the Specials, the Selecter, Madness and other bands went around the country on a 2 Tone tour that, simply by existing, was a direct challenge to the NF and British racism.

Although 2 Tone did not arise in London, the capital was the arena for the largest and most significant battles against organised racists. By 1981, after having been seen off in Brick Lane and Southall, the NF's main focus was in South Islington, where they proved adept at exploiting white working class grievances and dissatisfaction with the borough's Labour council. In 1980 the NF attacked a shop assistant in the left-wing Other Bookshop on Upper Street and fractured her skull.

The summer of 1981 saw regular street fights between fascists and anti-fascists in and around Chapel Street Market where the NF sold their newspaper. By 1983 resistance to the NF was so relentless that the fascists could no longer maintain a presence on Chapel Street, so they turned to easier targets, harassing and attacking Asian kids at local schools, a campaign of organised intimidation run out of a house on Avenell Road in Highbury.

Anna Sullivan, who by the early 1980s was NUT rep at Highbury Quadrant Primary School, led a determined fightback. Working with other teachers and local Bengali women, she formed Islington Anti-Racist Anti-Fascist Action (IARAFA) and set about defending the local Asian population from fascist violence, taking the fight to the NF by organising demos and marches past their Avenell Road HQ. The final blow to Camden and Islington NF came when eight of its members were sent to prison for armed robbery and the entire branch collapsed. With its stronghold defeated, the NF ceased to have an active presence in North London.

It could still cause harm, though, as it did in July 1987, when four petrol bombs were thrown through the living room window of Anna's house at 3.00 in the morning. She and her son got out of the house just before it went up in flames, running out in their dressing gowns, carrying their dog whose fur had burnt off her back. Anna vividly recalled:

> I stand watching my house burn and feel completely frozen, not crying, just shaking so much that I have to sit down and hold my body together...The middle section of my house is a charred shell, all my books, paintings, fragments of my life have perished in the flames.

The next day, when Anna told an unsympathetic policeman that she had received death threats from the fascists and that she was certain they were behind the attack, he responded *"What can you expect if you are one of these anti-racist teachers?"*[28]

2 Tone's message of working class unity in the face of divisive racism was wrapped inside a sparky and exuberant dance music to which bands like Madness, the Bodysnatchers and Bad

Manners added a distinctive London flavour. Nicky Summers, who in 1979 formed the all-female Bodysnatchers along with Rhoda Dakar and other singers, felt that 2 Tone was about people from different backgrounds making music together, something that came naturally from her own upbringing:

I had what might be considered a working class background: born in Hackney and grew up in Southgate. My mother was fairly bohemian and was into film, art, fashion and textiles. My father worked in Soho market as a greengrocer and had been a singer in his youth. I helped out on the stall and remember it as a village in which you met people from all walks of life.[29]

Initially, Madness were running to catch up with the likes of the Specials and the Selecter, and with Jerry Dammers, who in 1979 created 2 Tone Records. Of that time, Suggs remembered:

We were in Camden, getting into vintage things like Prince Buster. Ska had been out of fashion since the 60s. Then the Specials turned up at the Hope & Anchor wearing the same clothes as us. Neville was blowing holes in the ceiling with a starting pistol. Afterwards Jerry stayed on my mum's sofa and said: "I want to start a record label, like Motown." I said: "That's optimistic considering you've just played to 35 people in a pub." A few months later Jerry phoned and said: "I've done it!".

In the 1970s Suggs had moved to Camden after spending the fag-end of the 1960s living with his mum, jazz singer and later Colony Club barmaid "Big Eddi" McPherson, in a flat at the southern end of Tottenham Court Road and being taken as a seven-year-old to the Colony Room club, an experience that embedded him then and forever in the heart of London:

Mum always had books at home, things like Graham Greene and Anthony Burgess, so I always had a relatively good amount of words in my head, which was very helpful. English was always something that I was pretty good at. So when I later started

writing songs, it helped that I'd some sort of literary upbringing.
Mum herself was a good singer – when was younger she sang
at The Blue Angel in Liverpool and nearly had a go. But it just
didn't work out for her financially, so she ended up as a barmaid
in Soho.[30]

From his Camden council flat above the big Maples carpet
shop on the corner of Tottenham Court Road and Euston Road,
opposite Warren Street tube station, Suggs was perfectly placed
to enter Camden life. He met many of the lads that would
eventually be in Madness on the Regent's Park Estate, mixing it
up in the Cumberland youth club, going to the pubs of Camden
Town, eating at the Greek restaurants of Mornington Crescent,
buying clothes in Alfred Kemp's second-hand clothes store,
shoes in Holts and records at Rock On. His description of the
Duke of Hamilton pub in Hampstead nails exactly how North
London working class life evaded every cliché of what working
class life was meant to be:

> *I couldn't believe it when I first went in there, a real eclectic mix*
> *of kids into fifties and sixties clobber, Hampstead Teds, Kentish*
> *Town yobs, the Aldenham Glamour Boys, and the posh daughters*
> *of lefty intellectuals.*[31]

Suggs and his mates began their musical careers as the North
London Invaders but soon changed their name to Madness.
Over time they created a unique sound based on an experience
of growing up working class in a very specific part of North
London bordered by Euston Road, Regent's Park and Parliament
Hill Fields (the cover of their second album, *Absolutely,* was a
photo of the boys lined up outside Chalk Farm tube station,
literally next door to the Eton Club where Leon Griffiths was
writing *Minder*) that fused all of their influences together,
including a huge dollop of music hall, creating a Madness vibe
that was instantly identifiable.

Between 1980 and 1986 Madness produced a string of
classics — "One Step Beyond", "Baggy Trousers", "Grey Day",
"House of Fun", "One Better Day", "Wings of a Dove" — but

the one that most defined them was 1983's "Our House", an affectionate and nostalgic ode to working class family life:

Father wears his Sunday best
Mother's tired she needs a rest
The kids are playing up downstairs.
Sister's sighing in her sleep
Brother's got a date to keep
He can't hang around

It was a genuine picture of a functioning and basically happy family, of "our house in the middle of our street", but despite a level of universalism — parents, siblings, domestic chaos — it would have meant less to those living in "our flat in the middle of our block" whose father had never been there.

Despite their "Nutty Boy" image Madness were not a vaudeville act. "Baggy Trousers" and "Our House" celebrate a particular kind of working class existence, not privileged and sometimes stressed but kept afloat by the energy and stimulation of the modern city, whilst others such as "Grey Day" and "One Better Day" are soaked in urban melancholy. It was an inherently subversive *London* sensibility, a pride in the metropolis's history and diversity that would see its richest expression in their "late period" masterpiece *The Liberty of Norton Folgate* (2008).

Madness were not the only band turning London's working class culture into small slices of musical poetry. The London Irish community had always had its own music but it was usually a transplanted version of the old country's, literally so with bands like Big Tom and the Mainliners, perennial favourites at the Galtymore. But second and third-generation London Irish wanted something more, and the Pogues gave it to them. The Pogues themselves (Shane McGowan, Jem Finer, Spider Stacy) were not from London, although they all gravitated there in the 1970s, attracted to the punk scene, living in various squats around King's Cross, Kilburn and Camden Town. But they made the city their own, with their debut single "Dark Streets of London" (1984) creating a fresh London Irish punk sound driven by McGowan's raw and often drunken fury at the world. Their second album, *Rum, Sodomy and the Lash* (1985), was an opulent collection of revamped traditional songs, re-energised hard folk classics like "And the Band Played Waltzing Matilda" and "Dirty Old Town", and their own bitter and poignant working class ballads.

McGowan was a proud Irish Republican whose "Birmingham Six/Streets of Sorrow"(1988) savagely condemned the fit-up and conviction of the Birmingham Six, *"For being Irish in the wrong place and at the wrong time"*. But it was the intense, non-political songs like "The Old Main Drag", "Rainy Night in Soho" and "London Girl" that delineated the twin poles of his life since he arrived in the capital:

The devil moon took me out of Soho
Up to Camden where the cold north winds blow

Soho itself was changing rapidly. During the 1970s it was nearly overwhelmed by strip clubs, sex shops and XXX cinemas, many of them owned by Paul Raymond. But the Local Government (Miscellaneous Provisions) Act 1982 introduced stricter licensing of sex shops and the Cinematographic Acts of 1982 and 1985 did the same for sex cinemas. The effect was to reduce the number of sex shops in Soho from nearly two hundred in the late 1970s to thirty-five by the late 1980s, concentrated mostly around Brewer Street and Walker's Court (where they remain today). Yet Maxine White, who worked in a Soho sex shop in the 1980s that offered "under the counter", i.e. illegal, services and porn, found a camaraderie amongst those who worked in the business and a sense of safety in its permanently crowded night-time economy:

The strange thing about Soho was that I could walk around it any time of the day or night without fear. In most cities you would think twice about doing the same thing. We all looked out for each other, and it really was an extended family.[32]

The extended family generated both employment opportunity and a sense of community. In 1979 James Lebon opened a small one-chair hairdressing stall in Kensington Market called Cuts, a stall that became famous for the disciplined post-punk hairstyles of the early 1980s. Lebon soon expanded into a shop on Kensington High Street and in 1984 opened Cuts Barber Shop on Frith Street, next to Bar Italia. In 1985 21-year old Peter Dowland joined Cuts:

> At first we just rented two chairs – the other hairdressers were two old Italian boys. But we got busy pretty quickly. We were the young guns. The whole film industry and nightlife was here. It was the can-do era. People would go "Right. I'm going to be a video director" and just do it on whatever budget you could scrape together.[33]

Cuts soon became a social centre and meeting place as much as a barber's for all who worked in or frequented 1980s Soho, with Bowie, Boy George and Jean-Paul Gaultier amongst its customers. Peter worked there for the next few decades and through a temporary move to Dean Street before the salon came back to Frith Street in 2019.

Meanwhile, old Soho was slowly dying. In the 1970s some of the Dilly rent trade moved inside to clubs like Louise's in Poland Street, the Rockingham in Great Windmill Street, the Carousel Club in Orange Street and the Paint Box Club in Foley Street, Fitzrovia. These were mainly for boys lucky enough to find a sugar-daddy who treated them well. Those still working the Meat Rack, the public toilets at Piccadilly underground station or the Playland amusement arcade on Shaftesbury Avenue were less fortunate, abused by punters and constantly harassed by police who extorted money from them in order to be let off. The 1980s saw the devastating arrival of AIDS, which by 1984 had already taken the lives of many West End rent boys. It was the beginning of the end for the Dilly rent trade, soon to be erased by CCTV monitoring, online competition and a greater openness about gay sexuality.

By the 1980s Argyle Square in King's Cross was a notorious red-light area, choked by kerbcrawlers checking out the prostitutes who lined the pavements. The sex workers, harassed by pimps and drug dealers and aggressive policing, were represented by the English Collective of Prostitutes, formed in 1975 to argue for the decriminalisation of prostitution and a range of other protections. Based in a woman's centre on Torrington Square near Senate House, in November 1982 the Collective decided to occupy Argyle Square's nearest church, Holy Cross on Cromer Street, as a protest against the conditions local prostitutes endured.

Fifteen members of the Collective camped out in the church and put up a banner outside reading "Mothers Need Money", stressing they were workers not "vice girls" and should not be subject to arbitrary arrest. The occupation, which lasted for two weeks, quickly became a media story. Food was brought in by women from Faslane and Greenham peace camps. The occupiers had the sense to put forward a practical and realisable demand, the appointment by Camden Council of a monitor on Argyle Square to ensure that they were fairly treated by the police. When the council agreed to this the occupiers cleaned up and left, having gained enormous publicity for the cause of sex workers' rights.

Sex workers were not the only marginalised groups agitating for rights and protections. In 1984, following the success of Heaven and G-A-Y at the London Astoria, the Hippodrome in Leicester Square launched its Monday "gay nights". By 1987 London's annual Gay Pride march, which had begun in 1970 with 150 men staging a Gay Liberation Front (GLF) demonstration on Highbury Fields, was attracting 16,000 people (nothing near the size it would become but still significant). This did not prevent the passing into law of Section 28 of the Local Government Act (1988), which prohibited schools and local councils from "promoting the teaching of the acceptability of homosexuality as a pretended family relationship". Nor did it offset the stigmatizing of gay men that arose from media reporting of the AIDS epidemic as a "Gay Plague".

Section 28 had its genesis in the children's book *Jenny Lives with Eric and Martin*, published in 1982 and used by some London councils to illustrate circumstances when a child might live with same-sex parents. In 1986 Labour won control of Haringey Council on a manifesto that specifically mentioned its "commitment to fighting heterosexism", which the manifesto defined as "the belief that heterosexuality is the only form of sexuality". After the election the new council created a Lesbian and Gay Unit to highlight the rights of the borough's LGBT people and *Jenny Lives with Eric and Martin*, along with a list of other recommended works to be used at the teacher's discretion depending on children's ages, was made available to schools as an educational tool.

The storm broke when the *Sun* reported the Unit's "Positive Images" initiative under the heading "Bernie Kids Get Lessons in Gay Love", a hostile reference to Haringey Council's left-wing leader Bernie Grant, and followed it up with similar attacks on *Jenny Lives with Eric and Martin*. Worked up by the media, a group of homophobic local parents formed a Parents Rights group that campaigned for "a return to normal family values". Sides were drawn and a demonstration in support of the Positive Images campaign, attended by 3,000 people, took place on the Roundway in Tottenham. On 30th September 1986, during a debate on the work of the Lesbian and Gay Unit, protests occurred outside Haringey Civic Centre in Wood Green and a copy of *Jenny Lives with Eric and Martin* was ceremonially burnt by protestors. On 20th October, a debate in the council chamber on a Tory councillor's motion to allow parents to withdraw their children from sex education classes teaching a positive or non-judgmental view of homosexuality descended into abuse and violence between councillors.

Despite Section 28 and the appalling response to AIDS of the media and much of the medical profession, the sexual and cultural freedom offered in London still attracted young gay men from all over the country who could not find acceptance in more traditional communities. Paul O'Grady and Jimmy Somerville were just two of many talented, gay working class men and women who moved to London in the 1970s and 1980s,

O'Grady to work for Camden Council Social Services while developing his drag act Lily Savage, Somerville to live in a series of squats before forming the synth pop band Bronski Beat and releasing "Smalltown Boy" (1984), the quintessential anthem of provincial young gay men having to transplant themselves to London for a measure of personal freedom.

One important element of that freedom was Gay's the Word bookshop on Marchmont Street, Bloomsbury, next to the Brunswick Estate. Opened in 1979, it was for many years the only gay bookshop in England and functioned as much as a community and information resource as a bookshop, publicising gay and lesbian flatshares, political meetings, benefits, gigs and parties. The gay socialist group Icebreakers and the Gay Black Group, the first of its kind in the UK, were formed after meeting in the shop. Gay's the Word inherited the mantle of a gay information resource from Housman's left-wing bookshop at the south end of Caledonian Road, a non-gay shop which nonetheless had run the London Lesbian and Gay Switchboard out of its basement since 1974. By the 1980s the switchboard had become an around-the-clock service dispensing vital practical advice and emotional support.

Nearby, the first and for ten years the only lesbian centre in the country, the Camden Lesbian Centre and Black Lesbian Group (CLC & BLG), opened in October 1987 at 54-56 Phoenix Road, Somers Town, not without opposition from some of the area's older working class. When Camden Council's permission for the centre was announced at a public meeting, members of the Somers Town Tenants Association, who had petitioned against it, disrupted the meeting with homophobic jeers and threats of violence. Yet most of the centre's organisers were local women who ran campaigns such as the Lesbian Unwaged Club, which held its socials in daytime working hours to connect women who would otherwise have been marginalised or isolated, such as single lesbian mothers or caregivers.

The hostility that Gays the Word and the CLC & BLG attracted was utterly defied by the Bell pub on Pentonville Road near King's Cross mainline station, at the time a dog-rough area brimming with sex workers and the homeless. The Bell was a vibrant pub/disco full of every type of queer and bisexual, many of them students or unemployed, particularly renowned for its lesbian scene and women-only nights. As one regular customer recalled, these could get raucous:

> There was a disabled toilet in the ladies loo and you would see women going in there for sex. Then twenty minutes later a very upset woman would come in from the bar looking for her girlfriend.[34]

A retrospective on the *Gay in the 80s* blog remembered that occasionally pop and fashion stars would slum it in the pub, but stressed that

> no matter how bright their star, Bell punters were never dazzled by the icons who rubbed shoulders with them. Everyone was in it together whether they were a student, sex worker, activist or pop star. The vibe at the Bell was democratic, egalitarian, accepting, colourful, idiosyncratic. Its effect was like alchemy, getting under the skin and changing people forever.[35]

Some of King's Cross UBO's staff regularly popped down Pentonville Road to the Bell after work for its lively atmosphere.

Dawn Thorpe was born in 1965 in Hitchin, the daughter of a factory-worker mum and newsagent dad. She moved to London in 1987 when she was twenty-two, although she had often come down to the capital in the 1980s as a young lesbian goth to hang out at clubs like the Bat Cave and Gossips. Settled in London, she tried to find work, bouncing from one job to another:

> When I first moved to London I went for a job at Essex Food and Wine as a delivery driver! The ad said driving a 7.5 ton lorry. I didn't realise how big it was and on my test drive I couldn't even release the hand brake! They liked me though and offered me a job in the office. I didn't last long… I hated it… although they

were sweet people... I just didn't connect to anyone and found it hard. So in the early days I was on and off the dole... which was so much easier than today. I worked in theatre in and out of jobs with the producers of the Rocky Horror Tour, so would do Panto at Christmas and the odd UK tour, then I got a job at a ticket agency with my best friend from Rocky... then I worked on an "as and when" basis (early zero hour contracts) for TicketMaster. This was amazing because it meant we were at the theatre for free almost every night if we wanted... and we did.

Alongside almost nightly clubbing, Dawn took to political activism, initially against Section 28:

Alongside the clubbing, the political LGBT movement was strong, we were campaigning against clause 28, then for the equal age of consent. We attended marches in the centre of London, I remember one where we sat down in the Haymarket, blocking the street and I had loads of speed in my pocket... I was so scared of being arrested!... These times changed me. I had always been anti-Thatcher...a member of CND...anti-racist...I attended all the marches but I guess the gay movement felt closer to home... more personal.

Pride, its organisation and the day itself, was the symbolic and literal core of London's growing gay community:

Pride was our annual 'Christmas' event and it really did mean so much to us all. We were all happy, we all loved each other and we were fighting for our rights, the feeling of belonging and solidarity in the gay community back then was unlike anything I had ever known.[36]

The cultural diversity of 1980s London derived not only from a left-leaning middle class but from a new, increasingly multicultural working class, seen at its brashest in North London. Even football, notoriously tribal, opened up. In 1978, to general astonishment, Spurs signed the first two "foreign" players to play in English football, Ossie Ardilles and Ricardo

Villa from the Argentinian national team. Both men, Ardilles especially, became favourites with Spurs fans, helping the team to win the 1981 FA Cup and inspiring the absurdly popular song "Ossie's Dream", sung by the Spurs squad with accompaniment by Chas and Dave.

Ossie's dream turned into a nightmare when the Falklands War broke out. On 3rd April 1982, a day after the war began, Spurs played Leicester in the FA Cup semi-finals. Each time Ardilles touched the ball he was subjected to chants of "England, England, England!" from Leicester fans, to which Spurs fans instantly responded with "Argentina, Argentina, Argentina!". Spurs won the game and went on to beat Second Division QPR 1-0 in the final (after a barren period in the 1970s QPR had returned to form under Terry Venables and in 1983 gained promotion back to the First Division).

Like QPR, Spurs had a better 1980s than 1970s, winning the FA Cup in 1981 and 1982 and the UEFA Cup in 1984. This kept the fans as devoted as ever. Their informal HQ was the Bull pub on Tottenham High Road, previously Kartels, a sad attempt at a trendy bar named after its owners Karen and Terry. In 1985 Richard Cracknell, then a teenager, moved into the pub when his parents took over the tenancy and quickly made it Taylor Walker's most successful pub in North London. Richard remembered that his parents took over the pub on a Sunday, and on Monday lunchtime:

> After half an hour a bloke comes in with half a sawn-off shotgun under his coat and asks for some bloke by name. The old man never gets flustered by anything so he just says "Well, you can see who's in here". So the bloke says "I'll wait". Me dad says "You ain't waiting in here". So off he went. We never saw him again.

Richard was well placed to observe the evolving fashion sense of Spurs supporters, particularly the young men who made up the "firms" that would await visiting fans as they emerged from Seven Sisters tube station for the walk up Tottenham High Road to White Hart Lane:

There was a lot of Harrington jackets, sta-prest, Gabbicci and Sergio Tacchini tracksuits, Adidas mamba, samba and bamba, all that. The older ones didn't dress so much but the younger ones had what I call that London look, the sportswear.[37]

In 1988 the club decided that the Shelf, a stretch of raised terraces on White Hart Lane's East Stand, a favourite of the fans, would be removed and replaced with executive boxes. In response Spurs fans, helped by the London Football Supporters Association (FSA), formed a protest group called Left on the Shelf (LOTS) to campaign against a plan about which the club had not even bothered to consult fans. LOTS raised a storm, printing ten thousand leaflets and distributing them to fans on an away trip to Liverpool, so much so that Spurs had to hold a meeting with them and pretend to listen. While the Shelf was eventually removed and renovated, after a peaceful sit-in at the end of end of the season by five thousand fans a small part of it, nicknamed the Ledge, was allowed to remain until the ground became an all-seater in the aftermath of the Hillsborough disaster.

Arsenal managed its relations with its fans and the local community better. In 1985 the club set up "Arsenal in the Community", a scheme that provided opportunities to young people across three boroughs (but mostly Islington) to participate in sporting, educational and charitable projects, a community hub that has since grown to include a range of activities including mentoring ex-offenders from Pentonville Prison, a school pupil referring scheme, homelessness projects, a work experience programme and Saturday socials for older people, delivered to more than five thousand people every week.

In 1986 Arsenal appointed a new manager, George Graham, who ended a long run of under-achievement and in 1987 gave the club its first League title since 1971. While the big North London rivalry remained the Arsenal-Spurs Derby, on the ground there was not a total divide between fans. Despite coming from a fanatical Spurs-supporting family, with a Barbadian father and Jamaican mother, Shaznay Lewis, who in the 1990s became lead singer with All Saints, played for Arsenal Women FC Ladies team as a teenager.

The 1980s saw Chelsea hit the nadir of their fortunes when they narrowly avoided relegation to the Third Division. By now the club was infamous for an especially vicious and racist element amongst its fans, the Chelsea Shed Boys, many of whom came decked out in full skinhead gear with attitude to match. When Chelsea's first black signing, Paul Canoville, warmed up to enter his debut game in April 1982, some of the Shed Boys subjected him to loud and continuous racist abuse, as he recalled:

> As I'm stretching and running, I hear loud individual voices through the noise: "Sit down you black cunt!", "You fucking wog – fuck off!" Over and over again. Lots of different people. I hardly dared look around. They were right behind me. I snatched a glimpse. They were all wearing blue shirts and scarves – Chelsea fans, my side's fans, faces screwed with pure hatred and anger, all directed at me... I felt physically sick. I was absolutely terrified.

Chelsea's fortunes began to turn around when it was bought for £1 by Ken Bates, a canny businessman who had been raised by his grandmother on a council estate in Ealing and was himself a QPR supporter. Under Bates the club used its new money to purchase a succession of players who returned it to top-rank football. In the mid-1980s, in an attempt to control the Chelsea Shed Boys and prevent pitch invasions, he had an electric fence constructed around the pitch at Stamford Bridge but had to take it down when the local council denied him permission to turn it on.

The big football clubs offered their working class supporters a sense of community and social cohesion but it was not enough to counter economic recession and mass unemployment. In 1981 many of the UK's inner cities, subject to the twin ravages of Thatcherism and racist policing, were convulsed by riots, particularly Moss Side in Manchester, Toxteth in Liverpool, Chapeltown in Leeds and Brixton in London. In July 1981 the Met Police's Operation Swamp 81 (named after Thatcher's reference to immigrants "swamping" the UK and making a clear statement that the Met supported her) inundated Brixton with SPG vans, lifting young black men off the street on the "Sus" laws, i.e. being suspicious by virtue of being black.

The reaction was swift and violent, kicking off a wave of smaller scale riots across the capital. Long-term resentments, going back years and based on how local police forces routinely treated the non-white population, were ignited by the larger riots. On the evening of 10th-11th July 1981, Dalston Lane and Kingsland High Street in Hackney saw running battles between police and local youths. These were frenetic and violent confrontations, although as Paul Harrison, chronicler of Hackney's underclass during the 1980s, realistically summarised it:

> These were not the first skirmishes in the revolution, nor were they an organised protest against monetarism or mass unemployment. Many of the rioters were at school, some had jobs. The conscious motivation of those who were not just in it for the looting was, quite simply and straightforwardly, hatred of the police among the young and the desire to hit back at them for humiliations received.[38]

Yet unlike Brixton with its strong social core around Coldharbour Lane, Hackney was simply too fragmented and diffuse to act in concert. In true North London fashion even its ghettos were diverse, a multi-ethnic melting pot of Afro-Caribbeans, Whites, Asians, Cypriots and Turks. Aside from Tottenham, where local policing was exceptionally racist, North London as a whole didn't descend into more serious riots in 1981 for the same reason that it produced Spandau Ballet instead of the Specials.

London wanted radical new political leadership and in the GLC elections of May 1981, with the arrival of an explicitly socialist Labour administration led by Ken Livingstone, it got it. Hailing from a working class family in Streatham, Livingstone joined the Labour Party in 1968 and became active in local politics, first in his native Lambeth and later in Hackney and Paddington, as he did so moving north of the river to live in West Hampstead and Maida Vale. With the exception of

Lambeth Council, where he cut his political teeth in the 1970s, Livingstone's GLC was unlike any other Labour administration. Supported by his talented deputy and Head of Finance, John McDonnell, and a host of passionately committed socialists and feminists, during 1981-1986 Livingstone's GLC redefined what "socialism" meant in British politics.

The most newsworthy parts of the GLC's activities, especially for Tory newspapers who shamelessly distorted it to attack Labour nationally, was its anti-sexism, anti-racism and anti-homophobia educational work. But as important was its democratic arts policy, whereby it channelled GLC grants away from well-funded museums and art galleries to a range of less favoured initiatives such as street murals, fringe theatre, local radio, community arts groups, local history projects and helping LGBT people develop their own creative networks.

A key component of the GLC's work was "Popular Planning", a catch-all term for a programme that sought to bring workers, patients and welfare claimants into the policy-making process and build operational plans from the bottom up. One of its main advocates was Paul Philo, born in 1938 into an East Ham/ Streatham family not unlike Ken Livingstone's. In 1971, after working for a few years in Customs and Excise, Paul became a mature student at the LSE and an active member of Islington Labour Party, working with other members to replace its MP Michael O'Halloran, known to issue Labour Party membership cards as a prerequisite for work on big construction projects run by his cronies.

As a tutor at North London Polytechnic, Paul helped the TUC develop innovative training and educational courses for trade union reps. Because of this he was asked by Hilary Wainwright, head of the GLC Popular Planning Unit (PPU) to come work there:

Popular Planning was a hectic place to be at that time. It was like being back in student union politics. Some very keen hard working people with good left principles were recruited in that department as well as other places in the GLC during that time...My job was to plan, organise and teach courses so that the various sections of the GLC would develop their own Popular Plans on how they would like their section run. It was not an easy job as this was a new concept for many. The trade unions were suspicious of management trying to get the workforce to plan their work.[39]

The PPU attempted to bring ideas from rank-and-file trade unionists into all of the GLC's projects. It led to the creation of micro-firms and workers' co-ops in abandoned industrial parks and units, helping boost jobs and local economies. In 1984, when mass redundancies were threatened at the large Kodak plant in Harrow, the PPU tried to support the Kodak workforce by facilitating alliances with the trade unions of Kodak's European-based subsidiaries. As a result, the unions of Kodak Ltd and Kodak Pathé liaised at County Hall and agreed to support each other. Even so, nine hundred jobs were lost at Harrow and the operation was reduced to only five hundred staff where there had once been six thousand.

The PPU and the London Enterprise Board were attempts to create a socialist economic policy for the capital. But intervention did not extend to council housing. The New Left of Livingstone's GLC, scarred by the failure of the tower blocks, wanted to downsize and humanize housing provision but failed to appreciate just how much had been achieved in social housing by boroughs like Camden. Despite generous funding of new housing co-operatives and squats it left no legacy of smaller, more sustainable social housing schemes that could nurture and produce the next generation of politically literate working class Londoners, suggesting it was less interested in the input of ordinary working class constituents than it claimed.

Nonetheless, Livingstone's GLC became broadly popular in London. Above all, the bold and progressive Fares Fair policy—which attempted to fund a drastic cut in London Transport fares from increased property rates for more affluent Londoners, thus boosting public transport and reducing car use in the inner city, before being declared illegal by Tory Law Lords — generated mass support. In 1984, when a vindictive Tory government determined that the only way to destroy the threat of successful municipal socialism in London was to abolish the GLC itself, three quarters of Londoners opposed its abolition.

The 1981-86 GLC was not simply, as Livingstone put it, the emergence of the 1968 generation into politics. It was the arrival of a new London working class, or at least its politicised elements — a mixture of ethnic minority, women's and LGBT groups allied with the rank and file of the public sector trade unions, often led by activists of a working class background who had gone to university. It displaced the socially conservative white working class that had once dominated Labour's London machine, a demographic symbolised by the LCC Labour leader Herbert Morrison, a fervent censor of films and a strong opponent of de-criminalising homosexuality.

That older working class, presented today through rose-tinted spectacles by the likes of Paul Embery and Jon Cruddas, needed a shake-up. Ian Mikardo, the left-wing Labour MP for Poplar from 1964-70 and, after a spell as MP for Bethnal Green, again MP for Bow and Poplar 1984-1987, encountered amongst his constituents *"a racism which ran wider and deeper than I had expected"*. He was surprised by many things, especially

> *more hostility to their new Labour comrades from Benthal Green and Stepney than they ever showed to any Tory...I never saw a black face on any of the docks, or on any barge or tug or lighter. To the dockers, keeping out the "foreigners" was part of the operation of a closed shop, which excluded everybody who wasn't of their ilk.*[40]

This was not the politically conscious working class of 1936, inflated by a hard seam of East End Jewish socialists and an influx of fresh CP activists, that had driven back Mosley's Blackshirts at Cable Street. It was the insular white working class based around Docklands who in 1968 broke the heart of the CP and East End docker's leader Jack Dash when they marched to Parliament to demonstrate their support for Enoch Powell.

The politics of working class London were shifting radically in the 1980s. In 1987 the first black MPs, all from North London, were elected to the House of Commons. Bernie Grant, Paul Boateng and Diane Abbott were elected as Labour MPs for Tottenham (Grant), Brent South (Boateng), and Hackney North and Stoke Newington (Abbott). Grant, son of a Guyanan teacher, had arrived in London in 1963 and initially lived in Hornsey Rise. His first job was as a railway clerk in the Civil Engineers Department at King's Cross. After a couple of years he got a job with the Post Office as an international telephonist at the Garrick Telephone Exchange in Judd Street, Bloomsbury, where he led a strike against poor pay and conditions. As a result, he was asked to become a trade union representative.

In 1978, after passing some TUC courses, Grant became a full-time official with the National Union of Public Employees (NUPE). In the late 1970s and early 1980s some of NUPE's Post Office branches, notably Chapel Street in Islington, had a strong NF presence. A part of that presence was Ted's former best mate Ronnie Garrett, who turned into a racist bigot as he got older, an attitude which backfired on him when his daughter Tracy married a young black man and his colleagues at the Post Office, aware of his views, taunted him by continually asking after the health of his son-in-law. He also lost friends like Ted who, through reading and wider social experience, had no time for racism or far-right politics, and stopped socialising with his old friend.

Grant and others at the Post Office fought off the racists, sometimes literally. Of that time, he remembered:

My colour didn't matter at all, a lot of the workers were black, or from various foreign countries, because you spoke a number of languages in the Post Office. You had French-speaking people from Mauritius and so on...Our General Secretary was very much against racism and we were quite vocal at the time and the union was quite vocal. And one of the reasons for that, of course, was the fact that there were large numbers of black and other minority groups in the ranks of the union of Post Office workers, and in a number of post offices, there were black people who were shop stewards and district officials of one sort of another.[41]

Grant, who learnt his socialism from his uncle, the president of the Guyana Teachers' Union, was no crass populist. He was the first Labour MP to openly oppose Section 28, a year before it became law, even though a good number of his constituents in Tottenham's black working class were not enthusiastic about LGBT equality. As leader of Haringey Council from 1985 to 1987 he stood publicly against police harassment of his black constituents. But his biggest challenge as Council Leader came in October 1985 when the Broadwater Farm Estate was engulfed in a violent mass riot.

Broadwater Farm had been badly designed and badly constructed on land not fit for it. Built in the late 1960s out of the same prefabricated panels that had spectacularly failed at Ronan Point, it was put up on the poorly drained "Moselle Valley" (its name derived from the Moselle River, culverted over in 1906 and only glimpsed now as a wide stream running through Lordship Recreation Ground and Tottenham Cemetery) between Seven Sisters and Turnpike Lane. The soft foundations meant that its twelve blocks, connected by three miles of walkways, sat over dark, cavernous car parks which were a magnet for drug dealers and other undesirables. Soon after it opened in 1971 its problems magnified. By 1975 it was difficult to get people on the waiting list to accept housing there, which meant those with fewer options, like the elderly and BAME families, took most of the flats. By the 1980s its unemployment rate was over 50%.

The riot was ignited on 5th October 1985 by the death of forty-nine-year-old Cynthia Jarret. Earlier that day Cynthia's son Floyd had been arrested for theft and assault (he was later acquitted on both charges) and the police searched his mother's house near Broadwater Farm for incriminating evidence. In the search, in which a policeman pushed her to the ground, Cynthia died of a heart attack. Grant called for the local police chief to resign. Next day there was a protest outside Tottenham Police Station which escalated to a riot that consumed Broadwater

Farm and its surrounding streets. When riot police tried to clear the streets with baton charges, local youths retaliated with bricks and petrol bombs.

The main fighting took place at the centre of the estate itself, with police attacked by a group of about 150 people. Firefighters from Hornsey fire station, responding to reports of a fire on the elevated level of Tangmere House, away from the fighting, came under attack by rioters, as did the police sent to assist them. As the firefighters and police ran to safety PC Keith Blakelock, a beat officer in Muswell Hill sent in with other non-riot police to protect the firefighters, tripped and was surrounded by a mob with knives and machetes, who killed him in a frenzied attack.

The riot trailed off during the night as it began to rain and news of Blakelock's death percolated. The following morning Grant was asked by reporters for a view. In an attempt to explain its background and why local black youths so hated the police, he responded, "*The youths around here believe the police were to blame for what happened on Sunday and what they got was a bloody good hiding*". The media only reported the second part of his statement, with the *Sun* adding that he was "peeling a banana and juggling with an orange". Although in later years he would become a widely respected figure, when first elected MP for Tottenham in 1987 the Labour vote in the constituency dropped 7%, a sign of hostility from some of its white working class towards Grant.

The Tory media hated Bernie Grant almost as much as Ken Livingstone, but for Tottenham's black working class he was a hero. Zita Holbourne, who in later years would become one of the trade union movement's leading anti-racist campaigners as well as a major black poet and artist, grew up in Southwark, but by the late 1980s was living in a bedsit in Muswell Hill. Her boyfriend was working for the *Caribbean Times* based in Finsbury Park. After racist harassment from a neighbour they moved to Tottenham, which meant a daily bus journey down Seven Sisters Road to get the tube to work. She remembers seeing Grant for the first time on the local bus:

I was sat at the back of a bus on my journey to Seven Sisters tube station when he got on, and looking regal and elegant walked through the bus and greeted each passenger one by one. I didn't know who he was but was shyly enthralled to be greeted by this kingly looking and kindly acting man. I came to look forward to seeing him on the bus and learned from other passengers who he was. Years later a blue plaque was unveiled outside Tottenham Town Hall next to the Bernie Grant Art Centre and I was asked to write and read a poem to mark the unveiling. It was entitled Bernie on the Bus.[42]

Media coverage of the riot cemented a view of Tottenham and of Broadwater Farm as grim hellholes. These flowed from commonly-held racist assumptions but also from the activities of the Tottenham Mandem, the main organised street gang in Tottenham. Coalescing out of a number of gangs in the late 1970s, by 1985 the Mandem was established on the Farm as ruthless drug dealers and enforcers. It seems to have been its street soldiers, including future leader Mark Lambie, only fourteen at the time, who led the attack on Blakelock.[43]

The positive side of life on the Farm and in Tottenham itself garnered much less attention. Its sense of community was seldom mentioned, that most people knew each other even if indirectly, that even in the 1980s local working class artist Ben Robson, born in 1920, still cycled all over the borough with his window-cleaning equipment, providing an individual service to its flats and houses. In 1981 the Tryfonos family opened the Chick King fried chicken shop on Tottenham High Road, which over the next 40 years became the High Road's premier chicken shop and place to meet and hang out. By the 2020s the shop's owner Alex Tryfonos, who grew up in the area and who still lived there along with his parents and sister, had run the shop for decades. Chick King was just one of dozens of fried chicken shops including KFC and Dixy Chicken that would become as important to Tottenham's youth as shibeens and old cafes had been to their parents.

The early 1980s saw the formation of a Broadwater Farm tenants' movement led by local woman Dolly Kiffin and a worker at the Tottenham Law Centre, Martha Osamor, which set up a play centre, day nurseries, keep fit classes, a pensioners' lunch club, a community launderette and various workshops. After the 1985 riot, when the Farm was being demonised in the press and local youths were being rounded up indiscriminately by police looking for vengeance for Blakelock's murder, Kiffin and Osamor organised the Broadwater Farm Defence Campaign.

Like Bernie Grant, Martha Osamor, born in Nigeria, arrived in London in 1963. She settled in Tottenham and became active in community work, helping to form the United Black Women's Action Group. In 1986 she became Ward Councillor for Bruce Grove and, after Grant departed Haringey Council for Westminster, Deputy Leader of the Council. She later recalled how the Broadwater Farm Youth Association was created out of nothing:

> We got all the youths together to say what they wanted from this estate — jobs, training, to run businesses and so on. We set up a co-op to get people together, get the council involved because by the time we started most of the places were closed as it was seen as a bad estate. Whoever was alone in the laundry or the fish shop didn't want to run it. The grocers didn't want to run it because they were afraid of the young people around. When we realised a big space meant for a pub in the estate was forever boarded up, we asked for it to be opened as a centre for activities: to have the enterprise downstairs, a nursery, to have a women's centre. Downstairs, there was a tenants' room and the constitution was changed and we encouraged people to come and participate and say these are the programmes we need, this is what we're going to be using this place for.[44]

1982 saw the creation of the Ceddo Film and Video Workshop, created to empower local black filmmakers. Funded by Channel 4 and the BFI, it provided a range of grassroots film production and community training. In 1986 Ceddo made a documentary film, *The People's Account*, about the 1985 riot from the point of view of the black community living on the Farm, which called the riot a legitimate act of self-defence against the racist persecution of the police. The film was never shown on British TV as the Independent Broadcasting

Authority demanded severe editorial changes before broadcast, changes which Ceddo refused to make.

The Ceddo film was part of a new wave of self-created black media in and about London, literally so with the newspaper *The Voice*, first published in 1982 and still the only Afro-Caribbean weekly newspaper in Britain. Initially based in Mare Street, Hackney, the paper quickly became essential to London's black working class. Its success led to other publishing projects. Zita Holbourne recalled the importance of the *Caribbean Times*:

> *I used to visit the offices there. This was where I first met Arif Ali who decades later became my publisher. Arif founded the* Caribbean Times *and took on the* African and Asian Times. *He later established Hansib Publications publishing books written by Caribbean and Caribbean diaspora authors and others.*[45]

The new black newspapers mirrored the creation of an Afro-Caribbean music that wasn't simply performed in London for white people or as songs from the old country, but as part of the culture of the city itself. Following Osibisa's chart success in the early 1970s a new form of popular music emerged, a fusion of African drums and melodies with Western instrumentals and Caribbean jazz/funk that ignited an explosion of black London music in the next thirty years. It also celebrated African fashion and dress. Bernie Grant did the same, wearing a traditional Dashiki robe when he first entered the House of Commons in 1987.

Other black community leaders were emerging. John Oke was born in Nigeria in 1934 and first arrived in the UK in the early 1950s. After a period back in Nigeria he returned to London in the 1970s and settled in Kentish Town. The father of four children, he saw that black kids, especially boys, were being routinely failed by their schools and so in 1980 he set up the Camden Black Parents and Teachers Association (CBPTA) which he initially ran from his front room. The CBPTA had a real impact on Camden's educational institutions. On the back of its success John went on to form two other Kentish Town-based social initiatives that promoted African-centred education, the Kuumba Play Centre and the Winnie Mandela Supplementary

School. In 1986 he started the Odo-Dua Housing Association to help tackle homelessness amongst young single black men in Camden. It later expanded to cover Brent and Barnet as well, offering over three hundred flats at discounted rates, especially on the Lithos Road Estate in West Hampstead.

In 1980 the first Black British pirate radio station in Britain, Dread Broadcasting Corporation (DBC), started up in Neasden. Between 1980 and 1984 DJ Lepke (Leroy Anderson), using a sixty-foot high mast in his back garden, broadcast shows across North London aided by a network of other pirate transmitters, one of which was set up on the roof of Trellick Tower. DBC transformed London radio, bringing calypso, reggae, soca, lover's rock, soul, funk and hip-hop to a mass audience that rarely heard black music on mainstream radio. One of its prime movers, Lepke's sister Margaret Anderson, went on to present BBC Radio 1 as Ranking Miss P.

At the Notting Hill Carnival DBC broadcast from a sound system outside their mailing address in Portobello Road also known as the "pink shop", a second-hand clothes shop that had no name but was painted pink. By the 1980s sound systems, always an integral part of Jamaican music, were taking over from individual artists, operated by young black Londoners who had grown up with them at weddings, funerals, parties and other communal events. As the Met turned the screws on black communities across London — in Brixton, Notting Hill, Hackney and Tottenham — those communities turned more and more to their own music and their own means of making and distributing it, through pirate radio, sound systems or illegal warehouse raves. In doing so, their music became the foundation of London's entire working class youth culture.

Although Crackers closed in 1981, other clubs like the Electric Ballroom in Camden Town, the Horseshoe in Tottenham Court Road and the Africa Centre in Covent Garden took up the mantle of popularizing soul, reggae and jazz/funk. Casper Melville's *It's a London Thing* (2020) dissects how London's black music culture "remapped the city" by allowing a black presence where urban planners and the police didn't want one. Working class kids from East and South London who had to walk from the Electric

Ballroom to Trafalgar Square to catch the night bus home, were influenced and transformed — much as in the 1950s kids from Bloomsbury's council estates were educated despite themselves by their shortcuts through the British Museum — by a regular night walk through Camden Town, down Tottenham Court Road and through Soho, the West End and Covent Garden, so much so that, as one South London DJ put it, *"the journey home was as big as the club"*.[46]

One of the main drivers of the new black music scene, Jazzie B (Trevor Romeo), whose parents came from Antigua, was born in 1963 and grew up in Hornsey Rise. From an early age he understood how music formed and sustained marginalised people:

> *subconsciously I was becoming aware of how important music was to the lives of the immigrant communities— not just from the Caribbean but also the Irish and Greek communities that were all around us. We were all working class people, out all day, and the ultimate prize once you owned your own house or your own room was to get some entertainment in there.*[47]

In 1982, after several years DJ'ing around the city and working on his own and others' sound systems, Jazzie formed the Soul II Soul sound system. A true North London hustler, Jazzie used Soul II Soul as an umbrella brand name for several entrepreneurial projects on the go at the same time — the sound system itself, a clothing line and a record shop in Camden Town. Between 1985 and 1989 Soul II Soul performed at their Serious Shit sessions at Portlands on Great Portland Street and, legendarily, every Sunday night at the Africa Centre, the launchpad for the huge success they would go on to have in the 1990s.

Jazzie and Soul II Soul manipulated the media as skilfully as Spandau Ballet. In the early 1980s London's soul and funk scene was promoted by posters or flyers dropped off in cafés, shops, barbers and colleges. But Soul II Soul grabbed the limelight with a mélange of Afro-style and sci-fi imagery labelled Funki Dred, a brand name that caught on massively, including even its own comic book, *The Adventures of the Funki Dreds*, the sound system equivalent of *2,000 AD*. Soul II Soul shops and market stalls were dotted throughout North London, in Camden, the Angel, Tottenham Court Road and Dalston Kingsland, all selling clothes with the Funki Dred label.

Norman Jay, born in Paddington in 1957, was one of Jazzie's most important collaborators, and would become one of the most influential club and sound system DJs of the era. When promoting his own sound system, Good Times, a mainstay of the Notting Hill Carnival for thirty years, he took the direct approach:

> *I'd get my mate who was a burgeoning graphics student to scrawl something, then I'd go up to the photocopier place in King's Cross because they were open on Saturdays. Ten thousand copies, cut them up, then go down to all the trendy bars on the Kings Road and all the fashion shops and the hairdressers.*[48]

Sound system culture was a perfect fit for large house parties which in turn morphed into larger raves. In the mid to late 1980s, these fed into a wave of illegal warehouse parties held in areas that have since been gentrified but at the time were urban dead zones — the massive goods yard behind King's Cross mainline station, around Paddington Basin under the Westway, disused wharfs on either side of the Thames past Tower Bridge, and abandoned industrial units dotted all over Hackney Wick. Raves that had held two hundred people turned into mass events for two thousand people.

By the "Second Summer of Love" in 1988, London's warehouse parties were a derivative part of a national clubbing movement, fuelled by house music and Ecstasy, that had exploded out of Manchester's Hacienda club with help from Steve Hurley's Number 1 hit "Jack Your Body" (1987). The capital took a while to catch up, but when it did, it did so quickly. Clubs like Shoom (held first in Southwark and later at Tottenham Court Road YMCA, famously the easiest place to buy E in London), Labrynth in Dalston, Emergency on Rosebery Avenue, and the Battle Bridge Road squat in a disused school in King's Cross, allowed large raves to take place in the heart of London. On Monday nights, when Heaven turned into Spectrum, three thousand kids on E danced the night away under lasers and holograms.

More conventional venues were also revamping and reenergising. In 1988 Camden Town's historic Mother Red Cap pub opposite the tube station, recorded on maps as far back as 1690, was for some reason renamed The World's End with a new venue for bands called Underworld in its cavernous basement. The Good Mixer in Inverness Street, the Lock Tavern on Chalk Farm Road, the Stag's Head in Hawley Road and the Dublin Castle all got a new lease of life, the Mixer in particular alive with an unpredictable compound of musicians, market traders and the residents of Arlington House.

In April 1988, as acid house was taking off, Phil Potter, a regular Camden jack-the-lad, decided to check out the new scene. One Friday night, after the local pub chucked out at 11pm, he and a few mates headed down to the Camden Palace:

> By the time we got there hundreds were filing round the block! We made our way to the back looking at these people who looked as if they had just come out of a playground or Rainbow, the kids programme! Dungarees, very baggy jeans, long-sleeved day-glo t-shirts, Converse trainers or the old Kickers which I hadn't seen since the early 80s at football matches...It was the first time I'd see any of these so-called Acid Clubbers and thought what a state! I was sporting Adidas Gazelles and a button-down shirt, and thinking dungarees are for painting and decorating.

Once inside, it was a different clubbing experience from what he was used to:

> As we entered the main dance floor and bar, there were people dancing everywhere, on tables, stairs and even at the bar, it seemed that the whole of London was on to this new buzz. There was a smell of sweaty sock I'd get a whiff of every now and again, turned out it was the gay poppers, amyl nitrate. It made your

head have a 40 second instant head rush, the music was pumping hard, very hard to what we'd normally hear in night clubs around this time, also green and blue lasers raced across the dance floor.[49]

Scoring some E from a mate, Phil was transported by a feeling of immense euphoria and left a convert to both house music and E. He and his mates went to different clubs and raves and bought up as much acid house as they could. Soon he was living for the weekends, spending around £60-80 a week on records at Bluebirds on Edgware Road, Red Records in Soho and Flying in Kensington, all to bring it back to the Camden Palace every Friday night.

Des Penny, a working class lad from the Regent's Park Estate who went on to form and manage the house band Flowered Up in the early 1990s, recalled that from 1988:

For a stretch of two solid years there wasn't a night that I wasn't out in London. Pilled-up every fucking night, lapping it up, living it and loving it. Acid house quickly encouraged people's desire to push and experiment...More than just a music scene, there was a whole new economy emerging, one that provided a completely fresh starting point for a lot of people...Even if your life wasn't radically changed, the pills provided a colourful backdrop that made life more bearable.[50]

Pete, a small-time drug dealer from Streatham, knew exactly how to get the most from that economy. In the later 1980s he and some mates formed a tight-knit group of hustlers who called themselves the Family. In his memory, the Family

were out every weekend from Thursday to Sunday, at places like Babylon at Heaven, Go Global at Astoria, Dance Wicked in Vauxhall, Soul II Soul at the Africa Centre, and following wherever the Kiss DJs Paul "Trouble" Anderson, Mad Hatter Trevor and Norman Jay were playing. Put on top of that following the Arsenal home and away culminating in that magnificent night at Anfield, where we won the League in the fading embers of the match, and life was fucking good.

By 1989 Pete had sussed there was a massive opportunity waiting to be exploited. Once realised, Pete and his crew, who all had full-time jobs to tide them over, turned dealing in Es into the quintessential nice little earner. At Dance 1990 at the London Arena they *"smashed the place"*, milking Acid Heads for everything they could and then

> *pissing ourselves laughing as we head out of there at 7am with birds in tow and everyone is jangling with 800 quid's worth of pound coins in our sky rockets.*[51]

The media and moral panic about E in the late 1980s wildly missed the point. House was a sound, an *experience,* inextricable from its environment, from raves and E. Young people with energy to spare enjoyed it and mostly it did no harm. But its main legacy was neither a generation of hopeless drug addicts nor the advent of universal love but an increase in the wealth and power of the Adams crime family, who controlled the supply of the drug in London.

London's culture always revolved around wealth and power. On 19 July 1987 the Broadwater Farm Youth Association, encouraged by Martha Osamor and others, held a one-day conference, the first of what would become an annual event, to discuss the novel concept of "institutional racism" and how to combat it. It included speakers from the Broadwater Farm Residents Association, the Ceddo film collective and the Race Equality Unit of Haringey Council. The debate was given added urgency by recent events. By 1987 the British labour movement had suffered two massive and historic defeats, the Miners' Strike of 1984-85 and the crushing of the Fleet Street printers in 1986.

For obvious reasons the Miners' Strike did not directly impact London although left and trade union activists throughout the city took part in solidarity action, attending demos, collecting money and sending donations. Ted took pleasure in covertly redirecting food from Carlton's offices and properties to St Pancras Labour Party who added it to their regular collection for the miners. In early 1985, through the auspices of Poplar

Labour Party, I put up a Yorkshire miner and his wife in my council flat in Oban House near Canning Town for the night before we all headed off to a big demo the next day. Over a meal and drinks they told me about their experiences during the strike. They were friendly and polite although clearly hiding their astonishment at what a shithole Poplar was.

In April 1984 a small group of left activists brought together by Mark Ashton, a young member of the CP from Northern Ireland, formed Lesbians and Gays Support the Miners (LGSM). The group initially worked out of Gay's the Word bookshop but when the operation became too big to run from the shop it moved to the Fallen Angel gay pub on Graham Road, Islington, adjacent to City Road Basin. After a homophobic headline in the *Sun* attempted to smear the whole initiative, LGSM cheekily adopted the headline and held its famous "Pits and Perverts" fund-raising event, headlined by Jimmy Sommerville and Bronski Beat, at the Electric Ballroom in Camden Town on 10th December 1984.

The Fallen Angel was almost as important as the Bell to North London's gay community. Lisa Power, co-founder of the *Pink Paper* and Stonewall, was a regular at the pub in the 1980s. She remembered the night that Chris Smith, another regular and at the time Labour MP for Islington South, publicly came out, the first British MP ever to do so. The Fallen Angel's proprietor held a lock-in of the pub's regulars to greet him on his return from the announcement, Smith being greeted with cheers and a standing ovation:

> *The Mayor of Islington, Bob Crossman, also used to drink there with Martin his partner. My girlfriend would moor her narrowboat on the canal outside the pub (they let us use their loos) and we would party there. We were so rowdy one night that a resident came across to remonstrate with us.* "I'll call the Council" *he threatened.* "Call the Council?" *roared Bob.* "Call the fucking Council, then — I'm the fucking Mayor!"[52]

The 2014 film *Pride* tells the story of LGSM and the effect it had on wider labour movement attitudes. It captures not just this specific social milieu but the moment when London's culturally and sexually diverse working class geared up and went out into the world. Its gesture of solidarity with the struggle of an older, more traditional working class was welcomed and returned. Suddenly gay lefties from Camden found themselves in pit villages and Welsh miners found themselves dancing at the Electric Ballroom. Walls came tumbling down.

The defeat of the miners in 1985 was followed in 1986 by Rupert Murdoch's assault on the large number of Fleet Street's printers that worked for News International. The reason given for Murdoch's surprise mass relocation to Wapping and his derecognition of the printers union SOGAT was the legendary "Spanish Practices" of the printers. It was not that these did not exist. On the contrary, they were pervasive and some printers exploited them fully. But the underlying reason for the attack was that the printers had real control of the work process, with jobs secured only with a union card, decent wages and job security. This power could become political, as when *Sun* typesetters refused to print a slanderous attack on NUM leader Arthur Scargill during the Miners' Strike. SOGAT was perfectly aware that newspapers could not continue to be printed using "hot metal" forever, and its new General Secretary Brenda Dean assured Murdoch that the union could deliver a new deal on staffing levels and new technology if it was a fair one.

In early 1986 negotiations appeared to be proceeding smoothly but it was a simply a front, designed to persuade the union that Murdoch wished to reach an agreement. On 24th January 1986 Murdoch initiated a secret plan, Project 800, to transfer the operations of the *Sun,* the *News of the World,* the *Times* and the *Sunday Times* from Bouverie Street and Gray's Inn Road to a fortress complex in Wapping. When the printers realised that the agreements they were on the verge of signing were just a trick, they went on strike. This gave Murdoch a legal pretext to sack them. Five thousand staff were dismissed in one stroke, saving millions of pounds in redundancy payments and enabling Murdoch to start again with an almost entirely new workforce hired in secrecy and prepared for this moment.

Most journalists, but not all, went with him to Wapping, and for the next year there were mass pickets outside the plant as buses took the new staff in. On Saturday nights the pickets attempted to stop lorries taking out Sunday's newspapers. When mounted police attacked them, the pickets ran for escape into the Stephen & Matilda Estate where tenants of the new housing co-operative would shelter them from pursuit. In the end, despite a massive show of resistance and solidarity from trade unions and left activists across the city, the dispute was lost and London's trade union aristocracy were history.

Realising that politics had become a cultural battle as much as a political one, the Labour Party and a group of left-leaning musicians like Paul Weller and Billy Bragg set up Red Wedge, an umbrella organisation that tried to bring a socialist message to working class kids via popular music. By the mid-1980s Chip Hamer was a young musician, poet and aspiring writer, and up for the struggle:

> I got recruited by Porky the Poet (Phill Jupitus) at a Housemartins gig, at the Clarendon Hotel. The band I was in had split up, so I volunteered as a writer and started on Well Red, the Red Wedge magazine. I found that I knew quite a few people involved from my days following The Jam, but I was also able to put names to a few familiar faces and make a whole lot of new friends.

For a while Chip put most of his time into organising and writing for Red Wedge:

> I was a pretty average journalist but was out and about a lot at gigs - most of those brilliant little boozers that put bands on like the Falcon, the White Horse, The Bull & Gate, The Robey, have gone now - and demos and the like. We had a neat line in patter, flogging the magazine on the street. I remember properly pissing off the SWP paper sellers outside an LKJ AAA gig at Camden Town Hall opposite St Pancras. They never could take a joke.[53]

But Red Wedge couldn't stem the tide. With the loss of manufacturing industry in London and the defeat of one of the private sector's major areas of unionised employment, the public sector now became the heartland of labour movement values as well as one of the few sectors that actively welcomed a diverse workforce. By 1984 24% of LT's workforce were BAME. The welfare services and the NHS had a similar employee profile. The Metropolitan Police and the London Fire Brigade continued to provide relatively well paid and secure employment, but while the Met's "canteen culture" filtered out its few black and liberal-minded recruits, the LFB was more firmly rooted in London life.

The working pattern at Soho Fire Station was replicated in all London's fire stations. A rota system divided the firefighters into four watches — Red, Blue, White and Green. The watches worked a four-day shift of two-day duties (09.00-18.00) then two night duties (18.00-09.00), followed by four days off. The day duties included cleaning of the fire engines, testing equipment and checking health and safety, as well as daily drilling and a regular physical fitness regime in the station's gym. Firefighters also inspected buildings and fire hydrants on their patch.

Soho station was put to its biggest test on 18th November 1987 when a devastating fire took hold in King's Cross Underground Station, at the time London's busiest tube station. At 19.30 that day a passenger spotted smoke and sparks coming from under one of the old wooden escalators leading up from the Piccadilly Line platforms and pressed the emergency button to stop the escalator. When British Transport Police (BTP) Constable Ken Kerbey investigated he saw more fire but could not use his radio underground, so he ran up to street level and called in, "We have a fire on the Piccadilly line escalator at King's Cross. Request further assistance and fire service immediately".

Although Euston Fire Station was nearer to the scene its engines were all out on call so it was Soho Red Watch, led by Station Officer Colin Townsley, who arrived first. Fifteen minutes later a jet of high-pressure flames, burning at five hundred degrees, burst out from under the escalators and shot up into the main concourse in a "flashover" fireball, instantly killing passengers attempting to flee. No firefighters were killed but they had to retreat quickly out of the station. Townsley ordered his men out but himself returned down a smoke-filled escalator to rescue a passenger calling for help. He and the passenger, Elizabeth Byers, were later discovered dead at the foot of the escalator, she burned to death, he untouched but overcome by smoke as he tried to move her. As the fire took hold every fire station in North London was ordered to send "pumps" (fire engines) to King's Cross.

The flashover, the extreme heat and a wall of thick black smoke made for nightmarish conditions. Firefighters Steven Bell, Vernon Trefry and David Priestman were on the street when they heard screams and passengers crying for help below. They descended into the station and ran into a level of heat that none of them had ever before encountered. The three firemen dropped to the floor and slowly edged forwards to the main concourse where, as Bell recalled, the true horror of the situation dawned on them:

> We realised the trains were still running. The smoke was being sucked back down into the fire as they entered and left the platform. The sight that greeted us was completely unprecedented; the jet of water was simply turning to steam not more than ten feet after leaving the nozzle...Every time a train came into the station a great rush of air would fly up the escalator and feed the fire afresh. The waves of fire washed over us like a flamethrower.[54]

At the fire's height there were 150 fire fighters and 15 ambulances at the scene ferrying the dead and injured to UCH on Euston Road. Over the next few hours, the fire was gradually brought under control but the death toll was almost as high as the Denmark Place fire seven years earlier. On Friday 27th November central London came to a standstill as all four of Soho's Watches lined Shaftesbury Avenue for the funeral cortege of Station Officer Townsley. The cortege stopped outside King's Cross station for a minute's silence, where thousands of firefighters from all over London stood to attention, and then continued to St Paul's, Covent Garden for the service.

LT and the emergency services were traditional working class blue-collar occupations and would remain so. Other white-collar occupations, hitherto little regarded, were breaking with tradition. From the middle of the 1970s many sons and daughters of working class parents who had gone to university found themselves working in the social and welfare services, still with working class values but politically and intellectually primed to criticise their environment and employer. One of the structures of the state in which they ended up, often by accident or chance after a period of unemployment had introduced them first-hand to the benefits system, was London's large network of DHSS and Dole Offices.

In 1984, when Wham! had sung *"The benefit gang are gonna pay!"*, no one enjoyed its comic irony more than the "benefit gang" themselves, the harassed and under-paid staff on the front line of UBOs and DHSS offices, kept afloat by their camaraderie and after-hours drinking culture. By late 1987 the demands on them from national government to cut the total jobless figure (or, more accurately, the total registered as signing on) had become relentless. In London the Department of Employment saw CPSA's large and well-organised Central London Branch, which encapsulated most of North London up to Camden and Archway, as the main opposition to management diktat.

After UBOs and Job Centres were amalgamated into one entity called the Employment Service (ES) the ES's senior management decided that, contrary to previous agreements that transfers would be voluntary, staff at selected North London UBOs would be compulsorily re-deployed without filling the vacancies left behind. The policy was activated on 21st December 1987, when all of the "casual" (temporary) staff at North London's Job Centres were summarily sacked and those at Camden A UBO were transferred to take their place. Anger at the move and its timing was immediate and intense. On 11th January 1988 Camden A was joined on strike by Marylebone A and B and Westminster UBO. From there the dispute escalated to include thirty-five UBOs, Job Centres and DHSS offices across North London, culminating in a one-day, all-out strike across all of London's Employment Service offices on 18th February.

The initial enthusiasm for the strike across CPSA's Central London ES Branch drained away as it fell victim to internal union squabbles between the SWP, strong on the ground and wanting to extend the strike, and Militant, strong on CPSA's National Disputes Committee, who oversaw the wider strategy and were more cautious. The "Swerps" and the "Millies", although indistinguishable to most members, rarely got on or agreed on tactics.

Jean Richards, a second-generation Irish Londoner who worked in Marylebone UBO and belonged to neither faction, found meetings about the strike grew increasingly frustrating, with left activists more concerned with scoring points off each other than achieving victory:

> *The mass meetings became jargon-slanging matches with many determined and well-meaning strikers not realising what was going on. Generally, the same long-winded boring speakers would have their say every week. They weren't talking to the meeting but trying to prove themselves to their party. A lot of strikers felt too intimidated by this speechifying party atmosphere to ask questions...*
>
> *One excellent proposal suggesting there should be a mass picket targeting on a particular office decided secretly the night before, a tactic which would have terrified many scabs and possibly would have gained much needed publicity, wasn't even considered because it was a non-party proposal...Because all real discussion was suppressed, the meetings finally degenerated into mad debates on any unrelated, fashionable issue.*[55]

Even though DHSS offices refused to do the work of striking UBOs, the strike petered out at the end of March with no resolution. Towards its close CPSA's Central London Branch were banned from yet another social venue when a raucous solidarity evening for the strike held in a back hall of the Merlin Street Baths opposite Charles Rowan House in Clerkenwell(with Jeremy Hardy providing his usual unpaid routine for the strikers) got out of hand and ended with a urinal being ripped off its base.

London's borough councils, especially those historically run by Labour, also continued to provide jobs and opportunity to working class people. After finishing college in the mid-1980s, Sean McGlinchey had a series of temporary jobs including bartending, labouring with Murphy's and working at Madame Tussauds. In 1985 he saw a job advertised for Home Helping with Camden Council which led to taking up a post as a Warden in Denton, a tower block on the Denton Estate on Prince of Wales Road between Chalk Farm and Kentish Town, used as "sheltered accommodation" for older tenants:

> I had an affinity for Camden Council as I had worked regularly for them as a road sweeper in the university holidays. I got the job and really enjoyed being involved in the care of elderly people. After a year of doing it, I applied in 1986 as a resident sheltered Housing Manager...Throughout the years that I have worked for them, Camden Council has always been a progressive Labour controlled borough which has treated its staff with respect and rewarded us with good conditions.[56]

Like Sean and myself, Tony Kilshaw went to Queen Mary College, University of London, on the Mile End Road. Like other students from Queen Mary, he had a council flat on the Kingsbridge Estate on the Isle of Dogs where he was an active member of the Labour Party. But college was not for him. After a period working as a carpenter for Camden Council Tony moved to Leytonstone, discovered he had a deep affinity for maths and became a maths teacher. His sister Joan married Barry Howe, whose parents had come over to Britain from County Clare in the 1950s. Like many second- and third-generation London Irish, Barry also went on to university, later becoming a Quantity Surveyor.

Barry's brother Martin was born in 1959 and after taking law at Sheffield University he started his own law firm, Howe and Co, in two rooms at the back of his parents' off-license on the corner of Mozart Street and Bravington Road in Kensal Rise, immediately adjacent to the Mozart Estate. Martin and his younger brother Dave worked in the offy during school and university holidays. They and their parents were well known in the area and despite the Mozart's fearsome reputation there was relatively little trouble, although once when Dave was working the till a local kid came in and pointed a replica gun at him in an attempted robbery, whereupon the family's Alsatian dog jumped up and clamped his fangs into the kid's arm.

Further education remained the London working class's main route out of low pay and limited employment options. Ruth Quintyne was recruited in Barbados in the 1950s to work for British Railways, working at the cafeteria at Marylebone Station and living in BR's big hostel in Paddington. In 1978 she started work with Camden Council in a Day Nursery, looking after eighty children. At the time only nursery workers with formal qualifications were allowed further training but a Black Workers Group, supported by the local government trade union NALGO, pushed for training to be allocated to non-qualified workers like Ruth. As a result she was seconded for two years to a social work course, which developed into a course at the North London Polytechnic, a frequent route out of low-level admin jobs for working class men and women who wanted to push themselves educationally and professionally.[57]

The 1980s was the zenith of a period in which working class kids got paid to go to university and expand their social and intellectual horizons, using their new qualifications and self-confidence to enter professions hitherto closed to them, when not actively creating new professions and opportunities themselves. While some of London's young working class were trapped in long-term unemployment, many others forged new identities and less conventional working lives. Not all precarity was poverty. Some of it led out of poverty. Some of it was fun. Fashion and style became as important, *more* important, to working class youth than to the middle class.

As a result even the best dramas of London working class life at the start of the decade, like *Fox*, look anachronistic by its close. With rare exceptions, most dramatic presentations of working class life were filtered through the middle class biases of their creators. Two of the most critically lauded British films of the time, which include scenes and vignettes of North London working class life, Stephen Frears' *Sammy and Rosie Get*

Laid (1987) and Mike Leigh's *High Hopes* (1988) exemplify the problem.

Sammy and Rosie's narrative touches on urban deprivation, sink estates and how riots start, but Hanif Kurieshi's screenplay is really about London's liberal middle class. Its working class characters are colourful interlopers in the life of Sammy, an affluent Indian accountant, and his wife Rosie, a white social worker, whose "open relationship" is supposedly liberatory. The filmmaker's view of working class existence was best expressed in their use of the Howe family's off-license near the Mozart Estate, where they filmed a few scenes, adding a large chicken-wire screen to the serving counter where none existed in real life.

High Hopes is at least *about* working class London. Filmed around two old Victorian tenement blocks behind King's Cross mainline station, Culross and Stanley Buildings, managed by Shortlife Community Housing which at the time rented out flats on short leases to an eclectic group of working class tenants, *High Hopes* is an atmospheric record of the period and the place, but Leigh doesn't capture the *new* King's Cross at all, which at the time of filming was teeming with young people at house parties on Battle Bridge Court next to the Ice Wharf. Nor does he include or mention the long line of bedraggled sex workers lined up on York Road every night, as indisputably working class as his socialist hero and heroine. Neither *Sammy and Rosie* or *High Hopes* approach the authenticity of work produced by Euston Films or even that of a high-quality children's TV programme like *Tucker's Luck* (1983-85), filmed on North London locations including Trellick Tower and around Paddington, Kensal Rise and Harrow Road.

By historical accident, although Westminster City Council encompassed the capital's richest areas — the West End, St James's, Belgravia, Knightsbridge, Hyde Park and Marylebone— its neglected north-west quadrant, which borders Brent, includes Bayswater, Westbourne, Harrow Road and Queen's Park. In 1986, as in every local election from 1964 to 2018, Westminster elected a Tory-led council, but this time it had a historically low Tory majority (thirty-two to Labour's twenty-seven), with the Tories only holding on to the council by 106 votes when Labour failed to take one marginal ward. This was a situation Westminster's Tories, led by Council Leader Dame Shirley Porter, were determined to prevent happening again. The result was a policy called "Building Stable Communities" run in secret by Porter and a few trusted councillors, designed to alter the social composition of eight marginal wards to advantage the Tories.

These wards were three where Labour had narrowly won (Bayswater, Maida Vale and Millbank), three where the Tories had narrowly won (St James's, Victoria and Cavendish), one that returned an Independent (West End) and a ward where the SDP had taken Tory votes (Hamilton Terrace). In these wards the council housing stock was renovated and sold off instead of being allocated to those on the waiting list when they became vacant. A large number of homeless and vulnerable people, as well as students and nurses perceived as natural Labour voters, were moved to alternative accommodation outside Westminster or outside London entirely. In 1989, when this policy began to backfire, over one hundred homeless families were moved from hostels in the targeted wards to two dilapidated tower blocks in the safe Labour ward of Harrow Road.

Eventually this flagrantly political scheme was referred to the District Auditor who ordered it stopped pending investigation. In 1996 the Auditor declared the policy "disgraceful and improper gerrymandering". Porter had to pay back £12m to Westminster before she fled the country and the law. Her fall demonstrated there were limits, at the time, to a social cleansing policy in desirable parts of North London. It couldn't be done *explicitly*, as the result of deliberate council policy. It had to arise as the result of seemingly natural economic forces and the property market. That would happen soon enough.

THE 1990s

"We're steaming down the Westway, the welcoming sight of Trellick Tower as the sun's setting in the rear view mirror and we're heading into the most complex, sometimes unforgiving but beautifully diverse metropolis in the world. You get over the Edgware Road and you're steaming down the Marylebone Road and you know you're not far from your destination...Down through King's Cross, long been the haven of lowlifes, blaggers, brasses and pissed up Northern hooligans on their way back to insignificant backwaters. Down Gray's Inn Road...Round the corner into Holborn and there it is. Our destination. The Leisure Lounge...

6 hours of party time. 6 hours of living for the here and now. Fuck tomorrow. Fuck Work. Live Life. LOVE LIFE! This is London. My place, my town, my people."

Johnny Jarvis

On 31st March 1990, a huge demonstration against the introduction of the Poll Tax took place in London which turned into a violent riot in the centre of the city. It arose from the Thatcher government's desire to replace the rates, the long-established system to fund local government, with a flat rate levied on individuals, meaning that the poorest renter paid as much as the richest landowner. Under the rates, the higher a property's notional rental value the more the owner paid to the local council. Its replacement, the Community Charge (AKA the Poll Tax) was popular with Tories and businesses who saw the rates as a means by which Labour councils, particularly in London, took money from them to fund social housing or "loony left" equality programmes.

The introduction of the Poll Tax in Scotland in 1989 led to nearly one million Scots refusing to pay and the creation of the All-Britain Anti-Poll Tax Federation, mainly by activists from Militant, who had also been active in the North London Employment Service dispute of 1988. The Federation began to organise a campaign of mass non-payment of the Poll Tax which spread to the capital. In North London, the Unwaged Centre in Wood Green was used as a nucleus for anti-Poll Tax groups to come together and organise. By summer 1989 these had solidified into Tottenham Against the Poll Tax (TAPT), Hornsey and Wood Green Against the Poll Tax (H&WGAPT) and Green Lanes Against the Poll Tax (GLAPT), all operating under the umbrella of the Haringey Anti-Poll Tax Union. In early 1990 London saw turbulent demonstrations against the new tax outside town halls in Haringey (5th March), Newham (7th March), Hackney (8th March) and Lambeth (9th March), as well as across the country.

The campaign culminated on 31st March in the largest demonstration in London in the twentieth century, estimated at nearly a quarter of a million people, a vast coalescence of anti-Poll Tax groups from across the UK. When the front of the march approached Trafalgar Square the police blocked the top of Northumberland Avenue preventing marchers reaching the square. Up to that point there had been no trouble, but when marchers between St Martin's Lane and Whitehall were kettled, they fought back. In the fighting nearly four hundred shop and office fronts along Charing Cross Road, Oxford Street, Haymarket, Long Acre, St Martin's Lane and Covent Garden were trashed. Class War and other anarchists led the way, using materials from an unguarded building site on one side of Trafalgar Square to smash windows and attack police. It was the most violent demonstration in Trafalgar Square since "Bloody Sunday" 1887, when the Metropolitan Police viciously assaulted a huge labour movement protest against unemployment.

The resistance to the Poll Tax, with up to 18 million people refusing to pay, was the largest civil disobedience campaign in British history. But whilst its political significance was undeniable, the riot itself should not be blown out of proportion. On Saturday 31st March far more working class Londoners went to see a football match or to the pub or went shopping or did stuff around the house than attended the demonstration, much less took part in the riot. For many the riot primarily meant the closure of shops they either worked or shopped in and extra work for the cleaners who swept up the streets, the builders who boarded up broken windows and the ambulance and fire crews who dealt with the aftermath.

The anti-Poll Tax riots were also used to justify the further militarisation of the Metropolitan Police. In July 1991 the Met's national firearms training centre at Lippitts Hill in Epping Forest turned out its first cadre of ninety officers for the force's new Armed Response Vehicles (ARVs), adding another fifty within a year. On 3rd September 1991 the Met held a Female Officers Open Day at Lippitts Hill to redress the imbalance of only fifty armed female officers out of a total of over 2,000 officers in the Met authorised to use firearms. By 2011 at least seventeen ARVs were patrolling London's streets at any one time and the unit contained over 250 full-time armed officers.

The working life of most Met officers was very different that of the specialised ARV units. In 1987 Dave Blundell joined the Met as a cadet. Like all new entrants he trained at Hendon. Having grown up in a small town near Stockport, he particularly enjoyed being able to take a quick journey down the Northern Line to the West End. He recalled that once he graduated from Hendon as a Constable the kit available to him and his colleagues was basic. At the time beat cops wore tunics and carried a truncheon, handcuffs and a Storno channel 1 PR. Their patrol cars were Austin Metro Pandas. As a result:

The officer safety strategy tended to be 'all pile in' and we would act like a pack to bring down a larger animal. In the early 1990s…a lot of people took steroids along with all sorts of other drugs. Some of the men of violence were enormous. However, no matter how big the man we were facing we would overcome him with superior numbers…We did physical training every day and were as fit as we could be. I was really only armed with the foolishness of youth, and it was a matter of pride for me not to let a suspect get away.

289

In 1998 Dave was promoted to Sergeant and in 2004 to Inspector. In 2013 he became a Police Federation representative. As a beat officer in the 1990s he had a very different perspective on the Met's internal culture than those who collided with it on the streets:

> We had large reliefs in those days, and there would be 20-30 officers parading at each station. That meant back-up was usually near and there was a huge spirit of camaraderie. The canteens were an important source of advice, updates and knowledge and a place to speak about anything that was bothering you.[1]

The camaraderie of the Met could be lethal to others. On 23rd December 1990 an Irishman, Patrick Quinn, was amongst many drunken revellers rounded up and taken to Hammersmith Police Station on Shepherd's Bush Road, where he was almost certainly beaten to death by unnamed police officers. To cover up what had happened, the officers framed another Irishman, Malcolm Kennedy, who they had put in the same cell as Quinn and who woke up in the night to see three police officers giving Quinn such a beating that all his ribs were broken and his heart and spleen crushed. Kennedy had no previous history of violence, all the officers concerned cleaned their uniforms immediately after and the log books to record who visited Quinn's cell were "lost". Despite this Kennedy was convicted of murder and sentenced to life. An appeal led to a nine-year sentence for manslaughter, but Kennedy's sentence was widely perceived as a miscarriage of justice and a campaign to exonerate him carried on for many years.

Despite Thatcher's political demise at the start of the decade, it was in the 1990s that her legacy truly soaked into London life. If there was a crucial point from which all else followed it was in 1986, the year of the abolition of the GLC and the deregulation of the London Stock Exchange. The first meant the end of any attempt at a coherent jobs strategy for London. The second meant the domination of the City's financial services industry over any other aspect of London's economy.

In just nine years, between 1985 and 1994, London lost over a third of its remaining jobs in manufacturing, transport and infrastructure. Firms like Edward Barbers in Paxton Road adjacent to White Hart Lane, which since 1908 had manufactured taps, valves and other fittings for the water supply industry, closed forever in the 1990s. The same period saw an increase in employment in the hospitality, restaurant and retail sectors and, to a lesser extent, in the public sector, where opportunities existed for frontline, administrative and technicians' jobs in the NHS, welfare services and local government. But even with these increases London's unemployment rate during the 1990s was 2% higher than the rest of the country. The worst of it was concentrated in Inner London and amongst the young, male, black working class, whose traditional job opportunities were being switched off.

This put more pressure on the staff of the Employment Service who were supposed to find jobs where none existed and sanction those deemed to be not "actively seeking" work. In 1989 I became a Claimant Advisor at Archway Job Centre on the plaza beneath Archway Tower DHSS, interviewing the long-term unemployed and attempting to steer them towards a job, occupational training, the Enterprise Allowance Scheme (EAS) or attendance at a "Job Club". Some Claimant Advisors diligently followed the rules, referring claimants they suspected of working and signing to Fraud for investigation. Some didn't. All of us knew that putting the registered long-term unemployed on Sick Benefit (SB), even if they were not actually sick, or sending them to a Job Club was designed solely to cut the official jobless total, and as SB paid more than ordinary dole the claimant didn't mind either. Six months at a Job Club usually saw the claimant back at the office signing on but for that time they were off the register.

By 1991 I had transferred from relatively quiet Archway Job Centre to King's Cross UBO, a very different entity. But the political militancy and defiance of the 1980s had transformed into sullen acquiescence and juking the stats. On average a Claimant Advisor at King's Cross was scheduled to interview about sixteen claimants a day, usually less as some did not turn up. On one exceptionally difficult day, when several of my colleagues were off sick, I was obliged pick up the slack. By the end of the day I had interviewed forty-four claimants, a tsunami of individual cases and problems most of whom were impossible to help and who quickly became indistinguishable. When the office doors closed, I could barely recall the last person I had seen let alone any of the others.

Seasoned UBO staff, who often lived near the office and personally knew many of those signing on, either from school or from living on the same estate, were not naïve about those they dealt with. They were usually well aware when claimants were not being truthful or were working and signing on. Sometimes it was blazingly obvious. At King's Cross some claimants turned up to sign on in motorcycle despatch rider gear. Others could be seen by staff at lunchtime working a stall in Chapel Street Market, nodding to those who had signed them on a few hours earlier. In my experience, most UBO staff sympathised and did not report them to Fraud.

The fluidity of employment in London, the temporary and insecure nature of what was on offer, reflected a new type of economy based on new service industries. As older working class jobs disappeared, fresh opportunities opened up in unregulated and non-unionised areas such as the music business, the health industry including gym instructors and personal trainers, the capital's large leisure and entertainment sector, and the hard end of the creative and media industries including IT and technical repair work. The latter in particular threw up micro-firms and start-ups that were content to utilise raw working class talent but seldom had wider social goals.

Andy Wilson was born in 1959 and grew up in Coventry, the son of working class parents who were, in his own words, *"border line lumpenproletariat; my father worked in a factory but also ran a criminal gang"*. After a few years in the Navy, from which he was expelled on "security grounds", he worked in Liverpool for three years as a full-time organiser for the SWP. In 1989, at the SWP's behest, he moved to London and was put up in a comrade's flat in Finsbury Park. During the 1990s he regularly journeyed to the Screen on the Green on Upper

Street and to the Garage, a club on Highbury Corner, to see experimental noise rock bands like Boredoms, Shellac and Faust. The first time he saw Faust they used incendiary devices on stage and the club had to be evacuated.

Andy found London as exciting and cosmopolitan as he had always imagined it would be:

> I was unemployed for the first few years I was here, but then I got a job as a multi-media developer with a small company run by Andy Bereza, who had built the soundboards for Pink Floyd's live concerts and invented the four-track cassette recorder. I became involved in the new media industry as it took off...I also founded the first UK user group for multi-media developers, which became an active and influential technical community. Early on in my career I made attempts to unionise developers, but they were largely either hostile (on libertarian grounds) or indifferent to trade unions. They all made a lot of money, and if they lost one job they could pick up another immediately, so they felt no need for organisation.[2]

Although they usually paid poorly and provided few additional benefits, the new industries were hard to unionise. Despatch riders were treated particularly badly. Many companies demanded that workers provide their own gear including the bike, failed to pay on time or at all, and hired and fired at will. Working in central London, especially, had its trials, as an inside report by despatch riders revealed:

> London police almost daily put up road blocks for despatch riders. In important thoroughfares like Newgate Street, Soho Square or Pall Mall the police would stop and harass all couriers while allowing other traffic to pass freely. This is very frustrating and time consuming and costs couriers money because they are delayed and miss jobs. Officially the roadblocks are to check road worthiness of motorbikes hence the euphemism "Free MOT's", but the police use the checks to search for other things e.g. drugs, tax disks, immigration etc and generally to assert their nagging authority over couriers.[3]

After a feeble and aborted attempt by the TGWU in the mid-1980s to organise London's despatch riders, a few of them simply did it themselves. The Despatch Industrial Workers Union (DIWU), which tried to operate in a loose anarcho-syndicalist fashion devoid of hierarchy and bureaucracy, formed in 1989 and was active until 1992, making some impact in the industry. Within a year of its formation it had a small but loyal hard core and was known by virtually all of the 5,000 or so couriers in London through its free newsletter *Dispatches*. Adam, one of the DIWU's organisers, recalled that while verbal support for the union was usually solid, active engagement could be disappointing:

> *There were quite a few couriers around that described themselves as socialists or anarchists who did not join the Union. For example, I had one discussion with an Australian anarchist courier who said he liked everything about the DIWU except the word "Union". Another anarchist said he couldn't help the DIWU because Monday evenings were 'cheap night at the Rio Cinema"… You can give me your normal working class courier with mortgage and kids over one of those airheads any day.*

Hostility and victimisation from the courier firms made organising difficult. However, successes were gradually notched up. Two DIWU activists got a branch of ten members organised at Megacycles but the branch withered when they left the industry and Megacycles was taken over by West One. The DIWU began to get a reputation in the industry after an organised demo outside West One's office on Caledonian Road, after which new branches sprang up at First Courier, Cain Dispatch, ADC, Harley Street Runners and Cyclone.

The DIWU was hit hard in September 1991 when one of its key activists, despatch rider Peter Fordham, was killed in a collision with a lorry on Pentonville Road. By 1992 the others felt they had done all that they could and decided the DIWU had to be wrapped up. Alan, another one of its activists, remembered the final meeting of those who had started the initiative:

We had a good few bevvies and talked about the fun we'd had making monkeys out of the bosses. In the courier game you cannot be sure that all your friends and comrades will still be alive tomorrow. But here we all were, except for Peter Fordham, after three years, having survived the worst London traffic and the bosses could throw at us.[4]

Bad employers were legion. In 1994 Sue Richmond, who in the 1980s had been a CPSA activist at King's Cross UBO and had taken part in the 1988 North London Employment Service strike, returned from maternity leave to find her job as a trainer had been outsourced. She was offered a transfer to the Health and Safety Executive (HSE) as a Workplace Contact Officer. Her job was to find small firms, mainly on isolated industrial estates, which might be in breach of Health and Safety regulations and provide them the information needed to comply. With a remit spanning North London from Neasden to Barking, she visited many small firms, including the last existing furriers in the city in Finsbury Park, basement garment factories in Bow and numerous forgotten warehouses off the River Lea in Edmonton.

In summer 1996 HSE mounted a "targeted raid" on a series of sweatshops in Spitalfields, an area beginning to emerge from its mythic identity as the dark heart of the East End, the site of the Old Nichol slum and the haunt of Jack the Ripper. Although Spitalfields was still riddled with poverty and neglected housing such as the Rothschild Buildings, the post-war decades had been good for the City-owned fruit, vegetable and flower market, which had improved and extended its structure in 1961, and for Truman's Brewery at the northern end of Brick Lane. Spitalfields, in any case, was never quite as "east" as legend had it, as any map of London could attest. Its western edge along Bishopsgate was immediately adjacent to the City, miles from the real East End of Poplar and the docks.

But although Spitalfield's old market closed down in 1991, many other of its traditional practices remained. Sue, who took part in the raid, was appalled at what the HSE inspectors discovered:

> *In one basement I found about 20 South-East Asian men employed as sewing machinists, the electric cables trailing through pools of water on the floor and one disgusting toilet with no door in the corner. It was hot and humid and smelled horrible. They were employed on a sub-contact for a manufacturer who had a contract to supply a big chain store.*

Looking for more unregulated sweatshops, Sue investigated a nearby old eighteenth-century house on Folgate Street that looked run-down and found different companies on each floor:

> *I passed the 2nd floor only to bump into a very old lady who had rooms on the 3rd floor but who shared a bathroom and tap with the people employed in the workshops below.[5]*

This was not the last gasp of a dying industry but it's still standard practice. In 2003 the GMB union and the campaign group No Sweat reported that after a number of years' continuous activity in the Whitechapel and Spitalfields area they had uncovered at least ten garment factories that did not even pay the National Minimum Wage. On back streets and courtyards off Whitechapel Road and Mile End Road the union had found workshops where workers, virtually all Asian, earned as little as £3.50 per hour (the NMW at that time was £4.10) in unsafe and severely overcrowded conditions of the kind HSE uncovered in 1996.[6]

There were other ways for trade unions to protect workers. In 1995, having spent two years on the Construction Industry Training Board which ran health and safety training courses, Vic Heath was nominated by the TUC to sit on an Employment Tribunal (ET) hearing claims of breaches of employment law such as discrimination and unfair dismissal. Amongst many cases heard by the tribunal was a claim of "constructive dismissal", i.e. the employee had not been fired but had been left no option but to resign, brought by a gay man who had suffered homophobic abuse from his employer. However the Chair of the tribunal, a professional lawyer, was himself homophobic and subjected the claimant to a stream of derogatory remarks. When Vic objected to this the Chair snapped at him, *"What? Are you a poof lover?"*

Vic reported this behaviour to the Head of the London ET service and the Chair was swiftly removed, whereupon a new panel awarded the claimant the maximum amount of compensation. Vic found his time on the tribunal a political and personal education:

> *Most of the other cases I dealt with were on behalf of women experiencing harassment or other forms of sexism, though several involved racism...I always leant towards the side of the worker but we would go through every scenario and be unbiased. The thing is, though, that as a working class man your entire life it makes you aware of the kind of nonsense employees have to deal with, women especially.*[7]

Vic served on the ET until 2002 when he was seventy. On retirement he and his wife Vera moved from Camden to a bungalow in Leagrave with a bigger garden than any they had ever enjoyed in London. Vic's working life had seen him triumph over blacklisting and victimisation, yet those practices remained as entrenched as ever. Mick Lynch was born in 1962 in Paddington to Irish parents who came to Britain during the Blitz, and raised on an old LCC estate in the area with minimal facilities. Leaving school at 16, he qualified as an electrician but because of his trade union activities was subject to the construction industry's blacklist. Struggling to get long-term work, in 1993 Mick started a job with Eurostar, the beginning of a career in the railway industry that in 2021 saw him become General Secretary of the RMT.

Those employed in the older, more established parts of the public sector, such as the NHS and London Transport, faced new challenges. In 1990 the NHS and Community Care Act created the NHS "internal market" and separate NHS Trusts, independent bodies encouraged to compete to raise standards.

London became an immediate battleground when the 1992 Tomlinson Report recommended the closure of major hospitals such as Charing Cross and Barts. As Britain emerged from recession in the mid-1990s and better-paid jobs slowly began to appear, more nurses left the profession, leaving London hospitals heavily dependent on temporary and agency staff.

In May 1993 my daughter Elizabeth was born in the old Alfred Waterhouse-designed building of University College Hospital (UCH) on Gower Street, which opened in 1906 and where Elizabeth's grandfather Ted had been born in 1938. Although she was full-term, complications in the birth meant she was rushed to the Premature Babies Unit (PBU) to be monitored. Being in a PBU at 3am with your first, newly born child, only thirty minutes old, surrounded by premature babies so small you could cup them in the palm of your hand, with nurses who have been working all night ensuring they are safe and well, is a good place to appreciate the service. So I had a personal interest a year later when UCH became part of the University College Hospitals NHS Foundation Trust.

The move into a Trust was preceded by years of strikes and occupations. In November 1992, when it was announced that some UCH wards would imminently close, a spontaneous sit-in and occupation of those wards by nurses took place. Junior doctors and even some Consultants were reportedly sympathetic. The action was successful, with UCH management backing off and giving assurances that the planned ward closures would not go ahead. But it was only a brief pause. In August 1993, three months after I found myself in its PBU, over fifty nurses and porters at UCH went on strike against proposals to close the hospital entirely.

Management announced that any employee taking part in the strike would be banned from the building, making it impossible to organise an emergency rota. Unofficial support from other hospital workers such as ambulance crews kept the strike going. BT engineers refused to cross picket lines to begin disconnecting the closed wards. LT workers at nearby Goodge Street tube station used the station tannoy to tell commuters about the strike. An unofficial Day of Action on 16th September drew support from a wide range of other public sector workers such as teachers, postal workers, council and Job Centre workers, the last mobilised by the CPSA ES Central London Branch. But, in the end, it was not enough. Ill-thought-out ward occupations led by a handful of SWP activists led nowhere and the striker's trade union, UNISON, only recently created out of a merger of three smaller unions, was not keen to support unofficial action to keep an old building open when a new, state-of-the-art UCH on Euston Road was to be built following its closure.

London's transport network had also been "modernised". In 1982 the Tory government created London Underground Limited (LUL), turning the Underground into a separate business, making it more difficult for tube and bus workers to take joint strike action as they worked for separate employers. During the 1980s LUL's in-house works department, which employed 1,500 workers, plus its cleaning and catering services, were all outsourced. Between 1985 and 1997 the total number of people employed by LUL fell from over 21,000 to 16,000. One result of the cutbacks was that the North London Line, the "Magic Line" that whisked the young working class across North London from Hackney to Willesden via Camden and Hampstead, continued to run down.

The North London Line's magic was its route, not its service, which by the early 1990s was plagued by ancient infrastructure and worn-out trains. The service was further threatened by the government's plans for the new Eurotunnel to terminate at St Pancras, a project which utilised two of the NLL's four existing lines. Plans presented by Union Railways (UR), in charge of the project, envisaged the total closure of the lines between Dalston and Highbury and their replacement with a bus service. A confidential report from UR predicted this would provoke massive opposition, privately admitting that the NLL was

... highly political, running through several inner London boroughs and serving many low income passengers without access to cars... Several thousand people will suffer a 10 to 20 minute delay twice a day for two years...and it is quite likely that some of them will be very upset.[8]

A campaign to oppose the line closures eventually succeeded and it was decided that the route from Stratford to St Pancras would be entirely by tunnel. But the winters of 1991-92 and 1992-93 still saw no North London Line Sunday service at all because of long-postponed maintenance work. In 1994, when Network South East collapsed, its entire infrastructure (track, signals, bridges, etc.), including that of the NLL, was privatised under Railtrack. Run as a shadow franchise called North London Railways, it was further degraded by Railtrack's poor track maintenance, scaled back to ensure higher returns for its shareholders.

The introduction of Right to Buy and the selling off of the cream of London's social housing stock during the 1980s had been balanced, to an extent, by the completion of the last modern housing estates and greater availability of cheap rented or squatted properties. But in the 1990s these options shrank. The 1988 Housing Act abolished rent controls and introduced the Assured Shorthold Tenancy which removed protected or statutory tenure, whereby a renter could stay in a property indefinitely and pass it down to relatives, in favour of the landlord's right to evict at short notice. The 1996 Housing Act went further and introduced Buy to Let Mortgages. Rising house prices — between 1994 and 2000 house prices in Islington and Camden went up by 104% — made it almost impossible for the employed working class to buy a decent house in Inner London. Now it became harder to rent as well.

Two former GLC estates in Hackney, the Gascoygne on Well Street Common and the New Kingshold in Haggerston, demonstrated the problems of neglected council housing but also pointed the way to a partial solution. The Kingshold, a series of poorly constructed, asbestos-ridden tower blocks with connecting walkways, was built in the 1970s and soon showed its structural flaws. In 1986 it was transferred from the GLC to Hackney Council, another piece of collateral damage from the abolition of the GLC. Hackney could not afford to maintain the estate and it further declined. In the 1990s the council took the only way out and transferred the estate to a consortia of housing associations. Between 1995 and 1998 the towers were demolished. After consultation with the residents to determine their wishes, the bungalows were refurbished, creating a "Kingshold Mark 2" of new low-level flats, many with street access. A well organised tenants association meant the new estate had social facilities the old one sorely lacked.

In the 1940s and 1950s the Gascoygne, a redbrick LCC estate with additional flourishes like attractive Art Deco balconies, had been a beacon of new social housing. Working class tenants who had moved in from slum housing without indoor baths considered it a relative paradise. But in 1982 it transferred from the GLC to cash-strapped Hackney Council and, like the Kingshold, went into a rapid decline. By the 1990s, when many of its flats were occupied by squatters, it was regarded as a virtual no-go area. One of the squatters, Justine Pearsell, recalled the estate at its nadir:

I can even remember one morning outside my window, a man was crouched down with a gun. There were always burnt cars that had been joy-ridden around the estate, and our metal bins were always burnt out too.[9]

Until it was sold by the council in 1998 to the Sanctuary Housing Association and slowly began to turn itself around, the Gascoygne was a classic example of "residualisation", i.e. the increasing confinement of the capital's social housing not to a large assortment of working class families but to the poorest and most disadvantaged. The result was an increase in squatting not seen since its heyday in the 1970s, something the local state could no longer allow. In March 1988 fifty bailiffs, backed up by five hundred police, had evicted 250 squatters on the Stamford Hill Estate where 120 flats were occupied by squatters organised by the Hackney Housing Action Group. It took three days of fighting in and around the estate before the eviction was complete.

The eviction at Stamford Hill was a defeat for mass squatting but there were many other large squats across Hackney. By the early 1990s nearly all the houses in Ellingford Road and London Lane had been occupied for at least five years by squatters, some of whom were itinerant artists, including photographer Tom Hunter, who recalled:

> It was all very varied. Two doors down the guys were motorbike despatch riders – they'd save up enough money and then go off to the Far East for a few months. Next door to me there was a builder, and a girl who worked in a casino as a croupier. There were charity workers, people doing hardcore labouring jobs, and others who were saving up. It was a really good mixture.[10]

With the houses due to be demolished and replaced by an industrial zone including a frozen chicken warehouse, Hunter and his friend James Mackinnon constructed a replica model of the two streets made out of cardboard, wood, transparencies and photographs, which recreated in miniature the interiors of the houses and the people within. The sculpture, now on display in the Museum of London, caught the media's attention and forced the council to reconsider. It abandoned the demolition and allowed the squatters to become legal tenants in a "creative community" which the tenants then turned into a housing co-operative. Hackney's vibrant squatters' culture began to wither as squatters were either removed or absorbed into similar tenants' bodies. Even so, the last Hackney Homeless Festival held in Clissold Park in 1994 attracted 30,000 people.

Hackney's housing stock was not generally attractive, but in other parts of the capital Right to Buy continued to attract the "aspirational" working class. Ted knew a good thing when he saw it and was no hairshirt socialist. In 1990, utilising Right to Buy, he bought the flat on Haverstock Hill from Camden Council. He felt the hypocrisy and was mildly uncomfortable about it but did it anyway because, as a life-long working class grafter, he knew it offered opportunity to him and his family. Also, Joyce wanted for the first time in her life to live in a house with a garden. So in 1992 they sold the flat and bought a semi-detached house in Shepperton, technically part of South-West London but in reality a suburb.

The 1990s saw Ted living on the outskirts of London and working for the property services conglomerate Jones Lang

Wootton (JLW) managing the contractors, cleaners and security guards of Central House, a large building complex in Hounslow whose tenants included firms like Rockwell International. Joyce worked not too far away as Head Waitress of AGFA Photos HQ in Chiswick. Despite having his own office and a company car, Ted liked neither Hounslow nor Shepperton and yearned for what he had left behind. On most Saturdays in the next few years he travelled back up to Camden and Soho to drop into his favourite haunts. But in the end he had to accept there was no way back to city life except in 1998 to sell the house in Shepperton and move to Brighton, a mini-London much more to his tastes.

Meanwhile London's working class continued to transform. By 1991 about 1.35 million people, one in five of Greater London's population, were from BAME families, many of them born in London. One of the most public expressions of this multi-ethnicity was the construction in Neasden of the Shri Swaminarayan Mandir, the largest Hindu temple outside India, which opened to great fanfare in August 1995. By 2011, when 6.6% of London's total population was Indian and its Hindu majority was 5% of that total, the Mandir had become the centre of Hindu life in the capital.

Most immigrants from the Indian subcontinent settled in West and East London, leaving only outer London boroughs Havering, Bexley and Bromley with large "White English" majorities. North London's immigrants mainly came from Ireland, the Caribbean, Greece, Turkey, Hong Kong and, from the 1990s, failing states and conflict zones in the Middle-East and Africa such as Algeria and Somalia. Right-wing rhetoric of "alien", i.e. non-white, immigration threatening the indigenous culture was rooted in racist paranoia. In the early 1990s the largest non-British immigrant community in London remained the Irish at 256,000, with a quarter of those from Northern Ireland, ostensibly part of the UK.[11]

The first extensive Muslim communities in London arose in the 1970s in the old LCC council estates of Whitechapel and Limehouse. The NF and the BNP — and in the 1980s and 1990s, Tower Hamlets Liberal Democrats, whose cynical "Sons and Daughters" preference scheme was explicitly designed to appeal to white locals — sought to exploit the influx of Bangladeshi immigrants into these areas and persuade the indigenous white working class that the newcomers were being prioritised for social housing, initially with some success. By 2000 Indian Muslims, a separate enclave, lived mainly in Newham but with strong connections to their Pakistani and Bangladeshi co-religionists in Tower Hamlets, Redbridge and Waltham Forest. North London saw less Muslim presence but in the 1970s a small Bangladeshi community took root in Finsbury Park and Holloway, extending south to Somers Town in the 1980s.

By 1988 this community had grown sufficiently to open its own mosque in St Thomas's Road, Finsbury Park, at the time one of the largest in the UK. In 1994 a new, five-storey, completely modernised mosque opened on the site and functioned for a while as a genuine religious and community centre. Unfortunately for the mosque and the community, in 1997 the Islamic fundamentalist Abu Hamza became its Imam. In the 1980s Hamza had worked for a period as a bouncer at several Soho strip clubs and had seemed to enjoy what London had to offer him, but by 1999 he had been thoroughly radicalised and was supporting violent Jihad.

Hamza spoke for some Muslims, mainly angry and alienated young men, but Nasim "Nash" Ali represented a wider constituency. Born in East Pakistan in 1969, Ali moved to London in 1976 and grew up on the Regent's Park Estate. He left Sir William Collins Secondary School in Somers Town with one O Level in Art, after which he worked in a clothes shop in Kentish Town and then for British Telecom. From his early teens he was active in community and voluntary work, in 1984 helping to feed the protestors who had occupied St Pancras Town Hall and in 1989 setting up the Camden Monitoring Group to combat racial harassment. Ali's biggest challenge came in 1994 when a fifteen-year-old white boy was stabbed to death in Somers Town by boys from a local Bangladeshi youth gang.

The murder had its roots in the complex social situation in Somers Town at the time. By the 1980s the area was in a trough. Its main thoroughfare, Chalton Street, was strewn with boarded-up shops and office fronts. The Unity Theatre had closed, its old-fashioned agit-prop no longer popular. The 1990s saw the start of the regeneration that would eventually produce the new British Library, St Pancras International and the Francis Crick Institute, but these were grand public projects that barely touched working class life in the area. The quality and location of its social housing meant that some of the older white working class, who had been there for several generations, took up the option to buy their council flats and moved out. At the same time immigration created a new Bangladeshi community in the area.

Given the scale of immigration into London since the 1950s it is a testament to the city's fundamental tolerance and resilience that it did not produce more serious and destabilising social problems. Despite the racialised poverty and social exclusion of large estates like Broadwater Farm and Holly Street, at no point has London, or any other British city, created American-style ghettos or "projects" exclusively the preserve of black and other non-white minorities. The white riots of 1958 were the nearest the city ever came to a "race war". They were never repeated and by the 1990s London had become the most multicultural city in the world. The biggest obstacles to a better integrated multi-ethnic society in London were the decline of mass social housing, some serious misjudgements in the allocation and management of that housing, and the systemic racism of its police force.

But it would be naive to imagine that integration was not a difficult process. Most of the new immigrant families in Somers Town were concentrated in the area's worst housing like the Chenies or the Goldington Estate, producing resentment and friction between ethnic groups within the area. Integration, on both sides, was not always welcome, to the extent that dating and intermarriage was not encouraged. Most summers saw fighting between the young men of Somers Town and those of the nearby Regent's Park Estate, driven by a toxic mixture of turf and ethnicity. By that time the Sir Williams Collins School had transformed into the South Camden Community School. It was extremely mixed, with 50% of the pupils Bengali, 25% Afro-Caribbean and 25% white.

Amongst the pupils was Richard Everitt, born in Camden to working class parents who had moved to Somers Town in 1986. On 13th August 1994 Richard and two of his friends were the victims of an attack on Midland Road, next to St Pancras station, by a Bengali youth gang of ten to fifteen teenagers who believed that some white boys had earlier mugged one of their girlfriends. Richard, who had nothing to do with whatever had occurred, was stabbed in the back and died. Revenge attacks followed, with white gangs attacking Bengali kids and the firebombing of a Halal butcher. The police flooded the streets and Bengali parents told their kids to stay indoors.

At the height of the trouble a local reporter on the story talked to a worked-up fourteen-year-old white boy named Paul, sitting with his friends at the south end of Robert Street next to Rydal Water, who admitted:

"About 60 of us went up Somers Town on Sunday night to look for Asians. It doesn't matter if we get the ones that killed Richard. Any will do."

Nash Ali, at the time a twenty-five-year old working in the Surma Community Centre for Bengali kids, was also interviewed, and told the reporter:

My mother rang me and told me not to come home because white men and boys were out on the street. They passed right under our flat. Fortunately, all the Bengali boys were home from work by the time. But it's really tense. Two guys passed the community centre today in baseball caps and sunglasses and whispered to two staff that there would be revenge for Richard Everitt's death.[12]

It was widely believed that some of the gang that attacked Richard fled to Bangladesh. The murder, which took place a year after the racist killing of Stephen Lawrence in South London, was clearly racially motivated, but because it challenged the standard conception of such crime (i.e. it was committed by BAME people against a white person) and might have stoked racial tensions even further, Camden Council and the police denied this was the case.

A campaign to defend those charged with Richard's murder used rhetoric about the "King's Cross Two", demos to protest their arrest and trial, and representations made by groups such as Liberty and the Camden Legal Centre, to whom it was inconceivable that the defendants were not victims of racial prejudice. Richard's family were targeted by hate mail and had to move out of the area.

Somers Town would eventually move on but it took serious efforts by anti-racists on both sides to stop the BNP capitalising on the murder and its aftermath. Alan Walter, born in London in 1957, had been part of the Tolmers Square squat in the 1970s. A member of the SWP and a leading organiser in the Communication Workers Union (CWU), he was also a Camden council tenant who campaigned for more and better-quality council housing. After Richard's death he helped form the "Camden: Action Now" campaign group which set up new community youth groups to bridge the ethnic divide in the area. Nash Ali also learnt lessons from the Everitt case, establishing the Camden United Project to bring local kids together, using sport, particularly football, to forge common interests and friendships. In 1995 Nash became a youth worker with the King's Cross Brunswick Neighbourhood Association. Later in the decade he moved into local Labour politics and in the 2000s stood for Camden Council.

Turkish immigration into the United Kingdom increased in the 1980s after Turkey was subject to a military coup and the brutal repression of any who opposed it, especially those who wanted an independent Kurdistan. In 1989 over 4,500 Kurdish refugees arrived in Hackney alone. Many worked in the borough's textile sweatshops. These premises were often raided by the police, not to enforce health and safety but to arrest and deport "illegals". In response, the TGWU and the Union of Turkish Workers formed the TGWU North and East London Textile Branch, created not only to demand better pay and conditions but to campaign against police harrassment and deportation of migrants. Within a year it had 600 members and had taken strike action at Bacton Fashions, a firm that used the sweatshop labour of Turkish and Kurdish migrants awaiting Home Office decisions on leave to remain. When TGWU pickets outside Bacton got too large the police waded in and made arrests.

By the 1990s London's Turkish community was heavily concentrated in areas of North and North-East London like Edmonton, Tottenham, Walthamstow, Wood Green, Palmers Green and especially Stoke Newington. The first Turkish mosque in the United Kingdom was founded in 1977 in a converted synagogue in Shacklewell Lane, followed by the larger, purpose-built Suleymaniye Mosque on Kingsland Road which opened to great fanfare in 1999 and offered a very different kind of Islam to that brewing in the Finsbury Park mosque.

In the early 1990s many immigrants from impoverished, rural parts of Turkey arrived in London. Like their kinfolk who had arrived in the previous two decades, they looked for work in the textile industry but by the 1990s the old clothing factories of Hackney and Haringey were disappearing and new Turkish migrants had to take anything going. Cinar, who arrived in London in the late 1980s, found a job in a small clothing factory but before long it closed down. He recalled that in the early 1990s his life was challenging:

> I worked as a cab driver for a while. It was not a job suitable for me. I became a partner in a small business with the support of my co-ethnics. I did not have any idea about running the business. It was hard times. I became depressed.

Cinar persevered and eventually became the sole owner of an off-license in Stoke Newington. Turkish immigrants like Cinar had one great resource — the strong, informal support networks created by the Turkish community in North London. These enabled new arrivals and older established families to create opportunities, whether by taking seed loans at small interest, working all hours, or providing positions for friends and relatives from Turkey that others had vouched for. Olmez arrived in London in 1991 and like many others started work in textile factories and restaurants, but by 2000 he was already part-owner of a minimart, bought after he saw an advertisement in a Turkish weekly newspaper for a bargain buy. He admitted:

People started to search for alternative opportunities after the factory closures...Turkish people entered off-license, coffee shop, restaurant and market businesses. People who had £3-5 thousand and the ones who could borrow £3-5 thousand, from their relatives or co-ethnics, went into such businesses. It was the fear of becoming unemployed that oriented us to such businesses. We were affected by our surrounding. In reality, trade is not my business.[13]

Cinar and Olmez benefited from the operation of Halkevi, a mutual-support organisation in the UK of such influence within the Turkish community that Hackney councillors worked with it to sort out housing and school problems. This didn't stop the Met's paramilitary Territorial Support Group (TSG) raiding the Halkevi community centre on Stoke Newington High Street on 3rd January 1991, when 2,500 Turkish workers across London, particularly in Hackney, took solidarity action with a General Strike in Turkey that day. The TSG arrived in four vans at high speed, attacked a crowd of strike supporters, arrested people at random, battered many more both in the street and in the cells, and denied the injured access to Homerton Hospital's casualty department.

Halkevi recovered and carried on. Amongst its many services, it provided a credit union that used the modest subscriptions of its members to help fund buy-outs, start-ups and new firms within the community. Its operation was so successful that by 2010 Green Lanes contained hundreds of Kurdish and Turkish cafes and restaurants employing thousands of workers front and back of house, a large network of family and friends known as *Turkiyeli* (People from Turkey), a term created by the community itself to indicate a new, London-based ethnic identity.[14]

What was broadly perceived as "Arab" migration to the UK, with notable increases from Palestine and Lebanon and particularly from a war-devastated Iraq, shot up in the decade after the First Gulf War. The majority of these new arrivals settled in London, mainly in Kensington and Chelsea, Westminster, and Hammersmith and Fulham, in an area stretching from Church Street Market to Maida Vale and Kilburn, and west along Harrow Road. A strong concentration of Arab families could be found on the World's End Estate between King's Road and Cheyne Walk, next to the river. During the 1990s the western end of Uxbridge Road, from Shepherd's Bush to Acton, was transformed with new Arabic shops, Shisha cafes, restaurants, minimarts and market stalls.

Although most migrants from Middle-Eastern countries lived in council housing and worked in traditional working class occupations like catering, retail and taxicab work, they suffered a residual hostility from older Londoners (and not solely whites) arising from the widely reported misbehaviour of oil-rich sheikhs in London, a media cliché from the 1970s that survived because of its core of truth. In the 1990s my uncle Danny, after many different jobs in the 1970s and 1980s including driving a taxi and running a fruit and veg stall, settled into a comfy niche working the night desks of various West End hotels, where he was frequently asked to run expensive booze and other illegal extras up to rich Arab customers. On the other end of the scale, Jabir, who apart from his older brother was the lone Palestinian boy at a predominantly white working class school in North-East London in the late 1990s, was so beyond the ken of most of his schoolmates that he was simply called a "Pakistinian".[15]

The children and grandchildren of earlier immigration into London, the second and third generations, experienced different problems. Some of the modern estates they had grown up on had degenerated so badly they had to be destroyed. Between 1994 and 1997 three of the four towers of the Holly Street estate, and the "snake" that connected them, were demolished, replaced by street-level houses on a grid pattern. In 1996 Tom Hunter spent six months living on the estate and two years taking photos of the residents and their flats before they were moved out, recording a community that had, outwardly, collapsed, with burnt-out cars in the courtyards, broken down lifts and unpoliced crack dens, but had a hidden heart:

It was rough and violent and there was graffiti and rubbish everywhere, but then you went into peoples' homes and it was a warm experience — meeting these people who had put pride and effort into their homes and bringing up their kids.[16]

Robyn Travis was born in 1985 and grew up on the Woodberry Down Estate at the north end of Seven Sisters Road, technically in Hackney but spiritually Tottenham. When he was two his father left. At five he went to Tiverton Primary, a school with mainly Afro-Caribbean kids but with a good smattering of Turkish, Greek-Cypriot, Somali and Irish. Life on Woodberry Down could be hard, with only his grandmother to fall back on if things got difficult:

Sometimes there would be no food, gas or electricity in Woodberry Down. We would often have to walk from Seven Sisters to Dalston to Nan's place for that extra support. From N4 through N16 to E8. A couple of miles. That was a long arse walk as a kid. And it was always cold.[17]

In 1995, when he was ten, he moved to Holly Street and transferred to London Fields Primary. At the time the Holly Street Estate was being slowly demolished and rebuilt, massively disrupting the lives of the tenants being rehoused.

In May 1997 Robyn became aware that a popular sixteen-year-old boy from Tottenham nicknamed Popcorn had been killed by some boys from Hackney, apparently in retaliation for the shooting by the Tottenham Mandem of a sixteen-year old from Hackney, Guydance Dacres, at Chimes nightclub in Dalston. Others said the two killings were unrelated but what mattered was what angry young men *believed*, and they believed there was a beef between Hackney and Tottenham, that they needed to take sides, to "rep their Endz", to defend the dignity and reputation of their little slice of North London against attack and disrespect, even if it be from boys they had been playing football with a few years before. So the postcode wars began.

As a young man Robyn was sucked into the wars, being stabbed at different times in the head, legs, arms and stomach, and stabbing back. Luckily for him he always had other outlets, a sense of the world outside his estate. His Aunt Jay, who lived in Surrey, sometimes visited and took him and his family out to a restaurant or took Robyn to Highbury to see Arsenal. Even as the Hackney-Totty beef escalated, Robyn still had friends on the Tiverton estate in Tottenham and still visited them:

Even though there was a Hackney versus Tottenham war going on it didn't stop me and Geezer going to chill with Odz and our other Tottenham bredrins...My brother didn't like the idea of me going to Totty coz he didn't trust most of them. Neither did I, so I understood his concern. But I didn't like limiting myself to which areas I went to.[18]

In 1999, when Robyn ended up in Homerton Hospital after being stabbed in a street incident, his Aunt Jay got him a job as a server's assistant at Chiquitos on Leicester Square, cleaning the tables, washing cutlery and setting the tables. He was on the National Minimum Wage of £3.60 an hour, making more on tips, but it was the experience of working and socialising outside the Ends that was liberating. For the first time he talked to and became friends with white and Latino people, fellow workers:

Before I got stabbed I was always on the estate with my Holly Street boys because I didn't have anything better to do. I was always thinking of ways of making money without selling drugs or robbing people's phones. With this job I finally had that chance. It felt strange, coz from Monday-Friday I was repping my endz and backing my boys to the fullest and willing to ride on enemies from rival areas. Then from Friday-Sunday I was cleaning tables in a restaurant and asking customers "Can I take your order, please?"[19]

By 2000 the level of gang-related shootings on and around Upper Clapton Road and Lower Clapton Road led to the area being dubbed "Murder Mile" by the media, even though some parts of the infamous stretch, like Clapton Pond, retained the vestigial sense of a now-subsumed village (and does so even more today after receiving regeneration funding in 2004). Many incidents had nothing to do with post-codes. On 25th May 2000, in the middle of the afternoon, Memet Adiguzel, a 37-year old Turkish man, was shot six times as he sat in his car on the junction of Upper Clapton Road and Lea Bridge Road, a murder believed to be drug-related. Other assassinations in Shacklewell and Clapton were more to do with rivalry between drug gangs than kids repping their Endz, although the two could overlap. The Met's ARVs were heavily concentrated in the area on the assumption that this is where they would get their next call.

The problem wasn't London or even Hackney specifically. It was kids raised in the Ends with no good job prospects, constant police harassment, not many responsible male role models and gangs that offered easy money and a sense of identity. It wasn't a problem the police lost sleep over. In 1993 Stephen Lawrence was murdered in Eltham by a gang of white thugs in broad daylight, but the Met's investigation went nowhere. It failed Stephen because, firstly, he was black and so not important to them, and secondly, because many of their detectives in South London had close relationships with the area's major white working class crime families (some of whose sons were suspects in the murder) and didn't mind doing them a favour.

The situation was no better in North London. In January 1987, four years after Colin Roach was shot dead inside Stoke Newington Police Station, another young black man, Trevor Monerville, was arrested and held incommunicado inside the station. Seven days later he had to have emergency surgery to remove a blood clot on his brain. The reputation of Stoke Newington police station became so toxic that questions were asked in parliament. In April 1991 the Met was forced to set up Operation Jackpot to investigate allegations that up to fifty officers at the station up to the rank of Inspector were recycling crack cocaine confiscated from dealers on Sandringham Road and selling it on themselves.

In September 1990 Ida Oderinde was sitting in the kitchen of a friend's house on Sandringham Road when her friend, an occasional drug dealer, was visited by two detectives from Stoke Newington Station who dropped off a plastic bag full of crack cocaine. The detectives saw that Ida had recognised them and decided she was a threat. So, visiting her home later, they planted drugs and arrested her:

> At Stoke Newington police station, in the charge room, the sergeant was sitting in his chair, behind his desk, typewriter in front of him and loads of papers on one side of him. On the other side of the desk were scales, cling film and a roll of foil which they had taken from my kitchen. There was also their bag with their drugs in it. The sergeant took the self-sealing bag out of the carrier bag and placed it on the scales. It weighed 28 grammes. But, by the time we got to court they said it was 12 grammes. I was interviewed that same evening and charged with possession of heroin with intent to supply.[20]

Ida received a four-year sentence, one of many framed by Stoke Newington's corrupt police officers.

More than twenty-five officers were named in Operation Jackpot's first report, which included allegations of drug dealing, fabricating evidence and committing perjury. In November 1991 Detective Constable Lewandowski was sentenced to eighteen months in prison for stealing £3,000 worth of property from a murder victim. In July 1994 eight officers were disciplined and two were tried for perjury and conspiracy to pervert the course of justice, both being acquitted. The Hackney Community Defence Association called Jackpot an "insult to the community" and listed seventy-seven cases of police corruption that had not even been investigated. Shortly after, on 16th December 1994, "Shiji" Lapite was killed in the back of a police van by two officers from Stoke Newington. Even though an inquest found that Shiji had been "unlawfully killed", neither of the officers was prosecuted.

This was routine institutional racism, seen in all areas of the state. Kingslee James Daley, later known as the rapper and performance artist Akala, was born in 1983 to a white Scottish mother and Jamaican father. When his dad left the family soon after he was born he was raised by his mum in Kentish Town, sufficiently out of the way of both Tottenham and Hackney to avoid the worst of the postcode wars. As a mixed-race kid he was a puzzle to classmates, one white kid at primary school calling him a "Chinese black nigger bastard". When he was seven his white English teacher put him in a special needs class for those who needed help with English, despite knowing that he was reading *The Lord of the Rings* on his own at home.

Kingslee still saw his father, in regular visits to him and his new family in the school holidays. He also had other positive male role models looking out for him, an unofficial Greek Cypriot uncle and his godfather, Uncle Offs, who despite having three children of his own and living on an estate in Hackney acted as a surrogate father to him. Kingslee's step-father was the stage manager of the Hackney Empire and so he was exposed to regular theatre at an early age. Reinforcing these influences, he was sent to a Pan-Africanist Saturday School to supplement his official schooling. Like Robyn Travis, Kingslee had an indeterminate status that meant he could, if he wished, slip between postcodes and gang warfare:

I gravitated first to Hackney, where my earliest teenage best friend lived, then to Tottenham for the latter years of secondary and then finally in my later teens to Harlesden. I became a kind of ghetto nomad and because I was from Camden, an area that everyone knew had poor pockets but was not considered a rival hood in a way that any of the above mentioned areas would be, I could get away with it.

None of this saved him from police harassment. He had his first encounter with the Met when he was in his early teens, one evening about 7pm when he was walking home from the youth club. Suddenly a police car pulled over and told him to wait where he was. An officer got out and asked him *"Where are you from, Tottenham? What are you doing around here?"*. The meaning was very clear:

> Tottenham is a much rougher and distinctly blacker area than Camden, even though it's just a short bus ride away. We both knew what they were trying to say. The officer's question already let me know that in his eyes I was dirt; that is, matter out of place.

After holding his arms behind his back the officers searched him because *"someone matching my description"* had robbed somebody in the area earlier. They found nothing on him and then left with no apology. It was the first of many similar incidents in his life.[21]

Akala's upbringing, although leaving him as prey to police racism as any of his friends, demonstrated the social richness of black working class life, as replete with monuments, anniversaries, pubs, clubs, cafes and communal songs as the older white working class whose legacy it absorbed. Most of the time it had nothing to do with gangs, beefs and crime but was full of, in Akala's description of his own Caribbean family life:

> Weddings and funerals with the same soundtracks, the same rum cake with the white icing, Escovitch fish, hard food, carnival, sound-clashes, falling asleep at parents' "blues dance" parties, Saturday school, sometimes church, Rastafarian fathers clashing with Christian grandparents, reggae music, lovers rock, jungle.[22]

But while most of London's black working class tried to stay out of their way, the gangs could not be ignored. By the early 1990s the Tottenham Mandem (TMD) controlled most of the street-level illegal drugs trade in North London. By 1996 its unofficial "leader" Mark Lambie, who was a suspect in the murder of Keith Blakelock, was beginning to forge links with rival gangs in Brent and Notting Hill and was looking to expand. The late 1990s saw tit-for-tat shootings and murders erupt across the city, a cocktail of home-grown gang culture, the Hackney-Totty "beef" which was sometimes just over-excited kids but could become lethal if channelled through the TMD and Hackney Boys, and increasing violence from the "Yardies".

Some Yardies were serious armed criminals and drug-runners from Jamaica, while others were just young wannabe-gangsters aspiring to the status. Yardies didn't introduce guns and gun crime to London, that was already there, but until the 1980s it had been confined mostly to professional criminals, armed robbers and their more unruly counterparts such as those who carried out the 1966 Braybrook Street Massacre. But from the late 1980s the Yardies imported the style and methods of Kingston's violent street culture, where political parties routinely used hired posses of gunmen at election time, into London.

Victor Headley's cult novel *Yardie* (1992) turned this world into pulp fiction. Headley arrived in the UK from Jamaica as a twelve-year-old in 1971. Upon leaving school he worked as a market stallholder and a hospital porter before becoming a writer. *Yardie* was guerrilla-marketed by X Press, a new black publishing company aiming its product squarely at a working class black readership. With its garish and eye-catching cover, it was sold outside nightclubs and became a bestseller purely by word of mouth. Its story of D, a cocaine runner from Jamaica who decides to set up for himself in Hackney, is drenched in street patois, ultra-violence and acute social observation. Describing the clothes D cultivates as soon as he gets some money, Headley captures the aspiring drug king:

> *Several tailor-made suits, silk shirts, trousers and expensive soft leather shoes completed his style...As a final and compulsory touch, he had completed his look with an extensive range of expensive gold jewellery. For a newly arrived "immigrant", he looked like a million dollars.*[23]

The 2018 film of Headley's novel, directed by Idris Elba, was a mixed bag. Before he achieved film stardom, Elba — born and bred in Hackney, son of a Sierra Leonean father and a Ghanian mother — worked day shifts at Ford Dagenham whilst at night he was Big Driis, a popular DJ and MC. His slick and stylish film has a vibrant soundtrack but a strange air of unreality. Filming the exteriors at Chatham Historic Dockyard instead of on location gives Hackney and Green Lanes an artificial look. The only scenes that really convince are those filmed on an old LCC estate doubling as the Pembury, the sole point in the narrative that shows the non-criminal black working class simply living their lives and surviving as best they can.

The 1990s saw Harlesden rival Hackney as a centre of gang warfare and drug-related shootings. On 1st May 1999, a shoot-out occurred in broad daylight outside the Bridge Park Leisure Centre between two gangs, the Cartel Crew from outside the borough and the Lock City Crew based on the Stonebridge Estate, a Brutalist eyesore which the police only entered in convoys. The shoot-out resulted in one death and multiple arrests, after which the police discovered that the Centre, initially set up to help small businesses and unemployed youth but since turned into a community centre whose security was sub-contracted to a third party, was being used by the Lock City Crew as a depot for guns and drugs. From here they caused mayhem across Harlesden and Willesden, with shootings outside nightclubs and sometimes on the high street in the middle of the day.

The gangs of Tottenham, Hackney and Harlesden caused real suffering, but media coverage of their activities ignored that London had *always* had criminal gangs, back to the 1730s when Dick Turpin's Essex Gang carved up the city. In the 1920s Italian razor gangs fought on the streets of Clerkenwell, as did Billy Hill and the Whites in the West End in the 1940s. The Richardsons, who controlled South London in the 1950s and 1960s, were infamous for using torture to enforce compliance or punish grasses. Teddy Boy gangs like the Guvnors, although they lacked access to modern firepower, carried knives and used them as easily as their modern counterparts, fighting for their Ends just as viciously as the TMD and Lock City Crew.

Lambie and others like him were callous sociopaths but not all "roadsters" fitted the stereotype. Akala had several "uncles" who were serious gang leaders yet, seeing how bright he was, encouraged him to stay on at school and discouraged him from being like them:

> One of my "uncles" was a breed of roadman Britain has never admitted to the existence of — the politicised, well-read, suit-wearing black gangster. He could recite dissertations on the Russian Revolution, the troubles in Northern Ireland or Castro's Cuba, yet he was also as hard as they come. A natural leader with charisma and charm by the bucketload, he is the kind of man that other men follow into war. His crew robbed banks, banned the sale of Class A drugs from the estate they controlled, ran a security firm and built a boxing gym for the local children.[24]

London's older white working class criminal empires were starting to fray. By the late 1990s the Adams syndicate was being openly challenged. In March 1998, in a strike at the family by one of their rivals, their chief enforcer Gilbert Wynter "disappeared", widely rumoured to have ended up in the foundations of the Millennium Dome. Eight months later, on 27th November, the Adams' financial wizard Solly Nahomme was shot dead by a man on a motorcycle outside his home in Finchley, on the same street where Terry Adams lived. Shortly after, Terry's brother Tommy was convicted of drug smuggling and sentenced to seven years. By the 2000s the Adams brothers' strategy of maintaining a low profile, of keeping several layers between themselves and the firm's violence, collapsed entirely and in 2007 Terry Adams was jailed for seven years for money-laundering.

As ever, organised crime was demarcated by area and ethnicity. The Adams held sway over a lot of North London but they never attempted to carve up Hackney or Harlesden. Nor did they move on Chinatown, leaving it to the Triads, who had been active there since the 1970s. Several Triad gangs — notably Wo Sing Wo, the Sui Fong and 14 K — worked the streets of Chinatown on both sides of Shaftesbury Avenue, as well as Queensway in Bayswater, demanding protection money and running illegal gambling and prostitution rackets. By

1991 the Triads were such a threat to Chinese businesses and restaurants that the Chair of London's Chinatown Association asked the government to take action.

In 1997, when Hong Kong passed back to China and many Triad soldiers relocated to the UK, the problem got worse. The Snakeheads, a gang from mainland China consisting of ex-soldiers from the People's Liberation Army, arrived in Chinatown and immediately sought to take over. In the late 1990s Jian Ping Chen, known as "Sister Ping", began to dominate the Triad people-smuggling operation in the UK, aided by her boyfriend who ran the 14K in Rotterdam. Between them they are thought to have smuggled over 200,000 people into the UK, most of them to be exploited as casual labour in the restaurant trade or as sex workers.[25]

White criminality was as diverse as its BAME equivalent. Some of it was extremely professional, i.e. Billy Hill, the Adams firm and the kind of serious bank robber that pulled off major jobs like Baker Street Lloyds Bank in 1971, the Heathrow Brinks-Mat robbery of 1986 and the Hatton Garden safe deposit burglary of 2015. Some was as chaotic and hair-trigger as Murder Mile. The white equivalent of the postcode wars was expressed through organised football hooliganism of the type found in West Ham's Inter-City Firm or Chelsea's Headhunters, formerly the Chelsea Shed Boys. In the 1990s the Headhunters expanded their racism into overt neo-fascism, establishing links with the NF and Combat 18, as well as Northern Irish Loyalist paramilitary organisations.

For all this, by the 1990s the fanbase of the big North London clubs — Chelsea, Spurs and Arsenal, although not so much QPR — was beginning to shift towards the middle class, a process accelerated by the formation of the Premier League in 1992. But the most vociferous and most active element of the fans, defending ancient territory under social and economic threat, were still working class. A keen Chelsea fan, Tariq Goddard recalled the particular culture that sustained the club's zealous fanbase in the 1990s:

Chelsea FC was the land that time forgot, our own fans a terrifying presence who patrolled the place looking for new boys, fly by nights and other undesirables not sufficiently brutalised to belong. The Duke of Kendall pub was a place full of builders, sing songs on Sunday and also a slightly glamorous element amongst the actors and bohemians in the area.[26]

Spurs and Arsenal had a different culture, a more relaxed North London style. Spurs' hooligans tended to be a loose collective, an assortment of mini-firms all supporting the club. Unlike Chelsea, the fans formed around an explicitly *anti-racist* identity, the "Yid Army", in which they took the anti-Semitic racism flung at them by other teams' supporters and turned it around, embracing Spurs' Jewish support and wallowing in it, waving the Star of David flag, chanting back in unison, *"We are the Yids, we are the Yids, we are we are we are the Yids!"*

Spurs fans needed attitude in the 1990s because they weren't getting it from the team's performance. The decade began well, with a deeply satisfying 3-1 win against Arsenal in the 1991 FA Cup semi-final, the first ever played between the two sides, a North London Derby so significant it was played at Wembley. Spurs then went on to win the Cup 2-1 against Nottingham Forest. But despite the ambitious plans of manager Terry Venables and Chairman Alan Sugar, two London wide-boys made good, that was it for the decade. For the rest of the 1990s Sugar, like the fans, was consistently disappointed by the club's mediocre form. Sugar took it out on Venables, removing him in a boardroom coup in June 1993, prompting Arsenal fans to taunt Spurs with the chant, *"Just a spoonful of sugar makes the Venables go down...".*

As a Premier League member Spurs needed a new, bigger ground, but it was tied to the old White Hart Lane stadium, at the time notoriously difficult to get to with no nearby tube station. With little transport, many fans found themselves wandering the thoroughly ungentrified streets of North Tottenham. My brother Jamie, a life-long Spurs fan who like most of the club's supporters did not live in the immediate vicinity, had a season ticket and recalled:

The ritual was usually get the overground from Seven Sisters to White Hart Lane and then after the match to avoid the big crush at the station walk the half hour back down Seven Sisters Road to the tube. Of course you were walking with thousands of other fans. Even on midweek night games I don't recall being worried but Tottenham on match days was probably different from other days.[27]

Arsenal had more freedom to expand. In the 1990s it entered its glory years. Ian Wright, signed from Crystal Palace in 1991, became an instant Highbury hero when he scored a hat-trick against Southampton on his debut, going on to become a reliable goal-scoring machine. Arsenal was already performing well under George Graham, winning the FA and League Cups in 1993 and the European Cup Winners Cup in 1994, when in 1996 Arsene Wenger was signed as its new manager. Shaking the team up with a new line-up of international players like Dennis Bergkamp and Thierry Henry, Wenger took the club on to win the Double in 1998 and yet again in 2003.

For most fans football was a hobby, a passion and sometimes a party. Groups of organised football hooligans like the Headhunters, the Inter-City Firm and Millwall's Bushwackers were no more representative of the wider fanbase than professional criminals or Yardie gunmen were of ordinary working class men and women. Football also provided opportunities to working class kids to find a meaning in their lives. Sport often did so. Although the symbolic heart of London's boxing world is still York Hall in Bethnal Green, the city is dotted with boxing clubs and gyms that help working class boys, in particular, let off steam and develop emotional maturity.

One of its finest, the All Stars Boxing Gym and Youth Club at 576 Harrow Road was set up by Isola Akay, originally from Ghana, where he was one of the country's premier professional boxers. In 1974 Akay's ten-year-old son and a group of his friends were excluded from the local gym for being a "disruptive influence", so Akay trained them himself either in local parks or in his sixth-floor council flat in Paddington Basin. In 1981 he secured enough funding to convert an old, disused church on the Harrow Road near Westbourne Grove into a boxing club. It quickly took off.

After a period of political activism with Red Wedge in the 1980s, by 1990 Chip Hamer was working in the Lisson Grove area and needed somewhere local to train:

> ... so I rocked up at the All Stars boxing club. Mr Akay became a father figure to me (as he was to so many young men). I'd dabbled in my youth but the All Stars was serious business and it soon became apparent that my competitive days were behind me. So, wanting to give something back, I got into coaching work. Let's be clear, there's many have dedicated more of their time and effort than I have to that club, but I've met a lot of good friends and learnt an awful lot in my thirty years there.[28]

The Islington Boxing Club (IBC), originally known as the King's Cross Amateur Boxing Club, opened in 1974 in a community hall on York Way, later transferring to its current location on Upper Holloway. The IBC was founded by a dozen local men, including publican and former boxer Reg Topper, beat cop Bill McCourt and railwayman Jim Parodi, who wanted to give bored young men on the estates of Barnsbury and King's Cross better outlets than crime and vandalism. When Reg Topper died of a heart attack and Bill McCourt was promoted out of the area, the running of the club fell mainly to "Big Ron" Hagland. In 1981, after an agreement between the Bovis construction company and Islington Council, the IBC moved to Bovis's disused site offices on Hazelville Road on Hornsey Rise. With financial help from Bovis, the Variety Club of Great Britain, the Federation of London Youth Clubs and the ILEA, the site office was converted and redecorated throughout in the red and white colours of Arsenal FC.

By the 1990s Big Ron was feeling the strain of doing most of the management and he asked his son Lenny to assist (he now runs the club with his own son Reggie). Since its opening it produced hundreds of boxers at national and international level, but it has also acted as a surrogate family and support network for hundreds of working class kids who might otherwise have none, well known throughout the area for its sterling reputation and bright red frontage. Sports clubs such as the IBC were often an oasis and an escape for working class boys and girls who needed to express their energy and ambition.

As was music, although by 1990 the Second Summer of Love was history. It flared out in London in 1989 at a mega-rave at the Sobell Sports Centre in Highbury, after which the scene began to change. Phil Potter remembered:

> *Like most good things that come to an end our Friday night home started to decline. The club owners started to get a bit greedy and by 1990 it was all about chasing the dollar. The DJs started getting commercial and the management started putting the prices up on the door and charging about the same price for water as a pint of lager![29]*

The Baggy scene — Factory Records, the Stone Roses, baggy jeans and football shirts — emerged out of Manchester's frenetic "Madchester" period in the late 1980s, but London soon followed suit. In 1989 a group of lads from the Regent's Park Estate fronted by the mercurial Liam Maher, his brother Joe and Des Penny, formed Flowered Up. By 1990 they had signed with the new indie record label Heavenly Records, producing a strikingly original mash of acid house and North London pub rock. John Tuvey, their mainstay drummer between 1989-1992, recalled:

> *I grew up in King's Cross. My first school I went to was Netley Primary School in Camden. Also in attendance were Liam and Joe. Liam being 2 years older than me, Joe being 1 year older than me. Even though I lived in King's Cross my Nan lived on the Regent's Park Estate where the brothers lived and where Flowered Up was made. We all knew each other and each other's families for many years before the band was ever thought of.[30]*

In 1990 Heavenly Records released the debut singles of Flowered Up ("It's On") and Saint Etienne ("Only Love Can Break Your Heart"), both of which defined London house music.

"Weekender" (1992) was Flowered Up's big hit and major artistic statement. The song and its accompanying eighteen-minute video were a mini-*Quadrophenia* on the frustrations and despair of working class life in London. The video of "It's On", a utopian ode to getting pilled up and dancing, was part-filmed on Cumberland Market playground in the middle of the Regent's Park Estate, a lovely tribute to the place and its people. But the need to escape the estate became a need to escape everything and some of the band went far beyond E into heroin, scouring around King's Cross looking to score. "Weekender" was driven by a philosophy that could only produce burn out, and did. Liam and Joe Maher both died of heroin overdoses, Liam in 2009 and Joe in 2012.

House could be lyrical and rhythmic, but it was essentially music for white boys who needed to be off their heads in order to dance. London's black working class had better music and sense of self. They went to raves and danced with the best of them but they never wholly embraced house and they continued to draw on their past. Harlesden was the centre of London black music in the 1990s, led by Champion Records on the High Street; Lightning, a record distributor, wholesaler and owner of indie labels like Scope and Laser, on Harrow Road; Gangsterville, a record shop where Aswad used to practice and whose label released the hugely successful reggae medley "This Is Lovers Rock"; and Carib Records on Rucklidge Avenue. Their music was played and promoted by London's two big, black-owned pirate radio stations, the massively influential Kiss FM and WBLS.

Jazzie B continued to forge his own path. Soul II Soul led the way in providing new opportunities for new talent. Jazzie understood the reasons for its success in breaking through to the mainstream and for making black British music, black *London* music, so appealing:

They never got the idea that we were a collective, not a group in the accepted sense. We ran it as a sound system, whereas in the days of rock n' roll or, say, Eddy Grant, they could understand that and fix it, so it was the guy with the guitar who could sing who'd be out front, and he was the one they could concentrate on.[31]

The collective character of Soul II Soul, in addition to its relentless blending of reggae, techno and hip-hop, would influence how other music collectives such as Roll Deep and So Solid Crew operated, how free of big company pressures and commercial conformity they could be.

Jazzie was always on the lookout for people who could assist his vision. After a period living in Tottenham in the 1980s, Zita Holbourne moved to the US to live with relatives but in the early 1990s she returned to London and to Tottenham, where she lived in a flat in shared accommodation near White Hart Lane. Although she was beginning to emerge as a writer and poet, at the time she could only get some part-time work in the beauty industry, as a model and make-up artist, occasionally working as a backing vocalist and session singer. After a frightening experience with an intruder in her flat, she moved to East London and was lucky enough to get a council flat:

In this time I doubt another young woman like me could get emergency council housing like I did. But that flat in the tower block gave me a lifeline. Having somewhere safe, secure and stable that was my own meant I could rebuild the broken pieces of my life, grow stronger and get myself back on track. It was my first home that I could truly call my own and for months I used to walk in and out of each room in my flat pinching myself and silently expressing thanks that I had this roof over my head.

She also reconnected with some of her earlier friends, including one, Melissa Bell, with whom she had done a Saturday job at Marks & Spencer in the 1980s. Melissa was an aspiring singer and Zita started doing some backing vocals for her. Zita and Melissa used to go regularly to Friday nights at the 291 Club at the Hackney Empire, a talent show which was also televised. On one particular night:

We usually sat at the back at the top as that was the cheapest tickets. One night the compere shouted out asking if anybody in the audience could sing better than the act that had just been on and we screamed and screamed, "Yes, Yes, Yes!" as loud as we could from so far away until eventually the mic made its way to Melissa. The rest was history. She brought the house down from the few bars she shared on the mic and was invited to come down and sing on stage in the interval. She was then invited back to be a featured artist and me and another friend did backing vocals. Following that we gigged for a while there as backing vocalists.[32]

Following her breakthrough at the 291 Club, Melissa went onto record her debut single "Reconsider", which led Jazzie B to offer her the position of lead vocalist with Soul II Soul from 1993 to 1995. She followed a similar career path to Sonia Maria Clarke, AKA Sonique, born in 1965 in Crouch End to Trinidadian parents. In 1981 Sonia's mother remarried and moved back to Trinidad but Sonia refused to go with her and ended up living in the YMCA. Through a difficult period she attended Highgate Wood Secondary, an outstanding state school which nurtured many talented black working class kids including Chipmunk, Sway DaSafo, Laurie Cunningham and Oswald Boateng.

When Sonique was seventeen a youth worker spotted her singing talent and she embarked on the first stage of her singing career with some chart success. After a period spent refining her voice and working as one part of the S'Express dance music act she hit solo success in the 1990s with "I Put a Spell on You" (1998). Two years later she was even more successful with "It Feels So Good" (2000), winning the 2001 BRIT Award for British Female Solo Artist, widely recognised as a virtuoso chanteuse who fused a perfectly pitched voice with pumping dance music.

By 1990 illegal outdoor and warehouse parties were being replaced by organised raves in properly established clubs. Many had been putting on house events since 1988 but they had also varied their theme nights and provided other options. In the 1990s raves became the mainstream. In 1990 Turnmills in Clerkenwell became the first club in the country to be granted a twenty-four-hour license, followed in 1991 by the Ministry of Sound in a disused bus garage in Elephant and Castle. Others quickly followed. Black music was injected into the scene in the form of ragga, a fusion of reggae and electronic dance music.

Caron Liza Geary, born in Paddington in 1963, was exposed to reggae at an early age in the form of an almost continuous after-hours party next door. Later, as MC Kinky, she was one of the first white ragga DJs, mashing up slices of reggae and electronica with her own verbal overlay to create music for the London and Ibiza clubbing scene. Her era-defining hit "Everything starts with an E" (1990), with extra lyrics by Boy George, was banned by the BBC once they cottoned on to what it was about. It became such an anthem of the rave scene that, she recalled, *"when the screechy guitar on 'Everything...' began, the crowd would roar like a football stadium."*

Ragga and hardcore could not be contained in the rave scene. As the 1990s progressed it mutated into jungle, which grew spontaneously out of the pirate radio/DJ/MC scene in East London and outlier areas of North London like Hackney and Tottenham, added to and spiced up by the untutored musical experiments blasting out of illegal warehouse raves in the abandoned factories of Edmonton's Lea Valley. All of them were energised by the early example of Soul II Soul, living proof that the black working class did not have to compromise or dilute their music to gain success and recognition.

Junglists, those running with the new music and seeing where it took them, were the next stage of evolution after the conventional sound systems of Soul II Soul, but they always acknowledged their history. Record producer, DJ and remixer "Wookie", born Jason Chue in Hackney, was very specific about his influences:

The place to go was Music House in Finsbury Park, in that parade of shops that's opposite the park in Seven Sisters Road, by the Kentucky, there's a chemist shop that's been there for ages and Music House was above that, on the top floor. It was owned by Curtis Hanson, who used to be in the reggae group Black Slate... My dad and brother used to work there, so Curtis is literally like an uncle to me, and I used to hang out there. When I made my first tunes I used to take my keyboard into Music House and he put them on DAT for me.[33]

Jungle and hardcore were eruptions of urban working class creativity so forceful and demanding that they *became* the mainstream, a means of expression for a multi-ethnic working class that was being progressively denied the opportunities that had existed for their parents in the 1960s and 1970s to break through and make an impact. It could still be done, though, as many young jungle, garage and grime artists in the 1990s and 2000s would demonstrate.

Heartless Crew were a trio of multi-ethnic lads from Holloway, with two of the line-up of West Indian background and one mixed Palestinian/Iraqi. They operated as a collective with a mobile sound system, sampling different genres like R&B, hip-hop and ragga, before becoming one of the first UK garage crews. In 1996, after playing house parties and small clubs, they were offered a permanent spot at Chimes in Lower Clapton. Using the pirate radio stations Mission 90.6 FM, Freek FM 101.8 and Y2K FM 90 as a platform, they created a fusion of dancehall sounds with the older Jamaican sound system tradition. Their debut "Heartless Theme" (2002) opened the door to grime.

Akala vividly recalled the rush and excitment of the time:

In the mid-1990s, when I started to get hairs on my chest and I got my first job, I struck out and found my "own" hip-hop. I was thirteen years old, working for £20 per day at a local DIY store, and any week that my family did not need the money I'd be off to the West End to the nerdy record stores that stocked hard-to-get US imports, or up to our bootlegger in Tottenham, and I'd spend my entire £20 on CDs.

Starting with hip-hop, he rapidly moved on to jungle:

I loved Jungle for the rawness of the baselines, the speed and intensity of the drums and the incredible use of samples that gave it a totally unique sound, a sound laced with the grit of Bristol and London's council estates echoing the indelible, irreversible influence of Caribbean ex-pats on British music.[34]

It was a moment and a place perfectly expressed in the cult classic *Junglist* (1994) published by X-Press. *Junglist* eschewed grim sociology for a witty, stylish cyberpunk take of London's clubland. Laced with sly verbal banter and stream of consciousness prose, *Junglist's* four protagonists are part of a South London black working class that has friends in Camden where they routinely hang out and knows it is heading to college, absolutely refusing to be defined or constrained by poverty and race.

North London's working class had never been short of clubs on their doorstep, from Soho's in the 1950s and 1960s to Covent Garden's and Camden Town's in the 1970s and 1980s, but the 1990s saw a new phase, an explosion of new clubs in new venues, often using the abandoned infrastructure of its expiring industry. In the 1960s the Garage, at 22 Highbury Corner next to Highbury and Islington tube station, had been a Temperance Billiard Hall where local villains met and relaxed. In 1993 it opened as a nightclub with a capacity of six hundred. The Garage's resolutely down-at-heel look didn't prevent bands like the Red Hot Chilli Peppers, the Arctic Monkeys, the Killers, Oasis and Radiohead playing its small stage. But for many the ultimate 1990s club was Bagley's at King's Cross, created out of warehouses once used by the glass bottle maker of the same name. From 1992 Bagley's became the biggest rave venue in London, able to hold up to 2,500 people. Those who needed fresh air went out on to its long, curving balcony terrace to chill out and watch the sun come up over St Pancras.

Even Denmark Street experienced a resurgence of its former glory after its nadir in 1980 when the Spanish Rooms were consumed by fire. Number 1 Denmark Street, on the corner next to St Giles-in-the-Fields church, was home to a newly refurbished Job Centre specialising in vacancies for the West End's catering industry. It was managed by Sue Tilley, Lucien Freud's "benefit supervisor sleeping" who had previously worked at Camden and King's Cross UBOs. In the 1990s a slew of new music shops opened in the street, including Hank's Acoustic Instrumental Specialists, Argent's Keyboard Store, the HelterSkelter Music Bookshop, the World of Pianos and the PA Centre at number 23, where the first, non-franchise Forbidden Planet had operated in the 1980s.

All this made London jump like the 1960s, with a collection of clubs — Bagley's, the Garage, Clinks, the Limelight, It's On, Dungeons, Feet First at the Camden Palace, the Paradise Club at the Angel, the Cross on York Way, the Four Aces in Dalston, Syndrome in Oxford Street and Blow Up in Camden Town amongst many others — that were at their peak at this time. It was a culture that seemed to transcend economics. Defying poverty and unemployment and shrinking access to good housing, working class London, or at least major portions of it, displayed an energetic, self-confident swagger during the 1990s not seen since the height of "Swinging London". Tariq Goddard, in his twenties at the time, recalled:

> ... clubbing at Funkin' Pussy at the Africa Centre, Plastic People, the Leisure Lounge, Smashing, and the End, for hip-hop, jungle, indie and techno, everything was represented, as it evolved in real time. You would leave the house and feel as though cultural history was still happening, and you were in it.[35]

Sarah Lucas was born in Holloway in 1962, her dad a milkman and her mum a part-time cleaner, and grew up on an Archway council estate. As a kid she accompanied her mum to her employers' houses so that she could gawp at their furniture, carpets and coffee machines, much as Amanda Millhouse had done when babysitting middle class neighbours in the 1970s. With parents of "absolutely no ambition", she left school at sixteen. After falling pregnant at seventeen and having an abortion, she returned to adult education at the St Pancras Working Men's College in Camden Town to study fine art. By 1988 she was one of the "Young British Artists" (YBAs) and hung out with Damien Hirst.

In her thirties Sarah fetched up at the Colony Room with Hirst and a few other YBAs, most of whom were there to enjoy the wreckage of older Colony legends like Jeffrey Bernard, where she partied hard, sometimes working behind the bar just as Suggs's mum, jazz singer Big Eddi McPherson, had in the 1960s and 1970s. Sarah's upbringing and partying in Soho's least gentrified bar would later feed into scathing and unromantic self-portraits like *Human Toilet Revisited* (1998) and other radical deconstructions of notions of taste and femininity. Of her time at the Colony in the 1990s and 2000s she recalled:

> It stayed very much the Colony and not like other private clubs, because you could only get so many people in there. Unfortunately I can't remember the memorable nights because I was far too pissed.[36]

It was the golden twilight of a finely balanced community and the lifestyle that went with it, of places where class divides and class hang-ups dissolved, of a kind found all across North London but especially in Soho and Camden Town. Camden's febrile working class bohemia, based around the Market and the local pubs, had been too successful. By the 1990s Britpop and rising rents were beginning to choke it off. In the late 1990s Rock On, which had defined Camden's music emporia since 1975, found its annual rent of £36,000 too much and relocated to Harlesden. In 2000 the irreplaceable Compendium bookshop — which since 1968 had provided a truly unique collection of radical history, political theory, alternative and LGBT literature, and semi-legal Marxist, anarchist and Irish Republican publications to a wide customer base of cultural dissidents and curious locals — had to close due to steeply rising rents, a loss mourned by all its customers.

The danger to Camden's social mix and especially to its working class was clear and obvious enough that Camden Council took a specific stand against it. Dingwalls and the Market had been a great success but that still left fifteen acres of the old Goods Yard empty and undeveloped. In 1990 the property firm Hyperion put forward a scheme to convert it into expensive flats for young professionals, with no affordable housing, and a large office complex. Camden Council, supported by local residents and retailers, opposed the scheme and managed to defeat it. It also created a "Conservation Area" from Mornington Crescent to Inverness Street, an attempt to keep Camden Town and its immediate environs on a manageable and intimate scale, eschewing redevelopment that would destroy its character.

Bucking the trend of providing flats for middle class professionals and offices for them to work in, Camden instead built an attractive new council estate, Juniper Crescent, on the empty Goods Yard land immediately behind the Roundhouse and the new Safeways (now Morrisons) supermarket in Chalk Farm Road, which opened in May 1997. An access road was built from Chalk Farm Road through to the Goods Yard to connect to the new estate, an attractive sweep of pleasant, low-level yellow-and-buff-coloured flats with ground-floor entrances, whose balconies and gardens face inwards on a large communal garden and playground. The new development provided 202 homes for rent, run by a consortia of housing associations, a necessary device for Camden to get building permission past a violently anti-council housing Conservative government. The ploy worked and Juniper Crescent became a high-quality social housing project of maisonettes and flats, some specially adapted for people with disabilities, and a new working class community in the heart of Camden.

Camden, as Akala found when negotiating the postcode wars, could be a safe space for the itinerant working class, a zone of exploration and possibility. Laura Grace Ford, an art student from Halifax who took her degree at the Slade School of Art, found herself living a peripatetic life in London, floating from one squat or bedsit to another, notching up fifty different addresses between 1990 and 2010 whilst producing the *Savage Messiah* series of black-and-white printed zines between 2005 and 2009. Laura found that different zones of London produced very different working class experiences. A night out in Camden could end with a bunch of dodgy geezers in Trellick Tower and a one-night stand. Of a suffocating July night in 1995, Laura recorded she was:

wasted in Camden at a Selecter gig. I can't remember how it happened but suddenly I'm backseat joyriding with a bunch of

*skins into an unfamiliar zone. He lives ten floors up in that block
with the Meccano parapet and there's frantic kissing in a coffin-
sized lift, livid weals and fracture lines emerging on his skin.*

But it didn't end well. After waking up in the morning and
realising she didn't fancy him in daylight:

*We go the pub, a paranoid perambulation in the shadow of the
Westway to the Warwick on Portobello. There's the rest of his
crew there talking politics, sordid diatribes about immigration.
Panicked by a drunken mistake I pretend to go the ladies and run
out the back.*[37]

As the fight to defend the Goods Yard and the development
of Juniper Crescent demonstrated, Camden was in some
respects resisting gentrification. Queen's Crescent Market
was held every Thursday and Saturday and provided, as it
still does, a vibrant old-style fruit and veg market, spliced
with halal butchers and Arabic fruit and veg stores like the
Al-Habiib Food Centre and the Camden Fish Bazar, to the
local working class in the nearby council estates of Maitland
Park, Barrington and Lamble, Weedington Road, Denton and
Ferdinand. It was and remains a working class community
centred around the Fiddler's Elbow pub on Prince of Wales
Road and the Sir Robert Peel on Queen's Crescent, still served
by the positively ancient Victor Eagleton's Fishing Equipment
shop at 162 Malden Road, all essential parts of what the
Hidden London website describes as "one of London's hidden
cockney communities".[38]

In the 1970s and 1980s Queen's Crescent Estate had been an
integral part of the surrounding community but by the 1990s it
was experiencing the same kind of problems plaguing Maiden
Lane. Even so, the "proximity effect" that Robert Elms identified
still applied. Kadir, born in 1992, grew up on the estate, a
relatively pleasant low-level sprawl filling the space between
Queen's Crescent and Malden Road, a few minutes' walk from
Camden Lock. Queen's Crescent itself, running from Prince of
Wales Road to the market, exemplified the social intimacy of

old-style council estate and gentrified Victorian houses, in this case literally across the road from each other. Kadir didn't fail to notice:

> *Sometimes when I would walk to the park or something, I'd walk past these massive houses and think, "How have they got this?" Like, "What have they done to get this?" It made you think about how different people live, and it made me want that life as well. I don't know whether it made it better or worse, but seeing it was kind of inspirational, especially coming from my house.*[39]

The area was a vivacious melting pot that attracted ambitious working class youth. In 1995 Russell Brand, a likely lad from Grays in Essex with a precocious intelligence and razor-sharp wit, started at the Drama Centre London at 176 Prince of Wales Road, a converted Methodist church. As he recalled:

> *The social centre of Drama Centre was based around a fairly clear divide between the working class kids, who were there on grants, and those from middle class families who could afford to send their kids to a place like that. I'd managed to wangle myself a grant from Essex Council...There was also a fund, Friends of the Drama Centre, that gave the financially insolvent students, myself included, extra money for maintenance. I did my best to spend every penny of that money on drugs, while living on peoples' floors, wearing shit clothes, and drinking filthy five-quid-a-litre vodkas named after Russian authors.*

Russell ended up sharing a grotty flat with two other working class students above the Queen's Arms pub in Queen's Crescent. In lieu of rent, they were obliged to do three shifts a week behind the bar, a job which suited his mates but was fatal for Russell:

> *I had all the worst possible traits you could have as a barman: I gave drinks away for free, stole from the till, and got drunk at*

work. I couldn't pull pints, I didn't know how to change a barrel, and I was an alcoholic.[40]

The Queen's Arms pub was adjacent to the Queen's Crescent Estate, which had begun to degenerate from the days when my dad and I wandered in and out to access his lock-up, primarily because the 1977 Housing (Homeless Persons) Act mandated that families with "special needs" had priority for council flats. In the 1990s this had meant a large injection of Irish Travellers, none of whom wanted to be there, felt no connection to it, and who took it out on the estate and the local pub where Russell and his mates struggled and failed to maintain a semblance of order.

Yet a few minutes away the Denton Estate, part of Sydney Cook's legacy to generations of working class North Londoners, was holding up well. Sitting between Prince of Wales Road and Chalk Farm Road, the estate was constructed in the late 1960s and early 1970s on the same principle as the nearby Harmood Road and Queen's Crescent Estates, i.e. low-level flats with an individual balcony and garage lock-up for each unit. The Denton Estate was laid out in a hexagonal format, its four hexagons consisting of twenty-three connecting three- and four-storey blocks built around landscaped gardens and one central tower block, Denton, used as sheltered accommodation for older tenants who did not require full-time care but needed to live in a monitored environment where assistance was available if required.

Denton (the tower block) was the only high-rise block ever constructed under the regime of Sydney Cook. The nineteen-storey tower block was made up of ninety-one flats, mostly one-bedroom but with a few two-bedrooms, with a community room for social gatherings and a guest room if friends or relatives of the tenants wished to stay. Views of central London and Hampstead from the higher-level flats are spectacular. In 1986 Sean McGlinchey took up the post of Denton's resident Housing Manager. Until the mid-1990s he and his wife and young family lived in one of the block's flats. Nominally he had set hours, but if a tenant needed help or died then he had to be on duty to deal with it. Sean remembered Denton's special quality:

There was a genuine sense of community. There were so many people living in Denton that it was the size of a small village and it had a similar feel to living in a village with tenants coming together as they met spontaneously in the hallway for a chat as they came and went. The hallway at Denton was like a village high street with a constant stream of tenants, carers, health professionals, friends and family passing through...

It wasn't a place the elderly went to die; far from it:

There was something there for everyone with some of the more able and adventurous ones enjoying the lively nightlife that Chalk Farm and Camden had to offer. I would often bump into one of my tenants in the Marathon kebab house or the Enterprise pub opposite Chalk Farm tube station.[41]

Although not without problems of poverty and gang culture, the council estates in the area bordered by Chalk Farm Road, Belsize Park and Gospel Oak were and are an oasis of decent, secure homes for working class people in an "affluent" part of North London with excellent public transport and close proximity to Camden Lock and Hampstead Heath.

In the late 1980s my uncle Danny and aunt Josie, with my cousins Danny and Nicky, were living on the grim, intimidating Ingestre Estate just north of Kentish Town, but with two growing sons they needed an extra bedroom. The council agreed and moved them across Highgate Road to the newer and far more pleasant Carol and Sandringham Estate between Dartmouth Park and Gospel Oak. In the 1990s, when my uncle started working night shifts on hotel desks in the West End, he needed to sleep in the day. Carol and Sandringham was conducive as their three-bedroom, ground-floor flat looked inward on to a quiet garden in the estate and there were seldom the kind of youth-related problems that occurred elsewhere.

The attitude of Labour councils like Camden towards their tenants and staff were usually more progressive than London's Tory councils, but by the late 1990s the London Labour Party was changing from old-style paternalism, which for all its flaws instinctively favoured council tenants and trade unions, to New Labour managerialism. In May 1998 Islington's New Labour council announced a major restructuring and made every worker in its Housing Aid Centre reapply for their own jobs. When the process was complete, nine of the staff were rejected and slated for redundancy. All were BAME women.

When staff appeals were rejected workers staged a walk-out led by Cecilia Prosper, a fiery young black shop steward and SWP member. The council responded by sacking twelve of those who had walked out. Although their union refused to represent them because they had taken unofficial action, the sacked workers, welded together by Cecilia's leadership, took the council to an Employment Tribunal on grounds of unfair dismissal and discrimination. Just before Christmas 1998 the council offered to settle out of court. Seven workers accepted the council's offer of compensation but five, led by Cecilia, refused to settle and went on to the ET, which in 2000 found Islington Council guilty of indirect discrimination and institutional racism.

Political setbacks were, to an extent, offset by cultural advances. The 1990s saw the consolidation of a large and confident gay culture in London, especially in North London, which benefited all classes, expressed by publications like *The Pink Paper* and *Boyz* magazine. *The Pink Paper* started in 1987 as a fortnightly free tabloid given out in gay bars and clubs and went on to become the first mainstream gay publication, a weekly newspaper with job vacancies from local councils and the police. For those who found *The Pink Paper*'s serious politics and slant towards lesbian issues not to their taste, its owners started *Boyz*, a breezier magazine for young gay men that carried articles like "Up for it — the 50 fellas we'd most like to stuff".

Originally based above the Fallen Angel pub in Islington, in 1995 *Boyz* relocated to new offices on Holloway Road next door to Kiss FM. It survived and thrived on a newly emerging "pink pound" but other, less advantaged groups such as the Camden

Lesbian Centre in Somers Town were not as fortunate. In 1989 Camden Council announced a 35% cut in funding to the Centre but after protests this was reduced to a 12% cut. However, by 1993 cuts in funding meant that its core staff had been reduced to two part-time posts. In 1995 Camden, hobbled by cuts to its government grant and forced to make hard choices, removed the Centre's funding entirely, effectively shutting it down.

Gay clubbing had declared itself with the opening of Heaven, but it was during the 1990s that it really took off. In 1992 gay club night Bang! came under new ownership and changed its name to G-A-Y, expanding from two nights a week to four at the Astoria on Charing Cross Road directly across the road from Denmark Place. It quickly became London's largest gay-themed club night with up to six thousand clubbers a week, cementing its reputation in 1993 when Kylie Minogue performed there for Pride. After working at a range of jobs including as a box office assistant and stagehand, by the early 1990s Dawn Thorpe had a weekly spot on G-A-Y Radio as a stand-up comedian and was asked by its owner to provide more direct services:

> I also went on to work at G-A-Y as a 'Door Whore'. My job was to keep people entertained on the way in, oversee the guest and VIP list. I resented losing my nights out!...After G-A-Y closed we would all go and chill out at Compton's bar in Soho till daylight...[42]

Some clubs didn't *start* till daylight. Trade was a gay club in Clerkenwell based at an old warehouse that had been turned into a pub called Turnmills. Trade at Turnmills started life in 1990 and quickly became an infamous part of London's gay nightlife attracting, in the words of frequent visitor Philip Pederson, "*a top dedicated crowd of mega muscle men, club freaks, transgender and hardcore ravers. All searching for the ultimate ecstasy in dancing and sex, living only for the moment*". Trade's special niche was that it didn't open until 3am, almost exactly as other clubs like G-A-Y closed, providing an all-night music/sex/drugs bender for those with the stamina for it.

The re-emergence and widespread use of poppers on the London clubbing scene in the 1990s helped keep stamina up and bodies flexible. In Trade especially, as Philip vividly recalled:

The ultra-erotic music started out from the most funky House and every hour the music turned wilder and wilder and so did the atmosphere, and it culminated in hardcore industrial techno so distorted, so extremely hard that I felt sadness that it felt so good. Never before or after had I heard music that took me on such highs, never had I experienced a gay club that rough or seen so many gays not giving a damn, it was like a mega hardcore East End opium den full of raw lust.[43]

London gay culture was about sex, of course, but also about pride and politics. Dawn enjoyed clubbing but she felt the politics, the sense of community and identity, was the defining point of her new life in London:

I remember Pride in 1994. We got a limo to drive us around town for a bit before dropping us off in Soho... it was amazing... I can vividly remember being surrounded by my closest friends, being so happy I could have died! I can also remember the fear that this life would somehow change, and even end... I wanted to hang onto it forever. I also remember thinking that once we got equality...which we were fighting so hard for... we would lose this sense of belonging and community.[44]

The community was directly attacked on 30th April 1999 when a nail bomb set by neo-Nazi David Copeland detonated in the Admiral Duncan pub on Old Compton Street. Three people were killed and seventy-nine were injured, with four of the survivors having limbs amputated. Two other bombs had been detonated in previous weeks in Brixton and Brick Lane, the three bombs aimed at the heart of London's Afro-Caribbean, Bengali and LGBT communities. After his arrest Copeland wrote to a BBC reporter to explain, beyond any misunderstanding, his motivation: *"I bomb the blacks, Pakis, degenerates. I would have bombed the Jews as well if I'd got a chance"*.

But London's new society, for good and ill, couldn't be stopped. On 18th June 1999 the Carnival Against Capital, also known as J18, tried to disrupt and derail the working life of the City and its key institutions but only succeeded in creating a minor nuisance. The climax of the day was a march by five thousand people on the International Financial Futures Exchange which led to running battles in the City with mounted police. Sixteen people were arrested, and the day ended in a sit-down protest in Trafalgar Square.

J18 was an attempt to replicate the Poll Tax revolt, to widen it out to a general assault on the legitimacy of international capitalism and demonstrate that its financial centres were vulnerable to mass action from below. But despite a few exciting moments it was a relatively small street ruck contained and dispersed by bedtime. It didn't reach out to or influence working class London in any meaningful way, prompting one of its organisers to ask:

> What I want to know is where are the people that marched with us to Trafalgar Square on the March for Social Justice, the dockers, the RMT dissidents, disaffected trade unionists, Kurdish workers, pensioners groups, twice the number of people we attracted to the City?...Why have we failed to mobilise large swathes of people whose lives are touched everyday by the machinations of the City, whose communities have long traditions of resistance and whom we have worked with in the past?[45]

The answer was that a blanket anti-capitalism, unconnected to specific campaigns, had limited appeal. On the contrary, by the end of the 1990s London had the air of a Boom Town. The recession of the early 1990s was over and the cultural industries in particular achieved a critical mass which scooped up working class talent. Former pirate radio operators became major players in the music and entertainment industry, providing exciting jobs and lifestyles to those who had only dreamed of them before. Inevitably, some of this cascaded to workers at the lower end of the boom, shunting money their way, opening up new opportunities, forging new professional connections and social networks.

One of the nodal points for those opportunities and connections was the Sylvia Young Theatre School on Nutford Place, Marylebone. Since its opening in 1972 Sylvia Young has shaped and launched the talent of many London working class kids. Over the course of the 1980s, 1990s and 2000s the school saw Keeley Hawes, Shaznay Lewis, Ashley Walters, Dominique Moore, Emma Bunton, Nick Berry, Louisa Lytton, Matt Di Angelo, Dean Gaffney, Tamzin Outhwaite, Layla Anna-Lee, Denise van Outen, Amy Winehouse and Croatian child refugee Rita Ora come through its doors and take their first steps to career success.

In 1992 two lively sixteen-year-old Sylvia Young students, Emma Bunton, born in Finchley to her karate instructor mother Pauline and milkman father Trevor, and Marylebone cabbie's daughter Keeley Hawes became firm friends who for a while lived and travelled together. Before too long they had moved on to bigger things, Keeley to her acting break in *Our Mutual Friend* (1998) and Emma in 1994 to audition for a new band consisting of five working class girls — Mel B and Mel C from Leeds and Liverpool, Victoria Adams from Harlow, and Geri Halliwell from Watford — who after their mega-hit debut single "Wannabe" (1996) went on to become, for a while, the biggest pop group in the world.

The only rival to Sylvia Young as a maternity ward for working class acting talent was the Anna Scher Theatre School at St Silas Church on Penton Street near the Angel, adjacent to what was then King's Cross UBO and is now Barnsbury Job Centre. Beginning life as a drama club in 1968, the school is active in the local community, putting on drama workshops on issues such as child poverty and AIDS awareness. Over the years it has launched the careers of many London working class actors and actresses like Kathy Burke, Gillian Taylforth, Martin Kemp, Saffron Burrows, Gary Beadle, Phil Daniels, Naomi Harris, Natalie Cassidy, Sid Owen, Freema Ageyman, Pauline Quirke, Linda Robson, Joe Swash, Patsy Palmer, Tameka Empson and Daniel Kaluuya.

Contrary to Blue Labour's maudlin fantasies, these working class Londoners didn't particularly want to be "rooted" where they and their parents had always lived. They wanted to *uproot*, to explore, to enjoy what their middle class peers, no matter how ungifted and mediocre, were given on a plate. They might do that through music or sport or through more conventional career routes. They might do it themselves.

During the 1990s the small law firm that Martin Howe had started in a room at the back of his parents' off-license next to the Mozart Estate began to expand. Howe and Co would go on to become the UK's leading human rights legal firm employing up to one hundred staff, representing immigrants and refugees seeking leave to remain in the UK and not be deported back to life-threatening situations. They worked especially closely with the Turkish and Kurdish communities of Green Lanes, leading to some of the refugees they successfully helped coming to work for them as interpreters in similar cases.

After a period in which she had flitted from job to job and struggled to find her personal groove, Dawn Thorpe also found a way forward:

> As a result of my experiences — Comedy, The London Bubble, The Gay Community, etc.— I finally went to university at age 28 to study anthropology. I would never have gone to university had it not been for these years in London between 1989 and 1994. My lecturers were Marxists and Communists, they were active campaigners, they started The Radical Anthropology Group. Any struggle, they were there standing in solidarity with workers or minorities... and they opened me up again.[46]

After starting work as a cotton-cleaner in a Hackney clothing factory and then becoming a supervisor at Hackney UBO, Amanda Millhouse sought a new direction in her life by taking a degree in classical civilisation at North London Polytechnic. This led to her taking up a position at the newly-established Department for Culture, Media and Sport (DCMS) in Cockspur Street off Trafalgar Square. The senior civil servants with whom she worked were invariably charming and friendly, but not above deploying the "symbolic violence" that Bourdieu identified as one means by which the social elite keep working class interlopers in their place:

> It was the first time I had worked with really posh people and my first encounter with real politicians. To begin with I thought that all these people with plummy accents must be intelligent, and certainly more intelligent than me. It took me a year before I discovered that wasn't the case, but it made me realise how deeply embedded class is in the UK. I remember telling my boss in Media Policy that despite having a degree in Classical Civilisation I did not speak Latin or Greek. He laughed in disbelief and related this to the Director-General in front of me and they mused on how this could be at all possible.[47]

Danny Wright epitomised the schizophrenic nature of the North London working class's relationship with its middle class neighbours, simultaneously attracted and repelled by their lifestyle. In the late 1990s, after years spent exploiting gullible middle class acquaintances, Danny hit rock bottom as his hard drug addiction got the better of him. His usual modus operandi, summarised by his brother as *"find a posh girl, get her to fall in love with him...allow her to pay for everything and steal from her friends"*, had played out. He found himself squatting an empty flat on the Barnsbury Estate and signing on at King's Cross UBO.

Finally he lost even the squatted flat. Homeless and out of options, he tried to secure a room at Arlington House in Camden Town:

> Off to Arlington, where an overnight queue formed for morning registration. Before joining the happy campers, I knocked back a few drinks with Lucy...the queue was a mixture of young and old, most of the latter being Irish. Young ones were Northerners, unemployed, even some Londoners...I sank into a decent half sleep, awakening in the morning intensely cold and hungry. Eventually we were in through the door to be interviewed by a woman who resembled Lucy's mother, patronising, dogmatic,

*ignorant, middle class. She informed me that, frankly, I was
unsuitable material even for the dosshouse.*[48]

Yet somehow, between stays in dosshouses and squats,
Danny wrote his "autobiography" *Camden Parasites* (1999)
under the pseudonym Danny Lux. The book became a cult
success but Danny would never know it. In February 1999, as
the final proofs were being prepared for the printers, he died of
a heroin overdose.

With the exception of the BBC soap *Eastenders* — more
comic opera than serious drama — film, TV and literature
remained almost devoid of representations of working class life
in London. John King's *The Football Factory* (1996), often cited
by middle class critics enjoying a vicarious frisson as a brave and
disturbing portrait of working class Londoners, is a powerful
but deeply ambivalent novel. Like the violent hooliganism it
tracks, King's prose is dangerously addictive, capturing the
tribal instincts of a sub-section of football fans and how local
pride and identity warps into bigotry and hatred. But the object
of their hatred is modern London, which they are barely part of
and don't understand:

*We're Chelsea boys from the Anglo-Saxon estates of West
London. Your average Chelsea fan coming up to Tottenham from
Hayes or Hounslow is used to Pakis and niggers, but go up Seven
Sisters Road and it's all bagels and kebab houses. Greeks, Turks,
yids, Arabs.*[49]

The Football Factory's central characters are part of Chelsea's
Headhunters, who on closer examination turn out to be west-
of-London New Town boys rather than Inner London working
class. Its narrator-hero is a man who thinks Tottenham High
Road is too cosmopolitan. He works in a warehouse and lives in
Hammersmith but that is all we learn about his job and home.
The overt fascist politics of the Headhunters, their links to far-
right groups, is barely mentioned. For all its narrative force it is
never clear where the book, and the author himself, truly come
from.

Peter Watts, on the other hand, came from Sutton and knew exactly what London was and how to enjoy it. As a teenager, every Saturday during the 1990s he and two mates caught the train to London Victoria from where they immediately headed to Covent Garden for the clothes and music shops. Stopping off at Vinyl Experience and the Virgin Megastore on Oxford Street, they would check out the Selecterdisc, Sister Ray and Reckless record shops in Berwick Street, catching up with a schoolmate who worked a Saturday job on his uncle's stall in the market. Afternoons were usually football, either Arsenal at the Clock End or Chelsea in the Shed, followed by food at a suitable café and a gig at the Astoria or Marquee.[50]

Like Peter and countless others, Johnny Jarvis, a working class West London wide-boy whose vivid recollections of living it large in London in the 1990s top this chapter, travelled up from Southall every weekend to enjoy the clubs of central London. Unlike King's protagonist, he managed to do so without kicking the shit out of anyone not from his own enclave of Outer London, the difference being that Johnny was a *real* Londoner, unafraid of its diversity, alive to its rhythms and enjoying its culture.[51]

As was Courttia Newland, the most honest and engaging novelist to emerge from London's working class in the 1990s. Born in 1973 to Jamaican and Bajan parents, Newland grew up in the council estates of Shepherd's Bush. Leaving school at fifteen, he worked for a while as a shop assistant in Ryman's and then tried to form a band before deciding, at age twenty-one, to write a novel set in the world he knew. *The Scholar* (1997) introduced the fictional Greenside Estate in Shepherd's Bush and focused on how some young black men get enmeshed, despite themselves, in drugs and crime. But its genius was its credible characters and seamless invocation of London council estate patois, the fusion of cockney and downtown Kingston that had become the casual slang of London's working class kids. Newland's follow up, *Society Within* (1999) further explored this territory with a Dickensian range of characters including teenage girls out for a laugh, young drug dealers in over their heads, ambitious boys trying to start a pirate radio station and frustrated community workers.

British cinema, with a few honourable exceptions such as 1997's *Trainspotting*, barely tried to represent contemporary working class life, in London or anywhere else. Ken Loach's *Riff Raff* (1991) was another rare exception, an honest, funny and moving story of a collection of builders from across the country constructing "London Heritage Homes" out of the remains of the Prince of Wales Hospital in Tottenham, and their lives in the city, divided between those who have some capital and a home and new arrivals who are forced to squat in boarded-up council flats. *Riff Raff* is far from simplistic agit-prop. On the contrary, Liverpudlian builder Larry's (Ricky Tomlinson) pleas for socialist class consciousness are mocked by his workmates and the budding romance between its young leads simply dies of neglect.

Julian Henriques' *Babymother* (1998) goes where Loach seldom treads — London's BAME working class. Funded by the Arts Council and Channel 4, *Babymother* was filmed on location in Harlesden High Street, Craven Park Road and the Stonebridge Estate. Henriques' film, although tonally unbalanced, takes for granted the multicultural foundation of 1990s London working class life. Its girl-power story of a female reggae band battling against the odds and the sexism of their men is an inadvertent and important slice of social history, capturing the culture and atmosphere of 1990s Harlesden simply by being there.

The Football Factory, *Riff Raff* and *Babymother* all imply that North London's "traditional", i.e. white, working class evacuated the capital in the 1990s just as large parts of East London's working class had done in the 1950s and 1960s. If so, it was a different process, not the mass transference to Outer London and the New Towns (now not so new and with social problems of their own) driven by a wish to escape poor living conditions, but a result of working class *success*, of better careers and income secured through access to higher education. I was myself part of this process, moving to Brighton in 1996 whilst continuing to work full-time in London for the trade union movement. Around the same time Amanda Millhouse moved to Sevenoaks, Ray Picton to Salisbury, Tony Kilshaw to Tiverton, Helen Evangelou to Suffolk, Vic Heath to Luton. Others like

David Aaronovitch, Suggs and Robert Elms stayed in North London, where they had grown up, but by virtue of their income they enjoyed a middle class lifestyle, albeit influenced by the working class values of their background and upbringing.

There were and are deep patterns of genealogy and kinship in specific areas of London. In the previous two hundred years my dad's family had barely moved beyond an area bordered by St Pancras and Hoxton. Old retail shops such as Myalls Boot and Shoe Shop on West Green Road in South Tottenham, which closed in 2000, had been operating there, staffed by members of the Myalls family, for 175 years. Even longer than Blustons Coats and Gowns in Kentish Town High Street, which had been run by the Bluston family since the 1920s when it was set up by Russian Jewish émigrés who arrived in London at the end of the nineteenth century, and which finally closed in 2015 (although its old-style shop sign still sits above the Octavia Foundation charity shop).

These lineages of families and businesses established a level of historic continuity, but from a longer and larger perspective the city's working class had hardly ever *been* traditional. The Blustons were themselves immigrants to begin with. In 1700 about 5% of London's total population of 575,000 were refugee French Huguenots living in Spitalfields or Soho.[52] From its birth in the nineteenth century East London's working class was a fusion of southern English with Irish, Scottish, Chinese, Jewish, Russian, Eastern European and Asian immigrants, drawn to the West India and East India Docks constructed in 1802-1806 to absorb shipping that the Thames's wharves could no longer accommodate, and later to the Victoria Dock in West Ham opened in 1855 for new steam ships. "Bangladeshi" immigration into Spitalfields, especially from the Sylhet region of India, preceded the Second World War and was well under way in the 1950s.

If, nonetheless, we accept the dense web of extended families and urban lore exhibited by its white working class from the 1880s to the 1970s (the entire life span of my great-grandmother Phoebe) as "traditional" London working class culture, then this culture did fragment and dispel in the last two decades of the twentieth century. But like the ruins of Ancient Rome its monuments — its housing estates, pubs, street markets, cafes, fairs, boxing clubs and dance halls — were so embedded throughout the city that they remained an integral part of its life. In parallel, new structures arose — shibeens, basement clubs, kebab houses, community centres, pirate radio stations, chicken shops, gay pubs, refugee centres and communal gardens. North London's working class continued to evolve and adapt, a process fuelled by its ever-growing multi-ethnic subcultures. In the new century, this adaptability would be tested as never before.

2000-2008

"In the beginning was a fear of the immigrant."
Madness, "The Liberty of Norton Folgate", 2008

In May 2000, the first election for the newly created post of Mayor of London was won by the independent candidate Ken Livingstone, who had left Labour to run on his own after the party blatantly rigged an internal contest for its Mayoral candidate in order to exclude him. The result was a massive finger-up to all the established parties from London's electorate, especially its working class, for whom Livingstone had been a folk hero since Fares Fair and the abolition of the GLC. He took office in conjunction with the newly created Greater London Authority (GLA), the first time since 1986 that London had a single governing body, although the GLA's powers were not as extensive as the GLC's.

Livingstone and the GLA inherited a mega-city which had long abandoned the "Fordist" model of large-scale industry (quite literally when its last representative at Ford Dagenham closed in 2002) and whose small-scale industry was also under pressure. Excluding construction and the public sector, most of London's jobs were now in financial or consumer services. Some of London's working class had half-decently-paid jobs in local government, the civil service, the NHS, Royal Mail and London Transport, although their catering, cleaning and security staff were mostly outsourced, but a larger number worked in the hospitality and retail sectors, on check-out tills and front desks, serving or preparing food and drinks, or in warehouse and delivery. The higher-than-average wage levels of London's working class rarely compensated for the city's higher housing, travel and living costs.

Most of this Livingstone could do little about. The GLA's and Mayor's powers were limited to strategic planning of housing, transport and economic development, plus oversight of Transport for London, the Metropolitan Police, the London Fire Brigade and the London Development Agency. Livingstone's biggest political battle was against the Labour government's plan to turn London Underground into a Private-Public Partnership (PPP). Both the Mayor and the transport unions feared that the scheme's proposal to outsource maintenance of the tube's infrastructure to two PFI consortia, Metronet and Tube Lines, would degrade the service. Although Livingstone's legal challenge to the PPP scheme was unsuccessful, only a few years later Metronet, unable to fulfil its promises and failing to maintain let alone improve LU's infrastructure, went bankrupt and had to be taken into public ownership at a cost of £2bn.

During the Mayoral election campaign, Livingstone promised to keep the iconic Routemaster bus on London's streets. The last of London's 2,760 Routemaster buses rolled off the production line in 1968. In 1982 1,500 of them were taken completely out of service and by the mid-1990s only 600 were left working in London, prompting Livingstone to promise that the fleet would be retained and increased. But upon election he reversed himself, apparently persuaded by the need to make London's buses more accessible to the disabled. A phasing out began, the first public sign of which was their removal in 2003 from the cross-London number 15 from Paddington to East Ham. Their removal in 2005 from the number 73 from Tottenham to Victoria, a public transport staple for North London's working class, generated a petition against it from users, brushed aside by TFL.[1]

Livingstone's introduction of a Congestion Charge for central London, against hysterical opposition from the Tory media, reduced traffic in central London by 10% and was a notable success. So too was his expansion and investment in public transport, including the aggressive use of TFL to buy up failed and discarded private rail lines and add them to what would become the London Overground, the most successful updating of London's public transport network since the first tube lines were laid out in the nineteenth century. During his period of office Livingstone demonstrated that municipal socialism, even at its weakest, was still crucial to a decent quality of life in the city. In March 2001 the Labour Foreign Secretary, Robin Cook, in a speech on modern "Britishness", took London as the perfect exemplar of the new Britain, the quintessence of thriving multiculturalism. Of the UK's capital, he said:

> It is home to over thirty ethnic communities of at least 10,000 residents each. In this city tonight, over 300 languages will be spoken by families over their evening meal at home. This pluralism is not a burden we must reluctantly accept. It is an immense asset that contributes to the cultural and economic vitality of our nation.[2]

But Cook's praise of modern London ignored the growing cancer putting its health and viability at risk — the progressive winnowing out of the capital's vast reservoir of good quality social housing, i.e. where its working class lived, and the confinement of its remaining working class in what was left, with few other housing options and no way except Right to Buy to escape this trap. The combination of Right to Buy and Right to Let had paved the way for a crisis situation in which, by 2020, there were very few new builds of affordable social housing and where 42% of London's council homes bought under Right to Buy had been sold on to private landlords who then rented them out at exorbitant rates.

The effect of this on North London's working class was complex and contradictory. In some ways it left many of them untouched. If they owned, through having bought it or by family inheritance, a flat or a house in Queen's Park or Holloway or Stamford Hill or Kentish Town, they saw its value skyrocket just as did middle class homeowners. John Holland, a security guard who lived on the Whittington Estate in Highgate, bought his five-bedroom flat (valued at the time of purchase at £70,000) with his sister for £39,000 in 1983 under Right to Buy. Thirty years later it was worth £600,000. Not surprisingly, John was pleased with how things had turned out:

If it wasn't for Mrs Thatcher's policy, we couldn't have afforded to buy. There'd be no way we'd be property owners now if it wasn't for her. It was perfect, absolutely perfect.[3]

But if council tenants chose not to buy, because they did not wish to or could not afford to or their home was simply not worth buying, then it all happened elsewhere, a strange world just over the horizon which they could never enter. They were *still there*, living in North London and even in central London, but property prices did not raise them up. They just watched the world around them rise.

Livingstone made efforts to address this, but they were nowhere near sufficient. He stipulated that 50% of new builds be "affordable" but failed to specify what that meant. Granted flexibility to determine that for themselves, developers flouted the rules, putting a few smaller "affordable" units in expensive new developments or even building them somewhere else entirely so as not to spoil the overall effect for affluent buyers. These were usually studios or one-bedroom flats, not suitable for families to put down roots and raise kids. Even with a socialist Mayor pushing for affordable social housing, the days of fully integrated, high quality, council-run housing projects with a range of communal facilities seemed to be over.

The fight, for now, was to defend what was left. Faced with falling revenue and with a New Labour government as unenthusiastic about traditional council estates as the Tories, even London's Labour councils began to divest themselves of their social housing. They were virtually compelled to do so by the government's Decent Homes programme, launched in 2000, which set targets to raise the quality of social housing but only approved the money to meet them if councils either sold their estates to a Registered Social Landlord (RSL); transferred the estate to an Arms Length Management Organisation (ALMO) to run it on a commercial basis; or used a PFI scheme. The option of borrowing to build new council homes was expressly ruled out.

Islington Council fell for PFI's long con more readily than most. In the 1960s and 1970s it had municipalised many old Georgian houses, whose privately owned equivalents now commanded outlandish prices. The council-owned houses needed renovation and renewal but under the Decent Homes policy there was only one way to finance the work. So in 2003, in the first PFI council house regeneration scheme in England, the then Liberal Democrat Islington Council handed over the work to a PFI consortium called Partners for Improvement. In theory, the PFI scheme would bring £50m of investment to 2,348 Georgian and Victorian houses in Mildmay and Highbury, but the reality was quite different. From an early stage complaints flooded into the council, and to Islington's Labour MPs Jeremy Corbyn and Emily Thornberry, about the poor quality of the work.

One of the first properties to be subject to PFI "refurbishment" belonged to long-time Islington council tenant Daisy, who found that the contractors had hired people that didn't speak English and were paid only £30 a day. Seemingly unqualified for the work, they put a nail through a water pipe and brought part of her ceiling down. A worker mixing cement poured some down her toilet so that it became blocked. Compensation was not forthcoming. Edward, a self-employed carpenter who had moved with his family, including his disabled son, into a council-owned Grade II listed Georgian terraced house in Islington in the 1990s and who had used his skills to restore many of its historic features, had an even worse experience. When the PFI sub-contractors started on his home in 2005 he saw immediately that the work being done was extremely poor and discovered that other tenants had similar experiences.

Edward became the *de facto* spokesperson for the tenants, photographing the work done in his own home and putting it online, detailing breaches of health and safety and building regulations and generally demanding accountability from the contractors. As a result, Partners informed him that he and his family had to move out entirely until the work was finished.

No sooner were the family in temporary accommodation than Partners boarded up their house and did not start work on it for three months. Upon their return six months later, Edward found:

> *Everything was covered in dust. Previously nicely decorated walls had massive holes and beautifully varnished Georgian floorboards had been scratched and damaged with nails sticking out where floorboards had been lifted. As I inspected the basement a piece of plasterboard actually fell on my head and arm. There were clear signs that a major flood had occurred in the room above the kitchen, causing them to rip out my beautiful high-quality timber suite and replace it with cheap ill-fitting units which literally fell apart as soon as you opened drawers.*

Islington Council ignored his complaints even though they were backed up by reports by gas safety inspectors and the council's own listed building officer confirming multiple safety risks, breaches of listed building regulations and massive structural damage. It took seven more years for the main repairs to be properly completed, during which time welfare services found that the house was no longer suitable for his disabled son, who was sectioned and detained in a hospital. Neither Islington Council nor Partners ever apologised to Edward and his family or offered any compensation.[4] In 2006, well aware of Partners' record on what was known as PFI-1, Islington Council awarded the consortium the contract for PFI-2, an even bigger contract to renovate another 4,118 homes.

Even Camden Council, which had been so bold in letting Sydney Cook's team design and build truly new and high-quality housing estates in the 1960s and 1970s, bent with the prevailing wind. Camden's Chalcot Estate on Adelaide Road was not one of Cook's or inspired by his thinking. Because of its origin as a series of private high-rises it was hardly an estate at all, lacking a natural centre or communal facilities. It had always been an eyesore except to those living in it, many of whom, if their flats were high enough, had incredible views of Primrose Hill and Regent's Park.

In 2004 Camden Council informed the Chalcot's tenants that they could choose whether they wanted to be renovated through a PFI scheme overseen by the council, be transferred to an RSL, or run by an ALMO. The PFI option promised more money for regeneration of the old tower blocks but that amount reduced considerably when the Treasury scrutinised the proposal and found the investors' promises did not add up. In the end the tenants of the Chalcot voted to stay with Camden Council. For doing so, the tower blocks were subjected to a PFI-run renovation between 2005-2009 run by Partners for Improvement, who brought to the project the same level of care they had delivered in Islington.

Because Partners' initial estimate of the investment it could put in had proven inflated, it was allowed to deliver the improvements more cheaply, meaning that the five tower blocks of the Chalcot Estate were reclad in the same aluminium composite cladding that was later applied to Grenfell Tower, by the same company.[5] In 2012 one of the Chalcot's tower blocks, Taplow, caught fire in the same manner as Grenfell, but luckily was quickly extinguished. In June 2017, nine days after the Grenfell fire, and after the LFB informed Camden Council the tower blocks were an imminent fire hazard, all 4,000 residents of the Chalcot were temporarily rehoused while the cladding was removed. The cost to Camden was £92m, leading the council to stop all PFI contract payments to Partners, who then went insolvent. Control of the Chalcot transferred back to the Council.[6]

When not dabbling in disastrous PFI schemes, Islington Council could be determined and creative about defending its existing social housing stock. The Spa Green Estate just south of the Angel on Rosebery Avenue was and remained one of its finest, but even that had declined in the 1970s and 1980s with complaints from tenants about rubbish and lack of maintenance. In 1996, with overwhelming support from the estate's residents, the Spa Green Management Association took over day-to-day running of the estate from the council. Despite this, by 2005 Spa Green was in sad shape, with peeling paint and mesh covers to catch falling bricks.

However, in 2008 a £5m refurbishment project led by Homes for Islington (HFI), an ALMO established in 2004 to manage Islington's 21,500 council properties, restored the estate's three blocks to their 1940s constructivist ideal (which resulted in unwelcome large bills for the roughly third of Spa Green's tenants who had purchased their flats under Right to Buy and were therefore eligible to pay a portion of repair costs). Spa Green now stands as intended— an elegant, well-maintained social housing estate for mostly working class residents in the heart of London.

Laagering the wagons around the remaining council estates of North London, protecting their tenants against PFI pirates and cowboys, was essential, but it did not prevent the dissipation of an older working class culture. In 2001 tenants in the Culross and Stanley buildings, the Victorian tenements that had featured in Mike Leigh's *High Hopes*, were moved out as work to develop St Pancras International station began, either rehoused or offered compensation. Half of Stanley Building was demolished but following protests the other half was absorbed into the regeneration project and now exists as a quaint exterior feature of modern offices on Granary Square.

There were a large number of council-owned houses and flats in the area bordered by York Way and Caledonian Road that Islington Council had municipalised in the 1970s. Like all properties in the area, they were under threat in the 1980s and 1990s from British Rail's plans for the Eurotunnel that would terminate at King's Cross mainline station, plans that would have meant the demolition of much of York Way, Keystone Crescent, Balfe Street and the southern end of Caledonian Road. In response the residents organised in the South Caledonian Community Association. With support from their MP Chris Smith they managed to get the Eurotunnel re-routed so that it arrived at the newly constructed St Pancras International instead.

Free of the threat which had blighted the area for the last decade, in the mid-1990s the "King's Cross Regeneration Partnership" between Islington and Camden Councils made a bid for Single Regeneration funding. The bid was unashamedly in favour of a scheme which honoured the traditions of the King's Cross area, emphasising *"King's Cross has a robust and diverse population whose communities have demonstrated over many years their strong commitment to the area."* It stressed *"We must ensure that when investment comes it will bring benefit to, rather than alienate, the local communities of King's Cross".*[7] The bid was successful and in the late 1990s the King's Cross Partnership prepared schemes that not only saved and restored many of the historic buildings of the area but created new facilities for local residents.

In 2002 the regeneration got underway, erasing most of the Goods Yard and nightclubs, like Bagley's, that had arisen from its ruins. Soon the workshops and garages that once lined the western side of St Pancras station were also gone. The fear of local residents was what would replace them and if their own homes off York Way would even survive. After much discussion with residents, Islington Council and English Heritage, the final plans for what would be known as the Regents Quarter, which was restored and renovated between 2002 and 2005, included many of the old buildings like the Brassworks and Albion Buildings and made provision for affordable flats amongst the new offices. It wasn't social housing on the scale that Camden and Islington used to deliver, but it could have been much worse.

Similarly, the fortunes of Charles Rowan House in Clerkenwell began to turn around after it was Grade II listed in 1994. In 2001-2002 its courtyard underwent re-landscaping to designs by the landscape architects Farrer Huxley. It was the first stage of a major renovation project undertaken by Homes for Islington. By 2011 the renovations had cleaned up the exterior and common parts and entrances, and made an attractive settlement out of a neglected slum. It did what the earlier PFI-1 project had lamentably failed to do, the local state enabling a permanent change for the better in a social housing community and improving the quality of life of its residents.

Many of North London's council estates *needed* renovation and regeneration. The Market Estate adjacent to Caledonian Park, named after the cattle market that operated on the park until the early 1960s, had been constructed in the late 1960s. Dominated by three tower blocks called the Clock Tower Blocks, it quickly gained a reputation for crime and vandalism. Its problems were exacerbated when the first stage of the redevelopment of King's Cross displaced drug dealers and prostitutes from York Way and pushed them north to the Market. Attempts by Islington Council to reverse the decline of the estate by removing its walkways and creating new gardens never took hold. A new concierge's office was burnt out and CCTV was vandalised. It was only in 2003 that the Market Estate Tenants and Residents Association (METRA) chose a new Housing Association, Southern Housing Group (SHG), to entirely redevelop and regenerate the estate.

After a ballot in which 85% of the tenants agreed to transfer ownership to SHG, a complete redevelopment began in which the old blocks were closed and demolished, replaced with a mixture of houses and modern low-rise flats built on a traditional street pattern. The existing secure tenants were guaranteed a new home on the new estate, with ninety new for-sale and shared ownership units added to help subsidise the projects' costs. Between 2005 and 2010 the Market Estate was utterly transformed and Caledonian Park itself was given a major facelift. The main youth gang in the area, the Market Massiv, was progressively squeezed out of the estate's life although they did not depart without one final blow to the local community.

By the early 2000s the Stonebridge Estate in Harlesden had the highest rate of gun crime in the country. A number of young men in Harlesden, vying for control of territory to sell crack and other drugs, or simply to pay back or dominate another street gang, shot and killed each other with depressing regularity. In response their mothers, grandmothers, sisters and aunts, supported by Brent Council with Home Office funding of £1.5m, formed the campaign group Not Another Drop. The group had some impact in the area and beyond, organising vibrant street demonstrations and rallies with protest banners proclaiming "Young, Gifted and Dead".

There were deep social and economic reasons for gang crime on the Stonebridge and adjacent estates. Many of the big employers that once provided full-time employment to the area, like Heinz and Rolls Royce, had closed and moved away in the 1980s. By 2000 Harlesden's unemployment rate was nearly 50%. The physical environment of an estate was also a factor. Brutalist blocks and walkways created brutalised residents. Like Holly Street, the Stonebridge was a playground for drug dealing and violence, a concrete warren hidden from the street and impenetrable to the police except in major raids. It became a No Man's Land not unlike "Little Russia" on the border of Edmonton and Tottenham that, from the 1930s until its demolition in the 1970s, the police did not dare enter alone.

Kevin Georgiou was born in Harlseden in 1985 to Greek Cypriot parents and grew up on pre-renovation Stonebridge. A member of the rap group USG, he shot to prominence under his stage name K Koke after performing on the "Fire in the Booth" segment of Charlie Sloth's popular BBC Radio 1Xtra show. Sloth, born Ian Rouillon in 1981 in Liverpool to an electrician dad and taxi driver mum, moved down to London as a kid with his family. Initially they lived in Somers Town but by Ian's teens they had moved to a flat above the offices of the *Camden New Journal* in Camden Road. While Ian attended Haverstock School his mum worked as a domestic cleaner in Parliament Hill. After leaving school he spent a few years as a DJ and a Hypeman before eventually gravitating to Radio 1.

Although the Charlie persona could occasionally slide into Ali G, his show was immensely influential, attracting many different rappers to rap out their own personal Fire in the Booth. K Koke's was a powerful free-form poem on the emotional and psychological pain of growing up a young man in Stonebridge:

> *Check my lifestyle, this little white child*
> *Growing up hood, forced to live his life wild*
> *Yeah I might smile, on occasion*
> *But look into my eyes and see the fire blazing*
> *My heart is aching, life got me stressed fam*

Been through enough still these youts tryna test man
Trust, I seen life from a different vibe
Pissy stairways, crack houses and homicides
Huh, so try me fam I'm gonna ride
I fry beef, not a chief, never gonna hide
This street life's got these old peeps horrified
'Cause young Gs couldn't care if tomorrow dies
Look! I've seen hell through my mother's eyes
Ain't nothing worse than when you see your mother cry
Wishes it was different, wish we had another life
Mum you done your best please don't apologise
Yeah, stop looking with those worried eyes

In 2003, after another shooting produced headlines about the "law of the jungle" on the Stonebridge, Frank Downes, a youth worker on the estate who understood the reality behind what the media called the "worst estate in the country", tried to explain the background:

The facilities for young people on Stonebridge are appalling. If any money is spent on the area, the needs of the kids always come last…The last play area was covered over with a car park about 18 months ago. Now kids have nowhere to go except the stairwells and hallways…There are limits to what you can do in a hallway, so the graffitiing and that starts…I want a clubhouse here, just a normal clubhouse with sports facilities that offer something for everyone and the kids feel is theirs. A clubhouse would give the kids ownership, so they don't just think, "Oh, it's the council's" and give it a kick.

Frank saw a bigger picture than feral youth and scare stories about Yardies, one rooted in the social reality of how the Stonebridge and similar estates had been managed since the 1980s:

It is everything to do with how they are being treated… The government starves the estates of resources, then dumps them as cheaply as possible. They should have learned from my generation, the first to grow up on the big estates. When people know they are being treated in this manner, how can they be expected to respect authority?[8]

But the Labour government and Brent Council did not dump the Stonebridge as cheaply as possible. Between 2003 and 2009 a £225m redevelopment took place that transformed the estate. Unusually, the redevelopers consulted the residents on the kind of homes they wanted to live in and designed the new estate around their wishes. The tower blocks came down, replaced with low-level flats no more than four storeys high or terraced homes with gardens, surrounded by thoughtfully landscaped communal areas. Over 1,200 properties were demolished and rebuilt across a forty-six-acre site. About 4,000 people were rehoused, with no family compelled to move from the estate. Unlike the old estate, the new Stonebridge had integral, high-quality facilities — a health centre, a nursery, a sports pavilion and new community buildings. Problems of poverty and unemployment remained, but a community was retained and given greater dignity and safety than before.

By the early 2000s Harlesden was a polyglot mixture of Brazilian cafes, Portuguese restaurants, old Irish pubs, African and Caribbean takeaways, and established shops like Starlight Records on the High Street, the All Eyes on Egypt bookshop, Way 2 Save supermarket and Harlesden's specialty hair and wig shops. The combined barber shop/art gallery on the High Street near Willesden Junction was a popular fixture, run by Faisal Abdu'Allah (born Paul Duffus), whose parents had arrived from Jamaica in 1966. Faisal was born in 1969 and grew up on Tubbs Road which he recalled as a friendly place with mixed Caribbean and Irish families.[9] His dad worked in the Heinz factory in Park Royal until retirement and Paul attended the Rebirth Tabernacle Church in Leghorn Road every Sunday.

At sixteen Paul went to Harrow School of Art and then to Central Saint Martins in Covent Garden. After a few years in America, he converted to Islam and changed his name. As Faisal Abdu'Allah he embarked on two parallel careers, both equally important to him. He got into cutting hair and opened a men's barbers in Harlesden. At the same time he took the first steps in an artistic career that focused on representations of black, Muslim and working class life, was exhibited internationally and became a lecturer at the University of East London. In 2001, asked why he continued to work in the barber shop, he explained:

> If I gave up the barber shop, my work would die. It's a lived experience. I cut the hair of a circuit judge and a man who hasn't worked for 15 years as well as the son of a baronet. There's no end to the experience and stories that I inhale in the shop. And just to prove it's Harlesden, I've lost four customers. They were shot dead.[10]

Providing civilised housing estates and more social infrastructure was important but it did not eradicate gangs or postcode wars. The pattern was replicated in the ongoing war between the Mozart Estate in W9 in the City of Westminster and the nearby South Kilburn Estate in NW6 in Brent (or, more accurately, between a few young men on each estate). South Kilburn was one of the worst 1960s estates, dominated by eleven eighteen-storey tower blocks that drained life and joy from the area. Populated mainly by Afro-Caribbean tenants, South Kilburn had little going for it except its placement in London, an advantage that some of its young men squandered by confining themselves to a violent gang war with the nearby Mozart Estate off the Harrow Road.

The war had been brewing for a while but it exploded in August 1999 when a popular figure in the South Kilburn Mandem (SKM), O'Neal Laylor, known as Chicken, was murdered by a masked man who barged into a party at his flat at 03.15 in the morning and shot him dead with a laser-sighted Glock. It was never clear who had done it or why but it shattered what had been a largely unified gang of South Kilburn and Mozart gang members and led to the shooting in 2000 of Dino, another SKM member. The SKM blamed Mozart for Chicken and Dino and tit-for-tat shootings escalated, driven by personal grudges, male ego and a battle for turf to sell drugs. Micro-crews within

South Kilburn and Mozart, run by young men on the estates like Carlito, Young Tribez, Hurricane, Razor, Gizzy and Silence tore each other apart while everyone around them just tried to live their lives, not always possible when innocent bystanders were shot by mistake and the police response was to assume all young black men were tooled up gang members.[11]

The Mozart Estate, built by Westminster Council in the early 1970s as a fully integrated estate of forty redbrick buildings between two to six storeys, was by no means idyllic, but it was spared hugely depressive tower blocks and it had more facilities than South Kilburn, including the Jubilee Sports Centre where in the 1980s and 1990s Sean McGlinchey, Martin Howe and others, including myself occasionally, played five-a-side football for the Grey Horse pub in Kensal Rise. Most of the Grey Horse team came from the nearby Queen's Park Estate north of Harrow Road, including the long numbered Avenues, 1st to 6th, between Kilburn Lane and Harrow Road. The estate contained over 1,500 compact terraced houses built in the 1870s and 1880s by the Artisans, Labourers and General Dwellings Company for the "respectable" working class, and which in the twentieth century housed successive generations of local Irish families. The estate was sold to Westminster Council in 1964 and declared a conservation area in 1978.

Zuhair Hassan, later known as the grime MC Big Zuu, was born in 1995 and lived on the Mozart until he was sixteen when his family moved to Victoria. Zuhair's mother was a refugee from Sierra Leone and his father Lebanese, although like so many fathers on London's estates he largely abandoned his parental responsibilities (a consistent pattern going back to the older white working class, including both of my own ignoble grandfathers). After spending two years at Goldsmiths University studying for a degree in community development and youth work, Zuhair started his own rap group, the MTP Crew, with other grime MCs.

Looking back on where he grew up, he acknowledged the Mozart's problems, but also remembered:

But the area wasn't just pain and paigons, it's a place where you could have a good time with your lads, whether it's playing football in the cage at Ashmore Park, or swimming at the now-closed Jubilee Centre. We also had a park funded by the National Lottery called Paddington Recreational Ground where I used to play five-a-side footy every week. That's what I really loved and appreciated growing up in my area — how easy it was to access activities and sports without spending money. The good old days! I even remember going rock climbing in the Westway Sports Centre on Latimer Road, which was a mad ting.[12]

By the early 2000s the first postcode war, which began as a specific Hackney-Totty beef with the death of Popcorn in Dalston in 1997, had splintered into mini-beefs of no rationale at all. Now it wasn't Hackney versus Tottenham, it was a part of Hackney (Holly Street) versus another part of Hackney (London Fields). Since at least the Elizabethan era, if not before, Londoners often felt a strong affinity for the part of the city they grew up in but the postcode wars warped these loyalties to murderous effect. Boys who had been at school together and lived a hundred yards apart shot and stabbed each other because of imaginary slights to their Endz and fear of being seen to back down. The war wasn't much affected by the demolition of three of the original four Holly Street blocks and their replacement with a more welcoming, low-level modern estate built around a play area and school. Older residents and those not enmeshed in crews and gangs had a better environment in which to live, but for some young men, unwilling or unable to extricate themselves from a cycle of tit-for-tat violence, the changes meant little.

Robyn Travis, caught up in the war and getting a reputation as a hard man on the streets, started to comprehend its futility after he became a father in 2004:

I had a new hunger to change, and new dreams to make happen. I was ready to divorce the streets for good. I didn't give a damn about any past beef any more. Now I finally had reason to love my life. I just wanted to do the best I could for little man...It didn't make sense beefing with man over which area they came from any more. Coming from the roads we got life hard enough already. Why continue to make it harder by beefing a man just like me over his address?

In 2004 Robyn started boxing at the Islington Boys Club on Hornsey Rise. After his new family secured a flat in Bruce Grove near Broadwater Farm, he moved to the Haringey Boxing Club in Tottenham. As he saw boys he used to play with killed and imprisoned because of petty feuds, he became more alienated from life "on road" and determined to get out of it. In 2005, looking for any way out, he applied for a job in the London Fire Brigade. It never panned out and Robyn still had major troubles ahead, but after a couple of rough years he saw a future. In 2008 Robyn started to study for a BA in Youth Justice and Criminology and got a job as an outreach worker with Hackney Council.

It was the first step on a path that led to *Prisoner to the Streets* (2013), his visceral autobiography of how he got trapped in the postcode wars, and giving talks to schools, colleges and youth clubs about his life and avoiding the mistakes that he had made. Above all, Robyn was determined not to be an absent father and to stand for better values than those offered to young people by capitalist consumerism:

It's what's on our TV every day. It's about a certain lifestyle that not all of us will acquire, but it doesn't show the hard work that's put into getting that lifestyle, so when a child is not in a position to get certain things they get frustrated. With my son I'm there to de-programme him from what he's watching on TV and witnessing around him. You need to teach children the value of a work ethic.[13]

Boxing clubs often instilled that work ethic and provided an escape from the streets. The All Stars Boxing Gym and Youth Club on Harrow Road has grown into one of the most successful boxing gyms in the country, producing over thirty amateur champions, including female boxers such as Zaneta

Siertinski, Hannah Beharry and Lesley Sackey, the latter going on to win gold for England in the 2008 European Women's Championships. It was one of the few "neutral" places where young men from South Kily and the Mozart could meet and socialise.

Throughout the 1990s and 2000s Chip Hamer continued to train boxers at All Stars. As a political and trade union activist he appreciated the service it provided and the values it stood for:

The great thing about the gym, having been set up by a Ghanian Muslim man, is that it's the way I want London to be — everyone is welcome as long as they put in a shift. People like Ash Theophane, a local boy who did it the hard way and had a really good pro-career, prosper. Others do well at amateur level and then move on. Others just come to work out. There are all kinds of people train at the club, and if I've been able to pass on any kind of advice, whether it be about boxing or life in general, then I'd be proud of that.[14]

The All Stars and other clubs like it kept social life going, and gave young men an outlet and a focus beyond pointless turf wars. James DeGale, born in Hammersmith in 1986 to a white English mother and black Grenadian father, trained initially at the Dale Youth Boxing Club located in an old church hall called the Morgue, and from 2000 in a room on the ground floor podium of Grenfell Tower on the Lancaster Gate Estate. James represented Great Britain at the 2008 Olympics and went on to become a middle-weight champion at British and international level. In 2014-2016 the Dale Youth Boxing Club was completely refurbished with new premises on the walkway level of Grenfell Tower, opening in November 2016. Seven months later it was totally destroyed in the fire that consumed the building.

By 2000 Kilburn was far less Irish than it had been, although Jumbo's newsagent still stocked all Ireland's regional newspapers, Quex Street was still full of worshippers at Mass and Biddy Mulligan's was still packed to the rafters on St

Patrick's Day. But Lebanese, Moroccan and Somali communities were beginning to predominate along Kilburn High Road. By 2008 it had largely shed its old Irish image with the arrival of new Middle-Eastern restaurants, a renovated Black Lion pub and upmarket dance studios to sit alongside Poundsaver and assorted electrical shops. Going west on Willesden Lane were a procession of unglamorous small outlets like Ali's Scissors, a Housing Advice Centre, an Ethiopian delicatessen and Centro Brasileiro, a new Brazilian community centre.

Centro Brasileiro was the outward sign of a significant demographic shift in the area. From about 2000 Brazilians had become the largest Latin American nationality in London and a distinctive "Little Brazil" spread westward from Kilburn down Willesden Lane and Harrow Road towards Harlesden. From the 1990s the Willseden Junction Hotel, once a lively Irish pub, became a dark and neglected dive, but in the new century it transformed into a Brazilian restaurant, part of a process that included the Sabi Minerao Brazilian café on Tubbs Road, the nearby Brazilian Kero Coffee, Planete Brazilian hairdressers and, at the end of a corridor at the back of another hairdresser, Brazilian Lingerie.[15]

Whilst some of London's Latin American community were middle class professionals, a majority worked as office or domestic cleaners, kitchen assistants, security guards, hotel chambermaids, au-pairs, couriers and drivers. In the 1990s 10% of Brazilians in London worked either as a driver or a motorcycle courier.[16] Brazilian bars and eateries such as Made in Brazil on Inverness Street, Camden Town, or the Jazz Café around the corner on Parkway, served mainly middle class Londoners, but their working class equivalent appeared in the late 1990s when the Pueblito Paisa, or "Latin Village", emerged out of the closed and abandoned Ward's Department Store at the junction of Seven Sisters Road and Tottenham High Road. The derelict shop and office space, empty since 1972, had been subject to a Compulsory Purchase Order by London Transport, which in the mid-1980s began to let its space to Afro-Caribbean and Latin American locals who turned it into a rough and ready indoors market, a warren of no-frills, rigged-up hairdressers, money exchanges, shops, delis and cafes.

By 2008 the Latin Village was the heart of North London's Latin American community, a lively forum of sixty or so independent traders selling a wide range of food from Columbian coffee to Argentine meat to Frijoles and Parilla. Right next to Seven Sisters tube, the site was very attractive to developers, one of whom, Grainger PLC, secured Haringey Council's agreement to demolish it and to build a tower block next door with 190 flats, none of which would be affordable, and a shopping centre for corporate franchises. The battle to defend the Village was complicated by the fact that the land was owned by TFL. In 2021 Grainger withdrew from the site but its departure left the Village in limbo, temporarily closed down by TFL as an unsafe environment. Its most fervent supporters were unable to get the funds to implement their "Community Plan" and TFL were left juggling competing demands from market traders to either demolish Wards Corner and build an entirely new market or support a revived version of the old one. Either way the original, completely improvised Village, with all its quixotic charm, wasn't coming back.

The children and grandchildren of the Irish who had arrived in London in the 1950s had by now moved further afield. Many of them had gone to university and into middle class occupations, and simply had less interest in the old culture beyond a sentimental regard. There were hold-outs and there still are, like Harte's Irish Meat Market on Park Parade, Harlesden, but the pillars of the community were dissolving. In 2008 the last of the great old Irish dance halls, the Galtymore, closed its doors. Its last act, appropriately enough, was Big Tom and the Mainliners. When they finished the final set with "Auld Lang Syne", accompanied by the capacity crowd of two thousand, there wasn't a dry eye in the house.

Other parts of North London's diverse working class were putting down the roots the Irish were slowly extinguishing. By 2011 there were 124,000 people of Chinese ethnicity in London, 1.4% of the city's population. After a period in the 1950s and 1960s where it was heavily concentrated in central

London, it spread out across the city, its densest concentrations in Westminster, Barnet, Camden, Islington, Kensington and Chelsea, Haringey and Tower Hamlets. Spiritually, though, it still attached to Chinatown. A vibrant and successful advertisement for Chinese culture and food, Chinatown lived on an exploited workforce of illegal workers who for a variety of reasons were "undocumented", i.e. did not have official permission to reside in the UK and were therefore ripe for exploitation in a world where gangs like the Snakeheads and the 14K still operated with impunity.

A majority of London's undocumented, low-paid Chinese workforce were poor farmers and manual workers from China's Fujian province, its equivalent of Britain's "left behind" northern towns. After a perilous transit across international borders, they fetched up in Soho at the mercy of unscrupulous employment agencies who knew full well they were illegal and therefore without rights. It was easy to funnel them to Chinese restaurants to work in the kitchens or as waiters on an incredibly low "base rate" of pay, 11am to midnight, making them dependant on tips from customers. By 2008 they were at the bottom of a hierarchy that started at the top with the chef on about £500 a week, an assistant chef on about £360 a week, vegetable and meat choppers on about £300 a week and dishwashers on about £200 a week. All wages were paid in cash and there were no benefits beyond occasionally being allowed to grab left-over food.

Xiao Fan arrived in Britain in 2002, trying to make enough money to support his seven-year-old son. After three years in the kitchens of various Chinese takeaways, he got a job in the small basement kitchen of the Furama restaurant in Macclesfield Street connecting Shaftesbury Avenue and Gerrard Street. He recalled:

We weren't given any annual holidays. There's no such thing as a "paid holiday" in Chinatown...We were made to work non-stop throughout the year, with only two days break over Christmas but no pay. And if you're sick then you won't get paid at all.

This wasn't all meekly accepted. In 2001, after four kitchen workers at the New Diamond restaurant in Lisle Street were sacked for joining a trade union, they formed the "Justice for Restaurant Workers" campaign and went around Chinatown publicising their cause and asking customers not to eat at the restaurant. Hundreds of other kitchen workers joined them and marched through the area under banners proclaiming "We want to join a trade union" and "We want to be paid the Minimum Wage". With lost custom and public embarrassment, the New Diamond offered compensation to the sacked workers. As importantly, future battle lines had been drawn between the TGWU and restaurant owners who were entirely complicit in the exploitation of their workers.[17]

Chinatown's restaurants needed a ready supply of cheap labour to work long, unsocial hours but it would not have had these so easily if not for the Triads. The rivalry between the gangs went public in 2002 at the Hippodrome on Charing Cross Road during one of its "Monday Night is Chinese Night" events, when up to a hundred youths with allegiance to 14K and the Wo Shin Wo (WSW) fought each other on the dance floor. It escalated further on 3rd June 2003 when a Chinese man walked into the BRB bar on Gerrard Street and from a distance of fifteen feet shot and killed You Hi Lee, thought to be a member of the 14K. The prevailing theory about the murder was rivalry between the gangs for control of the people trafficking operation previously controlled by Sister Ping. Her empire had collapsed after the discovery of fifty-eight dead bodies in the back of a lorry at Dover in June 2000, and her subsequent arrest and imprisonment, leaving a power vacuum in Chinatown for the Triads to fight over.[18]

Anna Chen was born in the 1970s in Hackney to a Chinese father and English mother, a working class girl who largely educated herself and who by 1995 was making a name as a performance artist. By the late 1990s she was an active member of the SWP who brought her skills as a writer and publicist to a party that still didn't bother with things like press releases. Virtually alone she coordinated new national press activity, particularly for the Stop the War Coalition (STWC) that culminated in the million-plus anti-Iraq War demonstration in London of February 2003. Despite this she was regarded with suspicion by the grandees of the party, most of whom came from privileged white backgrounds with little idea of the reality of working class life. When she raised the issue of anti-Chinese racism, one of the SWP's Central Committee informed her that British-Chinese people could not be working class because they all worked in catering.

In early 2001 the Ministry of Agriculture, Fisheries and Food (MAFF), aware of the staff problems at the New Diamond restaurant in Soho, tried to blame it for the disastrous outbreak of Foot and Mouth Disease which led to mass culling on farms and much distress to rural communities. As a result, anti-Chinese bigotry increased, including assaults on Chinese people and restaurants. In response Anna organised a national campaign against racist scapegoating which led, on 8th April 2001, to the shutdown of London's and Manchester's Chinatowns in protest. Faced with this level of public opposition, the government backed down and retracted its allegations.

In 2003, appalled by its sectarianism and sexism, Anna left the SWP.[19] From there on she focused her art and work on challenging racist and "yellowface" stereotypes in the media and society, pointing out that despite covering British working class history from 1945 to the 1980s, literally every person interviewed in Ken Loach's *The Spirit of '45* (2013) was white, reinforcing an implicit narrative that the "real" British working class was "indigenous" while a new, not-quite working class of immigrants and migrants had disrupted its essential homogeneity. She did her best to counter this narrative with a ground-breaking ten-part Radio 4 series *Chinese in Britain* (2007) and her prize-winning blog *Madam Miaow Says*.

In the early 2000s immigration into London, both legal and illegal, redefined and transformed its workforce on a scale not seen since the 1950s. The 2004 enlargement of the European Union (EU), and the decision of the Labour government to allow unrestricted Freedom of Movement from new EU countries, led to a large influx of migrant workers from Poland, Hungary, Lithuania, Latvia, Slovakia, Slovenia, the Czech Republic and

Estonia. Of these the Poles had the largest pre-existing base in London, going back to the arrival of 128,000 Poles in Britain after the Second World War. A quarter of these were based in London, with a large concentration around the "Polish Corridor" of Cromwell Road in Kensington, particularly the Earl's Court end, a mostly working class population in which the men did manual labour and the women domestic work.

By 2011 the total number of Poles in the UK had increased to half a million, of which nearly 150,000 lived in London, the largest proportion in Ealing with significant numbers in Barnet, Brent, Haringey and Waltham Forest.[20] They worked in a wide variety of occupations, with large numbers in construction and care work, and in domestic services such as plumbing and building repair. Not all Polish migrants came for the long term, many came to make more money than they could at home and then return. Some came for the working week and went back to Poland at the weekend. But like Irish migrants in the 1950s, many of whom did not initially intend to put down roots, Poles began to integrate into British life. Polish delicatessens and food shops, the *Polski Sklep*, began to appear all over London and other cities.

Many of the job and housing opportunities available to Polish migrants in London arose from personal connections, either family or business. As more got work, the network expanded. Polish life in the UK was expressed and represented by the imposing modernist building of the Polish Social and Cultural Association (PSOK) on King Street near Hammersmith tube, which opened in 1967. The PSOK is a focus for cultural events and welfare advice of the kind performed by the London Irish Centre for Irish immigrants, which also houses the Polish Library (a unique collection of 100,000 Polish books, several hundred manuscripts and 40,000 photographs), the Polish University Aboard, an art gallery, bookshop, café, theatre and conference room. Despite its years of work to integrate Polish immigrants to the UK, in June 2016, a few days after the Brexit referendum result, the front entrance of the PSOK building was vandalised by racist graffiti.

The existence of PSOK did not mean that Polish arrivals had it easy. Piotr, a twenty-five-year-old man from Krakow's neglected housing estates who came from a broken family, his father an alcoholic tile fitter, and who had already served time for petty theft and burglary, arrived in the UK in 2006. Taking any work going, he ended up selling cigarettes on the streets and living in a room in a house in Acton shared by six other migrants. But still he saw life in London as better than any he might have had in Poland:

> I just want to live here. I want to work. Even what I have now, I am standing there (selling cigarettes)...I have £30 a day, I get £200 per week...That's fine for me...for food, accommodation, something else...just my needs...In Poland there is no middle class, there are those who are very poor and those who are very rich. Here you have a middle class like...All the blacks are middle class here.

As ever, race and identifiable ethnicity made the difference. Like Irish migrants decades earlier, Poles like Piotr had one advantage that many other immigrants lacked. They were white. If they and their children could more easily assimilate to British society, if they could avoid systemic racist persecution, it was not always because of their sterling work ethic. Michel P. Garapich's study of Polish migrants in London in the twenty-first century quotes a Polish Roma migrant who was explicit about how class and ethnic prejudice operated differently for him depending on where he lived, saying bluntly, "In Poland I was black. Here I am white".[21]

The Muslim community could not pull this trick. By 2018 London's Muslim population constituted 14% of its total, its largest concentrations in Tower Hamlets, Newham, Redbridge and Waltham Forest. North London contained a less heavy concentration, but there were still significant numbers in Brent, Hackney and Haringey. The 2000s saw the emergence of a new generation of Muslim political activists in North London, the most visible of whom was Nash Ali, who in 2003 became the UK's first Muslim Mayor when he was elected Mayor of

Camden. Nash went on to become the leader of Camden's Labour Group from 2009 to 2012 and Leader of the Council from 2010 to 2012.

By 2008 North London was home to a growing number of Iranian, Kurdish, Somali, Sudanese, Algerian, Morrocan and Lebanese refugees. Conflicts like the Algerian Civil War of 1991-2002 drove international migration. Where the number of Algerians seeking asylum in Britain during the 1990s was just over one hundred people per year, by 2002 that number had jumped to over 1,200 per year. Similarly, the 1983-2005 civil war in Sudan produced increasing numbers of people seeking asylum in Britain, as did the Ethopian intervention in Somalia of 2006-2009. The majority of these ended up in London, whose boroughs were obliged to provide some form of accommodation to those granted official leave to remain in the country.

Some did more than others. The Sudan Women's Association, founded in 1991, and which later changed its name to the South Sudan Women's Skills Development Group (SSWSDG), received a generous annual grant from Camden Council, which when added to other income amounted to £40,000 per annum. This greatly helped its work developing the self-sufficiency of Sudanese women in North London. The grant was allocated on a "funding-plus" basis, meaning that it was not simply doled out but came with additional logistical support to ensure the beneficiary made best use of it. In 2007 Elizabeth Ajith, a Sudanese refugee living in Somers Town and one of the founders of the original Sudanese Women's Association, became the SSWSDG's Co-Ordinator.

Based out of the Abbey Community Centre on Belsize Road between Kilburn and Swiss Cottage, the SSWSDG supplied teaching in English as a second language as well as top-up classes in English, Maths and Science for school-aged children, business start-up skills, and various arts and dance classes. It helped women such as Grace Oliver, born in 1954 in South Sudan near the Ugandan border. In 1994, when her husband was murdered and her children scattered, Grace fled to Egypt where she stayed until 2000. She finally ended up in the UK where she had relatives. In 2006, after staying in a number of lodgings around London, she was given official leave to remain. Camden Council offered her a small flat on the Weedington Road Estate next to Queen's Crescent Market where she lived on £125 a week Employment and Support Allowance. Every Saturday morning she took a bus to the SSWSDG for the company and to use their sewing and knitting equipment.

Khadiga Khogali arrived in London in 2000 as a political refugee from Khartoum. After securing a council flat in Cromer Street, St Pancras, she discovered the King's Cross Community Development Trust, who helped her to set up the Sudan Children in Need (SCIN) charity and point it to sources of funding in Camden Council. The charity, organised out of a neighbourhood hall in Argyll Square, assists the children of refugee Sudanese families with extra schooling and holidays. Both the SSDSWG and SCIN provide a vital sense of belonging and a welcome from the native English culture to outsiders looking for a home.

Other London boroughs, such as Tower Hamlets with Somali refugees and Lambeth with Syrians, were as proactive as Camden. Brent was second only to Tower Hamlets as a home to Somalis, where they could access the Somali Advice and Forum of Information (SAAFI) and other support services. Nonetheless, Somali immigrants in Harlseden sometimes encountered the same type of hostility from the older Afro-Caribbean population that they in their day had faced from the indigenous white population, i.e. that the newcomers were getting preferential treatment and jumping the queue for council flats. But by virtue of its culture and support structure, it was still home. As a Sudanese refugee living in Camden told Elizabeth Ajith:

To be honest, I strongly feel I belong in Camden Town. The place you feel accepted is where you belong.[22]

This was a sentiment well understood amongst London's Kurdish population. Although nearly thirty million Kurds live in eastern Turkey, that state's relentless persecution of its most significant minority had eroded any fealty to Turkish nationhood. Most of the refugees arriving in the UK from the 1980s who were classed as Turks by the Home Office were in fact Kurds. Political pressure meant that most of the nearly eight thousand applications per year from Kurds for political asylum during the 1980s and 1990s were refused, but this only meant they found other ways to enter and remain in the UK.

Over 40% of Kurdish migrants settled in London, mostly in Hackney, Haringey and Islington. The majority of them lived in either Council or Housing Association accommodation, with only 23% renting from a private landlord, and about 10% temporarily staying with relatives or friends.[23] Many received support from organisations such as Halkevi (Dalston Kingsland), the Kurdish Cultural Centre (Kennington), the Kurdish Community Association (Manor Gardens) and the Day-Mer Community Centre (Newington Green).Unusually, Halkevi offered advice services to both Turks and Kurds. It provided help on business, health, immigration, welfare, education, employment and housing, language courses, ICT training, drama classes, music classes, and sports activities for young people. It also contained a smaller organisation, Roj Women, a Kurdish women's rights movement that offered practical advice about the welfare system to Kurdish women whilst challenging the patriarchal values of traditional Kurdish culture.

Roj Women assisted women like Suna Parlak. Arrested in Turkey in 1994 for membership of the Kurdistan Workers Party (PKK), Suna was brutally tortured for information and sentenced to seven years in an overcrowded jail. After release she was subject to continual harassment from the police and in 2007 she came to England on a tourist visa. After being granted leave to remain in 2013 she started studying for a degree, earning enough money to get by in shop and restaurant work as well as interpreting for other Kurdish refugees applying for asylum.[24] One of the largest and most effective resources for Kurdish and Turkish asylum seekers was the Human Rights lawyers Howe & Co, which worked closely with the Halkevi in Green Lanes and other Turkish refugee groups, providing interpreters and advisors at first stage interviews at Heathrow and Gatwick, and representing asylum seekers in court when necessary. In September 2008 the firm won its biggest case yet, the fight to grant the legal right to remain in the UK of Gurkhas who had fought in the British Army.

The British imperial legacy continued to reverberate. Between 1992 and 2000, 10,398 Iraqi nationals, nearly double the amount that had settled in the UK in the previous thirty years, were granted British citizenship. In 2003 alone, following the Second Iraq War, over 14,500 Iraqi asylum claims were made, half of them allowed. These were a mixture of Shias, Christians and Kurds. This inevitably produced a significant increase in immigrants to London who were, to quote a 2005 GLA report, "born in the Arab world". But where once the major component of "Arab" migration into London had been from Egypt, by 2005 the largest numbers came from Iraq, Algeria, Lebanon, Palestine and Syria.[25]

By 2008 Uxbridge Road was London's centre for Middle Eastern food. Every conceivable ingredient was available at Al Dimashqi Supermarket and the best falafel wraps in the city were made at Zeit & Zaatar. But whilst the Uxbridge Road, from Shepherd's Bush Market to Acton, was pretty solid working class, Edgware Road had a different vibe. Running south from Church Street Market under the Marylebone flyover and down to Marble Arch, "E Road" had been the social and cultural centre of Arab London since the 1970s, a cross-class mélange of Arabic shops, supermarkets, cafes and restaurants surrounded by a close mix of council block and high-end penthouses. Its visitors and inhabitants intermingled on the street as customers, workers, bosses and employees.[26]

It was an area prone to the same kind of postcode gang war as the estates of Hackney and Tottenham, although not usually as lethal. The E Road Rude Boys fought with the Lisson Green Mandem over disputed territory north and south of the Marylebone flyover. It was a rivalry that could and did explode into violence, mainly after midnight outside the area's clubs and pubs. But while the gangs inflicted real hurt on some people, mainly rivals in other gangs, they were mostly legends in their own minds, ignored by most inhabitants on Edgware Road getting on with their daily life as restaurant and café owners, shop assistants, waiters, cleaners, dishwashers and cooks.

In *Becoming Arab in London* (2014), Ramy M.K. Aly describes two Shisha café workers he met in 2006 at the Downtown café between Baker Street and St Marylebone High Street. Wa'el Abu Isa, a Palestinian from the refugee camps of Lebanon, worked the counter while his friend, Mohammed Ali, a Syrian from Damascus who had only just arrived in the UK, had the harder job of preparing and serving the Shisha. Both Wa'el and Mohammed were illegals and so wide open to exploitation by the cafés, which paid about £30 a day at the time.

Mohammed could not speak English and so Aly recorded his work day for him:

Mohammed spends most of his day preparing the tobacco that rests in clay crowns on the top of the Shisha. It's a dirty job. The tobacco is sticky and pungent, so much so that it will give you a headache if you breath it in all day. His fingers are stained a reddish colour as a result of handling the tobacco without gloves. He cleans and refills the glass water vases that form the base of the Shisha as well as performing the menial tasks expected of anyone who works in a Shisha café, cleaning the toilets, stacking shelfs and so on...Part of his job is to inhale intensely to fire up the Shisha before passing it on to the customer...His clothes don't seem to change much from day to day, he is slightly dated wearing black denim from head to toe, his hair in a crew cut with a classic Ba'athi moustache, wide and bushy, attesting to his masculinity and recent arrival in the UK.[27]

Many new arrivals in London in the new century, especially those that had arrived illegally and could not therefore appeal to the authorities for rights such as the Minimum Wage, fell prey to exploitative employers. There were always exceptions, though. Child refugee Rita Sahatçiu, born in Pristina in the former Yugoslavia in 1990, arrived in London in 1991 with her Alabanian parents and older sister, fleeing ethnic persecution in what would become Kosovo. Initially the family lived in one room in Earl's Court overlooking Brompton Cemetery, her mother working as a waitress by day and studying to be a doctor at night, her dad working in and then running his own pub, the Queen's Arms in Kilburn, after the family moved to Kensal Rise. As a kid Rita sang in her dad's pub, which her father made sure served traditional Albanian spinach pies.

After a spell at the Sylvia Young Theatre School, Rita Sahatçiu went on to become the singer Rita Ora. There is now a pink "I Am a Refugee" plaque outside her old school, St Cuthbert's Primary School on Warwick Road, Earl's Court, that reads *"Rita Ora. Singer and Actress. Fled the war in Kosovo and studied here after arriving in the UK in 1991"*. Similar plaques were put up on the Urswick School in Hackney for the Sudanese refugee Alek Wek, who also arrived in London in 1991 and later became a supermodel; and also for Michael Marks, a poor refugee boy from Poland who fled the pogroms in 1882 and went on to found Marks & Spencer in 1894.

The ability of London to provide a new life to migrants and refugees was not a new phenomenon. Whether Huguenots, Eastern European Jews, Irish, Bangladeshi or Ugandan, it was why they came. Daniel Kaluuya was born in 1989 in London to Ugandan parents and grew up on the Camelot Estate in Camden Park Road between Kentish Town and Caledonian Road. The estate was an old LCC one with balcony access but was maintained and landscaped to a high standard, and is still a pleasant oasis of old-school social housing in an increasingly gentrified area. Daniel went to the Torriano Primary School in Kentish Town and then the all-boys St Aloysius Catholic School in Highgate.

St Aloysius had taught several generations of working class boys, including Joe Cole, who was born in Paddington in 1981 but moved to Somers Town when he was six and was adopted by foster parents, later going on to Premier League success with West Ham in the late 1990s and Chelsea from 2003. During Daniel's time there, 2000 to 2006, the school was going through a tough time, with falling standards and the closure of its entire sixth form. He would later achieve success as an actor, but of his secondary school he remembers:

It was a boisterous school, man—a lot of fighting energy. There was a time where we had all-year detention, where the school would lock up our whole year because there were fights and knife crime...I was that kid who could do schoolwork really easily—but I was bored, so I messed around a lot. My mum was strict, so she wanted me to get my grades. As long as I got the grades, I was thinking I could do whatever the fuck I liked. I just wanted to have fun and have vibes—to get grades to prove myself and carry on. If I got bad grades, I didn't see it as a reflection of me. I knew from an early age that school was a test of your memory, rather than a test of your intellectualism. It's not about learning; it's about retaining.

Given the limitations of his school, Daniel was fortunate to have another outlet for his talent at the Anna Scher Theatre School in Islington:

My mum got me into it to get me off the streets, and I just loved it. I took a class where you pay five pounds and improvise for two or three hours. There were people in class who were on TV, and I thought, Oh my God, this could be possible, so I kept at it. I thought I found my tribe—people who were from the estates who loved being creative but weren't flowery or lovey. That really resonated with me.[28]

While some working class kids would always find a way to express their talent and ability, many others left school with little or no qualifications and were stuck in dead-end jobs or semi-permanent unemployment. Low wage work presented more problems than simply a low income. The higher-than-average cost of living in London — of travel to work, of childcare, of rent — meant that low pay could leave someone worse off than if they had stayed on the dole. Even if a person's finances ultimately balanced, delays in administering changes in benefits, i.e. if someone took short-term work and then needed to return to Housing Benefit, were a disincentive to taking the work.

In 2005 the Guinness factory in Park Royal, one of the last remaining employers of what in the 1950s had been a substantial number of industrial jobs in London, closed and relocated to Dublin. Inevitably, London's de-industrialised economy produced a largely unseen underclass of migrant workers, unprotected by the law and, in most cases, by trade unions, who either couldn't reach them or never tried. Many worked in the thriving ethnic food sector, often with friends or relatives, in kebab and halal shops or in cafes and on market stalls, where if the money wasn't great at least the work was steady. The really isolated did the jobs nobody else wanted — cleaners, mini-cab drivers, carwashers, dishwashers, many of them locked into a black market of cowboy firms and dodgy employment agencies.

Nonetheless, some things improved. In 2005 the North London Line was transferred to Transport for London and its future was, at last, secure. A GLA report on the line, entitled *London's Forgotten Railway* (2006),found that "*Stations are often understaffed, which makes passengers feel unsafe*", citing the case of Thomas ap Rhys-Price, murdered shortly after leaving the unstaffed Kensal Rise station in October 2006 by men who had earlier assaulted a passenger on the station platform. TFL, now free of shareholders and allowed to borrow on the markets to avoid getting in hock to a PFI, could properly invest in the line and change travelcard zone boundaries so that Hampstead Heath moved from Zone 3 to Zone 2, and Willesden Junction from 3 to the 2/3 boundary, thus making many journeys cheaper.[29] In 2007 the NLL was incorporated into the new London Overground network and finally saw major investment in track, new trains and infrastructure.

This largesse seldom applied to those who kept London's transport network clean. Ben Judah's *This is London* (2016) follows the story of Akwese, who arrived in London on a student visa from Ghana in the early 2000s, seduced by stories of Ghanians setting themselves up in business after six months in the city. Instead he ended up sleeping on the floor of a crowded Peckham bedsit and doing the washing up in the back of a chic South Kensington brasserie that didn't spend its profits on a dishwasher. He hadn't intended to become illegal labour but he had not understood the legalities of work in the UK. He soon learnt that the engine of the illegal economy were cowboy employment agencies who sent cheap labour to clean kitchens and offices and then paid a pittance to those who signed on with them.

After five years working at a carwash, Akwese secured a job as a cleaner on London Underground, where 95% of the poorly paid agency workers were immigrants, mostly from Africa. He was stationed at Edgware Road, one of the largest and busiest tube stations, assigned to the late shift, the one that cleaned up after drunken late-night travellers. He was relatively lucky in being a "train picker", whose job it was to jump on and off the trains during their three-minute stops at Edgware Road and scoop up the *Standards, Metros,* lager cans and KFC boxes. There were worse assignments, like the train depot, where cleaners got to clean up vomit and blood.

Akwese got to know two other Ghanaian cleaners based at Paddington called Big Yaw and Baby Yaw. The older, Big Yaw, lived on the White City Estate with a Jamaican wife and was thoroughly disenchanted with his job and his life, but Baby Yaw, Paddington's RMT union rep, was more positive. Armed with street smarts and IT qualifications, he finally secured permanent leave to remain in the UK and began to dream of a life beyond cleaning up after drunken tube passengers:

> *These old guys they are down here picking...They are picking until the end. But me the only way I can go is up. I began at the bottom picking the rubbish. I can only break out into the streets and see the sun...Maybe even I can get as far as Customer Service...one day. I know a lot about the Underground.*[30]

By 2007 cleaners working on the Northern Line were employed by the cleaning sub-contractor ISS, who moved them around constantly to prevent any chance of organising in a trade union. At busy central London stations there was often only one cleaner, where there had previously been four or five. Only when the RMT began to recruit and organise ISS's cleaners, demanding better conditions and the London Living Wage of £7.20 an hour, did the company insist on checking their employees' National Insurance numbers. The RMT's support for the cleaners led to a big increase in recruitment of ISS cleaning staff, particularly by its active Finsbury Park Branch.[31]

After years of accepting the inevitability of privatisation and outsourcing and the cuts to pay and conditions that followed, workers in local government were beginning to kick back. In July 2006 refuse collectors at Haringey's large municipal depot on Ashley Road, Tottenham, took strike action against the private contractor Accord, to whom Haringey Council had outsourced its refuse collection services and who had eighty other similar contracts across North London. Despite making a £53m profit in 2005, Accord tried to make cuts to its Haringey service involving smaller crews and longer shifts, a move rejected by its workers who still had residual terms and conditions from their TUPE transfer from the council. In the five years since it took on the contract, Accord had already cut staffing levels on refuse collection work from seventy-three to forty-eight workers, with vehicle crews dropping from six people on each to only three.

The Ashley Road depot housed the bulk of Haringey's refuse collectors, with several hundred workers and over one hundred vehicles. The strikers were TGWU members dealing with domestic waste wheelie bins. Faced with solid and potentially indefinite industrial action, Accord recruited scab labour and fast-tracked "training" for the job, even though some required HGV licenses to meet health and safety regulations. Haringey Council claimed it had nothing to do with the strike as the strikers worked for Accord. As uncollected rubbish piled up on the streets, the Haringey Federation of Residents Associations offered support to the strikers and many residents deposited black rubbish bags outside Haringey Civic Centre. After three weeks Accord gave in and scrapped its plans to further cut collection crews, even offering a bonus to staff for clearing up the backlog.[32]

In August 2008 Unite called out bus drivers at multiple London garages to demand a 5% pay increase after years of below inflation deals. Despite an attempt by management at

Northumberland Park Garage in Tottenham to intimidate pickets by calling in the police, the strike held firm across London. The Westbourne Park Bus Garage, one of the largest in North London employing nearly one thousand drivers, was especially solid. Holly Eaton, a writer for *The Socialist* newspaper sent to cover the strike at Westbourne Park, reported:

> *The strike started at 3am that morning. I arrived at 6.45pm and there were still around 40 people there. I was told by one driver that he normally does a late shift and he had arrived at the picket line for 2pm. He estimated that there were 300 people on the picket line at that point. They didn't have much in the way of material — no leaflets, no posters, no placards, just a couple of A3 size signs saying "equal pay". However the mood was strong and it did seem that around half of all drivers at that garage had actually come to the picket line, rather than just stay off work.*[33]

The Labour government's proposals to privatise Royal Mail were paused when postal workers in Islington took strike action against local management for breaking a "pay and modernisation" national agreement negotiated in 2007 and ramming through cuts to the service. In June 2009 the Communications Workers Union (CWU) called out the Islington sorting office. When Mark Dolan, the CWU's North London rep based at the office, was informed that weekly earnings would be capped and delivery rosters extended, he called a meeting of CWU members. Mark told a reporter:

> *Over 100 of us met on Monday morning and unanimously refused to sign up for any unagreed duties. We're also pressing for more strike dates on top of those already announced. The feeling is the same at other offices across North London and at the Rathbone Place sorting office in central London.*[34]

Where economic capital was hard to come by, cultural capital could sometimes fill the gap. In 2001 Rowena MacDonald, a working class girl from Wolverhampton who had met plenty of arrogant Londoners at Sussex University, many of whom talked about their local bus routes with fetishistic passion, was lodging in the basement of a single mother's flat in Camden Town, so skint that she couldn't afford the tube to work. So she travelled by bus and discovered why Londoners were obsessed with them:

> I got to know the 24 very well and it was more exciting than the 501 from Wolves town centre. I caught it from Mornington Crescent station, opposite the old Black Cat cigarette factory, and it trundled down Tottenham Court Road, Charing Cross Road, around Trafalgar Square, down Whitehall and passed the House of Commons, where I got off for work. An iconic journey from start to stop, freighted with the weight of history and world-famous places on post-cards.[35]

This experience — cash poor but, by virtue of where they lived, culturally rich — applied especially to North London's working class, although it was hugely variable depending on specific locale. North Tottenham, for example, had a level of structural poverty heavily resistant to regeneration, let alone gentrification. But while South Tottenham was not a wealthy area, West Green Road between Seven Sisters and Turnpike Lane (both with tube stations) was a lively micro-economy of restaurants, takeaways and bars.

Even the boarded up shops at the north end of Seven Sisters Road fronted a hidden world on its backstreets, an interzone between the Tiverton Estate and the main road full of small car part specialists, air conditioner repairs and a variety of joiners and mechanics. It made a difference. The old Harringay Warehouse District on and around Hermitage Road, in particular the elegant Omega Works building, was transforming into a new eco-system of semi-legal live/work units for artists, craftsmen and a variety of small creative industries. Maynards had evacuated Tottenham in 1988 for Sheffield and its iconic factory chimney, seen for miles around the New River, was now adorned with the initials OCC for the Oriental Carpet Company, which had taken over its old building. The area was improving in other ways too.

Whatever other social problems afflicted them, the working class of South Tottenham enjoyed facilities like Lordship Recreation Ground and Downhills Park, the latter undergoing a major renovation in the early 2000s financed by Haringey Council and the Single Regeneration Budget that led to new footpaths, restored tennis courts and playgrounds, and its long-neglected Italian Garden being given a facelift.Work and employment in North London, perhaps even more than play, often expanded horizons. From the mid-1990s to mid-2000s Henry, a bit of a wide-boy on Camden Lock, worked on an outside clothes stall in the Stables Market. Amongst other things he recalled:

> ...always cold, dragging a ton of tweed jackets up the cobbles in the rain on a clothes rail with one wheel missing...My pal shouting at John-Paul Gaultier "Discount, qu'est que c'est fucking discount?"; mulled wine for breakfast; the guy next door smoking crack behind his stall; Cissy Strut by the Meters being played all day long by the bootleg tape sellers; the Israeli bloke two stalls up telling us about juggling live grenades during national service; the stench of non-specific "ethnic food"; the endless wall of people filing past; a job lot of 1970s Adidas tracksuits from a warehouse in Beirut; sitting on the radiator in a pub in Primrose Hill after work until I could feel my legs again.[36]

By the 2000s, house prices around Camden Town were far beyond the capacity of even the well paid, employed working class to buy from scratch, but Camden Town itself, its streets and bars and pubs, had not yet been gentrified (and Camden High Street remains impervious even today, nowhere near as middle class as, for instance, Fulham Broadway). Its idiosyncratic mixture of faded bohemian glamour and working class detritus remained intact, epitomised in the title and contents of Robert Lang's photographic collection *Filthy Gorgeous Camden Town* (2017). Lang arrived in Camden in 2001 as a teenager and divided his time between working at Offspring, a sports trainer shop on Camden High Street, and doing fashion reportage photography. *Filthy Gorgeous Camden Town* is a tribute to his friends, especially the young women, who between 2004 and 2011 tore up Camden's pubs and clubs.

One especially came to stand for them all. Amy Winehouse was born in Enfield in 1983 to her taxi driver dad Mitch and pharmacist mum Janis, and grew up in Southgate in far-North London. Her interest in music was bred into her. Her uncles were professional jazz musicians and her grandmother was a singer who once dated Ronnie Scott. In 1995 Amy started attending Sylvia Young where she stayed for three years, given her big break by Sylvia herself after she referred her to the National Youth Jazz Orchestra in 1999. Soon she was singing for the NYJA and acting as lead vocalist on its CDs. Her dad always knew she'd make it big, telling Robert Elms once in the late 1990s, as they were both enjoying a traditional Turkish bath at the Porchester Hall Baths on Queensway, that his daughter would be famous one day (when she was, she played a gig in the Baths).

After sharing a flat in her late teens in East Finchley, Amy's life shifted to Camden. With her parents' help she bought a small flat in Jefferys Street, where Kentish Town Road meets Camden Street, five minutes' away from her favourite Camden pubs, the Hawley Arms on Castlehaven Road next to Camden Lock and the Good Mixer on Inverness Street, where she played pool and listened to Motown and R&B on the jukebox. From then on it was her spiritual home while her albums *Frank* (2003) and *Back to Black* (2006) achieved global success. Even at the height of her fame she bought records at the Oxfam in Kentish Town and played live at the Dublin Castle on Parkway.

When Amy died in 2011 her image appeared on street murals all across Camden Town, most of which are still there. The Sylvia Young Theatre School set up the Amy Winehouse Scholarship in which one pupil is sponsored for the entire five years at the school. It received funding to do so from the Amy Winehouse Foundation run by her family, which also helped similar projects like the Pilion Trust Homeless Shelter in Holloway, the New Horizon Youth Centre in Euston, and an additional advice worker at the London Irish Centre down the road from Amy's final home on Camden Square.

Camden Town was Amy's adopted home, but N-Dubz, a contraction of NW1, were Camden from the cradle. Its three members —Costadinos Contostavlos, his cousin Tula Contostavlos and their friend Richard Rawson, better known as Dappy, Tulisa and Fazer — grew up on Camden's housing estates. Dappy and Fazer went to Haverstock School in the 1990s while Tulisa went to Quintin Kynaston in St John's Wood before transferring to Haverstock for her GCSEs. Dappy and Tulisa came from a Greek Cypriot family, Tulisa's mother an Irish immigrant from Dublin, while Fazer's mother was Jamaican and his father white English.

Tulisa's dad left when she was young. From eleven she spent much of her adolescence caring for her mother, who suffered from schizo-affective disorder and on one occasion had to be sectioned under the Mental Health Act. The stress of looking after her mum while still a child herself drove her to self-harm, eating disorders and depression. At fourteen she almost overdosed on pills and at seventeen she slashed her wrists. She began writing songs as escape and therapy. In the late 1990s, whilst still young teenagers, Tulisa, her cousin and his friend formed the hip-hop group N-Dubz under the tutelage and direction of Dappy's father Byron Contostavlos, known to all of them as Uncle B, who had once played for Mungo Jerry but later became a barber in Camden Town.

N-Dubz began to get noticed after their music videos played on the digital satellite platform Channel U. Their breakthrough came in 2007 when they won a MOBO for best newcomer. In 2008 their debut album, *Uncle B*, named for Dappy's father who died shortly before its release, shot up the charts and went Platinum, winning another MOBO for Best Album of the year. They would go on to global success with a succession of snappy, catchy hip-hop songs that wallowed in predictable clichés, working class kids whose triumph over upbringing and circumstances was intensely individualistic.

Other young North London working class women found their voices through music. In 2002 Akala's older sister Niomi,

AKA Ms Dynamite, released her debut album *A Little Deeper*. She won the Mercury Music Prize and the melodic "Dy-Na-Mi-Tee" shot to number five in the charts. Another single from the album, "It Takes More", used a deceptively smooth hip-hop rhythm to slate the vacuous gang and gun culture she saw all around her. Her signature smash hit, full of acute personal and social observation, rejected easy despondency:

> *Remember Sunday School and after go to granma's for lunch*
> *Macaroni, rice and peas, chicken and pineapple punch*
> *Never had much, my mum brother sister and me*
> *But love was enough to succeed*

Working class girls usually did accentuate the positive. In 2001 Sabrina Washington, born and raised in Harlesden, started a dance duo with Alesha Dixon in Fulham, both of them later forming the R&B girl group Mis-teeq with Su-Elise Nash. Melissa Bell's daughter Alexandra Burke, born in 1988 off the Caledonian Road in Islington, inherited her mother's singing talent and went on to win series five of *The X-Factor* in 2008 with her pop version of Leonard Cohen's "Hallelujah".

Alexandra was primarily an entertainer, but some of the music coming out of working class London was a cry of pain. Alex Holland, born in Leeds in 1974, moved with his mum and siblings to London when he was ten. He grew up on the Six Acres Estate in Finsbury Park where John Lydon had lived in the late 1960s and early 1970s and it had not improved one iota since then. On his first night on the estate his mum gave him their last £10 note to go out and get a bucket of KFC for dinner. He was mugged on the way back by local kids and lost the lot. Taking the street name Skinnyman, Alex spent a few years with the Bury Crew and Mud Fam hip-hop collectives, building a reputation as a battle rapper. In 2001 he was signed by the Talking Loud label and at the age of thirty released his first and only album, *Council Estate of Mind*.

A powerful lament about growing up in the marginalized North London working class of the Six Acres and Andover estates, *Council Estate of Mind* was a cult hit and has since had a subterranean afterlife, although Skinnyman himself never caught the break he deserved. The video to "Council Estate" was filmed around the Six Acres Estate, its tracking shots laid over a plaintive hip-hop chorus notable for its lack of aggression and attempt to simply be understood:

> Just look how this United Kingdom has come
> Within the council estates where man'll fight over crumbs
> You got young single parent mums
> Havin' the hardest time tryn'a survive for their daughters and
> their sons
> Be comin' out their youths, cause their youths are left out there
> Raised on the ways of these streets without care
> Now we're havin' our fair share of gun warfare
> And it's all gone nuts and that's just cause it's poor here
> People want more here, we're all on the floor here
> It's raw here, can't even sleep and ignore here
> Cause life's kinda militant, stuck in the grime
> Nothing's equivalent to this council estate of mind

Skinnyman's despairing verses were interwoven with a sweet female chorus that softened it still further:

> We know that we have been living our lives through the
> hardest times
> Still we know that we must keep up the faith in our hearts
> and minds

Skinnyman worked closely with Chester P, born Joey Coombs in Sunderland in 1976. When he was young Joey relocated to London where he grew up on the Highbury Quadrant Estate between Clissold Park and Highbury Grove, one of the better post-war estates, its unambitious low-level blocks surrounded by neat grass lawns well maintained by Islington Council. In 1998 Joey, his brother and some friends formed the hip-hop group Task Force and had a fleeting cult success in 2004 with their single "The Junkyard", a stark but over-dramatic monologue on the not-very terrible horrors of the Highbury

Estate. The world of Skinnyman and Task Force was broadcast to a mass audience in the three-part BBC3 documentary *Tower Block Dreams* (2004) which focused on the underground music scene on Britain's council estates. The first episode followed Skinnyman and Charlie Sloth in their attempts to re-orient their lives after serving brief prison sentences, to realise their dreams of escape through music.

Some dreams could be achieved. Ed Skrien was born in Camden in 1983 of mixed English and Austrian-Jewish descent and raised in the same world as Skinnyman in Camden, Islington and Haringey. As a teenager he got into gang-related trouble and when seventeen he was stabbed by kids from another gang. In 2004 and 2007, after working with hip-hop and Dubstep artists like Asian Dub Foundation and Plan B, he released his own rap albums. He got his first lead acting role in Plan B's *Ill Manors* (2012) before his big break as the villain in Marvel's *Deadpool* (2016). Despite acting success, Ed continued as a regular swimming coach at the Caledonian Road Gym and the Archway Pool and later opened his own swimming academy in Islington for disadvantaged kids, offering the kind of paternalistic discipline provided by boxing clubs like the IBC and All Stars.

Noel Clarke was born in 1975 in Notting Hill to Alf and Gemma from Trinidad. His dad worked as a carpenter and his mum as a nurse at St Mary's Hospital, Paddington. They divorced shortly after he was born and he was raised on an estate in Ladbroke Grove underneath Trellick Tower by his mum, a strict Christian who took on extra work as a part-time laundry worker. After a period working as a lifeguard at a leisure centre whilst studying media at college, he went into acting, in 2003 winning the Lawrence Olivier Award for Most Promising Newcomer. After getting noticed in the new *Doctor Who* he wrote and directed *Kidulthood* (2006) and *Adulthood* (2008), bringing the life of W11's estates to the big screen. Clarke went on to become a major player in British BAME culture, but his charm and talent obscured deep personal flaws which in 2021 saw him accused of multiple cases of sexual harassment.

The emergence in the early 2000s of young North London musicians, artists and actors like N-Dubz, Ms Dynamite, Sabrina Washington, Alexandra Burke, Skinnyman, Chester P, Daniel Kaluuya, Ed Skrien and Noel Clarke, amongst others, was an expression of the tenacity and energy of its working class. For the most part, though, it was an energy that followed trends rather than creating entirely new artistic and musical genres such as dubstep or grime. Dubstep's most outstanding artist, Burial, emerged from South London, as did many of his peers. Grime exploded out of East London, and a specific East London at that, not relatively genteel Bethnal Green but the grim high-rise estates of Bow and Canning Town.

Grime music, in particular the "road rap" coming out of South London's hardest estates bursting with gang anthems and gun porn, was accused of glamourising violent crime, and to an extent it did. But popular music has been accused of that in one form or another ever since John Gay's *The Beggar's Opera*, with its hero highwayman MacHeath, in the 1720s. If anything, grime was affirmative. Its heavy use of rapid-fire lyrics and rhyming schemes, of "spitting bars", opened the gates to a rush of urban poetry by working class boys and girls, most of whom had never been given poetry to study but found they had it in them anyway.

Akala pushed hip-hop and grime's capacity for poetic expression as far as it could go. His confidence in his ability to do so came from his own background. Raised mixed-race working class in Camden and Highgate, where he grew up with white kids, including middle class ones, he could see for himself they had no special qualities. Receiving additional education from his Pan-Africanist Saturday School, he always knew that Britain's institutional racism rigged the game against black kids and he would have to work twice as hard as white kids, be twice as good, to have any chance of success. In 2003 he started releasing music under his own independent label and in 2009 formed the Hip Hop Shakespeare Company, a musical theatre production company that fuses hip-hop and Shakespearean verse to explore the similarities of both forms. The company puts out its own material and delivers workshops to young people, furthering both cultural and political education.

Akala's first album, *It's not a Rumour* (2006), was recognised as a unique voice in black and hip-hop music, wining a MOBO award for Best Hip-Hop Act. Tracks like "Shakespeare" and "Bullshit" left many of his contemporaries looking frenzied and incoherent. After his third album in 2011, he went on Charlie Sloth's show and did a "Fire in the Booth" that blew away all its competitors and was widely praised for its structural and thematic maturity:

> *Judge no one, done many things wrong*
> *I just don't boast about it in songs*
> *But listen to my older bars*
> *I was just as confused as you probably are*
> *But you grow and you learn, travel and fuck up*
> *One too many man you know get cut up*
> *One too many man that could've been doctors*
> *End up spending their whole life boxed up*
> *You learn, if you study*
> *Its all set out just to make them money*
> *No cover, it's all about getting poor people to fight with one another*
> *So it's logical that us killing our brothers, dissing our mothers*
> *Is right in line with the dominant philosophy of our time*

Nor was he afraid to critique the more materialist and anti-intellectual elements of grime and its street culture:

> *All that you see me do I own*
> *But I won't hang what I make around my neck*
> *I know from where the diamonds came*
> *But I do quite literally own a library*
> *That definitely costs more than your chain*

Akala's hip-hop was similar to that produced by George Mpanga, AKA George the Poet, born in 1991 on the St Raphael's Estate in Neasden off the North Circular to a Ugandan family who arrived in the UK as political refugees in the 1980s. At the time he was part of an African minority within a Jamaican majority. As a disaffected teenager he gravitated to Harlesden. When he was sixteen a friend offered him the opportunity to make some quick money by selling drugs:

> I gave it some serious thought because I didn't have any money. But someone I respected shut this conversation down for me. It was a crucial moment for me. I respected him and so I didn't go ahead. It was the respect that did it. Young men don't have enough older role models around that they respect.[37]

After a first-rate education at grammar school and Cambridge, George put aside rapping for a while to concentrate on his spoken word and hip-hop poetry, a lively and demotic fusion of Dizzee Rascal and Maya Angelou. Amongst other awards, in 2018 he was elected as a Member of National Arts Council England. A few months later, after a successful sell-out gig at the Screen on the Green, he returned to his parents' house in Harlesden to chill but as he parked outside he was stopped and strip searched by the police for being black and in possession of a car.

Hip-hop and grime found a ready audience across all of London's multi-ethnic working class, especially Polish migrants who came to London from Poland's *Blokowisko*, the huge Communist-era blocks of flats known for their bare social infrastructure.[38] One of the things they transplanted to Britain was the popularity on the *bloks* of hip-hop, an anti-establishment urban music. By 2008 it was ubiquitous amongst London's young Polish working class, especially in West and North London, with at least one packed gig a week in the capital by Polish hip-hop groups like Kaliber 44 and Paktofonika. During a performance in 2007 by Kaliber 44, the group's lead singer screamed out to his ecstatic audience, *"We're conquering London!"*[39]

This didn't go unopposed. In 2005 the Met introduced "Promotion Event Risk Assessment Form 696", which all promoters and licensees of music events were required to complete and submit fourteen days in advance of an event or else have their license refused. Until 2008, when the question was removed following allegations of racial profiling, Form 696 even asked if a "particular ethnic group" would be attending the event.[40] For a while it seemed that Form 696 would suppress grime by denying it spaces to play live, but it adapted and found new ways to innovate and publicise itself.

In 2005 the Boy Better Know collective and independent record label was formed by grime artists Skepta and Jme, born Joseph and Jamie Adunega in 1982 and 1985 in Tottenham to Nigerian parents. Their mum had left Nigeria after the Nigerian Civil War and met their dad in London when they were both working shifts at the Top Rank Bingo Club. Jospeh, Jamie and their younger siblings Julie and Jason grew up on the Meridian Estate in North Tottenham where Little Russia used to be. They hit late adolescence just as grime took off in North London on pirate radio stations like Heat FM.

Inevitably, Joseph (Skepta) joined the Meridian Crew, a Grime Collective based on their estate. When in the early 2000s some members of the crew were implicated in a shooting, he detached himself from that life and started to work for Wiley's Roll Deep crew. Skepta did instrumentals for Roll Deep until Wiley suggested he branch out into MCing. He penned his first bars at age twenty-one and found he had an innate talent for it. His brother Jamie (Jme), a fiercely disciplined vegan teetotaller, ran the business end of Boy Better Know, turning his first independently released mixtape into a label of the same name that also released his debut album *Famous* (2008) and went on to release all of his brother's albums and mixtapes. BBK's debut single "Too Many Man" (2009), fronted by BBK members Skepta, Jme, Shorty, Frisco and Wiley, went straight for the strutting sexism of the genre by lamenting the lack of women in its club scene.

With a keen sense for the main chance and a flair for marketing similar to Spandau's and Jazzie B's, Jme turned BBK into a unified brand with its own clothing line. He controlled the design, marketing and distribution of all BBK material. Keeping all the merchandise in his parents' garage, Jme sold the clothes, CDs and vinyl the old-fashioned way — shifting them to local record shops from the boot of his car or posting them himself from his kitchen or lock-up. Gradually he built up a self-sufficient business infrastructure that protected his brother and himself from the traps and temptations of mainstream record company success.[41]

Skepta and Jme were hard-working black entrepreneurs in the tradition of so many working class Londoners. Their clothes and mannerisms may have been different but the ethos of ducking and diving, of grafting in the margins of society to make money or gain status, was the same. "Rolex Sweep" in 2008 was the start of Skepta's fame, a single that played in synergy with Wiley's "Wearing My Rolex" (2008) in which the classic watch is the ultimate symbol of male working class material attainment (it certainly was for my dad, who took great pride in his). Later songs developed and deepened his image and his style, particularly "That's Not Me" (2013) and "Shutdown" (2015), in which he turned his back on the flashier tropes of jungle and grime and went back to their purer roots. In the video for "Bullet from a Gun" (2019), Skepta sits waiting patiently with a baby buggy on a Camden Town tube platform and raps to the screen.

Skepta's and Jme's prominence in the Grime scene demonstrated not only that it had migrated from East to North London, but also the emergence of a newly assertive African identity within a black London music scene that had until then been dominated by Jamaican culture. The 2010s would see a vibrant "Afrobeats" genre — based on music from Ghana and Nigeria but fused with dancehall, house, R&B, soca and hip-hop — become so popular it threatened to eclipse grime. Of the crucial difference, Skepta remembered:

When I was a youth, to be called African was a diss. At school, the African kids used to lie and say they were Jamaican. So when I first came in the game and I'm saying lyrics like I make Nigerians proud of their tribal scars/my bars make you push up your chest like bras, *that was a big deal for me. All my early lyrics were about confidence. I can hear myself fighting back.*[42]

Fighting back took many forms. Ashley Thomas (AKA Bashy) was born in 1985 in Hammersmith to a Jamaican mother and a Dominican father but brought up around Kensal Rise and the Mozart Estate. After leaving school Ashley worked for a year as a postman but quit to concentrate on his music. With his controversial debut single "Black Boys" (2007) he challenged the prevailing negative stereotypes of young black men, sometimes repeated within the genre itself, by celebrating the professional successes of black men from Wiley and Kano to Lenny Henry and Trevor MacDonald. After giving Noel Clarke a mixtape of contemporary grime artists to listen to, Clarke employed Ashley as a music supervisor on *Adulthood* and from there he went into full-time acting.

London's working class in the first decade of the twenty-first century provided rich material for literature and the arts, but although it was occasionally used as the basis for films, novels and TV dramas, these were few and far between. Zadie Smith's *White Teeth* (2000), a serio-comic panorama of multi-cultural London, specifically the Willesden area, from the 1970s to 2000, was made palatable to the literary critics by its formal experimentation and satiric humour. By contrast, Amanda Craig's *Hearts and Minds* (2009), although receiving less critical attention than Smith's dazzling debut, shone a harsher and more affecting spotlight on the capital. A powerful and sympathetic novel of the immigrant experience of modern London, *Hearts and Minds* spins an intricate narrative linking well-meaning middle class teachers and lawyers with abused Romanian sex workers and illegal Somali cab drivers hanging on by their fingertips.

British cinema seldom noticed this reality. Ken Loach's *It's a Free World* (2007) was, again, an exception; an angry fable of how illegal migrants are brutally exploited by a neoliberal city. The film is fuelled by Kierston Wareing's powerful channelling of raw working class ambition and sexuality as Angie, creator of an employment agency that delivers a "multi-tasking, high energy female workforce" from Eastern Europe, but branches out into male manual labour as well. Based out of the back of a pub on the North Circular, the agency recruits Poles, Afghans,

Iraqis and Chileans, and expands into renting whole houses in which to cram its workers.

It's a Free World is a vivid depiction of a world without employment rights or trade union protection, reflecting the world of "beds in sheds" in Wembley, Neasden, Edmonton and other areas outside Inner London. A feminist Arthur Daley for the twenty-first century, Angie works to more malevolent economic forces than Arthur ever did. Seeing how she treats the migrant labour queuing up in the early morning to get casual work with her firm, her retired father, a voice from an older and more politically conscious white working class, is disgusted and tells her, "This is disgraceful. I thought these days were over."

Shane Ritchie's *Somers Town* (2008) is the flipside to *It's a Free World*. Told when St Pancras station was being expanded to encompass the Eurostar terminal, *Somers Town* focused on two teenage boys, Tommo, newly arrived in London from social care in the north, and Marek, son of a polish builder living in Somers Town. Unlike Loach's tale it's a fundamentally positive picture. Marek's dad and his mates drink socially in the Cock Tavern on Charlton Street, and father and son share a warm domestic life. The local Del Boy, whose lock-up is an underground garage, puts up Tommo when he is homeless. In the end, *Somers Town* is about getting what you can from urban multicultural life even if you're a sixteen-year-old straight from social care or a Polish adolescent out of place.

This world was dealt a hammer blow at 8.49am on 7th July 2005 when three bombs went off on the Underground within fifty seconds of each other, the first on a Circle Line train between Liverpool Street and Aldgate, the second on another Circle Line train just departing Edgware Road, the third on a Piccadilly Line train between King's Cross and Russell Square. An hour later a fourth bomb went off on a number 30 bus in Tavistock Square, en route from Marble Arch to Hackney Wick.

At Edgware, Big Yaw, the Ghanaian cleaner who lived on the White City Estate, was one of the first responders. He heard the bomb go off as he was sitting in the small white-tiled staff rest room at the station with his colleagues, and ran down to the platform:

There was black and smoke and glass all broked, and everybody crying and screaming. My uniform…it was covered in black and blood and everything. The body of the bomber was there…When we knew it was him, we just threw him. I went in to carry the bodies. But they did not scare me. When I saw the black people bodies in Africa…they scared me. But dead white people. They did not scare me.[43]

The bombs were set off by four Islamist suicide bombers. Fifty-two people were killed and hundreds injured, some very badly. The dead were a cross section of middle class and working class Londoners travelling to or from work, with a few visitors in the wrong place at the wrong time. Amongst the victims were Anna Brandt, a forty-one-year old Polish woman who had lived in London for three years and who was travelling on the tube from Wood Green to her job as a cleaner in Hammersmith when she was killed in the bomb blast at Russell Square; Giles Hart, a fifty-five-year old BT engineer who in the 1980s had worked so closely with the Polish Solidarity trade union that after his death in Tavistock Square on his way to work in Islington he was awarded Poland's highest posthumous honour; Ciaran Cassidy, a twenty-two-year old North London lad on his way to his job in a printing firm in Chancery Lane, killed at Russell Square; Shahara Islam, a twenty-year old bank cashier with the Co-operative bank in Islington, killed on the bus in Tavistock Square; and Gladys Wundower, a fifty-year old Ghanian cleaner at University College London, on her way home after a night shift when she too was killed on the number 30 bus in Tavistock Square.

Of the dead, thirty-two were British, three were Polish, and one each came from New Zealand, Iran, Afghanistan, Ghana, Kenya, India, Israel, France, Italy, Mauritius, Grenada, Turkey, Sri Lanka, Nigeria and Romania. The terrorist cell's leader, Shehzhad Tanweer, claimed in a statement written before the attack that the non-Muslims of Britain deserved this because they voted for a government which *"continues to oppress our mothers, children, brothers and sisters in Palestine, Afghanistan, Iraq and Chechnya"*, although three years before London had held the largest demonstration in British history *against* intervention in Iraq and most of its inhabitants were politically opposed to US policy in the other states.

It took a working class London politician, Ken Livingstone, reacting on his feet on the other side of the world, to find the right words, words not of nationalistic bombast but of a proud and unbowed metropolis:

> *I wish to speak directly to those who came to London today to take life. I know that you personally do not fear to give your own life in exchange for taking others — that is why you are so dangerous. But I know you do fear that you may fail in your long-term objective to destroy our free society, and I can show you why you will fail. In the days that follow look at our airports, look at our sea ports and look at our railway stations, and even after your cowardly attack, you will see that people from the rest of Britain, people from around the world will arrive in London to become Londoners and to fulfil their dreams and achieve their potential. They choose to come to London, as so many have come before because they come to be free, they come to live the life they choose, they come to be able to be themselves. They flee you because you tell them how they should live. They don't want that and nothing you do, however many of us you kill, will stop that flight to our cities where freedom is strong and where people can live in harmony with one another. Whatever you do, however many you kill, you will fail.*

This was London's best face, a British New York for the twenty-first century. Sadly, it did not always live up to this ideal. Nor did Livingstone. Throughout his terms of office he tried to get developers to provide "affordable" housing and succeeded in getting 35-50% of their builds to be so, but these numbers were so small that they did not offset the ongoing loss of social housing in London. To achieve this modest end he sold his political soul to big property developers, allowing them to build new skyscrapers — the Gherkin, the Shard, the Cheese-Grater, the Mobile, all of which were exclusively for office use and often, like Centre Point in the 1960s, left empty to accrue value — and private housing projects in return for a small number of supposedly affordable flats and houses that invariably ended up as shared ownership, studios and one-bedroom flats; the ones that didn't have nice views.

Existing council tenants were often left to look after themselves. The Andover Estate in Hornsey Rise, the newest parts of which were built in the 1970s, had the usual range of problems despite close proximity to an increasingly gentrified Finsbury Park and several tube stations. A few streets away from the Six Acres Estate, the Andover provided over one thousand homes in a sprawl of low-level housing units with front and back gardens, surrounding three larger blocks. Like the original Marquess Estate at the other end of Islington, Andover's maze of back alleys and interconnecting walkways made it hard to police except in large numbers. By the 1990s Andover had a reputation as a haven for crack cocaine dealers.

Andover was a ripe target for the new social authoritarians. In 2007 one of the most repellent of these, the far-right Tory MP Ann Widdecombe, spent three days and one entire night on the estate and then made an ITV programme about it. The programme, *Ann Widdecombe versus the Hoodies*, produced for the popular *Tonight with Trevor MacDonald*, made exaggerated and hysterical claims that the estate was a sinkhole run by feral youths. The programme was attacked by local residents and community leaders who said it fundamentally misrepresented the estate.

In response, some of Andover's young people worked with the filmmaker Michelle Golding on a film of their own, *Beyond the Hoodie* (2007), presenting a more objective and honest account than Widdecombe's, demonstrating that crime on the estate was actually falling and that its young people were more likely to be victims of crime committed by non-residents than perpetrators. It presented a community in which many residents knew each other, where the Arsenal Positive Futures programme (which funded Golding's film) helped with the local football team and other sporting opportunities, and where the intimate, village-like layout of the estate fostered a genuine community feeling among residents.[44]

Golding's film was a necessary corrective to politically motivated, anti-working class propaganda, but it did not deny that real crime took place. In June 2008 Ben Kinsella, whose dad was a taxi driver and mum a secretary and who lived locally, was celebrating the end of his GCSE's at Shillibeers nightclub on North Road between York Way and Caledonian Road. But when one of his mates accidentally bumped into a member of the local drug-dealing street gang, the Market Massiv, and failed to apologise, everything spiralled out of control. A fight broke out outside the club in which Ben was not involved. Faced with blatant "disrespect" three members of the Massiv— Jade Braithwaite, Micheal Alleyne and Juress Kika — followed Ben's mate and Ben himself down the street where Braithwaite stabbed Ben eleven times in five seconds, killing him. Prior to the murder, the Massiv, led by Alleyne, had terrorised the Market Estate and its residents for years, mugging school kids for mobiles and running Pitbull fights. With the Market being demolished and replaced by housing less congenial to their activities, Alleyne had started to make moves on the Andover Estate but had been rebuffed.

The Adams Syndicate, which still ostensibly controlled the area, did not much care about drug dealers on council estates, but they were displeased with the killing on their turf of a local white working class boy, well known as the brother of *EastEnders* actress Brooke Kinsella, by minor thugs of a small-time drugs gang. From his prison cell Terry Adams let it be known that his men were looking for Ben's killers to enact retribution. Such was the reputation of the Adams firm that Braithwaite immediately handed himself in to the police. Braithwaite, Alleyn and Kika all received life sentences.[45] After the murder up to four hundred teenagers from the Andover and Market estates organised a march from Islington Town Hall to Shillibeers, chanting on the way, *"What are we here for? Ben! Why are we here? No knives!"*

Ken Livingstone's efforts to address these issues may have been insufficient, but they were at least efforts. In comparison, under the new Tory Mayor Boris Johnson, elected in May 2008, there would be virtually no new affordable housing and even the existing social housing stock would be reduced, very few consents given for new social rented housing, the continued selling off of council properties without replacement, and an increase in insecure and unsustainable tenancies in the private rented sector. London's working class, who had for the most part not elected him, would suffer for it.

It was a period in which many other things, including some iconic landmarks of North London working class life, were ending or transforming to something new. In 2007 the Hammersmith Palais closed. Laurence Corner shut the same year. Trade at Turnmills closed in 2008. So did The Cross. So did Biddy Mulligan's. So did the Red Rose Comedy Club (although it re-opened in 2020). In the same year Rock On, which had left Camden Town in the 1990s for the Park Royal Industrial Estate, put out a compilation album of the best material it had sold on its once-legendary stalls.

Soho shifted gear dramatically when Paul Raymond died in 2008. In his semi-corrupt fashion he had preserved much of old Soho simply by buying it up and leaving it to do its own thing. His heirs only wanted to make money from their property portfolio and so sold much of it on to new developers. In the 2010s the number of licensed sex shops fell by a third in London and by 65% in Westminster. In Soho many of those remaining were concentrated on the main streets, particularly Brewer and Old Compton Streets, where they offered a range of LGBT and BDSM-themed products and services.

Those who worked there still had special attachment to its ethos and character. During the early 2000s Mark was working in a tastefully designed gay lifestyle store on Old Compton Street for his ex-partner Jason who ran the shop, while also working part-time in a bar around the corner. He had helped to design and set up the store, which had a licensed sex shop in its basement where gay porn played on screens next to the counter. In 2009 another worker in a "traditional" sex shop near

Walker's Court, who since the 1990s had been selling mostly pornographic DVDs, lamented the loss of the old vibe in the shop, of the banter with regular customers, brought about by the increasing commodification of sex and competition from online porn and other sexual services, admitting, *"When it was illegal it was good fun, but now it's just boring"*.[46]

After the unintended obstacle of Raymond's portfolio ownership was removed, gentrification crept up on Soho and its inimitable atmosphere began to dissipate, although its dark side was remarkably difficult to erase. In the new century organised Albanian gangs, many of whom arrived in Britain in the late 1990s falsely claiming to be Kosovan refugees, took over control of Soho's illegal vice trade (its brothels, saunas and "massage parlours") from the Maltese without much difficulty. By 2001 most of the young girls working in these places were trafficked sex workers from the Baltic and Balkan states. From their Soho base the Albanians quickly expanded into London's lucrative drugs business, taking over the cocaine, cannabis and heroin trades from South American, Jamaican and Turkish gangs, sometimes by offering more money to the suppliers, sometimes by violence.

The Albanians controlled their young sex workers with a cruelty not seen since the heyday of the Messina brothers. Unlicensed premises that fronted as lingerie or sex shops were actually selling extreme and illegal porn. Many clip joints were simply an organised con, whereby a £5 entrance fee got a punter a twenty-minute chat with a hostess followed by a £295 bill, which if he refused to pay led to threats of violence and being marched to the nearest cashpoint to cough up. Cleaners at Soho Parish School in Great Windmill Street began most days picking up discarded wallets which had been thrown over the school wall.[47]

But it was a complex picture. Not all sex workers worked for ruthless international cartels and not all locals were unsympathetic. In 2012, as a full-time PCS union officer sent to negotiate its annual pay deal, I visited the HQ building of the Valuation Office Agency (VOA) on Shaftesbury Avenue, the back of which overlooked Soho's Romilly Street and the rear windows of various brothels. The long-serving Chair of the VOA's PCS Branch, a decent and compassionate older man, told me that staff on the upper floors could sometimes see the transactions, and how sorry he felt for women who had to earn money this way. In 2009 the police tried to close a brothel on Dean Street, but following lobbying by the English Collective of Prostitutes and local residents who supported the sex workers as an integral part of the local community, were rebuffed. Meghan, a Soho sex worker who had worked there for twenty-five years, echoed local feeling:

> It's a little village here and we couldn't work in a better place...
> The community supports us.[48]

North London football also began to smooth out its edges. After the inauguration of all-seater stadiums, Arsenal uprooted entirely from Highbury in 2006 to a new, high-tech mothership, the Emirates, five hundred metres away in a perfectly positioned public space near Holloway Road tube. Spurs wouldn't and arguably *couldn't* leave White Hart Lane, such was its identification with that specific piece of turf. By the time White Hart Lane was refurbished to make it all-seater in 1998 it had lost 36,000 seats. In 2008 the club sought to buy land on the Wingate Trading Estate immediately to its north in order to emulate the Emirates. However, the plans fell through and it would be another decade, involving serious proposals for Spurs to move out of Tottenham entirely to a new ground in Stratford, plans defeated by popular outrage, before Spurs gave itself the major ground it deserved.

Others *had* moved out entirely. In 2008, after ten years in Brighton where he had recreated a bit of his old London life, working as a part-time concierge in a block of flats on the seafront and wangling the odd little fiddle, putting aside enough dosh to take Joyce on cruise ships around the Fjords or the Caribbean, Ted put his memories on tape for transcription. Of his home city, he admitted that it had moved on and left him behind:

Nostalgically, I miss London, but the city I knew no longer exists. Mine was a quieter, bomb-damaged London, lit for the most part by street lighting only, the exception being the West End. But even there I could walk the streets of Piccadilly at 3.00am and listen to the echo of my own footsteps.

In the end, after many good years, he left it. For himself that may have been right. Brighton carried the flame for a certain type of displanted working class bohemian whose life was moving from autumn into winter:

So here I am washed up on the shores of the south coast. It's a good place to live, and although the road ahead gets shorter and less inviting it's not a bad life.[49]

But London's working class history continued, and connected in unexpected ways. Islington's Royal Free Hospital, where I was born in 1962, closed in 1974 when its services transferred to the Royal Free in Hampstead. The building was then used as the headquarters of Camden and Islington's Community Health Council until it was purchased in 1986 by a partnership of the Circle 33 Housing Trust and the New Islington and Hackney Housing Association. From 1989 the site was converted into 178 flats and houses for social tenants at a cost of £10m, with four units specifically designed for wheelchair users and a set amount of sheltered accommodation. It was and remains one of the largest and most attractive housing association projects undertaken in London.

The socially progressive use of the old Royal Free building demonstrated that not all the landmarks of working class North London were slated for wreckage or erasure. In 2008, Madness, who could have rested on their laurels and trotted out "Baggy Trousers" forever, produced their greatest album, a distillation of all they represented for the culture of working class London. The title of *The Liberty of Norton Folgate* refers to a small district of Spitalfields, Norton Folgate, with the legal status of a "Liberty", i.e. a "non-parochial place" over which the Crown has no rights and certain inalienable rights accrue. In its way it was London in miniature, divorced from the United Kingdom and proudly independent. In 2008, by total coincidence, local residents who opposed another office block development argued successfully that the claimed abolition of the Liberty of Norton Folgate in 1900 was invalid and that it still existed, and thereby prevented the development.

The Liberty of Norton Folgate is a vigorous, subtle, playful fusion of musical styles, a celebration of working class London from Charles Dickens to Zadie Smith with a dash of *Minder* thrown in, all of it resting on a passionate and romantic love of the city. The title song on its own is a stunning mini-opera on the theme of London. Casting Spitalfields — that unique junction of East, City and North — as totem and exemplar of the capital, it skilfully dances through musical eras from Victorian music hall to Jewish jazz to Banglatown Bollywood, a joyous ode to the greatest ethnic and social melting pot in the world. It claims London for *working class* culture, even if that culture now survives buried and on the margins of the power and wealth that surround it:

> Cos in the Liberty of Norton Folgate
> Walking wild and free
> And in your second-hand coat
> Happy just to float
> In this little taste of liberty
> Cos you're a part of everything you see

In March 2008, Madness previewed the album at the Hackney Empire. An astonishing communal performance, it was turned into a film by Julian Temple that complimented Temple's other London-themed work, *Absolute Beginners* (1986), *Ray Davies: Imaginary Man* (2010) and *London: The Modern Babylon* (2012). Its mini-film of the title song, a montage of the show and film stock superimposed over London landmarks like Spitalfields Market and Camden Lock, is an anthem to a multicultural working class London that has always existed and still exists despite every attempt to extirpate it. Like the Fleet River, it is now encased in concrete and covered from view. But it still runs to the Thames. It's still a part of everything you see.

Madness's career-defining performance came only a month after the heart of their social world had been gutted. On Saturday 9th February 2008, the "Great Fire of Camden" broke out in Camden Lock. The fire, which took over one hundred firefighters to control, devastated the Old Stables Market. The damage caused by the fire was extensive. Six shops and ninety market stalls were totally lost, as was the Caernarvon Castle pub, famous for its live jazz and R&B (where in the early 1990s Sue and I had danced, sweating in leather jackets, to our King's Cross UBO colleague Dave's jazz band, none of us remotely ready to interview the long-term unemployed the next day). The Hawley Arms, though not destroyed, was severely damaged. The market was out of operation for fifteen months and the livelihood of its many workers hung in the balance.

A few years later, Wicksey, an Irish lad born just down the road from Camden Lock, looked back on the transformation of the area he knew and grew up in:

> I remember the first "silly boot" hanging outside the shops, the Irish poets who drank with me in the pub at 14 and told me to change my name back to proper Irish. Friends made things and sold them at the market. Camden Lock was where we met friends and made new ones. Thai food with hippies back from travels in the Stags Head...The vegetarian bulldog and the man sleeping under the pool table. I remember Burger King was the first fast food chain and no one ever ate the KFC...Mostly I remember that this was my home, but it's gone now and I can't go back at those prices.[50]

After the 2008 fire Camden Lock and its market would be rebuilt, renewed, renovated and expanded. In some respects, such as the range of food available, it would be improved. But it would no longer be what it had been.

What is?

It's a London Thing

Real poets don't wear Harringtons
Ben Sherman button-downs
Or step out in proper daises
Real poets don't rub-a-dub
With a damn fine Guyanese girl
Inna dance at the Betsey
Real poets don't eat pie n' mash
With an old china, at Clarks
At Exmouth Market
Not anymore they don't

Chip Hamer, "Death of a Pie n' Mash Shop", 2020

In August 2017 my uncle Danny died. By then he and my aunt Josie had lived on the Carol and Sandringham Estate in Kentish Town for twenty-five years. I travelled up from Brighton with my mum and dad for the funeral.

Kentish Town had changed from when we lived nearby in the 1970s and 1980s, but not that much. The Jolly Anglers pub was now a Nando's, but the Pineapple, once threatened with closure and demolition, had been saved by a community campaign and was better than ever. The area was, at most, semi-gentrified, although the value of the terraced houses all around it had of course skyrocketed. Kentish Town High Street was no Chalk Farm. Apart from a Gail's Artisan Bakery there were few outward signs of gentrification and none at all of hipsterism. On the contrary, Mem's Cafe, Tips n' Toes Nail Bar, Scratching Tattoo, an Iceland, a Greggs and the decidedly unglamorous flats above them, would have graced old Kentish Town. The Bengal Lancer, the mainstay of Indian food in the area since the mid-1980s, was still there, not much changed (as it still was in 2022). On Grafton Road the MAP (Music, Art and Production) recording studio/record label was still going strong, its ground-floor cafe doing good business while its auditorium played host to live gigs and occasional theatre.

The Carol and Sandringham was as it had always been. Trains on the North London Line went right past the estate between Kentish Town and Gospel Oak, but with minimal noise, not much disturbing the residents. The family congregated at the estate before the funeral cortege drove down to Somers Town and the service in St Aloysius Catholic Church. Aside from the enormous Francis Crick Institute, Somers Town still had the air of a slightly forgotten quarter of the city, dominated by good quality council estates, community centres, unglamorous shops and cafes, and the national HQ of the RMT. Outside the church a crowd of my uncle's old cronies gathered to pay respects, differentiated by their casual dress from the immediate family, severe in formal black, allowed inside for the funeral Mass. After the burial service at the great necropolis of Islington Cemetery we all went to the George IV pub in Holmes Road off Prince of Wales Road, almost totally obscured behind a wall of flowers and foliage. Inside, my cousin Danny, the absolute spit of his dad at his age, stood in the centre of the pub and received condolences.

Some of the family have died, of course; some have moved on and out; some have stayed. Aunt Josie worked on the check-out till at Marks & Spencer on Camden High Street from 1987 until 2020 when Marks put her on furlough, after which it offered her redundancy. She still shops there, though, as ex-staff get a 20% discount, and still lives on the Carol and Sandringham, an estate she appreciates for its quality of life (one night recently her hall flooded and Camden Council's emergency workers came out at midnight to fix it). Her youngest son, my cousin Nicky, lives in Hampstead in a council flat on Parliament Hill near the Hampstead Overground station. He works as a delivery driver for UPS and occasionally helps out at the fruit and veg stall outside the station.

Personal stories are revealing, but they can only tell so much. A narrative of this kind must ask if the social and economic conditions that gave rise to the North London working class of the second half of the twentieth century, that gave them good quality council houses in central London and enabled their children to leave home for decent jobs and their own homes, some to go on to university and cross the class divide, any longer exists? Or is this book simply a memorial for a moment and a place in working class life that is now gone, the conditions for its reproduction erased by neoliberal social policy?

The 2016 Housing and Planning Act demonstrated that this is the clear and conscious goal of the Conservative Party. An almost pathological display of calculated cruelty towards council tenants by Tories who no longer felt the need to disguise it, it legislated to eradicate lifetime tenancies and replace them by fixed-term tenancies of two to five years, thereby stripping council tenants of permanent homes and denying them spaces in which to raise families or create any kind of real, living community. The end of the fixed tenancy would mean that displaced tenants would have to resort to private renting, and if they could not afford to do so (as many could not, especially after the benefit cap put a ceiling on the amount of Housing Benefit a person could receive no matter how high their rent) then they would become homeless.

To further punish, the Act introduced "Pay to Stay" charges for those tenants whose total annual income exceeded £30,000 (£40,000 in London), the effect of which would, ironically, further deter Right to Buy, a policy only affordable to the well-paid working class. The other main plank of the policy, the provision of new "starter homes" for first time buyers aged between twenty-three and forty at 20% below the market rate, was utterly impractical as an alternative. As an afterthought, Right to Buy was extended to Housing Association tenants as well as local council tenants.

Although the Act was designed to remove any prospect of secure or affordable homes for social tenants, in London especially, a sustained fight against it by the Labour Party and public housing campaigners like Shelter watered down some of its worst aspects. In place of the original proposals, the Act stipulated that where there was a succession in a lifetime tenancy, the following tenancy, unless it were a spouse or legal partner, had to be fixed-term, although it might be longer than ten years for families with children. As a last-minute concession, Housing Associations were allowed to still grant lifetime tenancies.

The combined effect of boosted house prices and the 2016 Act heightened fears that London would soon emulate Paris, whose working class are pushed out of a centre reserved exclusively for a professional middle class to an outer ring of huge, socially deprived housing projects, the *banlieues*, that barely partake of the life of the city except to provide an invisible workforce. And if looked at from the perspective of privately owned and privately rented accommodation, then this process has started in London. They key difference, though, is that while most of central Paris's public housing and tenements were demolished in the late nineteenth and early twentieth centuries, great swathes of London's social housing are so deeply embedded in its centre and throughout "desirable" areas that a Parisian level of banlieue-ification is almost impossible. As of 2017 more than 40% of the housing units in Hackney and Islington were for social rent, i.e. a mixture of council estates and housing associations; in Camden it was 35%. These are significant concentrations of working class people who are living, working, shopping and sending their kids to school in the heart of "affluent" North London.

In comparison, the original gentrification of working class housing, the setting up of communal households in Ladbroke Grove or Elgin Avenue or Muswell Hill, the reclaiming and making beautiful of houses that had gone to seed, was almost benign. The first gentrifiers, like Michael Moorcock and Iain Sinclair, did not want to live in gated communities. They chose their houses precisely because they *were* in a working class area. If there were a counter-balancing stock of council houses, if councils could still buy up properties through municipalisation, it may even have been an overall good, a genuinely mixed community of the type envisaged by Aneurin Bevan when he was Housing Minister in the 1940s.

Instead, the 2008 economic crash unleashed a Tory assault on working class London, a British version (minus philanthropy) of the Robber Baron era of late-nineteenth-century America. Profits on London's land and property no longer had any relation to the real economy of GDP, inflation and wages. Central London was increasingly a playground for the five thousand or so "Ultra High Net Worth Individuals" (UHNWI) who bought property — houses, flats, entire buildings — at astronomical prices and then left them, mostly uninhabited, to inflate the overall market rate to levels unaffordable to Londoners not already well established on the property ladder.[1]

In the meantime, in the London not defined by permanently empty flats in Belgravia serviced by Filipino cleaners treated like domestic slaves, some working class Londoners were reduced to penury. In 2012 the Highgate Newtown Community Centre began serving 50p Sunday lunches to locals who, faced with the cap on benefits contained in the 2012 Welfare Reform Act, could no longer afford the basics. Linda Trahere, a sixty-two-year-old who lived on the Whittington Estate and had worked in the Community Centre since 1996 with her daughter and granddaughter, helped to serve the meals, often to her neighbours:

> The stigma is awful, because I know some of them, so they don't want to come in and ask. We had one girl over Christmas who came in for food for herself and the kids. She was so upset and embarrassed because she wanted to give something back that she begged me to let her do the washing up.[2]

In 2018 Cash Carraway was living with her young daughter in a tiny one-bedroom flat (actually a studio with a sliding partition) on the ground floor of a neglected estate in Kentish Town, for which the rent was £1,500 a month. Despite bursts of occasional employment in unregulated sectors of London's economy, including working in a Soho peep show, she found the financial pressure was relentless:

> And because I am so desperate to keep us in London, our beautiful yet poisonous home city of London, I will do anything. Tax returns are often dull, but mine depicts a sordid tapestry of life for the modern day working class: web psychic, writer of porn, sex-chat line operator, mystery shopper, e-bay seller, virtual assistant, miscellaneous anything – I'd sell my cunt if peak cunt-selling hours weren't in the evening and so require expensive childcare.

The estate had its own sub-tribes to which she adjusted, including the gang of boys who congregated on their mopeds at about 1am to distribute stolen iPhones and other goodies:

> Clifton (the guy who owns the boys) sits in his Volvo parked outside my flat eating a seemingly never-ending supply of KFC like some hungry Fagin draped in gold. He looks scary but he's always really nice to me, often helping me with my shopping bags when I'm struggling up the road and complimenting Biddy on her Arsenal shirt. He occasionally knocks on my door with a freshly rolled joint in exchange for use of my Wi-Fi. I save up the joints and sell them on to my friends who have spare cash lying around for things like getting stoned.[3]

At one point Cash had to use the Chalk Farm Salvation Army food bank, before finally netting a one-off £5,000 payment as an advance on some writing she had done describing the life of a single mother on benefits in North London. It was enough to pay off some debts and replace her one pair of shoes. Naively, she informed HMRC which led to the council misconstruing it as regular income and suspending her housing benefit entirely. She explained, but HMRC, convinced a working class single woman couldn't possibly earn a one-off payment of that kind honestly, decided to investigate her for fraud. Unable to pay her rent, she ended up in a homeless persons shelter in Kent to which London councils sent homeless single mothers.

The election of Sadiq Khan as London mayor in 2016 brought some respite. Khan, the son of a Muslim bus driver who grew up on a South London council estate, knew his city. Whilst studying Law at the University of North London (the former North London Polytechnic) he worked as a labourer on a building site and had a Saturday job at Peter Jones Department Store on Sloane Square. After college he went into law and local politics, becoming Labour MP for Tooting in 2006 before orchestrating Ed Miliband's successful campaign for the Labour leadership in 2011.

Unlike Johnson, Khan at least *attempted* to provide affordable social housing and control spiralling rents, with a goal of making 50% of new homes built in London affordable. Although much depended on the definition of "affordable" — Social Rent, set at 45% of existing private sector rent, or the more problematic London Affordable Rent, a better variation of the Affordable Rent introduced by the Tory-Lib Dem coalition but still not as affordable to those on lower incomes as Social Rent — more council housing was built under Khan than under Livingstone and Johnson combined, and in a shorter period. Sadly, though, the immense loss of available council housing in previous decades, and the failure to replenish it, meant the new build had little impact.[4] Khan also pushed hard for rent controls to cap the impossibly high rents afflicting the capital, where the average private rent for a one-bedroom home is more than the average for a three-bedroom home in every other region of England.

But Khan was faced with a Tory government implacably hostile to social housing and supportive of private landlords no matter how ruthless and extortionate. In Tottenham, Colin Edwards saw the results:

Estate agents claim that Tottenham is becoming gentrified because people cannot afford west of the borough. I saw no evidence of gentrification. My street was made up of Edwardian terraced houses. By the time I left in 2015 not one single house was still a family house. I had the ground floor, with a living room, two bedrooms, a kitchen, a bathroom and the exclusive use of the small back garden. My neighbour had the upper two floors with kitchen, bathroom, living room, and three bedrooms. They had the front garden, but that was completely filled with the recycling bins.

When my Cypriot family next door sold the house that they had raised their family in to return to Cyprus, it was bought by a developer who illegally turned it into eight bedsits, each with a small shower cubicle, and one small communal kitchenette on the landing and one toilet for up to 16 residents.[5]

Far from gentrification, the danger in Tottenham is that it will become a 2020s version of 1950s Notting Hill.

The 2010s saw a tentative re-emergence of council housebuilding by some Labour councils, including in London, as the most obvious way to address long waiting lists for social housing. These had to proceed under various different names and with some private sector involvement simply to avoid the sabotage of Tory central government. Inevitably, then, new schemes to build or regenerate council housing have been full of trade-offs. One of the most controversial, the Haringey Development Vehicle (HDV), a scheme which repackaged certain estates in Haringey as a "joint venture" between the council and private investors with the council retaining a 50% controlling veto, was scuppered by a vociferous campaign by local housing and Momentum activists. The HDV may have given away too much to the private sector but it was a genuine attempt to use the one remaining resource of local government, its land, to bring investment to some of North London's most neglected estates. Its critics, possibly not as representative of the tenants as they believed, had no real alternative except the arrival of a socialist government which, sadly, never did.[6]

Camden Council also had to get creative in order to generate finance to build council homes. Between 2009 and 2019 Camden launched its Community Investment Programme (CIP), or what others called its "North Sea Oil Strategy", in which it tried to get around cuts to local government grants by using its extensive land and property portfolio to play the markets, allowing private homes on some of its land in return for funds to build council homes, schools and other community facilities. The strategy was riven with unpleasant compromises. Despite building 330 council homes by 2019 and with 1,100 more to come, Camden was criticised for allowing the building of a twenty-two-storey block of fifty-four luxury flats in Brill Place, Somers Town, adjacent to St Pancras International, in return for funds for a local primary school and forty new council homes.

The CIP also funded the successful regeneration of Maiden Lane and the Bourne Estate, both of which have been turned into elegant and beautiful examples of social housing. On the other hand, its plans for the West Kentish Town Estate in Gospel Oak entail the demolition of the existing 316 homes on the estate, of which 240 are council properties, for a new development of 750 homes, 500 of which will be marketed privately. The biggest casualty of the new scheme will be the Wendling tower block at the centre of the estate, a mini-community of its own managed in the 1990s by my friend Bernie O'Hara, herself a product of Kilburn's immigrant working class who had gone on to university and a career in local housing. In 2020 the residents of the block passed a motion of no confidence in the scheme although they retain the right of a final say about proceeding in a yes/no ballot on the redevelopment.

In the circumstances it is surprising that North London's Labour boroughs do as well as they do, with tangible improvements to many estates in the last two decades. As a built environment, the new Holly Street is a vast improvement on the old blocks and the "snake", with communal and personal gardens and a sense of transparency totally lacking before. Broadwater Farm underwent major refurbishment and improvement in the 1990s helped by £33m from central government, including knocking down the concrete walkways and bringing the entrances of the estate's twelve blocks down to ground level, that had a noticeable effect on the security and atmosphere of the estate. The provocative police presence on the estate was removed and replaced with on-site housing officers. By 2016 Broadwater Farm, although it still suffers from high unemployment and poverty, had one of the lowest crime rates in Haringey.[7]

Even the notorious South Kilburn estate, one of the most run down and dysfunctional in North London, has seen tentative improvement with the construction in 2016 of 43 new street-level dwellings entirely different from the estate's original miserable blocks, which sought to reintegrate the estate back into the surrounding area instead of walling it off. At the same time the council is selectively and incrementally demolishing the blocks and replacing them with more communal alternatives. The new flats will include privately rented homes to help finance the entire operation (a necessity if anything is to be built at all, but one Brent Council has used as smartly and judiciously as has Camden) but will still contain more socially rented units than they started with. No existing council tenants have to move out of the development.

For all the benefits and advantages that some of North London's working class council tenants can sometimes enjoy, there are deep-seated social problems on the estates that cannot simply be fixed by renovation. In August 2021 a communal BBQ party held on Clarence Gardens in the middle of the Regent's Park Estate was fired on indiscriminately from a car that then sped off. Luckily no one was killed, but three young people and a seventy-three-year-old grandmother were injured. The shooting was almost certainly gang-related, although the four victims were not the intended target. As someone who grew up on the estate I find it inexpressively sad to see the priceless location and cultural capital of the place, which worked to the advantage of previous generations of its tenants and still does for many, pissed away in petty feuds and turf wars, whatever may have been the specific motivation for the shooting.

And yet, despite these problems, most of the estates across North London continue to provide a decent quality of life to their residents. As of 2022 those estates still contained a significant number of units for council tenants. Taking Camden alone they included, amongst others, the Westcroft Close estate in North Kilburn (73 units); the West End

Sidings estate in South Kilburn (154 units); the Lymington Road estate in Finchley Road and Frognal (161 units); the Alexandra and Ainsworth estate (516 units); the Holly Lodge estate in Highgate (226 units); Highgate New Town (73 units); Lissenden Gardens (137 units); the Ingestre Road estate (118 units); the Carol and Sandringham Close estate (81 units); the Waxham/Ludham estate near Gospel Oak (225 units); the Russell Nurseries estate off Belsize Park (152 units); the Fleet Road estate behind the Royal Free Hospital, Hampstead (172 units); South End Close estate in Hampstead (94 units); the Dunboyne Road estate (51 units); the Maitland Park estate off Haverstock Hill (92 units); the St Silas Street (Queen's Crescent) estate (192 units); the Weedington Road estate off Queen's Crescent (199 units); the Wendling estate immediately adjacent (180 units); the Denton estate on Prince of Wales Road (191 units); the Ferdinand estate off Chalk Farm Road (72 units); the Chalcot on Adelaide Road (575 units); Maiden Lane (387 units); the Curnock Street estate off Camden High Street (173 units); the Ampthill Square estate (295 units); the Regent's Park estate (1,200 units); the Godwin and Crowndale estate near Mornington Crescent (132 units); the Ossulton estate in Somers Town (262 units); Tolmers Square (55 units); the Brunswick Centre (304 units); the Cromer Street estate off Gray's Inn Road (150 units); the Regent Square estate off Gray's Inn Road (101 units); Tybald's Close estate off Great Ormond Street (162 units); Dudley Court off Shaftesbury Avenue (71 units); and the Bourne estate (342 units).[8]

The struggle for working class housing and infrastructure in North London can seem like a constantly losing battle, but it is not always so. The old Tolmers Square was lost in the 1970s but it was not replaced by a soulless office block as originally planned but by a peaceable, ground-level council estate built around a community garden and pub. The Ossulton Estate in Somers Town was going to seed in the early 2000s but has now had a through repainting and its Art Deco buildings gleam in pure white. The Brunswick Centre had the same treatment with the same result. The restoration work to Charles Rowan House, formerly a "hard to let" estate, were completed in 2015 and have turned it into a clean, beautiful communal housing project. The Peabody estates on Drury Lane and other locations such as Victoria and Clerkenwell now exude a sense of quiet, civilised sociability. Peabody's purchase from the Crown Estate of the Cumberland Market estate in 2011 has led to its tasteful redevelopment and improvement without losing any of its intimate charm, an oasis of social housing centred around hundreds of allotments made from the old Cumberland Basin, two minutes' walk from Regent's Park.

The biggest threat to the adjacent Regent's Park Estate is the work undertaken by the High Speed Rail 2 (HS2) project and the expansion of Euston station, which has already led to the total destruction of St James's Gardens and the demolition of the Eskdale, Ainsdale and Silverdale blocks on the north-west part of the estate. Camden Council, which campaigned hard against HS2's plans to demolish parts of the estate, is committed to providing 182 new homes for displaced tenants by a mix of regeneration (which has produced an improved and more attractive estate) and adding new floors to existing buildings. In addition to the replacement units there will be twenty-two new homes on the regenerated estate. Of the total of new and replacement homes only ten will be available at market rate, a line in the sand drawn by a council that, fifty years after the heyday of Sydney Cook, still seeks to provide good quality council housing to its working class tenants.

The nature and range of the work carried out by North London's working class, many of whom live in this network of social housing, has changed massively in the last half century. Since 1971 the number of manufacturing jobs in London as a whole has fallen by 85%, from 20% of London's employment to just 3%, whilst jobs in professional and real estate services have tripled in size. During this period jobs in administration, in information and communication services, in accommodation and food services, and in the arts and entertainment sector more than doubled. Jobs in retail increased but only slightly. Camden, Islington, Westminster, the City, Kensington & Chelsea, Hammersmith & Fulham, Southwark, Tower Hamlets,

Hillingdon and Hounslow (the last two benefiting from the Heathrow effect) saw overall increases in employment, but boroughs like Havering, Redbridge, Lewisham, Merton, Sutton, Harrow and Haringey saw low to no growth in jobs, with Hackney, Barnet, Croydon and Lambeth in an intermediate zone.[9]

Bare numbers of jobs tell us nothing about their pay, conditions or durability. The increase in the number of jobs in Tower Hamlets since the 1980s is mostly due to the development of Canary Wharf, which apart from a few jobs on the DLR and franchise food outlets has not been of much benefit to local residents, as demonstrated by nearby Newham which has seen far less employment growth. And the general increase in jobs in other boroughs is mostly due to rising employment in financial and business services. The area I have defined as "North London" has, in some parts, seen growth and opportunity for its working class, but in others, particularly Haringey and south Brent, continuing high unemployment and poverty.

One thing remains constant. The socio-economic transformation of these years has not erased London's working class, which continues to be essential to its functioning. The city's large hospitals and small health clinics; the buses and the tube; the emergency services; job centres and CABs; the welfare, caring, rubbish collection, street cleaning, home and park maintenance services provided by local councils; the vast range of private sector work in supermarkets, clothes shops, gardening centres, electrical and household appliance retailers; the hospitality and entertainment sectors; security; restaurants, pubs, bars, fast food outlets, nightclubs and sports centres; building construction, painting and decorating, plumbing and gas and electrical repair — it all depends on an employed working class. From 2010 a succession of Tory governments committed to economic austerity have produced a significant reduction in the take-home pay and quality of life of essential workers in the NHS, public transport and local government, workers who along with those in supermarkets and pharmacies were expected to keep London going through the Covid pandemic of 2020-2022, and did.

By contrast, better options sometimes opened up in the private sector. To take one example of a North London area that has seen growth in working class jobs and opportunity in the new century, what Islington Council call a Locally Significant Industrial Site (LSIS) in the Vale Royal/Brewery Road area between York Way and Caledonian Road just north of Granary Square, offers lasting employment for its non-middle class locals and tenants. It is an asset that Islington Council appears determined to use properly and not offer as a gift to speculators, with the *Islington Local Plan* (2019) specifically stating:

Any proposal which introduces additional offices, regardless of whether there is existing office use on-site, and which does not result in the building being in predominantly industrial use, will be refused. The encroachment of offices is considered to be the principal threat to the continued industrial function and balance of uses in the LSIS. The development of office use may be permissible as part of a hybrid workspace scheme, but it must only constitute a small proportion of the overall gross floorspace proposed.[10]

It is belated but welcome recognition by one London borough that "industry" and the jobs for working class people that accompany it, is at least as important as more office space and another Costa. At the same time, not all locals wax nostalgic about their old manor or workplace or regard its redevelopment as a bad thing. Fred Rooke, who worked for twenty-five years at King's Cross Goods Yards and still lives in his Islington council flat, sees the regeneration of Granary Square and Coal Drops Yard as a huge improvement on the industrial slagheap he used to work in:

King's Cross is so wonderful now, it's unbelievable, I'm so glad for the youngsters now... you look and there's all brand new buildings, all lovely bright colours... they've got gardens, they got activities going on there, it's a perfect place now... the difference between that and what I saw and I'm glad youngsters

didn't have to see what I saw. Now... it is absolutely beautiful...
everything now is so clean to look at but in my day all I saw was
dirt and filth.[11]

Transport for London (TfL) employs approximately 27,000
people in a wide variety of roles. The non-outsourced staff has
relatively decent pay and benefits, not least because they are
represented by Britain's biggest trade union Unite with whom
TfL routinely negotiate. The old Routemasters may be gone but
London's buses continue to run and numbers of passengers
are at record highs. In 2014 there were approximately 24,500
bus drivers employed by London Bus contractors, 7% of them
women, although the nature of the work — arduous shifts,
travelling to different and sometimes distant "pick up points"
to begin the shift, and frequent stress and harrassment— is
rarely compensated by a commensurate level of pay, with many
bus drivers having to work overtime to get by.

Joe Kerr (who arrived in London in the 1970s and started as
a driver on the 149 and 243 buses before moving on to the 19,
22 and the 38, and who later became Director of Critical and
Historical Studies at the Royal College of Art whilst still driving
a bus out of Tottenham Garage two days a week) acknowledged
the downside of change:

The privatisation of the buses has led not merely led to a
fragmentation of operations but of identity also. We no longer all
work for one monolithic corporation, driving the same buses and
wearing the same uniform, and I think something has been lost in
the relationship London has with its buses as a consequence of that.

Nonetheless he felt a keen awareness and personal pride in
what London's buses did for the capital:

I'm still acutely aware of my tiny but essential role in the provision
of a vital public service. I am merely one small cog in a vast and
complex machine that daily keeps London on the move, and I'm
proud of that.[12]

It isn't only London's daily bus services that are essential to its functioning. London's Night Buses have always been vital to the city's night-time economy, a service which in 2016 was enhanced and improved by a new Night Tube service. The Night Tube and the Night Overground run throughout Friday and Saturday nights on the Northern, Central, Jubilee, Victoria and Piccadilly lines, as well as a section of the East London Overground, a good 90% of it in the general North London area. Charging only off-peak fares, it immediately proved a massive success and now supports nearly 4,000 jobs directly and many more indirectly.

Like its daylight economy, London's night-time equivalent, which in 2014 contributed over £20bn to the UK economy and supported approximately 723,000 jobs, is kept going by an army of workers ranging from the unseen and unregarded such as cleaners, all-night cab drivers and sex workers making "out calls" to expensive hotels; to chefs, bar staff, waiters, croupiers, bouncers, firefighters, musicians and security guards. The mostly young staff of the bars and clubs are notoriously under-payed and overworked, a situation that trade unions are trying to address. London's clubbing scene continues to be a mostly North London affair, with the city's four main clubbing "hubs" — the West End and Soho, Camden Town, Stoke Newington and Hoxton/Shoreditch — containing the greatest numbers, although there are clubs all over the city, with smaller concentrations in Brixton and Peckham. The overall trend of clubbing in the city since the 1990s has been to transition north and east from the centre, but not as far as commonly supposed.[13]

Even London's pubs, for centuries the core of its working class life, are not immune to radical change. Between 2001 and 2018 a quarter of London's pubs closed. The majority of the remaining 3,500 were in North London, with the highest numbers in Westminster (430), Camden (230), Islington (215) Hackney (185) and the City (160). There are significant numbers in Southwark (175) and Lambeth (145) but other districts of south and east London such as Newham (45), Merton (40) and Barking and Dagenham (20) have lost more than half their number since 2001. Haringey's relatively low number of pubs (60) reflects its continuing economic disadvantage and the greater social pull of nearby Hackney and Camden. Yet despite a reduction in total pub numbers, employment in London's pubs has increased. In 2016 there were a total of 46,300 pub jobs in London, an 8.7% increase since 2001, traceable to the growing number of gastro-pubs which require more kitchen and serving staff.[14]

Working class employment in North London varies enormously between regulated sectors with recognised trade unions and the loosely regulated or unregulated. Some Uber or Deliveroo drivers might rent in North London and might be able to use the work as a jumpstart to other things, but the majority of workers toiling in an Amazon warehouse or a call centre on a minimum wage zero-hours contract, afraid to take a toilet break lest they be disciplined, will probably not be resident in North London even if their workplace is. And although those cleaning offices at night or driving cabs through its streets indisputably work at the heart of the city, the unrelenting nature of the work, the low pay and anti-social hours, negate any "proximity effect" that occasionally operates on those who do other work in central London and stop sometimes to enjoy its social life and absorb its atmosphere.

Ben Judah's *This is London* (2016) is, without question, the most important work on this aspect of London life. While *This is London* does not ignore the inner city, its core narrative is of semi-legal, semi-employed migrants and refugees barely existing in a sub-urban transit zone circling Inner London from Edmonton to Neasden to Catford to Plaistow, only entering central London to graft and clean. Telling a wide range of harrowing personal stories — Roma beggars sleeping rough in the underpass under Hyde Park Corner; Somali shop workers in Harlesden; Romanian and Polish builders lined up outside Wickes on the North Circular at 6 in the morning to tout for work, just as Irish navvies did in Hammersmith and Camden fifty years earlier — Judah's work is a bracing corrective to over-romantic conceptions of London as a successful multi-ethnic melting pot.

But his dystopian accounts of areas like Neasden, Harlesden and Peckham, with their implicit and sometimes explicit lament that these areas have declined since the old white working class moved out, make *This is London* a one-sided picture with as much utility to the racist right as the progressive left. His account of walking the Old Kent Road and finding "only one English shopkeeper left", seemingly unaware that most of the shopkeepers *are* English, just not white; or asserting that "the working class pulled out" of Edmonton, implying that the Turks, Poles and Ghanaians who live there now could not possibly be working class; or bemoaning that the King's Road is "one of the last very English streets in London", are naïve at best and problematic at worst.

Sometimes his pessimism leads him to miss what is in front of him, explained in strangulated but heartfelt language by Sabir, an Afghan migrant who runs a butchers shop in Neasden, who knows full well that it is not paradise, and yet contrasts it to where he and his friends came from:

Shafiullah is only miserable because he becomes like an English… he forgets why he walks five thousand miles to Neasden. Because when he looks out of his shop in Afghanistan…there was Americans and Russians fighting with machine guns…Shafilluh he was walking over many dead Afghans every day on his way to school. This is never going to happen to Neasden. This is a place that is so beautiful, because it is so boring. Neasden it's a rubbish in the London…but it's like a peace beauty in this world.[15]

Judah never answers Sabir. *This is London* is a fine work of boots-on-the-ground reportage but it contains no political analysis, no hint of industrial solidarity or self-organisation, no sense that while London can viciously exploit migrants and refugees it can also welcome and protect them. It skirts over the success stories of previous generations of immigrants, except to suggest that too much integration has turned them into gangsters ready to exploit more recent arrivals. There is hardly anything of the daily existence of NHS and council care workers, of Upper Street baristas and Kilburn shop assistants, of those who raise families on decent estates and send their kids to improved schools who then sometimes go to college, of mothers and grandmothers sitting outside a café in Wood Green Shopping Centre or Camden Town chatting over coffee and cake. It is all liberal despair, oozing sympathy and nothing but sympathy for an exploited underclass.

But this is a class capable of fighting back. Susana Benavides was born in Ecuador in 1975 and arrived in London in 2009, eventually securing a flat in social housing in Finsbury Park after a period as a cleaner working in offices from 4am to 7am and a hotel from 8am to 10pm. She managed to get a job with better hours in Topshop on Oxford Street but had problems with the cleaning company, Britannia, particularly a bullying sexist supervisor, so contacted the United Voices of the World (UVW), a trade union set up in London in 2014 to represent workers in low wage, outsourced industries, mainly migrants and with a heavy Latin American membership. Unlike the mainstream unions, who usually will not represent a new member until they have six months membership, the UVW immediately helped Susana. In time, after Britannia suspended her, Susana went to work for the UVW.[16]

The UVW was created out of a struggle to get the London Living Wage for outsourced cleaners at the Barbican Centre. In 2019 it staged a joint action with the PCS union to demand better pay and conditions for cleaners, security guards and receptionists at the Ministry of Justice (MoJ) and for general support staff at the Department for Business, Energy and Industrial Strategy (BEIS). In 2020 it secured funding from the German-based Rosa Luxemburg Foundation to employ a couple of full-time organisers and moved into office premises in Bethnal Green, where it established United Sex Workers, a separate Branch of the UVW. As well as Topshop, the UVW has staged visible and noisy walk-outs at Harrods, the Royal Parks and Sotheby's.

The UVW was following a trend of similar actions. In November 2013 outsourced cleaners at the John Lewis store on Oxford Street, employed by the sub-contractor Integrated Cleaning Management, took action against appalling pay and conditions. A previously unrepresented workforce paid the bare Minimum Wage, the cleaners had seen their hours and workload increase while their pay stagnated. Despite working in and for John Lewis, they did not share in the Mutual's employee profit-sharing scheme. The big private sector trade unions had ignored them until the smaller, more nimble Industrial Workers of the World (IWW) ran a successful recruitment campaign. After issuing a strike threat shortly before the Christmas period they won an immediate and backdated 9% pay rise and a commitment to pay the London Living Wage.

In March 2019 hundreds of sex workers in Soho went on strike to protest at unsafe working conditions, chanting *"Sex work is work"*, *"No bad whores, just bad laws"*, and *"What do we want? De-crim! When do we want it? Now!"* as they marched through central London. Their protest was just one part of ongoing work to support and protect sex workers in Soho, a key element of which is the NHS Health Clinic at 56 Dean Street which opened in 2009. Since then it has provided invaluable sexual health advice, seeing approximately 11,000 visitors every month. As well as providing a free weekly service to male and female sex workers that offers test results within ninety minutes, the clinic is as much an LGBT community centre as a health centre, providing free and anonymous sexual health results, including for HIV, within six hours.

On 7th April 2021, the first day that Deliveroo began trading on the London Stock Exchange, hundreds of Deliveroo drivers in London, galvanised by a February 2021 US Supreme Court ruling that Uber drivers are "workers" and not "independent contractors" who all happen to use the Uber app to find customers, went on strike. Organised by the Independent Workers' Union of Great Britain (IWGB), a new and relatively small trade union that seeks to recruit the exploited workers of the gig economy and to act for them, the drivers demanded the legal minimum wage, holiday and sick pay, and the right to collective bargaining with Deliveroo on terms and conditions.

The strike actions by migrant, sex and gig economy workers were the outward sign of a long-simmering discontent by London's hidden working class, many of whom, like the female

Irish cleaners interviewed in *Nightcleaners* in the 1970s, were yearning for a trade union to intervene on their behalf. Deliveroo drivers organised by the IWW had already taken protest action in May 2019 outside a Deliveroo "dark kitchen" (delivery-only kitchens, often on industrial sites) in Swiss Cottage. In September 2018 Uber drivers from across London assembled at an Uber "greenlight hub" in Aldgate to protest at earning less than the minimum wage when using the Uber app.

The cultural industry was also ripe for action. In 2017 workers at the independent cinema chain Picturehouse took nine days of strike action to try to secure the London Living Wage, sick pay for all staff, better maternity, paternity and adoption pay, and the reinstatement of four sacked union reps, despite a threat from their employer that if they did so they too would be sacked. Employees in Picturehouse cinemas in Crouch End, Hackney, East Dulwich and the Picturehouse flagship in Piccadilly planned to take thirteen more days strike action but had to call it off when the employer threatened them with loss of pay beyond just the strike days. The Picturehouse strikes attracted support and solidarity across London's trade union and socialist movement.

The most visible expression of this solidarity came from "Poetry on the Picket Line" (POTPL), an informal group set up by left-leaning poets to visit picket lines, entertain them with appropriate poetry and raise money for strike funds. POTPL arose out of a protracted dispute at the National Gallery in 2015 where PCS members had taken action to defend a sacked union rep. Chip Hamer, one of PCS's most experienced union reps and a published poet, recalled the wide range of strike actions POTPL have since supported, including strikes at the British Museum and the 2016 junior doctors' dispute, and that even an unglamorous picket line could throw up an unexpected North London conjunction:

> *The picket that we visited most often was the Hackney Picturehouse, on Mare Street. Towards the end of the dispute we did an evening gig for the strikers outside the cinema. After that we popped into a pub off Holloway Road for a bit of a lefty*

Xmas knees-up, where we bumped in to the then Leader of the Opposition. Which is how he got his picture into the Poetry on the Picket Line anthology.[17]

Campaigns and solidarity activity like the sex workers' strike, the John Lewis and Deliveroo actions and POTPL demonstrate that London's working class has not scuttled off in defeat nor lost its spirit. Not every employed or self-employed working class person in London is destitute. Some are organised in trade unions and fighting for better pay and a better life.

Jade Azim, whose father worked on London Underground and whose mother was a teaching assistant, was born in 1995 and grew up in Walthamstow in the 2000s in a family half-descended from Turkish migrants, playing under the North Circular with her mates because there were no other facilities. She recalled that friends who grew up in neighbouring Chingford would not come to visit:

We grew up in an ex-council terrace. There were no trees and the car park outside was full of holes. It felt as though the council and government completely ignored us. This feeling was amplified at school. I went to a mixed comprehensive with shaking walls, metal detectors at the door, and pass rates averaging 30%. Buses would not stop for you if you were wearing the uniform. We had well over 30 to a class and the rooms were too small. When the time came for us to benefit from the (albeit, PFI funded) Building Schools for the Future programme, the Coalition came into power and scrapped it. One of my first politicising memories was seeing a teacher cry at the news...Despite everything, I was very proud of being a working class Londoner. We wore our accent (a mix of ethnicities, Afro-Caribbean, Turkish, South Asian and distinctly Cockney) with pride. The accent today still makes me feel at home.

Jade's mum made a point of taking her kids in to central London to visit the museums, entry to which was made free by the 1997-2001 Labour government. The cultural and educational opportunities opened up by Labour's investment lasted just long enough to get Jade to university and into political activity, working for Sadiq Khan's mayoral campaign in 2015 and then other left-of-centre groups. By 2019 her social life was not that different from Jacky Hyams' in the 1960s, occasionally accruing unlooked for cultural capital along the way:

> There is nothing particularly glamorous about working in London when you're squashed against someone's armpit on the tube. It's definitely an incentive to go to the pub to avoid rush hour, so much of my working life in London is marked by after-work drinks. Which is part of what has moved my social life from local to central...I now frequent pubs in Westminster and talk to journalists who I admired growing up. I am very aware of how privileged I am when I suddenly find myself in conversation with Owen Jones at the Red Lion in Whitehall.[18]

This complex social experience goes hand in hand with urban poverty. Cash Carraway learnt this the hard way, ending up at the Chalk Farm Food Bank with what she called "the walking wounded of austerity". But at the same time, as if to demonstrate the protean nature of London working class life, especially that part of it embedded in its centre, in the early 2000s she found herself relaxing in Soho, sitting outside Bar Italia in Frith Steet with some friends after working by day as a theatrical agent and by night as a stripper:

> We sat outside chain smoking Marlboro Menthols and taking in suburbia's finest on a night out "up West" searching for sex and bohemia...and I ended up falling into conversation with a group of musicians who had just performed over the road at Ronnie Scott's and some trumpet player introduced himself as the "Soho legend" Reg Williams.

Reg Williams was an old, near-decrepit Soho jazz player who, through some forgotten kink of local housing, still had a council flat on the top floor of William Blake House, a thirteen-storey residential block that stood on the site of Blake's birthplace at 8 Marshall Street overlooking Carnaby Street. Cash was amazed that a property that could have gone for a million quid was, in Reg's hands, just an artist's doss house:

> He didn't have a bed, just a mattress on the floor, there was beer cans close to where he lay his head and an ashtray that looked as if it hadn't been emptied in months...Despite the chaos there was a surprising number of potted plants forming a jungle by the balcony which he obviously tended to in lieu of himself, and covering every wall were the most beautiful pieces of art I had ever seen.[19]

In their different ways Jade, Cash and Reg epitomise the complex lived experience of the North London working class, still alive in the heart of the city, still finding outlets and opportunities but struggling for air even as corporate capitalism envelopes and chokes it.

Its old culture also struggled to survive, even though some of it was literally written on the walls. The Fitzrovia mural in Whitfield Gardens, just off Tottenham Court Road, commissioned by Camden Council in 1980 and fully restored to glory in 2020, depicts a colourful assortment of street life in the area at the time. Not far away, a large mural on the side of a school in Polygon Street, Somers Town, funded in the 1980s by the GLC and Camden Council, depicts the social development of the area as a vivid montage including images of the Brill Market, Mr Darke's Dust Heaps at King's Cross, the Fleet River, Old St Pancras Church, Mary Wollstonecraft, the Elizabeth Garrett Anderson Hospital and Father Basil Jellicoe. Threatened with erasure in the 1990s and again in 2007, it was saved by a vote taken by the local community, and is now regarded as the finest street mural in London.

The working class cafes of central and North London have survived better than street murals and communal art, although one of the greats, the Stockpots of central London, a small chain of eateries serving cheap but good quality grub (their lamb chops a particular treat) in simple but clean surroundings, sadly closed in 2015. There were four Stockpots in central London, one in Old Compton Street, one on Panton Street off Haymarket, one on the King's Road and one on Basil Street behind Harrods. In the early 2000s when I was working for the Department for Culture, Media and Sport (DCMS) on Cockspur Street, Trafalgar Square, I often had lunch at the Panton Street Stockpot. At that time I was Chair of the DCMS National Branch of PCS, the successor union of CPSA and one of the more militant trade unions in the country. National industrial action by PCS always saw good picket lines outside DCMS from 7am to 10am, which then went off to the Stockpot for a late breakfast.

The Stockpot is history now, as is the New Piccadilly Café on Denman Street, which with its populuxe 1950s décor of yellow Formica and red booth seating was an iconic part of West End life from 1951 until 2008 when rising rents forced it to close. But many like it remain, like the Café Crescent on Camden High Street, the Workers' Café on Upper Street, Gino's Coffee Bar in Marylebone Place, Franx Continental Café on Shaftesbury Avenue, Café Bruno on Wardour Street, Café Plaka in King's Cross, the Smithfield Café in Smithfield Market, the Breakout Café on Caledonian Road opposite the prison, the Ferreira Delicatessen off Parkway in Camden Town, Delichio's Café on Queen's Crescent, the Royal Café on Fleet Road in Hampstead, Daisy's in Hoxton, Dino's in Spitalfields, Charlie's in Wood Green, Tachbrooke Café and Patisserie in Pimlico, Dolce Coffee on Essex Road, the Alpino in Chapel Street, the Crown Café on Crowndale Road off Mornington Crescent, the Valencia Café on Marchmont Street, the 101 Church Street Café and restaurant, the Kings Café on Brill Place in Somers Town— and hundreds more.

There are far fewer of the old pie and mash shops surviving, but still some. South and East London have their share, of course — Arments in Walworth, Harrington's in Tooting, G. Kelly on the Roman Road and Maureen's Pie and Mash in Poplar. In North London, Manze's in Chapel Street, where as kids my mum and dad both went shopping with their mothers, closed in 2019 after 108 years' existence, although there are other Manze's at the Elephant and Castle and in Peckham. F. Cooke on Hoxton Street is as popular as ever and shows no sign of extinction. Castle's Pie and Mash in Camden Road, regarded by many as the best in London, is still going strong (when I was fifteen or so I was taken there by my dad, who insisted I try jellied eels. I hated them). In 2022 you could get still a first-class pie and mash at Castle's for £4.95, paid for in cash only.

North London's street markets have followed a similar pattern— part-survival, part-adaptation, part endurance. The old three-storey Kensington Market was demolished in 2001 and Kensington High Street completed its transition to UHNW corporate blandness. Inverness Street Market still exists but only as a sad facsimile of its former self. With the last food stall closing in 2013 it is now full of cheap knock-off clothes stalls, sucking life from the Camden that surrounds it but giving little back. The Villiers Street Collectors Market has been literally driven underground, but it can still be found on Saturdays if you can locate the hidden door between the Costa and the mainline station at the bottom of the street and then descend three levels to the underground car park.

Chapel Street, though, is still healthy and thriving, as is Whitecross Street, North End Road, Swiss Cottage Market, Broadway Market, Leather Lane, Petticoat Lane, Tottenham Green Market on Sundays, Colombia Road Flower Market, Holcombe Market on Tottenham High Road, Goodge Place, Plender Street and Church Street. Queen's Crescent Market, open on Thursdays and Saturdays, has seen a return to its 1980s peak under the management of the Queen's Crescent Community Association (QCCA), a not-for-profit charity that took over its management in 2013. Running training courses and try-out pitches for new traders, it has a more diverse range of stalls than ever before, mixing spicy olive stalls, hot food takeaways like Dim Sum, authentic jerk chicken and freshly baked focaccia bread with discount clothing and duvet sellers.

Berwick Street may not be the throbbing heart of Soho it used to be, the vibrant street market that graced the cover of Oasis's *What's the Story, Morning Glory?* (1995), but it still retains a specific energy and quixotic charm, from the Blue Posts pub through Violet's café to Gosh Comics on the corner. Even some of the fruit and veg stalls are still there, the traders shouting to each other and to customers, but complemented by a large assortment of ethnic food stalls and takeaways. The impeccably tailored George Skeggs still walks Berwick Street, Dean Street and Old Compton Street every day, dropping into Bar Italia for a coffee.

Ungentrified cafes, street murals and urban markets are not the only elements of "old" London that have survived. The deep-seated failings of its police force remain almost untouched by seventy years of social progress. In September 2016 PC Joshua Savage stopped a car in Weedington Road off Queen's Crescent Market driven by Leon Fontana because he apparently looked like another black man, a drug dealer wanted by the police. When Fontana refused to get out of the car PC Savage smashed the windscreen with his baton and then used a multi-tool to saw through it. The attack, which left Fontana with a shard of glass in his eye, was caught on film. Savage, who resigned before he could be disciplined, claimed that all Met officers carried such unauthorised weapons. In February 2022 it was revealed that officers in Charing Cross Station, the West End Central of old, had been swapping sexist, racist and homophobic messages on WhatsApp. One officer said of other officers who might report such behaviour, *"There's a few of those grassing cunts I would like to knife"*. It was the final straw for a London Mayor who had grown up with racist policing and it led to the removal of a Commissioner who was as blind to the Met's failings as were her 1950s predecessors.[20]

This is a London that seldom receives its artistic due. *Essex Boys* (2000), a fictional recreation of the 1995 "Rettenden Range Rover murders" in which three professional drug dealers were shot dead at close range in a Range Rover in Essex, birthed an entire subculture of straight-to-DVD London and Essex-based crime films. Most are cheap nihilistic dross, as representative of London's white working class as an illegal pit-bull fight in a Dartford lock-up. Their inner-city black equivalent —*Bullet Boy, Kidulthood, Ill Manors* — are far superior as films but just as problematic as representative portrayals of contemporary London working class life. Far better is TV's *Top Boy*, which has a sympathy and authenticity unmatched by other portrayals of inner-London drug gangs and the community around them. Yet *Top Boy* is still a one-sided picture. Few alternatives to a life of crime are suggested or explored. The grim Summerhouse Estate is clearly meant to be Holly Street, except that in Hackney today the old Holly Street is gone (the scenes on the estate were actually filmed on an estate in Gravesend).

Literature does better but not massively so. Martin Amis's *London Fields* (1989) captured a particular zeitgeist with typically sour brilliance but Zadie Smith's subtle, humane *NW* (2012) reflected a deeper working class reality derived from personal knowledge of its subject. Born in 1975 to a white working class dad from East Croydon and a Jamaican immigrant mother, Smith was raised in Willesden and attended a comprehensive in Cricklewood before going on to Cambridge. Unlike Amis, she did not see working class characters as figures of fun or objects of fear. She knew them from school, her younger brother, also known as the hip-hop artist Doc Brown, became a youth worker working with the children of refugees and asylum seekers, and despite her literary success she continued to live in Willesden.

NW revolves around four characters (but mostly its two central female characters, Irish Leah Hanwell and Afro-Caribbean Natalie Blake) who grew up on the Caldwell Estate in "NW" somewhere between Willesden, Kilburn and Cricklewood. Smith is especially good on a subject Amis wouldn't touch with a bargepole — the employed, not well paid but just-about managing female working class, often single mothers or grandmothers who do all the heavy lifting. As Leah, the only white, Irish woman in the local council's Fund Distribution Team, observes of the team's admin grades at the end of the week, they are possessed of a life spark not easily suppressed:

> *In the corridor the women spill out of every room, ready for a warm night out on the Edgware Road. From St Kitts, Trinidad, Barbados, Grenada, Jamaica, India, Pakistan. In their forties, fifties, sixties, and yet busts and butts and shiny legs and arms still open to the sexiness of an early summer in a manner that the women of Leah's family can never be.[21]*

Other recent portrayals of working class North London, such as Guy Gunaratne's *In Our Mad and Furious City* (2016), Gabriel

Karuze's *Who They Was* (2020) and Jac Shreev-Lee's collection of short stories *Broadwater* (2020), explore the reality of life in working class Neasden, Kilburn and Tottenham respectively, complimented by John Challis's *The Resurrectionists* (2021), a collection of poems drawing out the invisible lives and historical legacies of London's labourers, porters and prostitutes.

With the exception of Dickens (and even he wrote in serial form and was sniffed at by the guardians of elite culture) since the beginning of London's rapid expansion in the early nineteenth century there has often been more of working class London in pulp and "non-literary" work, in George W.M. Reynolds' *The Mysteries of London*, in *A Child of the Jago* and Sherlock Holmes, in Gerald Kersh's *Night and the City* and Robert Westerby's *Wide Boys Never Work*, in Richard Allen's *Skinhead* and *Suedehead*, in Dan Kavanagh's Duffy novels and Nigel Fountain's *Days Like These*, in *The Sweeney* and *Minder* and *Top Boy,* in *Yardie* and *Junglist* and the entire strand of "London Gothic" from *Dr Jekyll and Mr Hyde* to early *Hellblazer* and *Neverwhere*. From that perspective the great London novel of our time is China Mieville's *Perdido Street Station* (2000), a radical work of art that whilst not about the "real" London captures its essence more accurately than most London-based contemporary fiction. To anyone who has ever lived, worked, loved or been politically active in the capital, Mieville's New Crobuzon is obviously London, and gloriously so.

This strand of London lore is presided over by two of London's greatest urban cartographers, Michael Moorcock and Peter Ackroyd, both born of the London working class. Moorcock's *Mother London* (1988) vies with *Bleak House* as the greatest London novel ever written, a rich mosaic of London life from the 1940s to the 1980s told through the eyes and disjointed memories of alienated petit-bourgeois intellectuals, failures and rejects. Yet while it sympathises with and offers cogent reflection on the working class experience of the capital, it does not portray it from the inside. It is accurate, true and telling because so much of London's working class, in North London especially, had a *similar* experience, or at least an experience that during those decades intersected and overlapped with the likes of Moorcock and his characters.

The dancing partner to Moorcock's psycho-drama is Peter Ackroyd's body of work on London's culture and history. Ackroyd's *London: The Biography* is a monumental hologram of a city over time, an x-ray, an autopsy and a dramatic reconstruction marred by one peculiar flaw, Ackroyd's facility to grasp and capture every aspect of London's two-thousand-year history except those decades he himself lived through. This mirrors his fiction. *The Great Fire of London, Hawksmoor, Dan Leno and the Limehouse Golem* are all historical novels leavened by magical realism, rarely touching on the post-war world, and when doing so in an elliptical and surrealistic fashion.

Iain Sinclair has followed and expanded on Ackroyd. Beginning with the provocative *Lud Heat* (1975) Sinclair created a manner of looking at London, a spatial-historical awareness that is now integral to its self-image. His finest books — *Lights Out for the Territory, London Orbital* and *Hackney, That Rose Red Empire* —combine that sensibility with sharp social vignettes and hard truths. But later work has been repetitive and increasingly jaded. Like the now dried up sub-genre of Soho memoirs, Sinclair is only interested in working class people who *work for his books*, with colourful eccentrics and semi-criminals, as well as déclassé middle class intellectuals, artists and drop outs. In one objective moment, Sinclair acknowledges his status as the chronicler of working class eclipse who would have no tale to tell, or motivation to tell it, if not for that eclipse:

> *If the lives of the flat dwellers had been undisturbed, I wouldn't be here. I'd be walking briskly south, heading towards Shoreditch, too much the aesthete of blight.*[22]

It is a common theme and a frequent lament. The Marxist historian Gwyn Williams ended his history of Wales, *When was Wales?* (1985), on a pessimistic note, concluding that at the time of writing the Welsh people were "a naked people under an acid rain". Many have said the same of London's working class.

The influential urban studies theorist Richard Florida went further and claimed, after redefining London's precariat "service class" as somehow not working class, that the latter barely existed, replaced by a new "creative class" of knowledge workers. In my view, this is a category error. If there is one consistent theme in this study of the North London working class since the 1950s, it is that they are not defined solely by their paid employment. There are whole other areas of their lives of equal importance — extra-curricular and voluntary work during the evenings or weekends, mentoring kids in a variety of sports, MC'ing sound systems or playing in bands, participating in adult education or trade union and political activity, and an endless range of personal hobbies and pastimes. Are these people not as "creative" as an advertising executive or an HR consultant?"

The socialist activist Ash Sarkar, herself from North London's working class, put creativity in a better context:

I love this country's pop culture! Grime, drill, house music — all that club culture — plus I think we do the best theatre, I think we make the best novelists. I genuinely feel this sense of, like, obnoxious flag-waving pride when I think about this country's cultural output, and in particular the creativity that comes from working class black and Asian people. I think that it's this ferocious engine of originality.[23]

This engine of originality works in mysterious ways. In North London it produced a large number of personal and professional success stories, born from an environment especially conducive to creativity and hustle. Living in, working in, constantly journeying around and through central London, the North London working class functioned as the hot core, the hyper-accelerated molecules, of a receptive, ambitious, open-minded, multi-ethnic and astonishingly diverse working class. The second half of the twentieth century, in particular, provided it opportunities to live lives as varied, colourful and exciting as those enjoyed by North London's middle class.

These opportunities were not evenly spread. During the last seventy years the "outlier" areas of North London — Hackney, Tottenham, Willesden — were so disfigured by poverty, sub-standard housing and street crime that their working class enjoyed less freedom to imagine and experiment than those who worked or lived nearer the centre. And yet, for all these difficulties and disadvantages, the working class of Hackney and Tottenham clearly have more in common with their fellows in Camden and Islington than they do with the working class of Hartlepool or Bolton. In the final analysis, it's a London thing.

This is not necessarily a privileged position. In 1994 one in six of London's workforce were on Income Support. In 1996 it was estimated that 2.1 million people, 30% of the city's population, were on or just above the poverty line. In 2012, the unemployment rate in London was 10.1%.[24] In 2020 the Joseph Rowntree Foundation found that London had the highest rate of poverty in the country at 28% (the North-East, the West Midlands and Wales all had 24%). It also found that those households in poverty in London have the least affordable housing available to them. London as a whole also contains two thirds of the UK's homeless.[25] Sometimes London's working class can also seem like a naked people under an acid rain.

But London's weather can vary immensely depending on personal circumstances, locale and luck. There are many elements of London working class life that offer advantage. The "proximity effect" still exists and has been spreading eastwards in the last two decades. For East End Grime artists like Tinchey Stryder the mere *sight* of Canary Wharf — not its function but its visual symbolism — is a motivation to achieve within their field, to maximise their talent, to be financially secure. In 2005 Roll Deep's DJ Target told an interviewer, "*Canary Wharf is like our Statue of Liberty. It pushes me on. It's like all the money is there and it's an inspiration to get your own*".[26]

London's state schools, failing and dysfunctional not so long ago, particularly in boroughs like Hackney and Haringey, are now producing some of the best outcomes in the country, especially for working class kids. In 2002 not one of Hackney's state-maintained schools even had a sixth form. Now they all do. In the same period the borough went from the bottom of the league on achieving Grades A* to C at GCSEs to near the top. In 2017 London as a whole, despite its problems of high housing costs and low wages, still accounted for nearly two thirds of the country's social mobility "hot spots".[27] It's a trend the Department for Education, in a report of November 2020, called "the London Effect", something most apparent amongst pupils from disadvantaged backgrounds. In 2015 disadvantaged pupils in London had an average "Best 8" score (equivalent to around eight GCSE grades) that was 46.7 points higher than that of disadvantaged pupils in the rest of England. The DfE found that:

> Compared to disadvantaged White pupils, disadvantaged Bangladeshi, Black African and "other" pupils were more likely to have higher aspirations and self-belief, to spend more time doing homework and to have parents with higher expectations and who were more likely to attend parent-teacher evenings.[28]

It's not an aspect of London life that Iain Sinclair, appalled by the aesthetics of a gleaming new library or busy mocking a passing hipster, ever bothers with.

It is one reason why people refuse to give up on London. Zita Holbourne, after forming the anti-austerity campaign group Black Activists Rising Against Cuts (BARAC) in 2010 with Lee Jasper and continuing to work within the trade union movement, is still committed to the city:

> I sometimes wonder why I am still living in London but despite the negatives I love being in a busy, active capital city, a centre of politics, activism and the arts. In the UK it is where I feel most comfortable and safest. In the past decade where racism has deepened, multicultural London provides something of a safety net to me. London is different including when it came to voting on exiting the EU. The aftermath of the referendum vote has been horrific, with labelling and scapegoating of migrant communities and deepening racism and xenophobia.[29]

Of the city where he grew up and has worked his entire life, Sean McGlinchey said:

I'm proud of how London is such a mixing pot for so many different ethnicities, faiths, cultures and sexualities and how you can be whoever you want to be largely without being judged and told it's wrong. London is constantly reinventing itself. For example, I grew up in Queen's Park near Kilburn, whose population was predominantly Irish immigrants. It had Catholic churches, pubs, dance halls and shops which catered for Irish tastes. Fifty years on the population is heavily Eastern European and Asian and there are mosques, Bazaars and all manner of shops catering for their cultural tastes. It is as vibrant and exciting as it has ever been.[30]

Big Zuu came from the Mozart Estate off the Harrow Road and his work and life still revolve around it. In 2018 he penned a "Love Letter to the Mozart Estate" that recognised its problems but refused to wallow in poverty porn:

Harrow Road really does have a great community spirit, regardless of the issues that always come to the front. Things like Notting Hill Carnival, the little market on Harrow Road and Portobello round the corner add that sick, diverse culture vibe in the ends. There are Arabs, blacks, Asians, whites. It's very unlikely to find any racism in Mozart, because most of us isn't really from England — so how can we diss each other? — and most people in the area are working class, so we're all in this together.[31]

To stress the positive aspects of a seventy-year history, to cite some examples of working class success or resistance, some successful campaigns and improved housing, is not to ignore residualisation, racism or other structural inequalities and oppression. The biggest problem facing London's working class is undoubtedly the lack of affordable housing. But there are glimmerings of hope. West Kensington and Gibbs Green Estate on North End Road near Earl's Court, home to 2,000 people in

760 flats and houses, sold to developers in 2011, was taken back into social ownership by Hammersmith &Fulham Council in 2019 after a long battle by tenants against private sector owners who wished to demolish the estate and relocate its residents as part of the "Earl's Court Masterplan". But residents were not keen on the Masterplan and after the Grenfell fire the council bought the estate back for the same sum it had sold it eight years before.

When the buy-back was announced Sally Taylor, Chair of the West Green Residents Association, told a journalist:

> People were absolutely cheering last night, it felt like New Year's Eve. Even the kids were going "is it true that we're really safe?"[32]

Similarly, after multiple complaints about the standard of the repair work under Islington's PFI 1 and 2 contracts, in 2022 Islington Council bought the management of the homes given over to the PFI projects back under local government control.

The battle never ends. In Tottenham, the High Road West redevelopment plan proposed by Haringey Council and Lendlease PLC claims to provide 2,929 new homes adjacent to the new White Hart Lane stadium. The developers claim that 750 of these will be at "affordable" rents but only 564 will be council-owned. The plans, which include a skyway linking a revamped White Hart Lane station and the Spurs stadium, involve the demolition of the Love Lane council estate and its 297 homes, the nearby Peacock Industrial Estate which contains over 30 industrial units, and shops like Chick King, a local favourite for the last 40 years with the reputation of being the best chicken shop in Tottenham. Not all tenants of the Love Lane Estate have been promised another council-owned property. The redevelopment *may* ultimately provide more and better homes for displaced tenants but at the cost of disrupting and erasing an existing community. Even Spurs, keen to redevelop the surrounding area to make it more palatable for visiting fans, criticised the plans as "not aspirational enough for residents".[33]

In 2019 the One Housing Group, managers of the Juniper Crescent social housing estate immediately behind the Roundhouse, entered into a joint venture with the developers Countryside Properties. The new partners proposed to demolish the estate, only built in 1996 and now a tightly knit, safe and pleasant working class community in the heart of Camden, as part of a massive redevelopment of the empty Goods Yard between Chalk Farm Road and the mainline railway. The scheme would eventually provide over six hundred high-rise flats in blocks as high as fourteen storeys to be built in the next decade, most of which will be unaffordable to local working class people. But as the regeneration scheme depends on GLA funding, One Housing was required, under new rules introduced by Mayor Khan, to ballot tenants about the proposal, which could not proceed if they did not agree.

The majority of Juniper Crescent's tenants rejected the plan and the proposal to eventually rehouse them on the new development. But One Housing did not accept this as final and in April 2021 it proposed to re-run the ballot. Meanwhile, residents have complained about slow repairs and maintenance, believing that these are not a priority for estate managers who hope to soon demolish it, a suspicion confirmed by One Housing's message to tenants during the ballot that if they voted against the scheme then their homes would in future only receive "essential" maintenance. Faced with unwanted pressure from One Housing and possible forced displacement, the tenants of Juniper Court are being defended by the GMB London Region, St Pancras and Holborn Labour Party and other tenants' rights advocates.[34]

For North London's working class the struggle for decent homes means its continuing ability to reproduce itself and thrive within the city as did previous generations. Kanya King was born in 1969 and raised in a crowded council flat in Kilburn, the ninth child of an Irish mother and Ghanaian father. Her dad died when she was thirteen and at sixteen she gave birth to a son, whose father disappeared a year later. Despite this she went on to study English Literature at Goldsmiths College and later founded the Music of Black Origin (MOBO) organisation. The first MOBO Awards took place in 1996 and are now amongst the most prestigious events in the annual music calendar. In 2013 Kanya was named one of the most influential women in the UK.

Savimbi Neto, AKA Ambush, born in Camden in 1994, had become one of the country's top rap artists by his early twenties. His 2018 single "Jumpy" was an instant classic, so much so that he worked on a remix with fellow North Londoners Chip and Skepta. In 2020 he moved on, in his debut album *Ask My Brother*, to reinvigorate and redefine grime and drill. Ambush's contemporary Awate, born in 1991, arrived in the UK as a child refugee from Eritrea and was raised on the Maiden Lane Estate, a legacy to Camden's working class from the days of Sydney Cook that he recognises and applauds. Influenced by his father, a former member of the Eritrean Liberation Front, Awate became a "conscious rapper", producing hip-hop songs and videos that, like Lowkey's music and Akala's educational projects, deliver mature critiques of neoliberal capitalism and institutional racism.

After the Met targeted, arrested and tried Awate four times, the first time for smoking a cigarette on the estate, failing to convict each time, he said:

> It's not my fault I'm black, it's not my fault I'm a refugee, it's not my fault I'm working class. If I just express myself in any way, it is labelled "political". I am not allowed to not be political, I don't have that privilege. Because of who I am, I'm not going to talk about brands and my Instagram profile, I'm going to talk about court cases and the beautiful perseverance in my communities.[35]

Awate was as clear about his influences as about his politics, acknowledging the debt he owed to his own particular part of North London and to its history:

> It's why my shit sounds like memories. The different subcultures and genres that have been developed and stuck in Camden are

*one of the characteristics of the area. People are still walking
around dressed like punks, mods and hippies.*[36]

Conservative social commentators, on the left as well as
the right, seek to divide the older white working class from
the more diverse working class of the twenty-first century. In
some parts of the country, they may have done so. But while
the social structures and lifestyle of that older working class
were, of course, products of their time and therefore different
from those of succeeding generations, they were not *that*
different, especially in North London, the cultural heart of the
metropolis. The continuities amongst the people whose stories
are told here may not be immediately obvious, but they existed
and they exist. It's why their shit sounds like memories. It's why
mine does.

These are the sons and daughters of Mother London. From
the Second World War to the twenty-first century the city has
birthed them, rescued them, housed them, educated them,
entertained them and sustained them. For the most part, it was
good for them. In time and with the right conditions, it could
be again.

NOTES

Maybe It's Because I'm a North Londoner

1. Stormzy, *Rise Up: The #Merky Story So Far*, #Merky Books, 2018, p.24
2. Karl Marx, *Capital Volume III*, quoted in David McLellan, *The Thought of Karl Marx* (Papermac, 1971), p.178
3. E.P Thompson, "Eighteenth Century English Society: Class Struggle Without Class?", *Social History 3*, May 1978, pp.147-149
4. Mike Savage, *Social Class in the 21st Century* (Pelican, 2015), p.366
5. Data on London housing in https://www.london.gov.uk/sites/default/files/housing_in_london_2019.pdf
6. Rachel Lichtenstein, *Diamond Street: The Hidden World of Hatton Garden* (Penguin, 2012), p.197
7. Gareth Stedman Jones, *Outcast London: A Study in the Relationship between Classes in Victorian Society* (Verso, 2013), first published by Oxford University Press 1971, pp.21-22

The 1950s

1. Ted is, of course, my father. Given the theme of this book it seems appropriate to outline my family's London antecedents, at least as far as I can unravel them.

   When Ted was born in 1938, his father, also named Edward Medhurst, was a general delivery man and commercial driver working in central London (I am told that Harry Edward Medhurst, West Ham United's pre-WWII goalkeeper, was a distant cousin, but am unable to substantiate that). Ted's dad was born in 1904 in Hoxton and had a family with a wife, Margaret Lannin, and children in the area from 1923 until his death in 1950. In the late 1930s he seems to have temporarily abandoned this family and lived with my grandmother Edith, a warehouse cleaner, in King's Cross, for a few years. After the war he returned to his first family. *His* father, my great-grandfather, *also* Edward Medhurst, 1877-1940, was a "Carman" (a driver of horse-drawn delivery vehicles) and "Housebreaker" who was born and died in Hoxton. In 1900 he married Florence Thorpe, daughter of George Thorpe, who worked as a waiter and who was born in the City of London in 1851. Edward and Florence had three children — Florence, Jessie and Edward.

Great-grandfather Edward Medhurst's father William Medhurst, a "Horse Hair Dresser", was born in 1851 in St Luke's, Clerkenwell. William's father, *also* William, recorded as a "Horse Hair Curler", was born in 1828 in St Pancras but later moved to Clerkenwell. He went to prison in 1861 for embezzlement and with no means of support his wife Ellen went into the St Pancras Workhouse. She died in 1868, and in 1888 her luckless husband is recorded as an inmate of Cleveland Street Workhouse in Marylebone. In 1872 William and Ellen's son married Emma Hooson of Clerkenwell, a machinist. Emma's parents were George Hooson, a painter and decorator born in Westminster in 1828, and Mathilda Mitchell, a dress maker born in Clerkenwell in 1834. Further back the London line is opaque, although the death of a Daniel Medhurst in Hoxton in 1758, at the age of seventy-two, is recorded in the Parish Register, so it is possible it goes back to the eighteenth and perhaps even the seventeenth century.

My grandmother Edith's family, the Byfords, moved to London from Ipswich in the latter half of the nineteenth century, where her grandfather Arthur Byford had been a newspaper agent. Edith's mother Phoebe Buck was born in 1883 in Bloomsbury. Phoebe's father Alf Buck, a warehouseman, was born in 1854 in St Pancras and died in 1893 in Holborn. His father, Stephen Buck, a shoemaker, was born in Yarmouth in 1810 and moved to London about mid-century. By 1861 he and his family, including young Alf, were living in Yardley Street, off Farringdon Road. Alf married Clara Gould on 25th December 1875. Clara was born in Battersea in 1854 and died in Wanstead in 1937. Clara's father Richard was born in 1813 in Sturminster Newton, Dorset, and became a tailor, maintaining a record of people with particular craft skills moving to London in the nineteenth century and then falling down the social ladder of the metropolis, sometimes to the very bottom where they encountered the Medhursts.

In 1903 Phoebe Buck married George Leonard Byford, who was born in Ipswich but, like Phoebe, grew up in an LCC building in Holborn. After marriage they appear to have moved to Clerkenwell because that is where their daughters Edith and Lily were born. In 1903 George was recorded as a Carman but by 1911 he was a driver for the Royal Mail. He almost certainly lost his job as a Carman in 1905, a year after his daughter Edith was born, when he attempted to steal a sack of tapioca and a few boxes of sugar and cocoa from his employer, for which he was sentenced to three months hard labour in Wormwood Scrubs prison. His wife Phoebe was remembered by my dad as Granny Phoebe, the woman who helped raise him as a child (and also by me as she lived until 1974).

The various lines of Goulds, Byfords, Bucks and Medhursts (and, of course, my mother's family, although they are impenetrable beyond her own parents, and not even then if certain suppositions are true) constitute my family background. I was born in the Royal Free Hospital in Liverpool Road, Islington, in 1962. Ted was born in University College Hospital on Gower Street in central London (where, in 1993, his grand-daughter Elizabeth was also born) and grew up in St Pancras. Parts of his life, as indicative of a certain type of North London working class existence in the second half of the twentieth century, but certainly not the only type, are referenced in this book. He died in March 2021 in Brighton as the book was being prepared.

2   Matthew Ingleby, *Bloomsbury: Beyond the Establishment* (British Library, 2017), p.73

3   Jerry White, *London in the Twentieth Century: A City and Its People* (The Bodley Head, 2001), p.53

4   Data on Holborn's housing shortage after the war can be found at https://municipaldreams.wordpress.com/2020/02/04/council-housing-in-holborn-part-ii/

5   John Boughton, *Municipal Dreams: The Rise and Fall of Council Housing* (Verso, 2018), p.3

6   Alan Johnson, *This Boy* (Corgi Books, 2012), p.21

7   For historical background on the Angel and Chapel Street area see https://www.british-history.ac.uk/survey-london/vol47/pp373-404#fnn175. Bert Lloyd had a rich and fascinating career, including a cameo in John Huston's *Moby Dick* (1956) singing an old English

sea shanty, joint publication with Ralph Vaughan-Williams in 1959 of the *Penguin Book of English Folk Songs*, and recording work with Ewan McColl.

8   For Christine's and others' memories of growing up in Camden see https://www.castlehaven.org.uk/static/uploads/documents/ Castlehaven_Community_History_Project_final.pdf

9   See Victor Heath, *Vic Heath: Just One of the Working Class* (LifeBook, 2019), for Vic's life.

10 Jacky Hyams, *Bombsites and Lollipops* (John Blake, 2011), p.17

11 Ibid., p.31

12 Michael Moorcock, *London Peculiar and Other Nonfiction* (PM Press, 2012), p.43

13 The standard of rubbish disposal in communal housing blocks, council and private, in deprived areas like Hackney and the East End did not improve for decades. Jacky's description of the chute of her childhood matches exactly the small, rusting rubbish chute of Oban House in Poplar where I lived in a "hard-to-let" council flat for six years in the 1980s. On one occasion, when it was once again blocked and over-spilling with clogged rubbish, the residents, sick of waiting for Tower Hamlets Council to come round to clear it, simply set fire to the contents of the chute, followed by an impromptu party in the courtyard as smoke billowed out of it on all the open landings. Surprisingly, it worked.

14 Steven Berkoff, *Free Association: An Autobiography* (Faber and Faber, 1996), p.13

15 Interview in Roger Rogowski, *The Other Side of Notting Hill: From Wartime to the Westway* (The History Press, 2018), p.32

16 Johnson, *This Boy*, p.36

17 Ibid., p.16

18 Rogowski, *The Other Side of Notting Hill*, p.77

19 Sid and Ann's recollections are in Stuart Deabill and Ian Snowball, *From Ronnie's to Ravers: Personal Situations in London Clubland* (Countdown Books, 2013), pp.48-49

20 Interview in Catherine Dunne, *An Unconsidered People: The Irish in London* (New Island, 2003), p.98

21 https://www.nomisweb.co.uk/census/2011/QS201EW/view/ 2013265927?cols=measures

22   Rogowski, *The Other Side of Notting Hill*, p.40
23   Samuel Selvon, *The Lonely Londoners* (Penguin Classics, 2006), p.167
24   Panikos Panayi, *Migrant City: A New History of London* (Yale University Press, 2020), p.83
25   Quoted in Miki Garcia, *Rebuilding London: Irish Migrants in Post-War Britain* (The History Press Ireland, 2015), p.70
26   Ibid., 2015, p.142
27   Dunne, *An Unconsidered People*, p.16
28   Clair Wills, *Lovers and Strangers: An Immigrant History of Post-War Britain* (Penguin, 2017), p.281
29   Garcia, *Rebuilding London*, p.69
30   White, *London in the Twentieth Century*, p.137
31   Helen Evangelou, *Tales from Riding House Street: A Faded London House and the Cypriots Who Lived in It*, www.ridinghousestreet.co.uk, 2018, p.2
32   Pip Granger, *Up West: Voices from the streets of Post-War London* (Corgi Books, 2009), p.42
33   Ibid., pp.71-72
34   Ibid., pp.68-69. When Pip Granger was researching her book, to date the only account of the post-war West End working class, she came across Ted's own self-published memoir and contacted him. They had a long and enjoyable phone conversation about their early lives. Pip died a few years later.
35   Ibid., p.125. It cannot be done today but I recall, as a teenager in the 1970s and later in the 1980s, that after my regular Saturday visit to my nan in her council flat in Hunter House off Brunswick Square, I would cross Russell Square and take the short-cut through the British Museum from back entrance to main entrance, to take me to Shaftesbury Avenue, Denmark Street and Soho.
36   Evangelou, *Tales from Riding House Street*, p.199
37   Mike Hutton, *The Story of Soho: The Windmill Years 1932-1964* (Amberley, 2013), p.125
38   Today the headquarters of the MU is in Southwark.
39   Granger, *Up West*, p.294
40   Barry Miles, *London Calling: A Countercultural History of London since 1945* (Atlantic Books, 2010), p.49
41   Ted Medhurst, *Charlie Potatoes* (Medhurst Books, 2008), p.24.

[42] Anna Sullivan, *People Like Us: A Memoir* (World of Inclusion Ltd, 2018), p.48,51

[43] Garth Cartwight, *Going for a Song: A Chronicle of the UK Record Shop* (Flood Gallery Publishing, 2018), p.32

[44] For Ken Weller's life and his recollections of the Suez demo of 1956 see https://pasttenseblog.wordpress.com/2021/02/07/ken-weller-an-obituary/

[45] Jeremy Reed, *The Dilly: A Secret History of Piccadilly Rent Boys* (Peter Owen Publishers, 2014), p.60

[46] Panayi, *Migrant City*, p.52

[47] Kenneth Coutts-Smith, *The Dream of Icarus: Art and Society in the Twentieth Century* (George Braziller, 1970), p.40

[48] Wensley Clarkson, *Billy Hill: Godfather of London* (Pennant Books, 2009), p.11

[49] Hutton, *The Story of Soho*, p.144

[50] Duncan Campbell, *Underworld* (Penguin, 1994, updated 2019), p.209

[51] Granger, *Up West*, p.358

[52] Barbara Tate, *West End Girls* (Orion, 2010), p.124

[53] Ibid., p.133, p.201,126

[54] Gilbert Kelland, *Crime in London* (Grafton, 1987), p.70

[55] Graeme McLagan, *Bent Coppers: The Inside Story of Scotland Yard's Battle Against Police Corruption* (Orion, 2003), p.8

[56] Colin MacInness, *Absolute Beginners* (Allison & Busby Ltd, 1959), pp.105-106

[57] Don McCullin's recollections of his youth in the 1940s and 1950s are in https://www.readersdigest.co.uk/culture/celebrities/i-remember-don-mccullin

[58] Johnson, *This Boy*, p.77

[59] White, *London in the Twentieth Century*, p.339

[60] Wills, *Lovers and Strangers*, p.168

[61] Denise Haynes' recollections are in *All in a Day's Work: Working Lives and Trade Unions in West London 1945-1995*, edited by Dave Welsh, Britain at Work London Project, 2015, p.198

[62] Hyams, *Bombsites and Lollipops*, pp.124-125

[63] Medhurst, op cit, p.27

[64] Ted did have his two sons (me and my brother Jamie) baptised Catholic, but otherwise reneged on his commitment.

The 1960s

[1] Dave Burn, *Rent Strike: St Pancras 1960*, Past Tense, p.6

[2] Newspaper report on St Pancras quoted in David Mathieson, *Radical London in the 1950s* (Amberley, 2016), p.25

[3] David Aaronovitch, *Party Animals: My Family and other Communists* (Vintage, 2016), p.82

[4] See report in *North London Press*, 23 September 1960

[5] As a kid, throughout the 1960s and early 1970s I visited Burton Street once a week with my mum, until 1973 when my nan and grandad moved to an old Camden Council block, Hunter House, just off Brunswick Square. I was very young but I can remember Burton Street's cold and unwelcoming outside loo.

[6] For George Skeggs's memories of living in the Bury and Wild Street estates in the 1960s see http://www.coventgardenmemories.org.uk/page_id__85.aspx?path=0p40

[7] Personal interview (2019)

[8] Alexander Baron, *The Lowlife* (Collins, 1963), p.22

[9] Gary Kemp, *I Know This Much* (Fourth Estate, 2009), p.11, 16

[10] Steve Jones, *Lonely Boy: Tales from a Sex Pistol* (Windmill, 2016), p.10, 13

[11] For Richard's fascinating and invaluable memories seehttps://www.richardgregory.org.uk/history/shepherds-bush-history.htm

[12] Boughton, *Municipal Dreams*, pp.159-160

[13] This soap opera story arose from the revelation that my grandmother Kathleen Delaney, whilst still a young Irish woman just over from Waterford, worked in the 1930s as a live-in maid/cleaner for Dr Linehan's father, also a doctor, and when her first child, my mother Joyce, was born in 1940 she and her baby were cared for at the doctor's expense at an expensive country retreat. This did not happen for any of my mum's other four siblings, understandably as the family were dirt poor. Family legend has it that this was because Joyce's father was not grim and monosyllabic IRA hitman Tom O'Connell, a man already married anyway, but the good doctor. I am inclined to believe this is true as until she was nine, when the family moved to Burton Street and Tom finally moved in with them, my mum went every Sunday to the doctor's grand house on Oakely Square near Mornington Crescent to play with his children in the large garden again something none of her siblings ever did. Doctor Linehan senio

also paid for her to go to Ireland for six weeks every summer until 1955 when he died.

14 Buchi Emecheta, *Head Above Water* (Omenala Press, 1986), p.65

15 Wills, *Lovers and Strangers*, p.201

16 Panayi, *Migrant City*, p.48

17 Evangelou, *Tales from Riding House Street*, p.115

18 Interview in Dunne, *An Unconsidered People*, p.35

19 Personal interview (2020)

20 Personal interview (2020)

21 Sean Sorohan, *Irish London During the Troubles* (Irish Academic Press, 2012), p.22

22 Wills, *Lovers and Strangers*, p.128

23 Medhurst, opcit, p.41

24 The Cumberland Adventure Playground can be seen exactly as it was in 1965 here: https://www.youtube.com/watch?v=mgH2F_rryNs

25 Derek's memories of Camden Town in the 1950s and 1960s are at https://www.castlehaven.org.uk/static/uploads/documents/Castlehaven_Community_History_Project_final.pdf

26 Adam Ant, *Stand and Deliver: The Autobiography* (Pan Books, 2006), p.6

27 Lynn's and Tracy's recollections of De Walden in the 1960s are recorded here: https://www.stjohnswoodmemories.org.uk/content/memories/personal-memories/de_walden_buildings_allitsen_road_ww2

28 See https://www.tes.com/magazine/archived/mr-bosley-john-barnes

29 Roy Porter, *London: A Social History* (Penguin, 1994), p.423

30 Heath, *Vic Heath*, p.133

31 Personal Interview (2021)

32 Gil Jackson, *The London Apprentice* (Blacktor Press, 2017), p.17, p 102, pp.159-60

33 Hyams, *Bombsites and Lollipops*, Introduction

34 Evangelou, *Tales from Riding House Street*, pp.218-220

35 In the early 1960s Ted and Razzle Basil did a PJ for the Nash family, installing iron grills on the windows of a new betting shop on Lamb's Conduit Street which for some nefarious reason the family had bought.

36 James Morton, *Gangland Soho* (Piatkus Books, 2008), p.154-155

37 Amber interviewed by Jeremy Reed, *The Dilly*, p.96

38 Mim Scala, *Diary of a Teddy Boy: A Memoir of the Long 60s* (Create Space, 2013), p.56

39 The most comprehensive examination of the Jack the Stripper murders is *The Hunt for the 60s' Ripper*, Robin Jarossi (Mirror Books, 2017).

40 Dave Wilson, *To Ride a Red Engine: Tales of a London Fireman* (Jeremy Mills Publishing, 2007), p.73, 140

41 For the post-war North London Line see Wayne Asher, *A Very Political Railway: The Fight for the North London Line 1945-2014* (Capital Transport Publishing Limited, 2014).

42 Gail Lewis's memoir is in Charlie Brinkhurst-Cuff, *Mother Country: Real Stories of the Windrush Children* (Headline, 2018), pp.84-94

43 Reed, *The Dilly*, p.81

44 Jones, *Lonely Boy*, pp.41-42

45 Lesley-Ann Jones, *Ride a White Swan: The Lives and Death of Marc Bolan* (Hodder, 2012)

46 Quoted in Mark Doyle, *The Kinks: Songs of the Semi-Detached* (Reaktion Books, 2020), p.63

47 Kemp, *I Know This Much*, p.45

48 Miles, *London Calling*, p.189

49 Personal interview (2019)

50 John Bird, *Some Luck* (Penguin Books, 2002), pp.312-313, 345, 351

51 John Marriott, *Beyond the Tower: A History of East London* (Yale University Press, 2012), p.247

52 For cited data see http://repository.londonmet.ac.uk/6143/1/OHJ_48-2_pp43-56_gabriel-harding_1st_NEW.pdf

53 Personal interview (2019)

54 Eddie Mence was interviewed in April 2018 for *Re-imagining Islington: work, memory, place and emotion in a community,* an oral history project by John Gabriel and Jenny Harding coordinated by Age UK Islington, Islington Local History Centre and London Metropolitan University.

55 Personal Interview (2019)

56 Medhurst, op cit, p.44

The 1970s

1 Chuck Anderson and Ray Green, *Save the Jubilee Hall!: The Battle to Preserve the Three-Hundred-Year-Old Tradition of Street Market*

Trading in the Piazza of Covent Garden (Random Thoughts Limited, 1992), p.52

2   See http://coventgardenmemories.org.uk/page_id__101.aspx?path= 0p40p for an interview with "Sarah Smith", not the interviewee's real name, conducted in 2013.

3   For an audio interview with Eileen Kelly and her sister Mary Ward, see http://www.coventgardenmemories.org.uk/page_id__76. aspx?path=0p40p

4   Data in White, *London in the Twentieth Century*, p.163

5   Keeley's memories quoted in https://www.thetimes.co.uk/article/ time-and-place-keeley-hawes-mzflxldr0d2

6   Boughton, *Municipal Dreams*, p.148

7   *Ibid.*, p.164-165

8   Robert Elms, *London Made Us* (Canongate, 2020), p.27, 28, 30

9   https://blackcablondon.net/2012/06/30/the-trellick-tower-from-doom-to-desire/

10 Boughton, *Municipal Dreams*, p.149

11 See Madness, *Before We Was We* (Virgin Books, 2019), p.1, 4, 36, 57, for a fascinating collection of life stories and oral histories by the members of Madness about growing up working class in Camden Town and Kentish Town in the 1970s.

12 The story of Lissenden Gardens is told in Rosalind Bayley, *To Paradise by Way of Gospel Oak* (Camden History Society, 2009).

13 Interview at https://pasttenseblog.wordpress.com/2017/01/

14 For an account of Hillview's struggle see Andrew Whitehead, *Curious King's Cross* (Five Leaves Publications, 2018), pp.37-42.

15 For Myra Scales's recollections of the Fidelity Radio strike in 1974 see *All in a Day's Work*, p.48

16 Fred Rooke was interviewed in April 2018 for the *Re-imagining Islington: Work, Memory, Place and Emotion in a Community* oral history project.

17 For an account of Vic Heath's life in the 1970s see Heath, *Vic Heath*, chapters 23-25

18 For a fascinating description of some of Earl's Court's eateries in 1974 see https://archive.commercialmotor.com/article/20th-september-1974/115/whats-cooking-at-earls-court

19 Panayi, *Migrant City*, p.42, 245

20 Elms, *London Made Us*, p.173

21 Suggs, *That Close* (Quercus, 2013), p.43

22 Personal interview (2021)

23 https://www.independent.co.uk/arts-entertainment/obituary-michael-o-halloran-1125332.html

24 Interview with Patrick in Sorohan, op cit, p.116

25 https://www.richardgregory.org.uk/history/shepherds-bush-history.htm#can

26 Personal Interview (2019)

27 See https://www.opendemocracy.net/en/opendemocracyuk/recalling-1970s-london-has-life-improved-since-for-young-poor-and-black/ for Janet Daley's recollections of Hackney in the 1970s and the 2010s.

28 Personal Interview (2020)

29 White, *London in the Twentieth Century*, p.65

30 Personal Interview (2020)

31 Tom Bolton, *Camden Town: Dreams of Another London* (British Library, 2017), p.89

32 Kemp, *I Know This Much*, p.70

33 https://www.kentishtowner.co.uk/2013/02/27/wednesday-picture-marine-ices-sold-the-truth/

34 Medhurst, *Charlie Potatoes*, pp.72-73

35 https://en.ejo.ch/ethics-quality/the-end-of-fleet-street-print-and-my-40-year-career-in-journalism

36 http://www.clanjames.com/print_unions.htm

37 Hyams, *Bombsites and Lollipops*, p.216

38 Suggs, *That Close*, p.119

39 Personal Interview (2019)

40 For Sheila Rowbotham's memories and a retrospective on *Nightcleaners*, see https://libcom.org/files/NightCleaners.pdf

41 I am indebted to Alec Forshaw's excellent *1970s London: Discovering the Capital* (The History Press, 2011), which is a treasure trove of North London social history in the 1970s. Although I grew up in Camden and spent a fair bit of my time in Holloway in the 1970s (and later, in the 1980s, when I was working there), Forshaw's book prompted me to recall specific details, shops and pubs etc, which had been lost in my memory.

42 Personal interview (2020)

43 Personal interview (2020)

44 Madness, *Before We Was We*, p.97

[45] Cartwright, *Going for a Song*, p.147

[46] Madness, *Before We Was We*, p.27

[47] Joe Kerr's memories of his time on London buses in the 1970s are in *Bus Fare: Writings on London's Most Loved Means of Transport*, edited by Trevor Elborough and Joe Kerr (AA Publishing, 2018), p.272-276

[48] Quoted in McLagan, *Bent Coppers*, p.10

[49] Elms, *London Made Us*, p.166

[50] Andrea Levy, *Never Far from Nowhere* (Headline Review, 1996), p.3

[51] Elms, *London Made Us*, p.279

[52] Melissa Tyler, *Soho at Work: Pleasure and Place in Contemporary London* (Cambridge University Press, 2020), p. 108

[53] Brian Dennis's memories of supporting Spurs are in Martin Cloake and Alan Fisher, *A People's History of Tottenham Hotspur* (Pitch Publishing, 2016), p.133

[54] John King, *The Football Factory* (Vintage, 1996), p.22

[55] Kemp, *I Know This Much*, p.62

[56] Personal interview (2020)

[57] See feature on Steve McQueen in *The Observer*, 15 November 2020.

[58] Suggs, *That Close*, p.121

[59] Personal interview (2019)

[60] Elms, *London Made Us*, p.163

[61] Medhurst, *Charlie Potatoes*, p.100

[62] For a more detailed account of the Crosfield occupation see https://pasttenseblog.wordpress.com/2021/03/26/today-in-london-industrial-history-1975-workers-occupy-crosfield-electronics-holloway/

[63] For Arthur Chaplin's memories of the time see *All in a Day's Work*, p.336.

[64] Personal Interview (2020)

[65] See Daniel Rachel, *Walls Come Tumbling Down: The Music and Politics of Rock Against Racism, 2 Tone and Red Wedge 1976-1992* (Picador, 2016), for Wayne Minter's and many other recollections.

[66] For Urmilaben Patel's recollections see *All in a Day's Work*, p.224

[67] See http://invereskstreet.blogspot.com/2012/01/simon-says-by-ian-walker.html for Simon's story.

[68] https://www.jacobinmag.com/2019/04/battle-wood-green-british-fascism-corbyn for an account of the Battle of Wood Green, including David Widgery's recollections.

[69] Sullivan, *People Like Us*, p.10

70 Jones, *Lonely Boy*, p.67, 69

71 Elms, *London Made Us*, p.73

72 For many vivid memories of the Punk years see John Robb, *Punk Rock: An Oral History* (Ebury Press, 2006) (Lydon's view of McLaren and Westwood on p.83).

73 Jones, *Lonely Boy*, p.146

74 Viv Albertine, *Clothes, Clothes, Clothes, Music, Music, Music, Boys, Boys, Boys* (Faber and Faber, 2014), pp.85-86

75 Madness, *Before We Was We*, p.147

76 Duncan Lloyd quoted in *From Ronnie's to Ravers*, p.88

77 Daniel Lux, *Camden Parasites* (Phoenix Press, 2007), p.14, 41

78 Suggs quoted in http://sevenraggedmen.com/1977-2/

79 Ant, *Stand and Deliver*,p.146

The 1980s

1 See Martin Lloyd-Elliott, *City Ablaze: Life with the World's Busiest Firefighters* (Bloomsbury, 1992), pp.145-158 for a full account of the Denmark Place fire, and https://www.independent.co.uk/news/uk/home-news/denmark-place-arson-why-people-are-still-searching-answers-35-years-one-biggest-mass-murders-our-history-10467987.html for an account of attempts by the victims' families to secure retrospective acknowledgment and a suitable memorial.

2 White, *London in the Twentieth Century*, p.239

3 Alec Forshaw and Theo Bergstrom, *The Markets of London* (Penguin Books, 1983, 1989), pp.54-55

4 Personal interview (2021)

5 Chris Scott, *The Street Riding Years: Despatching Through 80s London* (Chris Scott, 2018), pp.137-138

6 Lux, *Camden Parasites*, p.86

7 For an excellent account of the fire and occupation, including reports from the *Camden New Journal*, see Whitehead, *Curious King's Cross*, pp.21-24.

8 Data from Paul Harrison, *Inside the Inner City: Life Under the Cutting Edge* (Penguin Books, 1985), p.205

9 Ibid., p.31

10 Ibid., p.26. Harrison's powerful report on Hackney in the 1980s sits beside the work of Henry Mayhew, Charles Booth and George Orwell. His work is a damning indictment of how a London borough

was left to rot by cruel government policies, but equally impressive is his account of how working class life persevered in Hackney despite unemployment and poverty.

11   Personal interview (2019)

12   See http://www.unionhistory.info/britainatwork/about/about.php

13   One only has to walk around the western segment of Park Royal Industrial Estate on the wrong side of the North Circular, an area devoid of the main estate's corporate HQs and modern buildings, to be struck by how closely its small firms are connected to European and Middle-Eastern trade. The Easy Jet Foodstore (all items 50p!) and Hoo Hing Asian Food Ingredients dominate the area, but smaller firms like Middle-East Cargo Specialist and Mex Express Trans Crate are also international operators. These are firms whose workers were unlikely to have fallen for Brexit and were almost certainly hurt by it.

14   For David Lammy's recollections see *Mother Country*, p.xv

15   Lichtenstein, *Diamond Street*, p.283

16   Scott, *The Street Riding Years*, pp.221-222

17   Iain Sinclair quoted in Lichtenstein, *Diamond Street*, p.143

18   For an account of the struggles of the IAGOU see *Unwaged Fightback: A History of Islington Action Group of the Unwaged 1980-1886* (Past Tense, 1987).

19   Personal recollections.

20   *Mother Country*, p.xvi

21   *TV Times*, Oct 26-Nov 1 1991, p.87

22   Richard Cracknell's memories of the Bull pub in Tottenham are in Chapter 6 of Cloake and Fisher.

23   Elms, *London Made Us*, p.209

24   Gary Kemp quoted in Dylan Jones, *Sweet Dreams: The Story of the New Romantics* (Faber and Faber, 2020), p.214-215

25   https://shapersofthe80s.com/clubbing/1983-posing-with-a-purpose-at-the-camden-palace/

26   Personal interview (2019)

27   Quoted in http://sevenraggedmen.com/1977-2/

28   Sullivan, *People Like Us*, p.83, 77

29   Nicky Summers quoted in Rachel, op cit, p.304

30   Quoted inhttp://sevenraggedmen.com/1977-2/

31   Suggs, *That Close*, p.111

32   Maxine White, *Clipped: Inside Soho's Clip Joints* (VHC Publishing, 2009), p.105

33   https://www.theguardian.com/culture/2015/may/17/london-soho-stories-sex-drugs-rock-and-roll

34   Quoted in Whitehead, *Curious King's Cross*, p.99

35   See https://www.gayinthe80s.com/2017/09/pub-bell-kings-cross-london/2/

36   Personal interview (2019)

37   Quoted in Cloake and Fisher, op cit, pp.134-136

38   https://hackneyhistory.wordpress.com/2017/03/30/dalston-riot-july-1981/

39   Personal Interview (2019)

40   The quote from Ian Mikardo, taken from his autobiography, is in White, *London in the Twentieth Century*, p.392

41   Quote from an interview with Bernie Grant in Mike Phillips and Trevor Phillips, *Windrush: The Irresistible Rise of Multi-Racial Britain* (HarperCollins, 1998), p.264

42   Personal interview (2019)

43   Six people were charged with the murder of Keith Blakelock but the cases were undermined by the investigating officers cutting corners and fabricating evidence. Three minors had their cases dismissed when a judge ruled they had been denied legal rights whilst being held and questioned. Three adults — Winston Silcott, Mark Braithwate and EnginRaghip— were convicted and sentenced to life imprisonment, although no witness had confirmed they were part of the mob that attacked Blakelock and no forensic evidence linked them to it. In 1991 all three were cleared by the Court of Appeals. In 2013 another man, Nicholas Jacobs, was charged with Blakelock's murder, but was cleared at trial.

44   See the interview with Martha Osamor, from 2018 Baroness Osamor, on https://irr.org.uk/article/martha-osamor-unsung-hero-of-britains-black-struggle/

45   Personal Interview (2019)

46   Quote from Roger Drakes (DJ Dodge) in Casper Melville, *It's a London Thing: How Rare Groove, Acid House and Jungle Remapped the City* (Manchester University Press, 2020), p.102

47   Lloyd Bradley, *Sounds Like London: 100 Years of Black Music in the Capital* (Serpent's Tail, 2013), p.7

48 Norman Jay quoted in Ibid., p.317
49 Phil Potter's recollections are in Deabill and Snowball, *From Ronnie's to Ravers*, pp.110-120
50 https://thequietus.com/articles/29159-flowered-up-believe-in-magic-heavenly-records-book-extract
51 Pete's story is told in *From Ronnie's to Ravers*, pp.139-143
52 For the *Fallen Angel* and reminiscences from some of its customers in the 1980s and 1990s, see https://www.gayinthe80s.com/2012/09/1984-pub-the-fallen-angel-islington-london/
53 Personal Interview (2020)
54 For an account of the 1987 King's Cross fire, including recollections from several of Soho's Red Watch, see Lloyd-Elliott, Ibid, p.169-181. Both I and my future wife Sue had close calls with the fire. I passed through the station about an hour before the fire started. Sue, who at the time often went to the Bell pub after work, was planning to leave and catch the tube from King's Cross to Highbury Corner at about 7.30pm, exactly when the fire started, but at the last moment was persuaded to stay on at the pub.
55 This account is based on *I Haven't Had So Much Fun Since My Leg Fell Off: The North London Civil Servants' Strike 1987/88*, Past Tense, pp.8-9, and personal recollection.
56 Personal interview (2020)
57 Ruth Quintyne's story is told in *All in a Day's Work*, pp.99, 177

The 1990s

1 Dave Blundell is quoted at https://www.polfed.org/campaigns/centenary/metropolitan-police-dave-blundell/
2 Personal interview (2019)
3 https://libcom.org/library/the-couriers-are-revolting-the-despatch-industry-workers-union-1989-1992
4 All quotes from DIWU organisers are taken from the report on the DIWU at Libcom.org.
5 Personal interview (2021)
6 https://www.workersliberty.org/story/2017-07-26/exposing-east-londons-sweatshops
7 Heath, *Vic Heath*, pp.197-202
8 Union Railways internal report quoted in Asher, *A Very Political Railway*, pp.120-121

9   For an account of the Gascoygne Estate and Justine's memories, see https://www.eastlondonlines.co.uk/2017/02/exhibition-tells-50-years-of-hackney-estate/

10 See http://www.eastendreview.co.uk/2016/01/18/the-ghetto-tom-hunter/

11 White, *London in the Twentieth Century*, p.142

12 Cinar and Olmez are quoted in Olgu Karan, *Economic Survival Strategies of Turkish Migrants in London* (Transnational Press London, 2017), p.123, 124

13 Ibid., p.7

14 For contemporary reporting of the Richard Everitt murder and quotes from Nash Ali and Paul, see "Fear and loathing after 'racial' murder", *The Independent*, 15 August 1994.

15 For Jabir's story see Ramy M.K. Aly, *Becoming Arab in London: Performativity and the Undoing of Identity* (Pluto, 2015), pp.136-137

16 https://www.hackneygazette.co.uk/news/hackney-s-holly-street-estate-the-mile-long-corridor-that-3550952

17 Robyn Travis, *Prisoner to the Streets* (X Press, 2013), p.21

18 Ibid., p.63

19 Ibid., p.89

20 See https://hackneyhistory.wordpress.com/hcda/fighting-the-lawmen/ for a detailed analysis of the corruption at Stoke Newington police station in the 1980s and 1990s and the many wrongful convictions that resulted.

21 Akala, *Natives: Race and Class in the Ruins of Empire* (Two Roads Books, 2018), p.196, p.172

22 Ibid., pp.152-153

23 Victor Headley, *Yardie* (X Press, 1992), p.44

24 Akala, *Natives*, p.188

25 Morton, *Gangland Soho*, p.226

26 Personal interview (2021)

27 Personal interview (2020)

28 Personal interview (2019)

29 Phil's story is in *From Ronnie's to Ravers*, p.122

30 John Tuvey quoted in https://louderthanwar.com/flowered-weekenders-tale/

31 Jazzie B quoted in Bradley, *Sounds Like London*, p.335

32 Personal interview (2020)

33 Wookie quoted in Bradley, *Sounds Like London*, p.355

34 Akala, *Natives*, p.252

35 Personal interview (2021)

36 Sarah Lucas is quoted in Darren Coffield, *Tales from the Colony Room* (Unbound, 2020), p.295

37 Laura Grace Ford, *Savage Messiah* (Verso, 2011, republished 2019). The quote is in Issue 3 of the collected *Savage Messiah* zines.

38 https://hidden-london.com/gazetteer/maitland-park/

39 https://www.theguardian.com/cities/2015/aug/19/young-londoners-inequality-utopia-roundhouse-penny-woolcock

40 Russell Brand, *My Booky Wook* (Hodder, 2007), p.165,170

41 Personal interview (2019)

42 Personal interview (2019)

43 Philip's reminiscences of clubbing at Trade are at https://www.qxmagazine.com/2020/08/my-trade-experience-london-1990s/

44 Personal interview (2019)

45 For an account of J18 in London and the unusually self-critical analysis quoted, see https://pasttenseblog.wordpress.com/2020/06/18/today-in-londons-festive-history-1999-j18-the-carnival-against-capitalism/

46 Personal interview (2019)

47 Personal interview (2019)

48 Lux, *Camden Parasites*

49 King, *The Football Factory*, p.22

50 For Peter Watts's memories of Saturdays in London in the 1990s see https://greatwen.com/2015/02/15/a-saturday-in-london-in-the-early-1990s/

51 For Johnny's recollections of the 1990s London club scene see *From Ronnie's to Ravers*, pp.155-159

52 Dan Cruickshank, *Spitalfields: The History of a Nation in a Handful of Streets* (Windmill Books, 2016), p.147

2000-2008

1 *Bus Fare*, pp.216-221.

2 Robin Cook's speech is quoted in *London: From Punk to Blair*, edited by Joe Kerr and Andrew Gibson (Reaktion Books, 2012), p.33

3 John Holland is quoted in https://www.bbc.co.uk/news/business-22077190

4   Daisy and Edward are quoted in Stuart Hodkinson, *Safe as Houses: Private Greed, Political Negligence and Housing Policy After Grenfell* (Manchester University Press, 2019), p.94, pp.98-99. Edward's harrowing story is told on pp.96-101 and I have drawn upon it here. They are just two of a series of valuable in-depth interviews conducted by Hodkinson for *Safe as Houses*, an essential account of how the de-municipalisation policy of the New Labour government let private sector cowboys write their own rules and sign off defective work that was a clear danger to tenants' health and safety, a policy that led ultimately to the corporate crime of Grenfell Tower.

5   See Hodkinson, *Safe as Houses*, pp.107-116 for an account of what was done to the Chalcots, which I have used here amongst other reports.

6   http://www.camdennewjournal.co.uk/article/chalcots-was-model-for-work-on-grenfell-tower-inquiry-told-2

7   Angela Englis with Nigel Bruckner, *King's Cross: A Sense of Place* (Matador, 2012), p.66

8   https://socialistworker.co.uk/art/3988/Is%20this%20how%20to%20deal%20with%20gun%20crime

9   Rose Rouse, *A London Safari: Walking Adventures in NW10* (Amberley, 2014), p.119

10   https://www.theguardian.com/theguardian/2001/jun/30/features.jobsmoney4

11   For a garbled history of the South Kilburn Mandem, its affiliates and rivals, see https://www.reddit.com/r/ukdrill/comments/oegs53/the_history_of_the_south_kilburn_mandem/

12   https://crackmagazine.net/article/opinion/a-love-letter-to-the-mozart-estate/

13   Robyn Travis interviewed in "Former Hackney "bad-boy" reveals reality behind mythical image", *The Meddler*, 18 November 2009.

14   Personal Interview (2021)

15   Rouse, *A London Safari*, pp.123-126

16   Data in Panayi, *Migrant City*, p.66

17   Xiao Fan is quoted in Hsiao-Hung Pai's revelatory *Chinese Whispers: The True Story Behind Britain's Hidden Army of Labour* (Penguin, 2008), p.207. For details of the rates of pay in Chinese restaurants in Soho in the early 2000s, and the campaign at the New Diamond restaurant in 2001, see Pai, *Chinese Whispers*, pp. 206-212, 220.

18   Morton, *Gangland Soho,*, p.226

19 For Anna Chen's experiences as a young Chinese working class woman in the SWP, see https://madammiaow.blogspot.com/2013/10/why-is-left-failing-to-grab-popular.html

20 Data from the Office of National Statistics (ONS).

21 Piotr and the unnamed Polish Roma migrant are quoted in Michal P. Garapich, *London's Polish Borders: Transnationalising Class and Ethnicity among Polish Migrants in London* (Ibidem Press, 2016), p.192 and p.265

22 For background on the SSWSDG and Sudan Children in Need, based on the author's research interviews with Elizabeth Ajith and Khadiga Khogali, I am indebted to Cynthia Cockburn's excellent *Looking to London: Stories of War, Escape and Asylum* (Pluto Press, 2017), pp.148-153. Grace Oliver's story is on pp.156-159.

23 Data in *Kurdish Community Organisations in London: A Social Network Analysis*, Alession D'Angelo, Social Policy Research Centre, Middlesex University, 2008. Full data at https://core.ac.uk/download/pdf/17300875.pdf

24 Suna Parlak's story is in Cockburn, *Looking to London*, pp.46-52.

25 See data in Aly, *Becoming Arab in London*, p.61

26 My secondary school was five minutes' walk from Edgware Road. Sometimes at lunchtime I would stroll up and down it, looking in various shops. Revisisting E Road in 2019, it surprised me how little it had changed since the 1970s.

27 Mohammed's working life is described in Aly, *Becoming Arab in London*, p.105

28 Daniel Kaluuya interview at https://www.vice.com/en/article/53jbkn/daniel-kaluuya-early-works-interview

29 Asher, *A Very Political Railway*, p.139

30 Akwese's story is told in Ben Judah, *This is London: Life and Death in the World City* (Picador, 2016), p.86-100. Judah's interviews with Big Yaw and Baby Yaw are on pp.100-103. *This is London*, which I discuss in the conclusion, is one of the most important and challenging books written about contemporary London and I am grateful for the excellent reportage and indispensable personal stories it contains.

31 In *NightHaunts: A Journey Through the London Night* (Verso, 2007) Suhkdev Sandhu explored this territory further through the prism

of London's night-time occupations. Sandhu's revelatory book examines an eclectic range of work such as the Met's Air Support Unit (helicopters) policing the city's nightscape, Bargers working on the dark river, over-stressed volunteers for the Samaritans and the "Flushers" of the sewer network. Above all, Sandhu's evocative study captured the stressful work experience of London's migrant office cleaners and late night mini-cab drivers, a workforce figuratively and literally kept in the dark.

[32] For an account of the 2006 Haringey refuse collectors' strike, written by Alan Woodward, the Convenor of Haringey Trades Union Council and a regular contributor to the Radical History Network of North East London, see https://pasttenseblog.wordpress.com/2021/07/31/today-in-london-striking-history-2006-haringey-dustbin-workers-strike-begins/

[33] https://www.socialistparty.org.uk/articles/6368/03-09-2008/london-buses-strikers-pack-picket-lines

[34] Mark Dolan is quoted in "Waves of strikes to hit Royal Mail", Yuri Prasad, *Socialist Worker*, 16 June 2009.

[35] Rowena's recollections are in Kerr, *Bus Fare*, p.278. I can only echo her sentiment. All Londoners have their own "personal" bus route, the one they use or used the most, the one most associated with their lives. For me it will always be the 24, which for many years took me from Chalk Farm to central London and back again. That Michael Foot used the 24 daily, even when he was Labour Leader, to travel back and forth from Hampstead to Westminster, just adds extra poignancy to it.

[36] Henry's recollections of working life in Camden Market are in https://www.theguardian.com/cities/2016/dec/07/londons-subcultures-readers-memories-stories-camden-market-redevelopment

[37] George Mpanga quoted in Rouse, *A London Safari*, p.201

[38] From 1993 to 1999 I worked in the International Department of the Health and Safety Executive (HSE) delivering advice and "assistance programmes" to ex-Soviet Bloc countries establishing new occupational health and safety systems. Once on a visit to Warsaw, one evening after dinner with colleagues, I walked out from the restored, picture-postcard city centre lovingly rebuilt after the

Second World War, to the huge *blokowisko* estates that surrounded it. They seemed to me more like prison blocks than a community, although in reality they were both.

39 Garapich, *London's Polish Borders*, p.196

40 https://www.theguardian.com/culture/2009/jan/21/police-form-696-garage-music. The Met's attempt to contain grime was a backhanded compliment to its potential reach, but grime's biggest threat came not from a white power elite for whom it harboured justifiable hatred but from romantic middle class writers who ascribed it a Marxist politics it neither possessed nor desired, one of whom, getting over-excited in the aftermath of the 2011 riots, called it "Music to storm the Treasury to". But in 2011 the Treasury was left untouched, as were all other symbols of ruling class authority. It was the shops of Tottenham, Croydon and Clapham that burned, something that left the denizens of Pall Mall clubs completely unconcerned.

41 See Dan Hancox, *Inner City Pressure: The Story of Grime* (William Collins, 2018), p.186, easily the best book on grime as an integral part of London history.

42 Skepta quoted in https://www.thefader.com/2015/06/04/skepta-cover-story-konnichiwa-interview

43 Big Yaw's recollections of 7/7 at Edgware Road tube station are in Judah, *This is London*, p.101

44 Michelle Golding's excellent *Beyond the Hoodie* (2007) is on YouTube at https://www.youtube.com/watch?v=-gbX_wCHlzo

45 https://www.theguardian.com/uk/2009/jun/14/ben-kinsella-murder-underworld-gangs-adams

46 Taken from interviews in in Tyler, *Soho at Work*, pp.193-194, 115

47 https://www.standard.co.uk/hp/front/soho-s-russian-vice-lords-7220943.html

48 Meghan is quoted in Tyler, *Soho at Work*, p.206

49 Medhurst, *Charlie Potatoes*, p.162

50 Wickey is quoted in https://www.theguardian.com/cities/2016/dec/07/londons-subcultures-readers-memories-stories-camden-market-redevelopment

It's a London Thing

1 See Anna Minton, *Big Capital: Who is London For?* (Penguin, 2017), for an analysis of the impact of UHNWIs on London's property market.

2   https://www.hamhigh.co.uk/news/the-food-bank-family-highgate-residents-in-crisis-and-the-3437486

3   Cash Carraway, *Skint Estate: Notes from the Poverty Line* (Penguin, 2019), p.233, 235

4   Owen Hatherley, *Red Metropolis: Socialism and the Government of London* (Repeater, 2020), p.187

5   Personal interview (2019)

6   https://www.onlondon.co.uk/the-choice-before-labour-members-in-haringey/

7   Lynsey Hanley, *Estates: An Intimate History* (Granta, 2017), p.128-129

8   Data on the number and location of all Camden's socially rented housing units can be found at https://opendata.camden.gov.uk/Housing/Camden-housing-estates-containing-20-or-more-units/4mu9-qhqz

9   For a sector-by-sector breakdown of London's employment since 1971 see https://www.london.gov.uk/sites/default/files/wp92-borough-sector-jobs.pdf

10 See *Islington Local Plan: Strategic and Development Management Policies: Building a Fairer Islington*, September 2019, Policy SP3(C), p.34

11 Fred is quoted in *Re-imagining Islington: Work, Memory, Place and Emotion in a Community* oral history project, op cit.

12 Joe Kerr quoted in Elsborough and Kerr, *Bus Fare*, p.277

13 For recent reliable data on the number and locations of London clubs, see https://www.nesta.org.uk/blog/the-clubbing-map-what-has-happened-to-london-nightlife/

14 For data on numbers of pubs per London Borough in 2001 and 2018 see https://www.statista.com/statistics/777613/london-pub-numbers-by-borough-uk-united-kingdom/

15 Sabir is quoted in Judah, *This Is London*, p.67

16 Susana's story is told in *Invisible Britain: Portraits of Hope and Resilience* (Policy Press, 2018), edited by Paul Sng with photographs by Gordon Roland Peden.

17 Personal interview (2020)

18 Personal Interview (2019)

19 Carraway, *Skint Estate*, p.238, 240

20 https://www.theguardian.com/uk-news/2022/feb/01/met-officers-joked-raping-women-police-watchdog-racist

21 Zadie Smith, *NW* (Penguin, 2012), p.37

22 Iain Sinclair, *London Overground: A Day's Walk Around the Ginger Line* (Penguin, 2015), p.30

23 Ash Sarkar quoted in https://highprofiles.info/interview/ash-sarkar/

24 Reports by the GLA Intelligence Unit, May 2011, October 2012, November 2012

25 https://www.onlondon.co.uk/new-report-confirms-that-london-has-uks-highest-poverty-rates/

26 Hancox, *Inner City Pressure*, p.22

27 Jack Brown, *The London Problem: What Britain Gets Wrong About Its Capital City* (Haus Publishing, 2021), p.19

28 https://assets.publishing.service.gov.uk/government/uploads/system/uploads/attachment_data/file/937114/London_effect_report_-_final_20112020.pdf

29 Personal Interview (2019)

30 Personal Interview (2021)

31 https://crackmagazine.net/article/opinion/a-love-letter-to-the-mozart-estate/

32 Sally Taylor is quoted in https://www.bbc.co.uk/news/uk-england-london-50476286

33 https://www.mylondon.news/news/north-london-news/we-not-just-fried-chicken-23882615

34 For a summary of the Juniper Crescent situation as of late 2021, see https://www.estatewatch.london/estates/camden/junipercrescent/

35 https://www.vice.com/en/article/j5bgdg/awate-happiness-album-police-court-cases-activism-interview

36 Awate is interviewed at https://www.repeatmag.com/post/an-interview-with-awate

ACKNOWLEDGEMENTS

Many people helped me with this one. But first and foremost, I must thank Mother London herself.

I am very appreciative of all the biographies, autobiographies, personal memoirs, life stories and local histories, in print and online, that I accessed and used to compile this portrait of an under-examined subject. The richness of the material speaks for itself. I have only caught and presented a fraction of it.

I cannot thank enough those who agreed to be interviewed for the book and who gave me their personal stories and memories. Space and structure meant that not all of it made the final cut, but it was *all* useful. I am immensely grateful to Amanda Millhouse, Paul Philo, Chip Hamer, Ray Picton, Tony Kilshaw, Sean McGlinchey, Colin Miller, Tariq Goddard, Davy Jones, Andy Wilson, Lionel Welch, Alex Higgins, Clara Connelly, Imogen Radford, Ronnie Bridgett, Dawn Thorpe, Andy Coates, Colin Edwards, Yannis Gortsoyannis, Jade Azim and Zita Holbourne, as well as my mum, dad, wife, brother and aunt, for taking the time to do this and for what they provided.

I must thank everyone at Repeater Books, especially Tariq Goddard (co-parent of the original idea and strong advocate for it); Josh Turner, my meticulous editor; and Johnny Bull, for a perfect cover that has several layers of hidden meaning.

Finally, to my daughters Elizabeth and Eleanor, named after Elizabeth Eleanor Siddal, another Londoner with an interesting life story. And of course, to the most important person of all, my endlessly supportive and understanding wife Sue, who makes everything else possible.

Repeater Books

is dedicated to the creation of a new reality. The landscape of twenty-first-century arts and letters is faded and inert, riven by fashionable cynicism, egotistical self-reference and a nostalgia for the recent past. Repeater intends to add its voice to those movements that wish to enter history and assert control over its currents, gathering together scattered and isolated voices with those who have already called for an escape from Capitalist Realism. Our desire is to publish in every sphere and genre, combining vigorous dissent and a pragmatic willingness to succeed where messianic abstraction and quiescent co-option have stalled: abstention is not an option: we are alive and we don't agree.